IFIP Advances in Information and Communication Technology 796

IFIP Advances in Information and Communication Technology

The IFIP AICT series publishes state-of-the-art results in the sciences and technologies of information and communication. The scope of the series includes: foundations of computer science; software theory and practice; education; computer applications in technology; communication systems; systems modeling and optimization; information systems; ICT and society; computer systems technology; security and protection in information processing systems; artificial intelligence; and human-computer interaction.

Edited volumes and proceedings of refereed international conferences in computer science and interdisciplinary fields are featured. These results often precede journal publication and represent the most current research.

The principal aim of the IFIP AICT series is to encourage education and the dissemination and exchange of information about all aspects of computing.

More information about this series at https://link.springer.com/bookseries/6102

Antonios Papaleonidas · Elias Pimenidis ·
Ioannis Chochliouros · Stelios Krinidis
Editors

Artificial Intelligence Applications and Innovations

AIAI 2026 IFIP WG 12.5 International Workshops

B5G-Pine 2026
Chania, Crete, Greece, July 16–19, 2026
Proceedings, Part I

Springer

Editors
Antonios Papaleonidas
Democritus University of Thrace
Xanthi, Greece

Ioannis Chochliouros
OTE SA Hellenic Telecom Organization
Athens, Greece

Elias Pimenidis
University of the West of England
Bristol, UK

Stelios Krinidis
Democritus University of Thrace
Kavala, Greece

ISSN 1868-4238 ISSN 1868-422X (electronic)
IFIP Advances in Information and Communication Technology
ISBN 978-3-032-30506-0 ISBN 978-3-032-30507-7 (eBook)
https://doi.org/10.1007/978-3-032-30507-7

This Springer imprint is published by the registered company Springer Nature Switzerland AG
The registered company address is: Gewerbestrasse 11, 6330 Cham, Switzerland

AIAI 2026 Workshops Proceedings Preface

This volume comprises the proceedings of the workshops organized under the auspices of the 22nd International Conference on Artificial Intelligence Applications and Innovations, AIAI 2026.

The 22nd International Conference on *Artificial Intelligence Applications and Innovations* (AIAI 2026) continued a well-established tradition of promoting scientific excellence and fostering collaboration among researchers, academics, industry professionals, and practitioners working in the rapidly evolving field of Artificial Intelligence (AI). Technically supported by the *International Federation for Information Processing* (IFIP) Working Group 12.5, AIAI is an internationally recognized forum for presenting innovative research, exchanging ideas, and discussing emerging challenges and opportunities in AI-driven technologies and applications.

Artificial Intelligence (AI) has become one of the most influential technological paradigms of the modern era, affecting nearly every sector of society and industry. From environmental sustainability and telecommunications to education, healthcare, cultural analytics, and intelligent infrastructures, AI technologies are increasingly transforming the way organizations operate and individuals interact with digital ecosystems. At the same time, the widespread adoption of AI raises important scientific, ethical, and societal questions, creating the need for interdisciplinary dialogue and collaborative research initiatives. In this context, the workshops organized within AIAI 2026 provided focused venues for in-depth scientific discussion on specialized themes of strategic and societal importance.

The workshops included in these proceedings reflected the diversity, maturity, and interdisciplinary nature of contemporary AI research. They brought together experts from different scientific domains to explore novel methodologies, practical implementations, and innovative applications of Artificial Intelligence capable of addressing complex real-world challenges. Through the presentation of cutting-edge research contributions, experimental studies, industrial experiences, and visionary ideas, the workshops contributed significantly to advancing both the theoretical foundations and practical impact of AI technologies.

The response of the international scientific community to the AIAI 2026 Workshops call for papers was more than satisfactory, with 98 papers initially submitted. All papers were peer reviewed by at least two independent academic reviewers. 35 papers (36%) were accepted as full papers (12+pages) while 2 more papers were accepted as short papers (up to 11 pages) due to their high scientific quality. Reviews were single blind, with an average of three reviews per submission.

Among the workshops organized within AIAI 2026, the **3rd Workshop on "AI Applications for Achieving the Green Deal Targets"** (**AI4GD**) focused on the crucial role of AI in supporting sustainability and climate-neutral development. The *European Green Deal* has established an ambitious roadmap for transforming Europe into a climate-neutral continent by 2050. Achieving this objective requires advanced digital technologies, capable of supporting efficient resource management, environmental monitoring, sustainable urban planning, and intelligent energy systems. The AI4GD workshop explores innovative AI applications related to energy efficiency and flexibility, smart and resilient infrastructures, waste management, renewable energy integration, marine and underwater monitoring, and biodiversity conservation.

The workshop emphasizes advanced AI methodologies and technological approaches, including distributed machine learning, neural networks, Generative AI, and Agent-based modelling. These technologies contribute significantly towards the improvement of energy systems efficiency.

The 11th Workshop on "B5G – Putting Intelligence to the Network Edge" (B5G-PINE)

B5G-PINE stands for "**Putting Intelligence to the Network Edge**". It was the 11th workshop in the series, organized by the *Hellenic Telecommunications Organization* and dozens of EU scientific partners. It took place under the auspices of the AIAI international conference. The workshop was established to disseminate knowledge obtained from ongoing EU projects as well as from any other action of EU-funded research, in the wider thematic area of "*B5G/6G Innovative Activities – Putting Intelligence to the Network Edge*" and with the aim of focusing on Artificial Intelligence (AI) in modern 5G/B5G telecommunications infrastructures. This should take place by emphasizing associated results, methodologies, trials, concepts, and/or findings originating from technical reports/deliverables, from related pilot actions and/or any other relevant 5G-/B6G-/6G-based applications, intending to enhance intelligence to network edges.

The 15th Workshop on "Mining Humanistic Data" (MHDW)

The Mining Humanistic Data workshop (MHDW) aims to bring together interdisciplinary approaches that focus on the application of innovative as well as existing artificial intelligence, data matching, fusion, and mining, and knowledge discovery and management techniques to data derived from all areas of Humanistic Sciences.

The abundance of available data which is retrieved from or is related to the areas of Humanities and the human condition challenges the research community in processing and analyzing it. The aim is two-fold: on the one hand, to extract knowledge that will help us to understand human behavior, creativity, ways of thinking, reasoning, learning, decision making, and socializing, and even biological processes; on the other hand, to exploit the extracted knowledge by incorporating it into intelligent systems that will support humans in their everyday activities.

The 6th Workshop on "Artificial Intelligence and Ethics" (AI & ETHICS)

This interactive workshop has been organized for the last 6 years by John Macintyre. The workshop explores the profound ethical dilemmas emerging from information security challenges in Generative AI adoption. As GenAI tools become ubiquitous in research, education, and enterprise, we face urgent questions about responsibility, trust, and the moral obligations of institutions and individuals deploying these technologies.

A distinguished panel of three experts debated these ethical tensions through real-world cases.

- Larry Medsker, University of Vermont, USA, and Co-Editor-in-Chief, AI and Ethics
- Jack Fisher, NASSTAR, UK
- Romit Choudhury, Questa-AI, Luxembourg

The workshop concluded with audience Q&A, encouraging vigorous discussion about navigating the moral complexities of securing GenAI in an increasingly AI-dependent world.

We would like to thank all contributors to the AIAI 2026 workshops. The workshops of AIAI 2026 successfully highlighted the dynamic evolution of AI and its impact across science. The workshop proceedings reflect a collection of innovative ideas, achievements and practical applications. We hope that the research presented in this volume will inspire further research, and that it will contribute to the development of sustainable and trustworthy AI.

July 2026

Antonios Papaleonidas
Elias Pimenidis
Ioannis Chochliouros
Stelios Krinidis

Organization

General Co-chairs

Ilias Maglogiannis	University of Piraeus, Greece
Michalis Zervakis	Technical University of Crete, Greece

Program Co-chairs

Lazaros Iliadis	Democritus University of Thrace, Greece
Antonios Papaleonidas	Democritus University of Thrace, Greece
Efthyvoulos Kyriacou	Technological University of Cyprus, Cyprus

Steering Committee

Ilias Maglogianis	University of Piraeus, Greece
Lazaros Iliadis	Democritus University of Thrace, Greece
Eunika Mercier-Laurent	EPITA, IFIP, France

Honorary Chair

Eunika Mercier-Laurent	EPITA, IFIP, France

Organizing Co-chairs

Antonis Papaleonidas	Democritus University of Thrace, Greece
Anastasios Panagiotis Psathas	Democritus University of Thrace, Greece
Marios Antonakakis	Hellenic Mediterranean University, Greece
Andreas Menychtas	University of Piraeus, Greece

Advisory Co-chair

Serafin Alonso	Universidad de León, Spain

Doctoral Consortium Co-chairs

John MacIntyre	University of the Commonwealth Caribbean, Jamaica
Dario Malchiodi	Università degli Studi di Milano, Italy

Publication and Publicity Co-chairs

Antonios Papaleonidas	Democritus University of Thrace, Greece
Anastasios Panagiotis Psathas	Democritus University of Thrace, Greece
Nikiforos Mpotzoris	Democritus University of Thrace, Greece

Liaison Chairs

Ioannis Chochliouros	Hellenic Telecommunications Organization S.A. (OTE), Greece
Stelios Krinidis	Democritus University of Thrace, Greece
Andreas Kanavos	Ionian University, Greece

Workshops Co-chairs

Andreas Andreou	Cyprus University of Technology, Cyprus
Konstantinos Votis	CERTH, Greece
Vassilis Plagianakos	University of Thessaly, Greece

Special Sessions and Tutorials Co-chairs

Massimo Mecella	Sapienza Università di Roma, Italy
Manuel Domínguez	Universidad de León, Spain

Local Organizing/Hybrid Facilitation Committee

Aggeliki Tsouka	Democritus University of Thrace, Greece
Anastasios Panagiotis Psathas	Democritus University of Thrace, Greece
Anna Karagianni	Democritus University of Thrace, Greece
Athanasios Saliakouras	Democritus University of Thrace, Greece
Christina Gkizioti	Democritus University of Thrace, Greece

David Akoda	Hellenic Mediterranean University, Greece
Dimitrios Giannoulakis	Democritus University of Thrace, Greece
George Livanos	Technical University of Crete, Greece
Iasonas Konstantinos Kazakos	University of Piraeus, Greece
Ieremias Thimianidis	Democritus University of Thrace, Greece
Ioanna–Maria Erentzi	Democritus University of Thrace, Greece
Leonidas Skopelitis	Democritus University of Thrace, Greece
Melina Tezia	Democritus University of Thrace, Greece
Nikiforos Mpotzoris	Democritus University of Thrace, Greece
Stelina Naka	Technical University of Crete, Greece
Tassos Giannakopoulos	Democritus University of Thrace, Greece
Theodoros Koutrakis	Democritus University of Thrace, Greece

Program Committee

Adnan Yaramis	Asterion Biotechnology, Turkey
Advait Patel	Broadcom, USA
Afef Mdhaffar	National School of Engineering of Sfax, Tunisia
Akhil Eppa	Adobe Inc., USA
Alexander Ryjov	Lomonosov Moscow State University, Presidential Academy, Russia
Alexander van Grootel	Leverpoint, USA
Alexios Papaioannou	Democritus University of Thrace, Greece
Ameya Wagh	Rivian Automotive Llc, USA
Anastasios Panagiotis Psathas	Democritus University of Thrace, Greece
Andreas Christoforou	Cyprus University of Technology, Cyprus
Andreas Menychtas	University of Piraeus, Greece
Andres Iglesias	University of Cantabria, Spain
Angel Lareo	Universidad Autónoma de Madrid, Spain
Anna Wiewiora	Queensland University of Technology, Australia
Antonio Morán	Universidad de León, Spain
Antonios Kalampakas	American University of the Middle East, Kuwait
Antonios Papaleonidas	Democritus University of Thrace, Greece
Aristidis Likas	University of Ioannina, Greece
Arnaud Lewandowski	LISIC, Université du Littoral Côte d'Opale, France
Asimina Dimara	Democritus University of Thrace, Greece
Asma Mekki	Université de Sfax, Tunisia
Athanasios Kallipolitis	University of Piraeus, Greece
Athanasios Koutras	University of Peloponnese, Greece
Athanasios Tsadiras	Aristotle University of Thessaloniki, Greece

Balakrishnan Natarajan	Sona College of Technology, India
Banafsheh Rekabdar	Portland State University, USA
Bernhard Jung	Freiberg University of Mining and Technology, Germany
Binyu Zhao	Heilongjiang University, China
Bisola Kayode	Independent Researcher, UK
Bo Mei	Texas Christian University, USA
Bujar Raufi	Technological University Dublin, Ireland
Chandra Sekhara Reddy Adapa	Labcorp, USA
Charalampos Liapis	University of Patras, Computer Technology Institute and Press "Diophantus", Greece
Chia-yi Su	University of Notre Dame, USA
Chokri Slim	Manouba University, Tunisia
Christos Makris	University of Patras, Greece
Chunyu Yuan	Graduate Center CUNY, USA
Claudio Giancaterino	Independent Researcher, Italy
Cyril de Bodt	University of Namur, Belgium
Cyril Drocourt	Université de Picardie Jules Verne, France
Damien Lolive	University of Southern Brittany, CNRS, France
Daniel Perez	University of León, Spain
Daniel Stamate	Goldsmiths, University of London, UK
Daniel Vašata	Czech Technical University in Prague, Czechia
Darshan Mehta	AT&T Services Inc., USA
Davide Zambrano	Sportradar, Switzerland
Delwar Hossain	Angelo State University, USA
Denise Gorse	University College London, UK
Dhivya Kalaiinban	National Institute of Technology Puducherry, India
Diana Laura Borza	Babeş-Bolyai University, Romania
Dimitrios Michail	Harokopio University of Athens, Greece
Dionysios Koulouris	University of Piraeus, Greece
Doina Logofatu	Frankfurt University of Applied Sciences, Germany
Douglas McLelland	Brainchip, France
Dulani Meedeniya	University of Moratuwa, Sri Lanka
Efstratios Georgopoulos	University of the Peloponnese, Greece
Eleni Gerasimidi	Democritus University of Thrace, Greece
Eleni Vlachou	Ionian University, Greece
Eleni Vrochidou	Democritus University of Thrace, Greece
Elias Pimenidis	University of the West of England, UK
Ercan Atagün	Düzce University, Turkey
Faisal Alvi	Habib University, Pakistan

Farhin Farhad Riya	University of Tennessee, Knoxville, USA
Federico Corradi	Eindhoven University of Technology, Netherlands
Fei Zuo	University of Central Oklahoma, USA
Flora Ferreira	University of Porto, Portugal
Florian Mirus	Autonomous Reply, Germany
Florin Leon	Gheorghe Asachi Technical University of Iaşi, Romania
Fnu Neha	Kent State University, USA
Fotios Kounelis	Imperial College London, UK
Francesco Marcelloni	Università di Pisa, Italy
Francesco Trovò	Politecnico di Milano, Italy
Gaetano di Caterina	University of Strathclyde, UK
George Magoulas	Birkbeck, University of London, UK
Georgi Tsenov	Technical University of Sofia, Bulgaria
Georgios Alexandridis	National & Kapodistrian University of Athens, Greece
Georgios Drakopoulos	University of West Attica, Greece
Gerasimos Vonitsanos	University of Patras, Greece
Guillem Rodríguez	Artificial Intelligence Research Institute (IIIA-CSIC), Spain
Hafez Abdolkarimi	Islamic Azad University, Iran
Hanae Belmajdoub	Mohammed V University in Rabat, Morocco
Haopeng Chen	Shanghai Jiao Tong University, China
Hugo Camacho Cruz	Universidad Autónoma de Tamaulipas, Mexico
Ignacio Díaz Blanco	Universidad de Oviedo, Spain
Ilias Maglogiannis	University of Piraeus, Greece
Ioannis Chamodrakas	National and Kapodistrian University of Athens, Greece
Ioannis Chochliouros	Hellenic Telecommunications Organization S.A. (OTE), Greece
Ioannis Karampinis	Democritus University of Thrace, Greece
Ioannis Karydis	Ionian University, Greece
Ioannis Livieris	University of Piraeus, Greece
Jacopo Rossi	Sapienza University of Rome, Italy
Jan Treur	Vrije Universiteit Amsterdam, Netherlands
Jeyadev Needhidevan	New York University, USA
Jiaming Hu	Boston University, USA
Jiaxun Tang	University of Massachusetts Amherst, USA
Jinling Wang	Ulster University, UK
Juan Fuertes	Universidad de León, Spain
Kamil Dedecius	Czech Technical University in Prague, Czechia
Konstantinos Delibasis	University of Thessaly, Greece

Konstantinos Moutselos	University of Piraeus, Greece
Kostas Karatzas	Aristotle University of Thessaloniki, Greece
Krati Saxena	Kyushu Institute of Technology, Japan
Lazaros Iliadis	Democritus University of Thrace, Greece
Madalina Erascu	West University of Timisoara, Romania
Madhavi Kannan	Tempus AI, USA
Magda Friedjungová	Czech Technical University in Prague, Czechia
Markus Aho	Funlus Oy/University of Eastern Finland, Finland
Melih Doğanay Sazak	Roketsan, Turkey
Michail-Antisthenis Tsompanas	University of the West of England, UK
Michel Salomon	Université Bourgogne-Franche-Comté, France
Miguel Prada	Universidad de León, Spain
Mirjana Ivanovic	University of Novi Sad, Serbia
Mohamed Elleuch	University of Manouba, Tunisia
Naim Terbeh	University of Lille, France
Narayana Sivateja Gollapudi	Meta, USA
Naushin Nower	University of Dhaka, Bangladesh
Neeyati Anand	Illinois Institute of Technology, USA
Nichat Kiourt	Democritus University of Thrace, Greece
Nikolaos Mitianoudis	Democritus University of Thrace, Greece
Nikos Karacapilidis	University of Patras, Greece
Noémi Gaskó	Babeş-Bolyai University, Romania
Oke Oluwasegun Babafemi	National Open University of Nigeria, Nigeria
Oluwakemi Temitope Olayinka	University of Arkansas at Little Rock, USA
Panagiotis Gratsanis	Ionian University, Greece
Panagiotis Pintelas	University of Patras, Greece
Panthadeep Bhattacharjee	National Institute of Technology Rourkela, India
Paul Stefan Popescu	University of Craiova, Romania
Paulo Cortez	University of Minho, Portugal
Payam Farhadi	Islamic Azad University, Iran
Petia Koprinkova-Hristova	IICT, Bulgarian Academy of Sciences, Bulgaria
Petr Hajek	University of Pardubice, Czech Republic
Phivos Mylonas	University of West Attica, Greece
Pin-Yen Huang	Academia Sinica, Taiwan
Qi Zhao	Nanjing University, China
Roman Mouček	University of West Bohemia in Pilsen, Czechia
Rong Lu	Viridien, USA
Sanchit Hira	Independent, USA
Satyam Raj	Arizona State University, USA
Saurabh Deochake	SentinelOne, USA
Selvine George Mathias	Technische Hochschule Ingolstadt, Germany
Serafin Alonso	Universidad de León, Spain

Sheshananda Reddy Kandula	Adobe, USA
Shu Eguchi	Honda Staffing Services Co., Japan
Shuozhe Li	University of Texas at Austin, USA
Sie Long Kek	Universiti Tun Hussein Onn, Malaysia
Sotiris Kotsiantis	University of Patras, Greece
Stefanos Nikiforos	Ionian University, Greece
Stelios Krinidis	Democritus University of Thrace, Greece
Taibiao Zhao	Louisiana State University, USA
Takuya Kitamura	Toyama National College of Technology, Japan
Tenny Enoch Devadas Chandrasegar	Fidelity Investments, USA
Thanasis Moustakas	ITI - CERTH, Greece
Theofanis Kalampokas	Democritus University of Thrace, Greece
Tomoyoshi Kimura	University of Illinois Urbana-Champaign, USA
Tony Tona Landu	University of Thiès, Senegal
Vandana M. Ladwani	PES University, India
Verner Ferreira	Universidade Federal do Rio Grande do Norte, Brazil
Vijay Rao Duddu	Mahindra University, India
Vilson Dallemole	Universidade Tecnológica Federal do Paraná, Brazil
Wanchun Dou	Jiyang College of Zhejiang A&F University, China
Weifeng Liu	China University of Petroleum (East China), China
Weiheng Bai	University of Minnesota, USA
Wenxin Long	Penn State University, USA
Xingpeng Zhang	Southwest Petroleum University, China
Xuewen Wang	China University of Geosciences (Wuhan), China
Yang Shao	Hitachi, Japan
Yijing Wei	Northwestern University, USA
Yisong Chen	Georgia Institute of Technology, USA
Yuchen Cao	Northeastern University, USA
Yuning Yang	Food and Drug Administration, USA
Zhaoyun Ding	National University of Defense Technology, China
Zhichao Lian	Nanjing University of Science and Technology, China
Ziad Doughan	Beirut Arab University, Lebanon
Zoran Obradovic	Temple University, USA

Keynote Lectures

Modeling Interactions in Temporal Multiplex Networks

Zoran Obradovic

Computer and Information Sciences Department, Statistics Department, Temple University

This presentation will discuss our machine learning approaches for identifying, categorizing, and forecasting events of interest from limited data and imprecise labels. This is accomplished by integrating structured and unstructured multimodal information and jointly modeling multiple types of interactions within temporal multilayer networks.

Seeing Humans Through AI: Advances in Human-Centered Computer Vision

Antonis Argyros

Computer Science Department, University of Crete

Human-Centered Computer Vision (HCCV) is a rapidly evolving research domain at the intersection of computer vision and artificial intelligence, focusing on the observation and interpretation of humans and their interactions through visual data. In this talk we will present key contributions from our research group on the HCCV research landscape, highlighting computational methods for modeling and understanding aspects of human presence such as body pose, hand articulation, facial expressions, gestures, activities, and social interactions. We will showcase state-of-the-art systems for real-time human tracking, interaction analysis, and semantic scene understanding. We will also discuss recent advances in 3D human pose and shape estimation, visual-linguistic modeling for action anticipation, and sensing humans in context using multi-modal approaches. The presentation will also discuss applications of the developed technologies that span healthcare, robotics, ergonomics, digital culture, and entertainment, demonstrating the transformative potential of HCCV.

Impacts of AI on Humanity: Utopia Versus Dystopia

Hojjat Adeli

Ohio State University

The author has been doing research in the area of artificial intelligence (AI) and machine learning (ML) for over four decades. This lecture delves into his long journey in this field and its wide-ranging impact and pervasive influence on society. The popular media tends to claim we are living in the age of AI with the *largest economic and technological transformation in human history*, but we are actually living in a new golden age of *algorithms* rooted in Greek mathematician Euclid and formalized by the ninth-century Persian polymath Al-Khwarizmi, the father of algebra. AI is simply a subset of that. AI models are algorithms, but not all algorithms are AI. It is fallacious to assume AI can solve nearly all intractable problems. AI algorithms, in fact, have to be integrated with other types of algorithms such as image processing, signal processing, nonlinear dynamics, and chaos theory, just to name a few, to solve complex intractable problems. Examples of such synergistic integration will be presented.

A personal view of what is good, bad, and ugly about AI is presented. The lecture explores how the power of algorithms including AI/ML can be used to increase humanity's quality of life, for example in medical fields, such as predicting seizures, automated detection of hyperglycemia and hypoglycemia from facial images, and creating smart capsules. On the other hand, the author is concerned about increasing misuse and abuse of the technology used as a trustworthy source of advice and problem solving from social media addiction to spreading falsehood on a scale never imagined before, increase in inequalities, eroding people's sense of purpose, erosion of democracies, and in the extreme control of world affairs by AI agents.

AI for Trustworthy Autonomous Systems from Reactive Machines to Reasoning Agents

Anastasios Tefas

Department of Informatics, Aristotle University of Thessaloniki

Most current AI-powered autonomous systems rely almost exclusively on fast, intuitive reactive processing, that is pattern recognition from large datasets, while lacking the deliberate reasoning needed for planning, adaptation, and trustworthy decision making. This imbalance limits adaptability, safety, and explainability in dynamic, real-world environments. In this talk recent advances in General-Purpose AI for robotics that integrate reactive efficiency with deliberate analytical capabilities, both in inference and learning, will be presented. This enables autonomous systems to estimate confidence levels and detect anomalies while maintaining fast reactive behavior, escalate to advanced sophisticated behavior when needed, plan over long horizons, adapt to domain shifts, and make explainable and trustworthy decisions aligned with European values and the AI Act.

Plenary Talk

Information Security in Generative A.I.

Led by John MacIntyre

University of the Commonwealth Caribbean and Democratus University of Thrace,
Co-editor-in-Chief, AI and Ethics

Panel Members:

- Larry Medsker, University of Vermont, USA, and Co-Editor-in-Chief, AI and Ethics
- Jack Fisher, NASTAAR, UK
- Romit Choudhury, Questa-AI, Luxembourg

This talk explores the profound ethical dilemmas emerging from information security challenges in Generative AI adoption. As GenAI tools become ubiquitous in research, education, and enterprise, we face urgent questions about responsibility, trust, and the moral obligations of institutions and individuals deploying these technologies.

John MacIntyre will give a presentation examining critical ethical dimensions underlying information security in GenAI:

Consent and Transparency: When users unknowingly expose sensitive data to AI systems, who bears ethical responsibility? What obligations do institutions have to inform students, staff, and clients about data risks in AI tools they recommend or require?

Equity and Access: Do robust security measures create a two-tier system where only well-resourced organisations can safely use AI, while others face impossible choices between innovation and security? What are our ethical duties to those who cannot afford secure AI infrastructure?

Trust and Accountability: When AI systems leak confidential research, student data, or proprietary information, where does moral culpability lie—with users, institutions, or AI providers? How do we rebuild trust after breaches?

Professional Ethics: Are professionals who use insecure GenAI tools violating duties of confidentiality to clients, patients, or students? What ethical frameworks should guide AI use in sensitive contexts?

Surveillance and Control: Does institutional monitoring of AI usage to ensure security create new ethical problems around academic freedom, privacy, and surveillance?

Power and Vulnerability: How do security risks disproportionately affect vulnerable populations whose data appears in training sets without their consent?

Contents

The 11th Workshop on "B5G – Putting Intelligence to the Network Edge" (B5G-PINE)

Preface to B5G-PINE 2026 Proceedings

The **eleventh B5G-PINE Workshop**, following the great success, the wider market- and research-oriented impact and the good tradition of its predecessors, was established and organized in a concrete and efficient way to disseminate knowledge obtained from actual B5G/6G EU-funded projects (mainly coming from the Horizon Europe framework and the Horizon SNS-JU framework, both covering 5G and "Beyond 5G" (B5G) aspects) as well as from other research actions (such as DIGITAL, I3-PJG) in the wider thematic area of "B5G Innovative Activities – Putting Intelligence to the Network Edge ("B5G-PINE")" and with the aim of focusing upon Artificial Intelligence (AI) applications in modern 5G-/B5G-oriented telecommunications infrastructures.

Based on its selected research papers that have promoted a highly competitive framework of reference in the modern 5G/B5G environment, the 11th B5G-PINE Workshop had again a strong and deep impact on the broader context of the **AIAI 2026** (the 22nd International Conference on Artificial Intelligence Applications and Innovations), which has been hosted by the *Conference Center of CIHEAM MAI.Chania, Crete, Greece* (July 16-19, 2026). For once again, the preparatory work was mainly driven by the hard organizational effort, the dynamic coordination and the continuous supervision of **Dr. Ioannis P. Chochliouros** (Head of R&D Labs Section, Hellenic Telecommunications Organization S.A. - OTE, Greece), also coordinator of the SNS-JU project "6G-PATH", who has been the main organizer of the event for 11 consecutive years.

Support has also been provided by: **Dr. Latif Ladid** (Founder and President of IPv6 Forum and Researcher of SnT/University of Luxembourg, Luxembourg); **Prof. Christos Verikoukis** (Industrial Systems Institute (ISI)/Athenà Research Center & University of Patras, Greece) also coordinator of the SNS-JU projects "6G-BRICKS" and "FLECON-6G"; **Mr. Luis Cordeiro** and **Mr. João Fernandes** (OneSource Consultoria Informática Lda, Portugal); **Dr. Lechosław Tomaszewski** (Orange Polska S.A., Poland); **Prof. Vishanth Weerakkody** (University of Bradford, United Kingdom); **Prof. Almudena Díaz Zayas** (University of Malaga, Spain); **Prof. Qi Wang** (University of Leicester, United Kingdom); **Prof. José M. Alcaraz-Calero** (Aston University, United Kingdom); **Prof. Nancy Alonistioti** (National and Kapodistrian University of Athens, Greece); **Prof. Pavlos Lazaridis** (University of Huddersfield, United Kingdom); **Dr. Christos-Antonios Gizelis** (Hellenic Telecommunications Organization S.A. - OTE, Greece); **Dr. Zaharias Zaharis** (Aristotle University of Thessaloniki, Greece); **Dr. Michail-Alexandros Kourtis** (National Centre for Scientific Research "DEMOKRITOS", Greece) and; **Mrs. Anastasia S. Spiliopoulou** (Lawyer and IT expert, Hellenic Telecommunications Organization S.A. - OTE).

Special thanks also to Mrs. Anastasia S. Spiliopoulou (Hellenic Telecommunications Organization S.A. - OTE), Lawyer and IT expert, for her valuable support in a multiplicity of issues covering, *inter-alia*, administration and organizational management, relevance to European policy, technology and direct market impact and/or applicability.

Apart from the above members of the Workshop Organizing Committee, the entire process was also supported by more than 126 European experts, several of whom came from the relevant EU-funded projects (such as "6G-PATH", "FLECON-6G", "ELASTIC", "6G-BRICKS", "6G-SENSES", "AMBITIOUS", "DATAMITE", "COP-PILOT", "3D-CIRCULAR", "ELIXIRION", "VIGILANCE" and "SM4RTENANCE". These projects formed the "core" of the corresponding effort towards realizing a "joint" B5G-PINE 2026 Workshop, purely "5G/B5G"-oriented.

Among the originally submitted 37 papers, **20 papers** have finally been accepted as full papers (**acceptance ratio of 54**) due the high quality of the works and, *most importantly*, due to their strong relevance to ongoing EU-funded research activities. The accepted papers promote important innovation aspects from current – and in most of cases already validated and tested – 5G/B5G/6G research activities, thus "delineating" incentives for growth in the converged digital telecoms and IT market sector, especially emphasizing upon dedicated verticals with strong market impact.

The 11th B5G-PINE Workshop promoted, *inter-alia*, the context of **modern 5G/B5G/6G network infrastructures** and of related innovative services in a complex and highly heterogeneous underlying wireless communications ecosystem, strongly enhanced by the inclusion of cognitive capabilities and intelligence features, with the aim of significantly improving network management and orchestration. Furthermore, based upon the well-known Self-Organizing Network (SON) functionalities and related cognitive features, the 11th B5G-PINE Workshop not only identified but also promoted network planning and optimization processes through **Artificial Intelligence- (AI-) based tools,** able to smartly process input data from the surrounding environment(s) and come up with extended knowledge that can be formalized in terms of models and/or structured metrics, to explicitly "depict" the network behavior to a satisfactory level. This allows, *among others*, in-depth and detailed knowledge to be gained about the whole underlying 5G/B5G ecosystem; also understanding of hidden "patterns", data structures and relationships in a diversity of (interactive) sectors and, ultimately; their use for more efficient network management to respond to a multiplicity of situations and requirements to provide new market offerings and/or related innovative solutions. Inter-alia, the 11th B5G-PINE Workshop takes into account the fact that AI technologies have experienced remarkable growth in recent years, transforming industries with their ability to analyze data, automate processes and deliver intelligent solutions. This rapid evolution has been fueled by advancements in machine learning and neural networks, making AI a cornerstone of innovation. Specifically in the converged telecommunication sector, AI has the capability to profoundly change the way future networks operate by enabling autonomous and predictive functionalities on multiple network layers. As such, AI has already been nominated as one of the major building blocks of future 6G networks by prominent standardization bodies and associations while the vast majority of global telecommunications stakeholders are prioritizing research into AI-based technological enablers, as 6G is expected to offer AI-native functionalities.

In parallel, related **Key Performance Indicators (KPIs)** were also discussed, evaluated and assessed to the extent possible, to demonstrate progress implicated by the ongoing – or even by the expected – 5G/B5G growth. Among the "core objectives" of the B5G-PINE 2026 Workshop was to support **"delivery and implementation of intelligence" directly to the network's edge**, by exploiting the emerging paradigms of Network Functions Virtualization (NFV), Software Defined Networking (SDN), Network Slicing (NS) and Edge Cloud Computing. Moreover, the Workshop also supported promotion of rich virtualization and multi-tenant capabilities, optimally deployed close to the end-user(s) and, consequently, enhancing network and service opportunities towards establishing a competitive and innovative telecoms market with flavours to multiple verticals. The latter has also strongly influenced the entire effort towards introducing, discussing and analyzing the modern concept of **Key Value Indicators (KVIs)** which is the "next step" for the efficient incorporation of meaningful use cases in the market sector and offer innovations for the benefit of all involved end-users (i.e., corporate, residential, state and local authorities, etc.); indeed, the notion of KVIs as means to assess the impact of technology advancements on various dimensions of life and environment sustainability has gained attention during the last years and offers a reliable means to assess 6G networks from the sustainability dimension.

Among the "core" pillars of the 11th B5G-PINE Workshop was the innovative background of the ongoing Horizon SNS-JU **"6G-PATH" ("*6G Pilots and Trials through Europe*") project**, whose goal is to help foster the further development and integration of new and improved tools and/or products from EU companies within the B5G/6G framework, while also measuring relevant KPIs and KVIs in selected scenarios of use. To achieve this target, seven (7) dedicated testbeds are actually part of the project consortium, which are used by ten (10) use cases spread across four (4) key verticals of the market, that is: Health, Education, Smart Cities and Farming. Moreover, in the detailed context for Financial Support to Third Parties (FSTP) the project has already integrated two (2) extra pilot sites and has extended the testbeds with ten (10) additional technologies, while it also included thirty (30) new Use Cases through a dedicated Open Call procedure, to further involve the community and obtain more metrics and outcomes. 6G-PATH works closely with other ongoing/starting SNS-JU Stream-B and Stream-C projects in a "feedback" loop, to promote innovation, particularly via the assessment of KPIs/KVIs. The involved testbed facilities shall play a critical role in advancing the development and deployment of B5G/6G networks. They provide a reliable means of testing and validating new technologies, applications and services before their deployment in real-world scenarios. Therefore, 6G-PATH explores KPIs (such as, for example, latency, bandwidth, outage probability and energy efficiency) and KVIs that are critical to assess effectiveness of modern networks. Additionally, the project will investigate the evolution of capabilities including, *among others*, location accuracy and timeliness, end-to-end measurements, latency and AI network energy efficiency. Furthermore, 6G-PATH aims to explore throughput, latency, reliability and quality of experience (QoE), which are essential KPIs in assessing how end-users "perceive" the quality of a 6G-enabled application or service. Lastly, the project will look at deployment flexibility and service availability, which are crucial indicators in reducing barriers for developers and product adoption.

Seven papers have been relevant to the broader 6G-PATH scope, focusing either on the innovative architecture of the project or upon the dedicated verticals, that is:

(i) A joint paper (composed by OTE, the University of Malaga, OneSource Consultoria Informática Lda, University of Leicester, Aston University, ACTA Ltd. and Fraunhofer FOKUS Institute) discussing *"6G-PATH Experimentation in the B5G/6G Era via a Federated Approach"*. The 5G system has the ambition of responding to the widest range of services and applications in the history of mobile and wireless communications. Addressing the question of how a platform can host and integrate verticals and concurrently deal with reconciling their competing and opposing requirements, requires operational 5G/B5G infrastructures that can host various vertical industries' applications. The validation/assessment of use cases (UCs) via suitable experimentation platforms is fundamental in the development of any new mobile network technology, especially when the corresponding UCs are explicitly correlated to real market needs. After assessing the recent European initiatives in the H2020/5G-PPP and the SNS-JU frameworks, the paper focuses upon the innovative ecosystem created by the 6G-PATH project. In particular, the paper analyses the 6G-PATH experimentation environment that has been designed as a distributed, multi-testbed platform enabling coordinated experimentation across geographically dispersed infrastructures while preserving local autonomy and technological diversity. The work identifies and discusses the corresponding experimentation framework, as it is realized via a federated architectural approach consisting of distinct layers that collectively enable secure access, orchestration, and observability. All involved components, per layer, have been assessed as of their specific roles and functionalities.

(ii) A joint paper (composed by OTE, OneSource Consultoria Informática Lda, eBOS Technologies Limited, the University of Bradford and Kingston University) being about *"Smart Cities Evolutionary Progress in the B5G/6G Era: The 6G-PATH European Paradigm"*. The paper focused upon the specific ecosystem created by the innovative 6G-PATH EU-funded research framework, via assessing three selected use cases within the smart cities vertical sector and being relevant to: (a) connected and sensing city; (b) automated logistics, and; (c) security coordination. Having identified the major role that smart cities perform as an "enabler" of innovation, the authors have provided a closer look at sector-specific market dynamics by highlighting concrete demand drivers, strategic challenges and adoption barriers. Then they identified potential pathways for businesses by assessing strategic visions and value propositions, market commercialization channels and related key challenges for growth. The successful transition of the 6G-PATH project's innovations in the smart cities' vertical, from research excellence to real market deployment, requires a comprehensive understanding of market dynamics, business opportunities and strategic commercialization approaches within the rapidly evolving 6G telecommunications landscape.

(iii) A joint paper prepared by OTE, bSpoke Solutions and Diakinisis S.A., entitled as *"Network Slicing-Enabled Architecture for Autonomous Inventory Verification in Smart Warehouses"*. This paper presented a B5G-enabled architecture designed for autonomous inventory verification in warehouse environments, with a primary focus on network slicing. A detailed use case was introduced, where mobile robots perform real-time validation of load positions by interacting with Warehouse Management Systems (WMS). The proposed slicing framework ensures service differentiation, efficient resource utilization, and high system reliability.

(iv) A joint paper prepared by Fraunhofer FOKUS Institute and Slicefinity, entitled as *"Applying Trustful APIs for Quality on-Demand and Traffic Influence"*. Based on the original framework of the 6G-PATH ecosystem, this paper proposed a Trusted Application Function that "bridges the gap" between programmable network exposure and practical application experimentation. The solution provides controlled access to CAMARA-aligned Network APIs, integrates authorization and policy enforcement, and enables end-to-end validation within a real testbed environment. The approach is validated through healthcare and automotive traffic-influence scenarios, demonstrating measurable improvements in latency, prioritization and service reliability. The results underline the importance of trusted middleware for accelerating Network API adoption toward 6G programmable and intent-driven networks.

(v) A joint paper prepared by the University of Bradford, in cooperation with Kingston University and OTE, entitled as *"Bridging the Adoption Gap: A Techno-Economic and Strategic Commercialization Framework for 6G Across European Verticals"*. This paper draws on early findings from the Horizon Europe SNS JU 6G-PATH project, which studies ten use cases across Smart Farming, Education, Healthcare, and Smart Cities verticals. The use cases are positioned on the Technology Readiness Level (TRL) and Technology Adoption Life Cycle (TALC) scales on the basis of secondary market analysis, refined through expert panel review. All use cases occupy TRL 4-6, constrained by rural connectivity gaps, regulatory fragmentation, skills deficits, and uncertain return on investment. Six recurrent commercialization pathways are then comparatively assessed, and a Transformative Commercialization Model (TCM) is proposed, building on existing European telecom policy tools, universal service obligations, spectrum coverage requirements, and co-investment rules. Findings are linked to verified real-world outcomes measured through Key Value Indicators (KVIs).

(vi) A joint paper prepared by Fraunhofer FOKUS Institute, the Clinical Research Unit for Geriatrics at Charité Hospital Berlin, BlackDrop Biodrucker GmbH, Pinakashield Tech and OneSource Consultoria Informática Lda, entitled as *"6G-PATH: Architecture Validation via Internal and Open-Call Trials"*. This paper presents the 6G-PATH architecture and its validation through internal deployments and open-call trials in a healthcare scenario for chronic wound management. Starting from requirements derived with clinical partners and a survey of nursing personnel the authors identify high availability, security and seamless access to medical data as primary needs, while futuristic ultra-low latency features rank lower. These findings "drive" the design of an end-to-end platform that combines a beyond5G core network with edge capabilities, a secure experimental testbed, and healthcare-specific enablers. A realistic testbed with on-premises central and edge nodes, private 5G and integrated SDR-based access enables trials under strict time and budget constraints. The validation confirms that the proposed architecture can meet clinical workflow needs while demonstrating how B5G/6G capabilities such as network slicing, MEC, federated learning for attack detection and traffic influence for its mitigation can be concretely exploited in safety-critical healthcare environments.

(vii) A joint paper prepared by OneSource, Consultoria Informática Lda, Politecnico di Torino, the Technical University of Crete, Ericsson Research Finland, MOSA!C Lab, TU Wien and Ruhr University of Bochum, discusses an objective *"Towards AI-Driven*

Security in the Edge-Cloud Continuum: A Unified Architectural Perspective". Artificial Intelligence (AI)-driven security is emerging as a "key" approach for enabling adaptive monitoring, intelligent threat detection and automated response. This paper presents an integration-oriented perspective on AI-driven security in the Edge–Cloud continuum. It identifies the main security requirements and design dimensions and analyses representative building blocks, including extended Berkeley Packet Filter (eBPF)-based monitoring, hardware-accelerated intrusion detection, federated intelligence and privacy-preserving mechanisms. Based on these elements, the paper outlines a unified architectural framework that integrates telemetry collection, AI-driven detection, distributed learning, and trusted orchestration into an end-to-end security pipeline. The approach is further supported by insights from the **Horizon ELASTIC *("Efficient, portabLe And Secure orchesTration for reliable servICes")*** and **6G-PATH** projects, highlighting its applicability in realistic deployment scenarios. Finally, the paper discusses key challenges related to scalability, trust and robustness in next-generation Edge-Cloud systems.

There is also one more joint paper prepared by OTE and AgroApps –and presented by OTE – based on the **Horizon COP-PILOT ("*Collaborative Open Platform for PILOTing services across energing smart IoT and Edge computing environments*") project**. It is entitled as "*5G-Enabled Smart Agriculture: Requirements, Architecture and Key Benefits*". COP-PILOT, develops a Collaborative Open Platform framework geared towards orchestrating end-to-end services across diverse industry domains. To this aim, COP-PILOT provides a flexible solution designed to effectively manage various industry sectors while ensuring robust security, automation and intelligence features. Regarding interoperability, the framework seamlessly integrates with underlying technologies, ranging from IoT platforms to core infrastructure and facilitating collaboration across the compute continuum. Furthermore, this project empowers the development of advanced cross-sector applications by offering support for cutting-edge network services, thereby enabling heightened security, resource management and automation capabilities. The paper presents a comprehensive review of recent AI techniques applied to container orchestration and Kubernetes-based scheduling, analyzing their impact on cost reduction, performance optimization and resource efficiency. Key challenges such as model interpretability, real-time adaptability and integration with existing cloud and edge infrastructures were also discussed.

The paper presents an analysis of the advantages of 5G network technology in the agricultural domain, focusing on its ability to support complex, data-intensive and distributed agricultural applications. The study is grounded in the context of Cluster 3A, which aims to demonstrate how digital, autonomous and interoperable solutions can improve productivity, sustainability and resilience across the agri-food value chain. A representative use case is examined, integrating precision crop monitoring, autonomous agri-robotics, secure data management and smart logistics. Based on this UC, the key system requirements are identified, including real-time data processing, reliable connectivity in rural environments, interoperability and data sovereignty. The paper then analYses how 5G architectural features, such as network slicing, edge computing and massive machine-type communications, can effectively address these requirements. The findings highlight the critical role of 5G as a foundational infrastructure for next-generation agricultural systems, enabling scalable, efficient and trustworthy digital farming ecosystems.

Another essential "core" of the 11th B5G-PINE Workshop has been the framework promoted by the Horizon SNS-JU **"FLECON-6G" ("*Flexible Open Architecture and AI-driven Enabling Technologies for a Novel 6G Connectivity Platform*") project**. FLECON-6G "gathers" key participants from Phase-1 and Phase-2 SNS JU projects, aiming to make the "Intelligent 6G Network of Networks" vision a reality, with Trustworthiness and Generalisability of Native AI and Network Digital Twins (NDT) assisted approaches. It aims to deliver "key" technological assets in the form of collaborative and distributed frameworks offering scalability and support for multi-domain, multi-stakeholder infrastructures, jointly with network infrastructure programmability that supports the offloading of network application logic. The project provides groundbreaking research to "drive" the next phase of 6G Native AI research, addressing Trustworthiness and Generalizability via novel intent-driven frameworks and robust Foundation Models, that not only deliver zero-touch orchestration but also performance guarantees and robustness in multi-stakeholder infrastructures. In line with EU's policies, FLECON-6G will design, develop and validate through relevant proofs of concept (PoCs), several secure, trustworthy, resilient and reliable solutions across 4 heterogeneous verticals that require 6G performance capabilities. The work will strongly impact standardisation, with significant contributions to 3GPP, ITU, ETSI, GSMA and O-RAN and open-source communities.

A joint paper (prepared by OTE, Telefónica Innovación Digital S.L., Iquadrat Informatica S.L. and Industrial Systems Institute (ISI)/Athenà Research Center) has been presented by OTE. The context was about *"Key Value Indicators in 6G for Societal Evaluation"*. FLECON-6G envisions an "Intelligent 6G Network of Networks" that seamlessly integrates Native and Trustworthy AI. This vision empowers the automated and scalable orchestration of services and capabilities across diverse networks, subsystems and technological domains, fostering collaboration among multiple stakeholders. In this paper, the authors initially discussed four fundamental UCs of the project and then they proposed a set of the Key Value Indicators (KVIs) for evaluating the societal aspects of the above FLECON-6G use cases. Feedback from "key works" in the area such as those coming from **HEXA-X II, FIDAL, CENTRIC** and **SAFE-6G** has been taken into account. Probable extensions for future work have also been identified.

The 11th B5G-PINE Workshop has also taken care of innovative aspects coming from the ongoing EU-funded Horizon SNS-JU **"6G-BRICKS" ("*Building Reusable testbed Infrastructures for validating Cloud-to-device breakthrough technologieS*") project**. 6G networks, currently only existing as concepts, are envisioned as portals to a fully digitized society, where the physical and virtual world are "blended" via boundless Extended Reality (XR) and also as an "enabler" for the Digital and Green transformation of the European Industries. To support this vision, the network capacity must be increased at least by an order of magnitude, while infrastructures must be transformed into a very dense continuum. In order to "win this race" towards shaping the next-generation communication ecosystem, a new generation of testbed infrastructures and breakthrough research and technology development is needed, as well as a new generation of testbeds to support future research initiative. To this end, 6G-BRICKS aims to deliver a new

6G facility, building on the baseline of mature ICT-52 EU-funded platforms, that bring breakthrough cell-free (CF) and RIS (Reconfigurable Intelligent Surface) technologies that have shown promise for B5G networks. Moreover, novel unified control paradigms based on Explainable AI and Machine Reasoning are explored. All enablers will be delivered in the form of reusable components with open APIs (Application Programming Interfaces), termed as "bricks".

A joint paper (by OTE, Satways Ltd., Iquadrat Informatica S.L., Industrial Systems Institute (ISI)/Athenà Research Center and Space Hellas S.A.), presented by OTE and entitled as "*6G-BRICKS – Defining Objective Indicators Towards Elaboration of the Key Value Indicators*", focused upon the need for the evaluation of the Key Value Indicators (KVIs), aiming to "capture" broader societal, environmental and economic impacts of emerging technologies, within the transition towards B5G/6G networks. The issue of defining measurable and reliable indicators that integrate technical performance with broader value creation remains a key challenge. This paper focuses on objective indicators (OIs) as core elements for KVI evaluation, proposing a structured classification into three categories: (i) Network and system-level KPIs; (ii) application/services related metrics, and; (iii) questionnaires/surveys based indicators. Moreover, a comparative analysis of pioneer 6G initiatives (including projects like **ADROIT-6G**, **TrialsNet**, **6G-SANDBOX** and **Hexa-X II**) highlights diverse approaches. The 6G-BRICKS methodology is also presented by emphasizing upon a holistic, application-driven and user-centric evaluation approach. Although experimental validation is ongoing, the proposed 6G-BRICKS innovative framework contributes to the development of robust and scalable methodologies for KVI evaluation, efficiently supporting the alignment of 6G technologies with real-world value creation

Another pillar of the Workshop has been the dynamic framework promoted by the I3-PJG **"AMBITIOUS" ("*Advanced CoMputing Continuum Solutions for Boosting DigITalization across European RegionS*") project**, intending to offer a fundamental technological infrastructure, which will provide advanced data aggregation and clean-up, analytics, AI-enabled forecasting and secure information exchange mechanisms, via a transparent computing continuum infrastructure, to be integrated with existing, mature services (of at least TRL6) of the relevant stakeholders (i.e., mainly SMEs), unleashing for them yet unforeseen functionalities and opening up new pathways of commercial exploitation. The envisaged fundamental infrastructure is provided via the deployment of technological "pillars", which interact with existing services towards supporting the envisioned functionalities. Pillars are technological solutions answering crucial challenges of customers in different real-life situations that require reaction and prevention. The corresponding solutions aim at advancing the European companies in areas such as data analytics, AI, 5G, computing continuum and IoT. The solutions are demonstrated by a diverse set of specific use cases in the sectors of safety, smart water management, precise agriculture, and innovative digital health and wellbeing services.

A joint paper (prepared by OTE, Sammy IKE, the University of Patras and Egaleo Municipality of Attica), presented by OTE, was about discussing "*AI-powered Wildfire Detection*". In this paper, the authors focused upon the surveillance and monitoring use case, employing an AI-based framework for data driven applications. The work presents the overall architecture and pilot setup and also investigates the proposed AI-based wildfire detection system together with the pilot evaluation process. Further potential extension are also discussed.

The framework of the 11th B5G-PINE Workshop has also been enriched by the concept of the on-going EU-funded Horizon SNS-JU **"6G-SENSES"** (***"SEamless integratioN of efficient 6G wireleSs tEchnologies for communication and Sensing"***) **project.** This project provides a detailed exploration of innovations in the forthcoming sixth generation (6G) wireless systems, focusing on their dual role in communication and sensing. It proposes the integration of novel 6G RAN technologies such as Cell-Free Massive Multiple-Input Multiple-Output (MIMO) and Joint Communication and Sensing (JCAS) to support the 6G vision that is sustained by the current (and future) architectural framework based on 3GPP and O-RAN. The project considers a multi-technology RAN ecosystem with technologies that are able to offer sensing functionalities. These technologies are Sub-6, Wi-Fi, millimeter wave and 5G NR, which will coexist in a JCAS framework whose goal is to retrieve as much information as possible from the surrounding environment to improve energy efficiency, reduce power consumption and favour communication at high data rates. Additionally, some of these technologies will be amenable to be integrated in the first implementation of a fully distributed CF-mMIMO scheme using mmWave and Sub-6 technologies.

A joint paper (prepared by OTE/COSMOTE Mobile Telecommunications S.A., the Institute of Accelerating Systems and Applications from the University of Athens and 3IHP GmbH – Leibniz Institute for High Performance Microelectronics) has been presented by OTE. The work was about *"Techno-economic Factors affecting Deployment Options of Network Sensing"*. 6G networks will rely on highly heterogeneous and disaggregated infrastructures, while access networks must meet stringent coverage and performance requirements while incorporating Integrated Sensing and Communication (ISAC) as a native capability, introducing challenges in sensing performance, coverage and resource requirements. AI/ML techniques are so expected to play a key role in enabling adaptive and efficient network operation. To this end, transport networks will need to support diverse deployments, including macro- and dense micro- radio units as well as distributed and cloud-based RAN architectures (D-RAN, O-RAN), while converging fronthaul, backhaul, and sensing traffic over multi-technology wireless and optical infrastructures. Such complex deployments depend on geography, feasibility, traffic demand, technologies' availability and scalability and cost. Therefore, early-stage techno-economic evaluation of alternative deployment options is essential to identify cost drivers, optimize design choices, and assess sensing-related architectural options, enabling sustainable and economically viable 6G network planning. The paper provides insights on techno-economic factors affecting deployment options of network sensing in 6G networks, as retrieved through the techno-economic analysis performed in the context of 6G-SENSES project, and discusses their applicability based on **"MULTI-X"** ***("Multi-layer Network Digital Twin for Industrial Manufacturing")*** project.

Strong feedback has also been provided by the framework of the Horizon **"DATAMITE"** ***("DATA Monetization, Interoperability, Trading & Exchange")*** project, that foresees to revolutionize the European Data Market by helping users (such SMEs, large enterprises and public administrations) to better monetize, govern and enhance the trust of their data, empowering them to become new relevant players in the data economy. The project understands the precise nature of existing barriers and develops a simple but impactful technical framework that enables European enterprises and public administrations to overcome existing challenges and facilitate the monetization of their data. The core target consists of helping users to better monetize, govern and enhance the trust of their data by developing a set of key modules: Data Governance, quality, security, sharing & supporting tools. Interoperability with current leading storage technologies is achieved by building them on top of existing open-source component. DATAMITE empowers European companies by delivering a modular, open-source and multi-domain framework to improve Data Monetizing, Interoperability, Trading and Exchange, in the form of software modules, training and business materials. DATAMITE will validate its results in three (3) different use cases with a total of six (6) pilots (covering sectors of agriculture, energy, industrial and manufacturing and climate), demonstrating that the related framework is interoperable and usable in different domains and user needs, as: (i) Intra-corporate, multi-domain data exchange; (ii) data trading among Data Spaces, and; (iii) integration with other initiatives such as Data Markets, EU AI-on-demand platform or Digital Innovation Hubs (DIHs).

The following three papers have been presented:

(i) A paper prepared by OTE was about *"ReUse-Telco: Turning Regulatory Compliance into Data Value"*. Telecom operators process petabytes of distributed data daily, yet much of this potential remains buried under regulatory uncertainty and internal silos. Traditionally, the evolving European landscape, defined by GDPR, the Data Act, and the AI Act, has been viewed solely as a compliance hurdle. This paper argues the opposite: these regulations are actually the "blueprint" for a new era of sovereign and trusted data exchange. The authors introduce ReUse-Telco, a pragmatic framework designed to shift the industry from a "one-off" data usage mindset toward a sustainable Circular Data Economy. The framework is built on three integrated pillars: privacy-preserving monetization, regulation-by-design and data circularity. Instead of treating information as a disposable byproduct of network operations, the authors propose the creation of "Data Products", managed, reusable assets that carry their own Data SLOs, semantic definitions, and embedded compliance metadata. Drawing from the operational objectives of EU-funded initiatives like **DATAMITE** and the workforce-reskilling focus of the **DIGITAL 3D-CIRCULAR,** this research provides a comprehensive technical and governance roadmap. In addition, the works provides detail actionable architecture patterns, including secure enclaves and Privacy-Enhancing Technologies (PETs), alongside a measurable KPI model for value capture and reuse readiness. By treating data as a circular resource that evolves through multiple lifecycles, operators can finally bridge the gap between strict legal compliance and sustainable commercial innovation.

(ii) A paper jointly prepared by the Hellenic Electricity Distribution Network Operator (HEDNO) S.A. and the Centre for Research & Technology Hellas (CERTH) and presented by HEDNO S.A. It was about *"Energy Data Sharing through Data Spaces with DATAMITE: Supporting Digital Transformation"*. This paper evaluates the DATAMITE framework as an enabler for automated, secure, and standardised energy data exchange within the context of an energy Distribution System Operator's (DSO) network operations. Through a pilot involving a DSO and an energy service provider, the authors demonstrate how DATAMITE supports end-to-end processes, from data ingestion and quality validation to anonymisation, harmonisation, policy definition and publication to an Energy Data Space catalogue. Eight validation scenarios are implemented to test the framework's capabilities to support the process of preparation and sharing of data products through an Energy Data Space. The results showcase substantial reductions in manual effort and time-to-consumption, while improving data product compatibility and governance, compared to previous workflows and underscore the DATAMITE framework's role in enabling scalable, trustworthy data exchange and supporting the improvement of energy efficiency in the sector.

(iii) A joint paper (prepared collaboratively between Eötvös Loránd University (ELTE), OTE, FIR e. V. an der RWTH Aachen and the University College Cork), presented by ELTE. This was entitled as *"A Business Blueprint for Data Monetization"*. This paper presents a novel action blueprint for data monetization for commercial use. It consists of three modules that were developed as self-contained work packages, namely the Data Monetization Maturity Model (DMMM), a set of strategy archetypes for data monetization including a corresponding business canvas tool, and a novel data valuation model. Together, these elements form a coherent framework that enables companies to assess their readiness for data monetization, quantify the value of their data assets and design viable, value-based business models. The authors presented these three components and reported the results of a pilot deployment with practical use cases in an industrial setting. The paper summarized key results of the DATAMITE project and added further transfer insights.

The 11th B5G-PINE Workshop has also been supported by the DIGITAL **"3D-CIRCULAR"** ***("Digital Deep tech Driven Circular Economy")*** **project**. This project holds a central position in the strategic thinking and the successful implementation of the EU strategies, regulations and directives for the realisation of the EU green and digital transition, which depends on reskilling and upskilling of future young talents, professional experts and the EU workforce in general (as well as beyond the EU borders). The project's objective is to build the next generation of the educational and certification ecosystem for exercising expert-level, interdisciplinary capabilities within the context of promoting a European, digitally native, circular economy. To this end, 3D-CIRCULAR intends to create new educational master-level and doctorate programmes and certification components that strongly relate to the ongoing innovation aspects promoted by the European Commission and the research performed in the various EU funding programmes. Such programmes embrace the development of innovative curricula and the respective courses and self-standing learning components, which emphasise the role of deep tech technologies to drive the operational aspects of sustainable growth through circular economy principles. The project brings together industrial and research communities into a sustainable and ambitious partnership to promote excellence and support workforce upskilling and reskilling towards a digital and green EU economy that will ensure the sustainable development and the digital transformation of the business ecosystem in the Europen Union.

A joint paper has been prepared by OTE, AiNTIGONE and the Center for Research and Technology Hellas (CERTH) and presented by OTE. This was entitled as *"Optimizing Digital Resources Usage in Large Industries: a Telecommunications Use Case"*. This paper describes the results of an innovative solution that aims to optimize the use of digital resources within a large industry in the telecommunications domain. It attempts to address the challenge of managing large amounts of data by a group of companies, which consists of many subsidiaries that collect, process and store their own data across heterogeneous systems. The solution is part of an open-source modular framework, the main goal of which is to assist European companies in preparing their data for trading, exchange and potential monetization. The proposed architecture is based on distributed data management for big data analytics, follows the data product paradigm, and has been validated against real-world business case scenarios. The findings presented show how enterprises can benefit from cutting-edge technology and data-driven insights to achieve both economic growth and cost effectiveness, while respecting the principles of the digital circular economy. In this way, companies make a significant step towards achieving their sustainability and environmental goals, by reducing digital waste and making more efficient usage of their existing data and infrastructure resources.

The Workshop has also been supported by the ongoing **Marie Sklodowska-Curie Actions (MSCA) programme "ELIXIRION"** ***("rEaLIzing healthcare 4.0 eXploIting the 6G netwoRk evolution")*** **project**. The project's mission is to pioneer a four-year effort focused on establishing a training and research network, by leveraging cutting-edge 6G technologies, for the improvement of healthcare systems laying the foundation for a future where healthcare is advanced, inclusive, and responsive to the needs of individuals and society as a whole. The project's vision encompasses providing diverse healthcare services to all citizens/patients, fostering a secure, efficient, and profitable healthcare ecosystem for all stakeholders.

A paper has been prepared jointly by Orange Polska S.A. and the University Clinical Hospital No.1, Medical University of Silesia in Katowice. The paper has been presented by Orange Polska S.A. and it was about *"Healthcare 5.0 and challenges for 6G mobile technology"*. Indeed, Healthcare (HC) 5.0 conditions and use cases create demands addressed to Information and Communication Technologies (ICTs, particularly mobile networks. The paper confronts HC 5.0 service requirements with the current state-of-the-art 5G System (5GS) and future 6G System (6GS) whose standardisation has only just begun. There are technological barriers to implementing extremely-high data rate and very-low jitter HC services in 5GS, but more importantly, legal barriers ("Network neutrality") for mobile operators and their market strategies (focus on mass consumers and delayed deployment of network slicing support causing disappointment to industrial customers). 6GS has the technological potential to support HC 5.0 depending on the mutual synchronization of 6GS and HC 5.0 development roadmaps. Examples of **ETHER**, **6G-PATH** and **ELIXIRION** projects show how research initiatives contribute to the creation of specific 6GS enablers for HC 5.0 support.

Among the supportive concepts for the 11th B5G-PINE Workshop was also the framework promoted by the on-going DIGITAL **"VIGILANCE"** **("*Versatile Intelligent aGents for Interconnected Ledgers and Autonomous Next-gen Cybersecurity Ecosystems*") project.** The main goal of VIGILANCE is to lower the effort and cost for cybersecurity vendors and Critical Infrastructure (CI) operators to establish, deploy and operate intelligent cyber-defence strategies based on Zero Trust Architectures (ZTA), which will be characterized by a considerable degree of autonomy and scalability. The project will enable the development of autonomous and intelligent cybersecurity systems grounded on ZTA principes, that will be able to operate across multiple administrative domains to secure entire digital supply chains of interconnected CIs in different industrial sectors. The project will revolutionise the cybersecurity landscape by delivering a highly innovative, scalable, incremental, integrated, and operational 5-layer platform that leverages breakthroughs in next-generation digital technologies including Adversarial Artificial Intelligence (AI), Generative AI (GenAI), Blockchain and Quantum computing. At its core, the platform ensures end-to-end cybersecurity governance by transforming fragmented insights into accessible, actionable, and proactive CTI, empowering organisations to collectively anticipate, mitigate, and neutralise threats before they materialise and escalate. To this end, VIGILANCE will enhance continuous verification, real-time anomaly detection, and adaptive risk and vulnerability assessment, resulting to the transformation of the cybersecurity approaches from a reactive defence model to a proactive, self-sustaining, and scalable security ecosystem.

A joint vision paper has been prepared by OTE, UBITECH Ltd., the National Kapodistrian University of Athens, eBOS Technologies Limited, INNOV-ACTS and STAM SRL. The paper has been presented by OTE and it was about *"Designing the Future of Secure Intelligence: A Vision for AI-Enabled Cyber-Resilient Ecosystems"*. In the accelerated evolution of digital ecosystems, there is a demand for a new synthesis of Artificial Intelligence (AI), cybersecurity-by-design and autonomous decision-making in diverse settings. The above paper provides a consolidated view, formulated by six European initiatives (i.e.: **VIGILANCE**, **CyberAId**, **ENFORCE**, **Act4Food**, **CTIS4NIS** and **5G-TACTIC**) that contribute jointly to the evolution of intelligent, cyber-resilient, and trustworthy next-generation systems. Employing common methodologies, prototypes, immense pilot deployments and trials, the EU initiatives through the collective, present in this paper, formulate a coherent roadmap to install these components into future large-scale digital infrastructures: automation driven by AI, proactive threat detection, zero-touch operational paradigm and any type of trustworthy data flow. Also, the vision engulfs related topics like federated and collaborative AI, guarding all the cyber-physical continuum, secure and interoperable data spaces, and after that application-driven intelligence, forwards the range across the domains from critical infrastructures to the food systems guaranteeing a mechanism to bring what has been described to the physical world. The paper concludes by presenting a common architectural blueprint and starts highlighting open research issues and policy considerations that could build an environment where AI-driven cyber resilience intelligence would become a rudder of European digital autonomy and societal resilience in forthcoming decades.

One more among the supportive concepts for the 11th B5G-PINE Workshop was also the framework promoted by the on-going DIGITAL **"SM4RTENANCE"** (**"*European Deployment of Smart Manufacturing Asset 4.0 MultilateRal DaTa Sharing SpacEs for an AutoNomous Operation of CollAborative MainteNance and Circular SErvices*") project.** Industry has shown the potential of data-driven and AI powered algorithms for predictive maintenance (PdM) & dynamic asset management services in small scale trials. In parallel embryonic data spaces & strategic European infrastructures for digital sovereignty in manufacturing are now set; i.e. EDIH (European Digital Innovation Hub) network, AI Testing and Experimentation Facilities (TEF) facilities; Data Spaces Support Center (DSSC); DOME (Distributed Open Marketplace for Europe) marketplace, OSS

(Open Systems Solutions) Data Space connectors & evaluation facilities. To bring such potential at scale, SM4RTENANCE exploits all those manufacturing assets to deploy a data space federation. The development of collaborative PdM solutions demands a cross-sectorial approach that cannot be achieved by just individually extending services and capabilities of individual data space initiatives. SMARTENANCE objective is to: (a) Harmonise and facilitate a data space federation bringing together embryonic data spaces DAW Aero Data Marketplace, SCSN (Smart Connected Supplier Netrwork), Catena-X, BAIDATA and new Manufacturing-X initiative; (b) modernise asset IoT and PdM service platforms to provide native connection and support to data sharing solutions; (c) demonstrate and evaluate the performance of multi-lateral digital value chains for collaborative and circular maintenance business applications in 5 sectors of strategic business impact for European industrial sovereignty; (d) support data space participation with dedicated skill up programmes, EDIH services and clear guidelines, code of conduct and industrial agreements across the data space federation.

OTE has prepared a paper entitled as *"Smart Manufacturing Meets Data Spaces: A New Paradigm"*. Data is, indeed, a critical asset in today's world. As the global data environment is rapidly evolving with substantial proportion of internet data to be machine-generated, the extensive volumes of real-time industrial data have the potential to improve operational efficiency and to drive innovation enabling transformation in the manufacturing landscape. The paper examines the role of data as a "key driver" of economic growth within the European data economy, highlighting the strategic vision behind the European Strategy for Data. It also explores the concept of data spaces as decentralized, trusted ecosystems that enable secure and sovereign data sharing across sectors. Additionally, it outlines "key initiatives" such as IDSA (International Data Spaces Association), DSSC and Gaia-X. Finally, it explores the SM4RTENANCE EU-funded project, which is designed to exploit cross-sector manufacturing assets to deploy a data space federation that will enhance collaboration within the industrial ecosystem strengthening data sovereignty.

One more joint paper prepared by the University of Coimbra and OneSource Consultoria Informática Lda. The scope of the work was supported by national funds through the **COMPETE 2030 Programme**, co-financed by the European Union through the **European Regional Development Fund (FEDER)**, under the CoParticipation project (**COMPETE2030-FEDER-02208000**).

The paper, presented by the University of Coimbra, was aboiut *"Harmful Content Moderation in e-Participation Platforms"*. Moderating harmful textual content in e-participation platforms requires balancing user safety with the protection of legitimate democratic expression, procedural fairness and deliberative quality. The proposed paper reviewed the evolution of automated moderation approaches, from rule-based and classical machine learning methods to transformers and large language models, while highlighting the contextual, explainability, bias and governance challenges that are especially salient in civic settings. Building on this review, the paper presented a multi-Large Language Model (LLM) moderation workflow with council-based consolidation and human oversight. Experimental results using a test set of 150 examples showed that while individual model accuracy peaked at 0.6267 with Llama 3.2, an oracle accuracy of 0.9467 highlights the potential for improved results. Aggregating judgments through a council yielded 0.5733 accuracy, suggesting that refining consolidation rules is a “key path” forward for robust decisions. The proposed workflow was further situated as a possible moderation component within the broader Co-Participation platform. The study positioned harmful content moderation in e-participation as a socio-technical governance challenge rather than a conventional text classification task, and emphasised the need for evaluation methods aligned with deliberative and institutional goals.

All the above projects cover a wide variety of technical and business aspects and explicitly promote options for growth and development in the respective market(s). All accepted papers are fully aligned to the explicit objectives of the 11th B5G-PINE scope and purely introduce innovative features, able to “influence” a 5G/B5G/6G effective deployment.

In addition, interactivity “liaisons” between the above projects have either been created and/or strengthened, allowing for exchanging of information and experiences between the participating entities, so that to further promote research and development towards the B5G/6G “path”.

Organization

Co-chairs

Ioannis P. Chochliouros	Hellenic Telecommunications Organization S.A. (OTE), Greece
Latif Ladid	IPv6 Forum and University of Luxembourg, Luxembourg
Christos Verikoukis	Industrial Systems Institute - Athenà Research Center and University of Patras, Greece
Luís Cordeiro	OneSource Consultoria Informática Lda, Portugal
João Fernandes	OneSource Consultoria Informática Lda, Portugal
Lechosław Tomaszewski	Orange Polska S.A., Poland
Vishanth Weerakkody	Bradford University, UK
Almudena Díaz Zayas	University of Malaga, Spain
Qi Wang	University of Leicester, UK
José M. Alcaraz-Calero	Aston University, UK
Nancy Alonistioti	National and Kapodistrian University of Athens, Greece
Pavlos Lazaridis	University of Huddersfield, UK
Christos-Antonios Gizelis	Hellenic Telecommunications Organization S.A. (OTE), Greece
Zaharias Zaharis	Aristotle University of Thessaloniki, Greece
Michail-Alexandros Kourtis	National Centre for Scientific Research "Demokritos", Greece
Anastasia S. Spiliopoulou	Hellenic Telecommunications Organization S.A. (OTE), Greece

Program Committee Members

George Lyberopoulos	OTE, Greece
Alexandros Kostopoulos	OTE, Greece
Dora Politi	OTE, Greece
Maria Belesioti	OTE, Greece
Michalis Rantopoulos	OTE, Greece
Christina Lessi	OTE, Greece
Elina Theodoropoulou	OTE, Greece

Ioanna Mesogiti	OTE, Greece
Fofy Setaki	OTE, Greece
Eirini Vasilaki	OTE, Greece
Achilleas Marinakis	OTE, Greece
Nina Mitsopoulou	OTE, Greece
Dimitrios Arvanitozisis	OTE, Greece
Kostas Ramantas	Iquadrat Informatica S.L., Spain
Adlen Ksentini	EURECOM, France
Konstantinos Filis	OTE, Greece
Michalis Kefalogiannis	OTE, Greece
Betty Charalampopoulou	GeoSystems Hellas S.A., Greece
Adonis Bogris	University of West Attica, Greece
Nikolaos Melis	National Observatory of Athens, Greece
Uthayasankar (Sankar) Sivarajah	University of Kingston, UK
Jing Li	University of Bradford, UK
Imesha Devindi Wedikkara Gedara	University of Bradford, UK
Anastasios Kourtis	National Centre for Scientific Research "Demokritos", Greece
Susana Sargento	Instituto de Telecomunicações, Portugal
Pedro Rito	Instituto de Telecomunicações, Portugal
Nils Lahmann	Charité - Universitätsmedizin Berlin, Germany
Simone Kuntz	Charité - Universitätsmedizin Berlin, Germany
Fihmi Mousa	MCS Data Labs GmbH, Germany
Celine Mousa	MCS Data Labs GmbH, Germany
Gregor Liebscher	MCS Data Labs GmbH, Germany
Tarik Taleb	ICT-Ficial Oy, Finland & Ruhr University Bochum, Germany
Yan Chen	ICT-Ficial Oy, Finland
Eduardo Fullea Carrera	Telefónica S.A., Spain
Arturo Torrealba Carrera	Telefónica Innovation Digital S.L., Spain
Christos Skoufis	eBOS Technologies Limited, Cyprus
Marilena Paraskeva	eBOS Technologies Limited, Cyprus
Ioan Constantin	Orange Romania S.A., Romania
Cristian Patachia-Sultanoiu	Orange Romania S.A., Romania
Marius Iordache	Orange Romania S.A., Romania
Elena-Madalina Oproiu	Orange Romania S.A., Romania
Ana Ciobanu	Orange Romania S.A., Romania
Filipe Cabral Pinto	Altice Labs S.A., Portugal

Carlos Marques	Altice Labs S.A., Portugal
Alexandre Moron	Airbus DS SLC, France
Laurent Drouglazet	Airbus DS SLC, France
Pedro Merino-Gómez	University of Malaga, Spain
Anna Brunstrom	Karlstad University, Sweden
Mohammad Rajiullah	Karlstad University, Sweden
Ovidiu Ana	Fundatia Orange, Romania
Carmen Lazar	Fundatia Orange, Romania
Juan Manuel Losada Rodriguez	Agencia Estatal Consejo Superior de Investigaciones Científicas, Spain
Andreea Corici	Fraunhofer FOKUS, Germany
Hemant Zope	Fraunhofer FOKUS, Germany
Marius Corici	Fraunhofer FOKUS, Germany
Jorge Gallego Madrid	OdinS Solutions SL, Spain
Ana Hermosilla	OdinS Solutions SL, Spain
Evi Tziola	App-Art S.A., Greece
Katerina Tziola	App-Art S.A., Greece
Efthymios Serpentzoglou	App-Art S.A., Greece
Samuel Almeida	F6S Network Ireland, Ireland
Mirana Khanom	F6S Network Ireland, Ireland
Evgeny Bogdanov	Gamaya/Terraview GmbH, Switzerland
Piyush Harsh	Terraview GmbH, Switzerland
Peter Gray	CloudSigma AG, Switzerland
Blagovest Tushev	CloudSigma AG, Switzerland
Tilemachos Doukoglou	ACTA Ltd., Greece
Panayiotis Verrios	ACTA Ltd., Greece
Nicola di Pietro	Hewlett-Packard Italiana S.r.l., Italy
Daniele Munaretto	Hewlett-Packard Italiana S.r.l., Italy
Donal Morris	CEO, RedZinc Services, Ireland
Daniel Alcaraz Mora	RedZinc Services, Ireland
Jeanne Caffrey	RedZinc Services, Ireland
Vaios Koumaras	Infolysis P.C., Greece
Marina Koulaloglou	Infolysis P.C., Greece
Nikolaos Vrionis	Infolysis P.C., Greece
Ioannis Neokosmidis	INCITES Consulting S.A.R.L., Luxembourg
Theodoros Rokkas	INCITES Consulting S.A.R.L., Luxembourg
Monique Calisti	Martel Innovate, Switzerland
Dimitrios Brodimas	Independent Power Transmission Operator, Greece
Ralitsa Rumenova	Entra Energy, Bulgaria

Verzhinia Ivanova	Entra Energy, Bulgaria
Georgi Hristov	Vivacom, Bulgaria
Atanas Velkov	Vivacom, Bulgaria
Irina Ciornei	University of Cyprus, Cyprus
Ioannis Giannoulakis	Eight Bells Ltd., Greece
Stamatia Rizou	Singular Logic Systems Ltd., Greece
Cedric Crettaz	Mandat International, Switzerland
Tinku Rasheed	TriaGnoSys GmbH, Germany
Rodoula Makri	National Technical University of Athens, Greece
Antonino Albanese	Italtel, SpA, Italy
Claus Keuker	Smart Mobile Labs AG, Germany
Begoña Blanco	Universidad del Pais Vasco/Euskal Herriko Unibertsitatea (EHU), Spain
Jose-Oscar Fajardo	Universidad del Pais Vasco/Euskal Herriko Unibertsitatea (EHU), Spain
George Agapiou	National Centre for Scientific Research "Demokritos", Greece
Stylianos Trevlakis	InnoCube I.K.E., Greece
Christos Zaroliagis	University of Patras, Greece
Spyros Kontogiannis	University of Patras, Greece
Ioannis Panaretou	SAMMY IKE, Greece
Ioanna Papafili	OTE, Greece
Dimitra Vali	OTE, Greece
Christos Mizikakis	OTE, Greece
Kelly Georgiadou	OTE, Greece
George Tsiouris	OTE, Greece
Stefanos Chatzipantelis	OTE, Greece
George Tsiouris	OTE, Greece
Dimitrios Mouroukos	OTE, Greece
Stylianos Androulidakis	OTE, Greece
Alexandros Stathakis	OTE, Greece
Stamatios Perdikouris	OTE, Greece
Evangelos Tompras	OTE, Greece
Antonis Georgiou	ACTA Ltd., Greece
Angelos Antonopoulos	NearBy Computing S.L., Spain
Nicola Cadenelli	NearBy Computing S.L., Spain
Dimitrios Tzempelikos	Municipality of Egaleo, Greece
Panagiotis Kontopoulos	National & Kapodistrian University of Athens, Greece
Sotiris Nikoletseas	University of Patras, Greece
Vasilios Vlachos	University of Thessaly, Greece

Srdjan Krčo	DunavNET, Serbia
Nenad Gligoric	DunavNET, Serbia
Luca Bolognini	Italian Institute for Privacy, Italy
Konstantinos Patsakis	University of Piraeus, Greece
Dimitris Diakakis	OTE, Greece
Jason Diakoumakos	OTE, Greece
Dimitris Salmatanis	OTE, Greece
George Pappas	OTE, Greece
Simos Hinopoulos	OTE, Greece

5G-Enabled Smart Agriculture: Requirements, Architecture and Key Benefits

Christina C. Lessi[1(✉)], Gregory Mygdakos[2], and Ioannis P. Chochliouros[1]

[1] Hellenic Telecommunications Organization (OTE) S.A, Athens, Greece
clessi@oteresearch.gr
[2] AgroApps, Kalamaria, Greece

Abstract. The agricultural sector is undergoing a significant transformation driven by the integration of digital technologies, automation and data-driven decision-making [1]. Emerging paradigms such as precision agriculture, agri-robotics and smart supply chains require advanced communication infrastructures capable of supporting massive connectivity, ultra-reliable low-latency communication and secure data exchange [2, 3]. Fifth-generation (5G) network technology is widely recognized as a key enabler for these requirements, offering enhanced performance compared to previous generations [4, 5]. This paper presents an analysis of the advantages of 5G network technology in the agricultural domain, focusing on its ability to support complex, data-intensive and distributed agricultural applications. The study is grounded in the context of the COP-PILOT project and in particular Cluster 3A, which aims to demonstrate how digital, autonomous and interoperable solutions can improve productivity, sustainability and resilience across the agri-food value chain. A representative use case is examined, integrating precision crop monitoring, autonomous agri-robotics, secure data management and smart logistics. Based on this use case, the key system requirements are identified, including real-time data processing, reliable connectivity in rural environments, interoperability and data sovereignty. The paper then analyses how 5G architectural features, such as network slicing, edge computing and massive machine-type communications, can effectively address these requirements. The findings highlight the critical role of 5G as a foundational infrastructure for next-generation agricultural systems, enabling scalable, efficient and trustworthy digital farming ecosystems.

Keywords: Smart Agriculture · 5G networks · Edge Computing · IoT · Agri-Robotics · UAV · Low-Latency Communications · Massive Machine-Type Communications

1 Introduction

Agriculture is facing increasing pressure to enhance productivity while simultaneously addressing sustainability, environmental impact and resource efficiency. Climate change, population growth and the need for more resilient food systems are driving the adoption

Published by Springer Nature Switzerland AG 2027
A. Papaleonidas et al. (Eds.): AIAI 2026 Workshops, IFIP AICT 796, pp. 23–33, 2027.
https://doi.org/10.1007/978-3-032-30507-7_1

of advanced technologies in the agri-food sector. In this context, the transition toward smart and digital agriculture has become a key priority, leveraging innovations such as the Internet of Things (IoT), artificial intelligence (AI), remote sensing and robotics.

Modern agricultural systems are evolving into highly interconnected and data-driven ecosystems. Precision farming applications rely on heterogeneous data sources, including satellite imagery, unmanned aerial vehicles (UAVs), in-field sensors and weather stations, to monitor crop health and optimize inputs. At the same time, autonomous systems such as unmanned ground vehicles (UGVs) are being deployed to perform tasks like crop scouting and targeted interventions. Wearable plant sensors represent a further dimension of this sensing ecosystem, enabling direct physiological monitoring at the leaf level and providing fine-grained data on crop health and nutritional status (Fig. 1). In parallel, the integration of secure data management solutions and smart logistics enabling end-to-end visibility across the agri-food value chain [5–8].

However, the effective deployment of such complex and distributed systems introduces significant communication challenges. Agricultural environments are typically characterized by large geographic areas, limited infrastructure and highly dynamic conditions. The need for real-time data exchange, ultra-reliable connectivity, support for massive numbers of devices and secure data sharing exceeds the capabilities of traditional communication technologies.

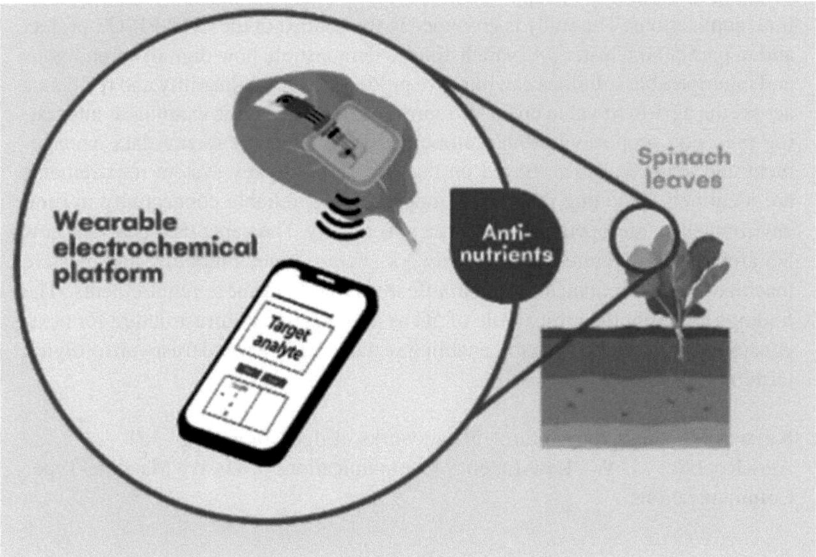

Fig. 1. Wearables use in Smart Agriculture

Fifth-generation (5G) mobile networks are emerging as a key enabler for addressing these challenges [9]. By offering enhanced mobile broadband (eMBB), ultra-reliable low-latency communications (URLLC) and massive machine-type communications (mMTC), 5G provides the necessary technological foundation to support advanced agricultural applications. Additionally, architectural features such as network slicing and edge computing enable flexible, scalable and application-specific network deployments, which are particularly relevant for heterogeneous agri-food systems [10–13].

This paper builds upon the context of the COP-PILOT research project and specifically Cluster 3A, which focuses on demonstrating how digital, autonomous and interoperable solutions can improve productivity, sustainability and resilience in modern agricultural systems. During its initial phase, Cluster 3A established the technical and organisational foundations for innovative agricultural pilots, integrating precision farming, agri-robotics, secure data infrastructures and smart supply chains.

In particular, the project developed and integrated multiple components, including advanced farm management platforms, UAV-based monitoring systems, wearable plant sensors, autonomous robotic platforms and blockchain-based data management mechanisms. These components collectively form a complex, distributed system that requires robust, low-latency and secure communication capabilities.

2 Architecture of an Integrated Smart Agriculture System

2.1 System Overview

The proposed smart agriculture system is designed as a multi-layer, distributed architecture that integrates heterogeneous technologies and services across the agri-food value chain. The architecture supports end-to-end data acquisition, processing, decision-making and actuation, enabling a fully digital and interconnected agricultural ecosystem.

At a high level, the system follows a layered approach consisting of: (i) the data acquisition layer, (ii) the communication layer, (iii) the data processing and service layer and (iv) the application and actuation layer. These layers interact seamlessly to enable real-time monitoring, autonomous operations and optimized supply chain management.

Data Acquisition Layer

The data acquisition layer is responsible for collecting information from diverse and distributed sources deployed across the agricultural environment. These include satellite-based observations, unmanned aerial vehicles (UAVs), in-field sensors and local weather stations. In addition, wearable plant sensors are utilized to monitor physiological parameters directly at the leaf level, enabling fine-grained assessment of crop health and nutritional status.

This multi-source sensing approach ensures high spatial and temporal resolution of data, allowing the system to capture both macro-scale and micro-scale variations in environmental and crop conditions [14].

Communication Layer

The communication layer enables reliable and continuous connectivity between all system components, facilitating data exchange across geographically distributed elements. It supports bidirectional communication between sensing devices, autonomous machinery, cloud infrastructures and end-user applications.

Given the large number of connected devices and the need for real-time data transmission, this layer must support high device density, low latency and reliable connectivity, particularly in rural and infrastructure-limited environments. The communication layer acts as the backbone of the system, ensuring seamless integration between physical and digital components [10].

Data Processing and Service Layer

The data processing and service layer is responsible for aggregating, storing and analysing the collected data. A multi-cloud infrastructure is employed to support scalable data management, while an orchestration framework coordinates the interaction between different services and platforms.

Advanced analytics and artificial intelligence (AI) services are deployed to extract actionable insights from the collected data [15]. These include crop health assessment, stress detection, weed identification and predictive analytics for decision support. Data from multiple sources—such as UAV imagery, satellite data and field sensors—are fused to generate a unified and coherent representation of the agricultural environment.

To ensure secure and trustworthy data exchange, blockchain-based mechanisms are integrated into the architecture, enabling immutable logging of critical data and events across the agri-food value chain. In parallel, interoperable APIs are implemented to facilitate communication between heterogeneous subsystems.

Application and Actuation Layer

The application and actuation layer provides interfaces and tools for end-users, including farmers, agronomists and supply chain operators. Through farm management platforms, users can visualize real-time data, monitor crop conditions and receive decision support recommendations.

This layer also enables the execution of automated and semi-automated actions. Autonomous systems, such as unmanned ground vehicles (UGVs), receive processed information and perform targeted interventions, including precision spraying and field scouting [7, 16]. This creates a closed-loop system in which data-driven insights directly trigger physical actions in the field.

Furthermore, the architecture extends to supply chain operations, where logistics platforms utilize real-time data for tracking, coordination and optimization of transportation processes. Telemetry and geolocation services provide continuous visibility into product movement, supporting efficient and transparent farm-to-fork operations.

2.2 System Requirements

The architecture described in the previous section introduces a complex, distributed and data-intensive agricultural system that integrates sensing, analytics, autonomous operations and supply chain management. The effective operation of such a system imposes a set of stringent technical requirements on the underlying communication and computing infrastructure.

These requirements arise from the need to support real-time monitoring, large-scale device connectivity, secure data exchange and reliable operation in geographically dispersed and often infrastructure-constrained environments.

Real-Time Data Transmission and Low Latency
Many system functionalities rely on near-real-time data exchange and processing. Applications such as UAV-based crop monitoring, AI-driven weed detection and autonomous robotic interventions require timely delivery of data to ensure accurate decision-making and effective actuation.

In particular, closed-loop operations—where sensor data is processed and immediately translated into actions (e.g., precision spraying)—demand low end-to-end latency. Delays in communication could lead to suboptimal decisions, reduced efficiency, or even operational failures in autonomous systems.

Massive Device Connectivity
The system incorporates a large number of heterogeneous devices, including sensors, UAVs, robotic platforms, telemetry units and user interfaces. As agricultural deployments scale, the number of connected devices increases significantly, especially in large farming areas.

Therefore, the network infrastructure must support massive device connectivity while maintaining performance and reliability. This requirement is particularly critical for IoT-based sensing environments, where thousands of low-power devices may simultaneously transmit data.

High Data Throughput and Bandwidth
The integration of high-resolution UAV imagery, satellite data and real-time video streams from robotic systems generates substantial volumes of data. Efficient transmission and processing of this data require high bandwidth and throughput capabilities.

For example, UAV-based monitoring and AI-driven image analysis depend on the rapid transfer of large datasets to processing units, whether in the cloud or at the edge. Insufficient bandwidth can lead to bottlenecks, limiting the effectiveness of data-driven applications.

Reliability and Coverage in Rural Environments
Agricultural operations typically take place in rural or remote areas, where network infrastructure may be limited or unreliable. As a result, the system must ensure robust and continuous connectivity across wide geographic regions.

High reliability is especially critical for mission-critical operations, such as autonomous navigation of unmanned ground vehicles and real-time logistics tracking. Network disruptions or coverage gaps could negatively impact system performance and operational safety.

Support for Heterogeneous Services
The system simultaneously supports a wide range of services with different communication requirements. For instance, real-time robotic control requires ultra-low latency, while environmental sensing may tolerate higher delays but involves massive numbers of devices.

Consequently, the network must be capable of handling heterogeneous traffic profiles and service requirements in a flexible and efficient manner. This includes the ability to prioritize critical services and allocate resources dynamically.

Security, Privacy and Data Sovereignty

Given the sensitivity and economic value of agricultural data, ensuring secure data transmission and storage is a fundamental requirement. The system must protect against unauthorized access, data tampering and cyber threats.

In addition, compliance with data protection regulations necessitates mechanisms for controlled data access and data sovereignty. The integration of blockchain-based logging and secure data management frameworks further reinforces the need for a trustworthy communication infrastructure.

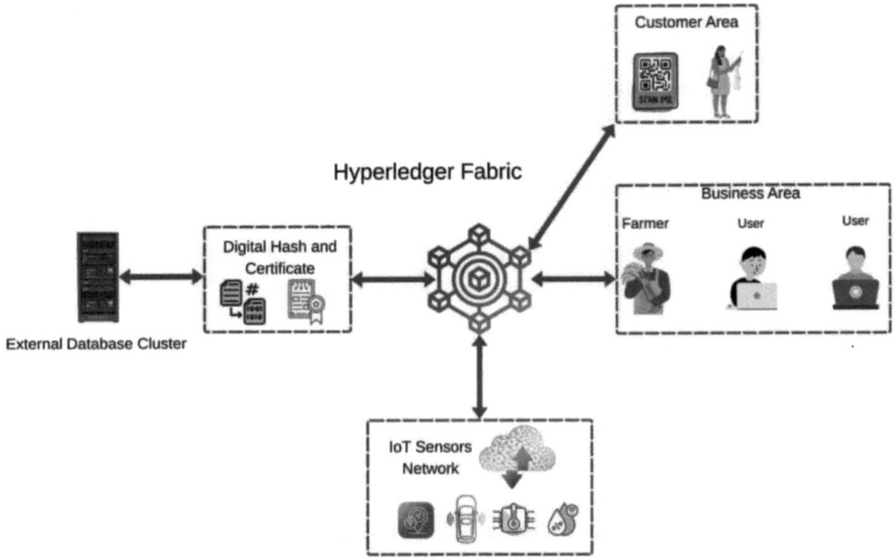

Fig. 2. Secure Data Management and Interoperability

Interoperability and Scalability

The system integrates multiple platforms, devices and services developed by different stakeholders. Therefore, interoperability is essential to ensure seamless communication and data exchange across heterogeneous components (Fig. 2).

At the same time, the architecture must be scalable to accommodate future expansion, including additional devices, services and geographical coverage. This requires flexible and modular infrastructure capable of adapting to evolving system demands [17].

3 The Use of 5G Networks in Smart Agriculture

3.1 5G Network Architecture

To address the stringent requirements of modern smart agriculture systems, a 5G Standalone (SA) architecture is considered, aligned with the specifications of 3GPP Release 16 and beyond. This architecture enables full exploitation of 5G capabilities, including ultra-low latency, high reliability and flexible service provisioning, which are essential for data-intensive and mission-critical agricultural applications.

The overall 5G system follows a modular and service-based design, consisting of four main components: the Radio Access Network (RAN), the 5G Core (5GC), the cloud infrastructure and a network slicing management framework. These components jointly support end-to-end connectivity, computing and service orchestration across the agricultural ecosystem.

Radio Access Network (RAN)

The RAN constitutes the access layer of the 5G architecture and is responsible for connecting end devices—such as sensors, UAVs and autonomous agricultural machinery—to the core network. It is based on 5G New Radio (NR) technology, which provides enhanced flexibility, improved spectral efficiency and support for diverse deployment scenarios.

Advanced radio technologies are employed to improve performance and coverage, including Massive Multiple Input Multiple Output (Massive MIMO) and beamforming techniques. These mechanisms enable efficient utilization of the radio spectrum while enhancing signal quality and extending coverage, which is particularly important in large and sparsely populated agricultural areas.

The RAN infrastructure typically includes distributed radio units and centralized or virtualized baseband processing units (gNBs), enabling scalable and flexible deployments. As the entry point to the network, the RAN plays a critical role in determining the end-to-end performance, particularly in terms of latency, throughput and reliability.

5G Core Network (5GC)

The 5G Core network is designed based on a cloud-native, service-based architecture (SBA), where network functionalities are implemented as modular and containerized services. This approach allows dynamic deployment, scalability and efficient management of network resources.

The core network separates control plane and user plane functionalities, enabling flexible traffic routing and supporting both centralized and distributed deployment models. This separation is particularly important for enabling edge computing capabilities, where user plane functions can be deployed closer to the end devices.

Key network functions defined by 3GPP include:

- Access and Mobility Management Function (AMF): responsible for user equipment (UE) registration, connection management and mobility handling across the network.
- Session Management Function (SMF): manages session establishment, modification and release, as well as the allocation of user plane resources.
- User Plane Function (UPF): handles user data traffic forwarding and routing and can be deployed either centrally or at the network edge to reduce latency.
- Authentication Server Function (AUSF): provides authentication mechanisms for secure access to the network.
- Unified Data Management (UDM): manages subscriber data, authentication credentials and user profiles.

This service-based and modular architecture enhances flexibility, allowing the network to adapt dynamically to the varying requirements of agricultural applications.

Cloud and Edge Computing Infrastructure

The 5G architecture is complemented by a cloud computing infrastructure that hosts applications, services and network functions. This infrastructure is typically based on virtualization technologies and supports containerized workloads, enabling efficient deployment and management of services.

A key feature is the integration of edge computing capabilities, where computational resources are placed closer to the data sources, such as agricultural fields or farming facilities. This reduces the need for long-distance data transmission and significantly lowers latency.

Edge computing is particularly beneficial for applications such as real-time crop monitoring, AI-based image analysis and autonomous robotic control, where rapid processing and immediate response are required. Additionally, cloud infrastructure supports centralized data analytics, long-term storage and system-wide coordination.

Network Slicing and Slice Management

Network slicing is a fundamental capability of 5G architectures, allowing the creation of multiple virtual networks over a shared physical infrastructure. Each slice is tailored to specific service requirements, with dedicated resources and Quality of Service (QoS) parameters.

A slice management framework is responsible for the lifecycle management of network slices, including their creation, configuration, monitoring and optimization. This enables the simultaneous support of diverse applications with different performance requirements.

In smart agriculture, network slicing allows the isolation of critical services—such as autonomous vehicle control—from less time-sensitive applications, such as environmental monitoring. This ensures that performance-critical operations are not affected by network congestion or competing traffic.

The combination of RAN, 5GC, cloud infrastructure and slicing mechanisms forms a cohesive end-to-end architecture that supports seamless connectivity and service delivery. Secure access mechanisms, including VPN-based connectivity and authentication frameworks, enable controlled access to services and infrastructure components.

Furthermore, monitoring tools and performance measurement mechanisms can be integrated across different parts of the network (e.g., RAN, core and edge) to evaluate key performance indicators such as latency, throughput and reliability. This facilitates continuous optimization and ensures that the system meets the operational requirements of smart agriculture applications.

3.2 5G Capabilities for Smart Agriculture Applications

The architectural components described in the previous section collectively enable the simultaneous support of heterogeneous agricultural services through network slicing. For the use case under examination, three functionally distinct slice types are defined, each aligned with a specific category of performance requirements: an ultra-reliable low-latency slice, a massive IoT slice and an enhanced mobile broad-band slice. These slices operate concurrently, with resources dynamically allocated in response to evolving operational demands.

- Ultra-Reliable Low-Latency Slice (URLLC Slice): The URLLC slice is designed to support mission-critical and time-sensitive applications, such as autonomous agricultural machinery and real-time control of unmanned ground vehicles (UGVs). These applications require extremely low end-to-end latency and very high reliability to ensure safe and accurate operation in dynamic field environments.
- Massive IoT Slice (mMTC Slice): The mMTC slice supports large-scale connectivity for massive numbers of low-power devices deployed across agricultural fields. These include environmental sensors, soil moisture sensors, wearable plant sensors and weather monitoring stations.
- Enhanced Mobile Broadband Slice (eMBB Slice): The eMBB slice is dedicated to high-bandwidth applications that require the transmission of large data volumes. In the proposed system, this includes UAV-based high-resolution imagery, satellite data integration and real-time video streams from robotic platforms.

Beyond network slicing, several intrinsic 5G capabilities are essential for fulfilling the requirements of the smart agriculture system.

- Low Latency Communication: Low latency is a critical requirement for autonomous and real-time agricultural applications. 5G achieves this through optimized radio protocols, edge computing integration and reduced network traversal times. In the presented system, low latency enables rapid decision-making in autonomous robotics, real-time response to sensor inputs and immediate execution of precision farming actions. This is essential for maintaining system accuracy and operational safety in dynamic environments.
- Support for Massive IoT Connectivity: 5G networks are designed to support massive machine-type communications, allowing the simultaneous connection of a large number of heterogeneous devices. In agricultural scenarios, this capability is crucial for integrating distributed sensor networks, wearable plant monitoring systems and telemetry-enabled logistics assets. It ensures continuous and scalable data collection across large geographical areas without network congestion.
- High Reliability and Extended Coverage: Agricultural environments often span wide rural areas where network infrastructure may be limited. 5G addresses this challenge through improved radio technologies, advanced interference management and flexible deployment architectures. High reliability ensures uninterrupted operation of critical services such as autonomous machinery control and logistics tracking. Extended coverage guarantees consistent connectivity across entire farming regions, enabling seamless system operation even in remote locations.
- Security and Trust Mechanisms: Security is a fundamental requirement for digital agriculture systems, given the sensitivity and value of agricultural and supply chain data. 5G incorporates advanced authentication, encryption and identity management mechanisms to ensure secure communication between all network entities. In the proposed system, these mechanisms are complemented by higher-layer security frameworks, including blockchain-based data logging and access control policies. This

combination ensures data integrity, traceability and trust across the entire agri-food value chain.

4 Conclusion

This paper presented an analysis of the role of 5G network technology in enabling next-generation smart agriculture systems. The study was structured around a representative end-to-end agricultural architecture that integrates precision farming, autonomous agricultural operations, secure data management and smart supply chain optimisation.

The analysis first introduced a layered system architecture composed of data acquisition, communication, processing and application layers. This architecture highlights the increasing complexity of modern agricultural ecosystems, which rely on heterogeneous data sources such as UAV imagery, satellite observations, in-field sensors, wearable plant devices and autonomous robotic platforms. The integration of these components creates a highly distributed and data-intensive environment that requires advanced communication and computing capabilities.

Based on this architecture, a set of stringent system requirements was identified, including ultra-low latency for real-time control, massive device connectivity for large-scale IoT deployments, high bandwidth for data-intensive applications, strong reliability in rural environments, interoperability across heterogeneous systems and robust security and data sovereignty mechanisms.

To address these requirements, the paper examined the capabilities of 5G network technology, focusing on its Standalone architecture, service-based core design, edge computing integration and network slicing framework. It was shown that 5G is particularly well-suited for smart agriculture due to its ability to simultaneously support heterogeneous services with different performance requirements. Ultra-Reliable Low-Latency Communication (URLLC), Enhanced Mobile Broadband (eMBB) and Massive Machine-Type Communications (mMTC) were mapped to key agricultural functions such as autonomous machinery control, UAV-based monitoring and large-scale sensor networks.

Furthermore, network slicing was identified as a critical enabler for isolating and optimizing different service types, ensuring that mission-critical operations are not affected by non-critical traffic. Complementary features such as edge computing enhance system responsiveness, while built-in security mechanisms support trusted and secure data exchange across the agri-food value chain.

Overall, the findings indicate that 5G technology provides a comprehensive and flexible communication foundation for smart agriculture systems. By enabling low-latency control, scalable connectivity, high data throughput and secure interoperability, 5G acts as a key enabler for the transition toward fully digital, autonomous and data-driven agricultural ecosystems. Future developments are expected to further enhance these capabilities, particularly with the evolution toward 6G networks and more advanced AI-native infrastructures.

Acknowledgments. This work has been performed in the scope of the COP-PILOT European research project under Grant Agreement No. 101189819.

References

1. Food and Agriculture Organization: Digital agriculture and innovation trends. FAO Report (2023)
2. Wolfert, S., Ge, L., Verdouw, C., Bogaardt, M.-J.: Big data in smart farming – a review. Agric. Syst. **153**, 69–80 (2017)
3. Liakos, K.G., Busato, P., Moshou, D., Pearson, S., Bochtis, D.: Machine learning in agriculture: a review. Sensors **18**(8), 2674 (2018)
4. Zhang, Y., Wang, L., Wang, Y.: Internet of Things for smart agriculture applications. IEEE Access **5**, 18995–19003 (2017)
5. Qin, Z., Zhang, S., Cao, X., et al.: UAV-based remote sensing in precision agriculture. Remote Sens. **12**(7), 1200 (2020)
6. ITU-R: IMT-2020 requirements and evaluation criteria. International Telecommunication Union Report (2017)
7. Mendes, J., Oliveira, A., et al.: Smart agriculture systems: architecture and applications. Comput. Electron. Agric. **168**, 105–112 (2020)
8. Ordonez, C., et al.: Network slicing for 5G networks: concepts and challenges. IEEE Commun. Mag. **57**(3), 24–30 (2019)
9. ETSI: Multi-access Edge Computing (MEC): An introduction. ETSI White Paper No. 28 (2019)
10. 3GPP: 5G System (5GS) Stage 2 and Stage 3 Specifications, Release 16. Technical Specification (2020)
11. Saad, W., Bennis, M., Chen, M.: A vision of 6G wireless systems: applications, trends and enabling technologies. IEEE Commun. Surv. Tutor. **22**(4), 1955–1988 (2020)
12. Andrews, J.G., Buzzi, S., Choi, W., et al.: What will 5G be? IEEE J. Sel. Areas Commun. **32**(6), 1065–1082 (2014)
13. Gupta, A., Jha, R.K.: A survey of 5G network: architecture and emerging technologies. IEEE Access **3**, 1206–1232 (2015)
14. Ayaz, M., Ammad-Uddin, M., Sharif, Z., Mansour, A., Aggoune, E.-H.M.: Internet-of-Things (IoT)-based smart agriculture: toward making the fields talk. IEEE Access **7**, 129551–129583 (2019)
15. Kamilaris, A., Fonts, A., Prenafeta-Boldú, F.X.: The rise of blockchain technology in agriculture and food supply chains. Comput. Electron. Agric. **162**, 725–743 (2019)
16. Shafi, M., Molisch, A.F., Smith, P.J., et al.: 5G: A tutorial overview of standards, trials, challenges, deployment and practice. IEEE J. Sel. Areas Commun. **35**(6), 1201–1221 (2017)
17. Klerkx, L., Jakku, E., Labarthe, P.: A review of social science on digital agriculture, smart farming and agriculture 4.0. NJAS: Wageningen J. Life Sci. **90–91**, 100315 (2019)

6G-BRICKS – Defining Objective Indicators Towards Elaboration of the Key Value Indicators

Michalis Rantopoulos[1](✉), Ioannis P. Chochliouros[1], Anastasia S. Spiliopoulou[1], Ioanna Karampelia[2], Christos Verikoukis[3], Kostas Ramantas[4], and Nicholas Zafeiropoulos[5]

[1] Hellenic Telecommunications Organization S.A. (OTE), 99 Kifissias Avenue, 15124 Maroussi, Athens, Greece
mrantopoul@ote.gr

[2] Satways Ltd., Iraklio-Athens, Greece

[3] Industrial Systems Institute (ISI) / Athenà Research Center, Athens, Greece

[4] Iquadrat Informatica SL, Barcelona, Spain

[5] Space Hellas S.A., Athens, Greece

Abstract. The transition towards 6G networks introduces the need for the evaluation of the Key Value Indicators (KVIs), aiming to "capture" broader societal, environmental and economic impacts of emerging technologies. The issue of defining measurable and reliable indicators that integrate technical performance with broader value creation remains a key challenge. This paper focuses on objective indicators (OIs) as core elements for KVI evaluation, proposing a structured classification into three categories: (i) Network and system-level KPIs; (ii) application/services related metrics, and; (iii) questionnaires/surveys based indicators. Moreover, a comparative analysis of pioneer 6G initiatives (including ADROIT-6G, TrialsNet, 6G-SANDBOX and Hexa-X II) highlights diverse approaches. The 6G-BRICKS methodology is also presented by emphasizing upon a holistic, application-driven and user-centric evaluation approach. Although experimental validation is ongoing, the proposed 6G-BRICKS innovative framework contributes to the development of robust and scalable methodologies for KVI evaluation, efficiently supporting the alignment of 6G technologies with real-world value creation.

Keywords: 6G · digital inclusion · Key Performance Indicators (KPIs) · Key Value Indicators (KVIs) · Objective Indicators (OIs) · Sustainability · next-generation networks

1 Introduction

The world confronts multi-level threats spanning diverse societal and environmental dimensions, including: (i) the rising cost of living; (ii) natural disasters and extreme weather events; (iii) geo-economic tensions, and; (iv) cyber-attacks targeting critical infrastructures. These are identified among the top global risks in the Global Risks Report

Published by Springer Nature Switzerland AG 2027
A. Papaleonidas et al. (Eds.): AIAI 2026 Workshops, IFIP AICT 796, pp. 34–48, 2027.
https://doi.org/10.1007/978-3-032-30507-7_2

2023 [1]. Technology researchers have extensively discussed the role of technological developments when "facing" such threats, targeting not exclusively performance metrics but in a more holistic view addressing the impact to societal and environmental challenges [2, 3]. As time progresses, research engineers and scientists are already considering the impact to UN Sustainable Development Goals (SDGs) [4] when designing the new technological developments starting from the architectural defining works. The relatively recently introduced KVIs which aim to measure the alignment of new technologies with greater societal and sustainable goals are becoming an increasingly important topic for researchers and engineers [5]. Growing awareness of KVIs among professionals is driving their incorporation into early-stage architectural developments, resulting in tangible outputs reflected in architectural specifications. While still at an early stage, this trend is promising [6, 7].

From the scientific perspective, assessing the impact of technology research and development on societal values has become a "key priority" in EU-funded research activities [8] and is explicitly mandated within R&D project frameworks. In this context, the Societal Needs and Value Creation (SNVC) subgroup of the Vision Working Group (WG) of the 6G Industry Association [9] as well as the Test, Measurement and Validation (TMV) Working Group [10] addressing KVIs, have been established. The aim of the SNVC subgroup is to inter-exchange knowledge and experience between representatives from: (i) EU-funded projects; (ii) the social sciences field, and; (iii) ICT industry towards aligning the activities at EU-funded research level. Similarly, the TMV WG aims to promote common approaches across projects with a strong focus on testing and monitoring (T&M) methodologies. It serves as a platform for sharing best practices to support 6G trial use cases, including the development of test methods, procedures and the formalization and validation of Key Performance Indicators (KPIs) [11, 12] and KVIs.

The EU-funded 6G-BRICKS project [13] is actively involved in both the SNVC and TMV Working Groups, aiming to foster knowledge exchange with the respective communities and support the development of KVI evaluation methodologies. 6G-BRICKS aims to deliver a trusted, flexible and scalable 6G experimentation facility by integrating platforms in Belgium and France, and federating them under a core site in Greece that provides public cloud and experimentation services. In particular, the project focuses around two essential use cases (UCs): (i) UC1 – Metaverse as an Enabler of a Modern Workplace [14], and; (ii) UC2 – 6G Applications for Industry 4.0 [15]. For each one, 6G-BRICKS proceeds with the verification of two Proofs-of-Concept (PoCs) which aim to increase adaptability of the UCs to the corresponding verticals. In more detail, the two PoCs under UC1 demonstrate: (i) A novel "holoconferencing" scenario set in a meeting room, referred to as UC#1-PoC#1 – Holoconferencing in a Virtual Meeting Room, and; (ii) virtual team-building activities that leverage ultra-high-density (uHDD) communications and Joint Communication and Sensing (JCAS) capabilities, referred to as UC#2-PoC#2 – Virtual Team Building Activities. Similarly, the two PoCs under UC#2 showcase: (i) How 6G technologies will enable autonomous robots in Industry 4.0, referred to as UC#2-PoC#1 – Autonomous Robots in Industry 4.0, and; (ii) how 6G will support remote digital twin (DT) visualization via an augmented reality (AR) interface, referred to as UC#2-PoC#2 – On-site AR Inspection of an Industry 4.0 Digital Twin.

Under the prism of the 6G-BRICKS UCs, it was decided during early works of this project [16] to distinguish between the KVIs methods of measurements under two distinct categories termed as *Objective* and *Subjective* Indicators [17] (as depicted below in Table 1):

Table 1. KVIs Template – OIs

Key Value Indicators - Methods of measurement		
Metric	Metric	Evidence
OIs	OIx: An objective metric is a measurement that is based on observable, quantifiable data, not on personal feelings, opinions or interpretations	An example could be measured incidents obtained from the logs
Subjective Indicators	A subjective metric is a measurement based on personal opinions, perceptions, feelings, or judgments rather than strictly quantifiable data	Surveys or Questionnaires of relevant stakeholders

This paper focuses on the first category of indicators, namely OI, which rely on observable and quantifiable data derived from newly developed applications or experimental testbeds capable of providing such measurements. It is important to note that, unlike other studies [18], this work does not concentrate on general experimental frameworks for KVIs but instead provides an in-depth examination of the methods used to obtain objective data measurements. Section 2 discusses various identified categories for OIs. Section 3 examines the way how other fundamental EU-funded projects deal with OIs. Section 4 discusses several OIs as defined upon the PoCs of the 6G-BRICKS project. Finally, Sect. 5 concludes the paper.

2 Identified Categories for OIs

Based on the authors' analysis, the OIs employed in the definition of OIs can be systematically categorized into three principal groups such as follows: (i) KPIs, which "capture" core system-level performance and network capabilities; (ii) application-related metrics, which reflect the behavior and efficiency of specific services and use-case implementations, and; (iii) Questionnaires/surveys based metrics, which provide structured, quantifiable representations of user perceptions and stakeholder feedback. This classification enables a more comprehensive and multi-dimensional evaluation of the indicators, facilitating the integration of technical performance measurements with application-driven insights and user-centric assessments [19].

In addition to the above, it has been observed that, in many cases, the design of OIs does not rely on a single category, but rather on a combination of two or more of the aforementioned categories. This hybrid approach allows for a more comprehensive evaluation framework, capturing both quantitative system performance and qualitative user-centric aspects.

As will be discussed in detail in Sect. 4, the 6G-BRICKS framework falls within this multi-dimensional approach as it incorporates both application-related indicators and questionnaires/surveys based analytics to assess the impact of the proposed solutions. In the following subsections, each of the categories is analyzed in detail, outlining their characteristics, scope and contribution to the formulation of KVIs.

2.1 KPIs as OI Metrics

According to the Recommendation of ITU-R [20], IMT-2030 is expected to provide enhanced and new capabilities beyond IMT-2020, guided by overarching design principles including: (i) sustainability; (ii) security and resilience; (iii) connecting the unconnected and; (iv) ubiquitous intelligence. As it can be deduced from Fig. 1, below, there are newly created technical performance requirements – denoted in blue colour – such as: (i) area traffic capacity; (ii) composite requirement; (iii) sensing-related requirements; (iv) AI-related requirement; (v) energy efficiency for sustainability, and; (vi) resilience and extended connectivity. In the search of defining a clearly-structured KVI, researchers are already utilising both the previously and newly introduced KPIs as a means of objective indicator metrics [21, 22].

Within this expanded performance landscape, the definition of KVIs increasingly relies on both legacy and newly introduced KPIs as objective indicator metrics. Researchers are leveraging this enriched KPI set to construct multi-dimensional evaluation frameworks that go beyond pure technical performance, incorporating aspects such as sustainability impact, service relevance, and societal value.

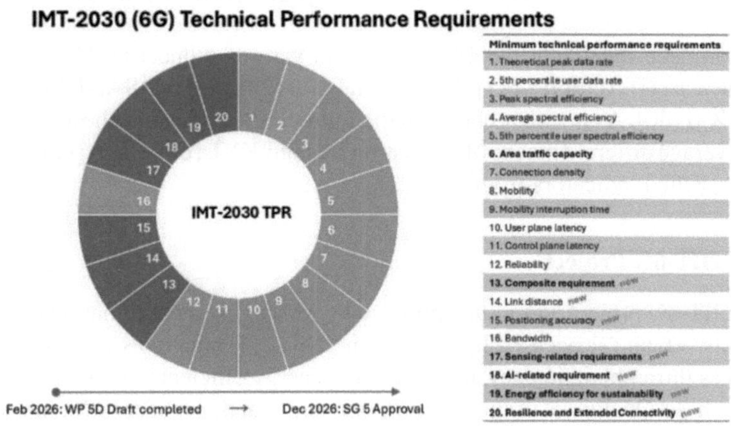

Fig. 1. IMT-2030 (6G) Technical Performance Requirements [23]

2.2 Application/Service-Related Indicators as Metrics

Application – or often called as – Service Related metrics fall into a category of OIs focusing on the performance and efficiency of the newly developed applications within use-case implementations [24]. They are typically obtained from application logs, custom monitoring tools or embedded mechanisms within experimental testbeds. They aim to integrate technical performance with actual service delivery towards a more contextualized evaluation of indicators, thus contributing to broader societal and operational objectives.

In Sect. 3, examples of application-related indicators are presented to provide the reader with a clearer understanding of how this classification is applied in practice. These examples illustrate how different projects leverage application-level metrics to support the definition and measurement of OI, thereby enhancing the comprehensibility and practical relevance of this category.

2.3 Questionnaires/Surveys Indicators as Metrics

Questionnaires based on Likert-scale [25] based metrics provide the means to "capture" user perceptions and stakeholder's feedback in a quantifiable manner. The surveys "bridge the gap" between subjective evaluations with objective measurement frameworks [26]. The metrics are derived from surveys or questionnaires to assess aspects such as user satisfaction, perceived quality of experience and ease of use.

Despite the fact that they are rooted in subjective input from stakeholders, the actual output of the analysis is a tangible indicator; thus, this type of metric is included in this classification of OIs. Towards the evaluation of KVIs, Likert-scale based metrics play a crucial role in incorporating human-centric feedback into the evaluation process, complementing technical and application-level measurements to a more holistic assessment of developed technologies.

3 Survey on How Other Horizon Projects Deal with OIs

This section deep-dives into the OIs engaged in various pioneering Horizon SNS-JU projects such as: (i) ADROIT-6G [27], (ii) TrialsNet [28]; (iii) 6G-SANDBOX [29] and; (iv) Hexa-X II [30]. As it will be shown in the following subsections, the aforementioned projects leverage different means of evaluation for their KVIs, employing either 1 or more types of classified indicators from Sect. 2.

3.1 ADROIT-6G Project

The ADROIT-6G project adopts an approach by leveraging a combination of OI definitions of network and service KPIs. As seen in Table 2, it integrates traditional network KPIs such as throughput, latency, reliability and energy efficiency with service-oriented metrics such as Quality of Experience (QoE) and Random Access Memory (RAM) needed per stream rendering.

This combined use of OIs enables ADROIT-6G to evaluate in a holistic manner the technical performance with the effectiveness of service delivery. Such an approach "highlights" the importance of bridging infrastructure-level measurements with user-centric perspectives in the assessment of next-generation 6G systems. Table 2 depicts KPIs as have been defined for all PoCs of this project.

Table 2. ADROIT-6G Network and Service Key Performance Indicators [31]

Indicator	PoC1	PoC2a	PoC2b	Poc3
Network and Service KPIs as defined in [27]				
Peak throughput (Gbps)	√	x	x	x
Experienced upload throughput (Gbps) per device	√	x	x	√
Experienced download throughput (Gbps) per device	√	x	x	√
Maximum bandwidth (GHz)	√	x	x	√
Jitter (μs)	√	√	√	√
Energy efficiency (Tb/J)	√	x	x	√
Device density (devices/m^2)	x	√	√	√
Reliability (packet error rate)	√	√	√	√
Positioning accuracy (cm)	x	x	x	√
End-to-end latency (ms)	√	x	x	√
Visualized user experience	√	x	x	x
QoE (Quality of Experience)	√	√	√	√
AI Model Selection Latency	√	x	x	x
System Scalability	√	√	√	√
Service Recovery Time	√	x	x	x
Orchestration Efficiency	√	x	x	x
Computing power needed per stream rendering	√	x	x	x
RAM needed per stream rendering	√	x	x	x

3.2 TrialsNet Project

TrialsNet assesses KVIs by connecting KPIs derived from use case trials with broader societal value outcomes. This is achieved through a structured framework that integrates quantitative metrics, qualitative feedback and evaluation across economic, environmental and social dimensions.

As illustrated in Fig. 2, KPIs encompass quantitative analyses at both the network and application levels, contributing to the evaluation of Quality of Service (QoS). It is important to distinguish that "application KPIs" are collected at the user equipment level and should not be confused with "network KPIs". This distinction aligns with the findings of this work and the classification presented in the previous section.

Based on this framework, it becomes evident that OIs influence the perceived Quality of Experience for each user. This perception can be assessed through user feedback and subsequently translated into KVIs.

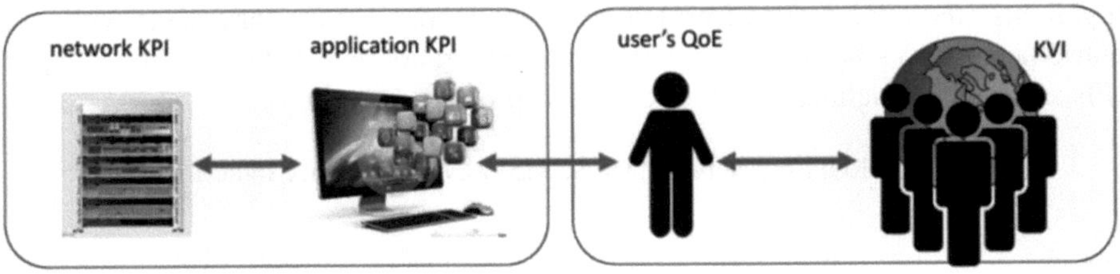

Fig. 2. TrialsNet Relation between KPIs and KVIs [32]

3.3 6G-SANDBOX Project

6G-SANDBOX adopts the 6G-IA SNVC methodology for the elaboration of the Key Values (KVs) of its context, therefore the focus is around three core values: (i) "resilience", as the ability to adapt and recover from challenging and unforeseen situations; (ii) "sustainability", as the ability to meet the needs of the present without compromising the ability of future generations to meet their own needs, and; (iii) "inclusiveness", which is the recognition that every member of society should have equal access to opportunities, resources, and services in the context of 6G network. These KVs are indicated in Table 3. 6G-SANDBOX declares as "enablers" features such as open access to infrastructure and the usage of energy efficient solution technologies with neutral environmental footprint. Moreover, for the inclusiveness key value, the project declares as "enablers" the remotely accessible facilities and the high reliability of facilities.

In a similar vein to TrialsNet, the 6G-SANDBOX project adopts a balanced evaluation approach by combining traditional network-related "key" KPIs with more user-centric metrics [33]. These include aspects such as remote accessibility, usability and service reliability, thereby extending the assessment beyond purely technical performance. This integrated perspective enables a more holistic alignment with societal needs, thus ensuring that technological advancements are not only efficient and robust but also accessible and relevant to a wide range of stakeholders.

Table 3. Selected KVIs targeted by 6G-SANDBOX [34]

KV	KVIs	Enablers
Resilience	**KVI1:** Improved response times for critical and emergency service providers **KVI2:** Improved effectiveness of services in the event of disruptions	Open access to infrastructure Resilience related capabilities incorporated in the testbeds
Sustainability	**KVI1:** Reduction of the energy footprint, materials usage and environmentally neutral materials lifecycle of telecommunication solutions	Energy Efficient Solution Technologies

(continued)

Table 3. (*continued*)

KV	KVIs	Enablers
Inclusiveness	**KVI1:** Accessibility of infrastructure from remote locations with no 6G facilities (for experimentation and testing) **KVI2:** Accessibility of infrastructure to under-represented or marginalized communities	Remotely accessible facilities. High availability of facilities

3.4 HEXA-X II Project

Hexa-X II "distinguishes" itself from other pioneering initiatives by not relying on KVIs [35] for sustainability assessment. Instead of a strictly quantitative approach, this project adopts a qualitative evaluation framework designed to capture broader and more nuanced impacts. This specific framework focuses upon identifying core values and systematically examining the potential effects associated with specific use cases.

Within this approach, impacts are divided into two main categories: Positive contributions are described as "sustainability handprints," reflecting the benefits generated by a technology or application, such as improved efficiency or reduced environmental burden. Conversely, negative impacts are termed "sustainability footprints" [36], representing the associated costs, including resource consumption or environmental strain. This dual perspective enables a more balanced and comprehensive understanding of sustainability outcomes. Table 4 provides a clear illustration of this conceptual framework, demonstrating how benefits and costs are mapped across different value dimensions.

For the purposes of this research, Hexa-X II is positioned across all three categories within the broader classification of OIs. Although its evaluation framework is primarily qualitative in nature, it aligns as well with operational performance assessment through Network and Service/Application-related KPIs.

Table 4. Hexa-X II: Sustainability Analysis

Term	Definition
Sustainability Analysis	Provides a qualitative analysis by outlining the key values and hence the potential effects relevant to a use case. These effects are grouped by benefits as "sustainability handprints" and cost as "sustainability footprints"
Sustainability Handprint	In the context of Hexa-X-II, the term "handprints" refers to the positive effects enabled by a 6G-enabled solution. These encompass positive first-order, second-order and higher-order environmental, social and economic effects that not only help mitigate and reduce direct negative effects but also generate additional positive contributions to the environment, society and economy [37]

(*continued*)

Table 4. (*continued*)

Term	Definition
Sustainability Footprint	In the context of Hexa-X-II, the term "footprint" is defined in alignment with ITU-T L.1480 [38], encompassing direct (first-order) negative environmental effects, extended to direct negative social and economic effects. Furthermore, the Hexa-X-II definition of sustainability footprints includes second-order and higher-order environmental, social and economic negative effects

4 6G-BRICKS – PoCs Defined OIs

This section presents a comprehensive analysis of the KVIs defined by focusing on the measurement methods within the 6G-BRICKS PoCs. In parallel, Tables 5, 6, 7 and 8 provide a detailed overview of the validation methodologies applied to the OIs across the different PoCs.

Table 5. 6G-BRICKS – UC#1-PoC#1 – KVIs OIs

KVI	Description	Measurement Method	Survey Questions/Indicators
Digital Inclusion	Tech and platform for under-served/represented audiences	Questionnaires to end-users (live demo) and to stakeholders (demo video)	Percentage of users from underserved demographics who can access and use metaverse applications under realistic conditions
Trustworthiness	Interaction with real-time captured holograms, not avatars	Questionnaires to end-users (live demo) and to stakeholders (demo video)	Stakeholder Satisfaction Index (SSI): Valuates user satisfaction levels across different expertise levels
Energy Efficiency	Allows saving costs, travel, time…	Application Related Indicators + Questionnaires to end-users (live demo) and to stakeholders (demo video)	Resources Usage Load, including Central Processing Unit - CPU (%), Graphics Processing Unit - GPU (%) and RAM (MB)

A cross-analysis of these tables reveals a consistent methodological approach: the primary measurement techniques rely on qualitative and application-level data collection. Specifically, stakeholder and end-user feedback is gathered through structured questionnaires, while application-specific KPIs are extracted directly from the demonstrator applications developed within each PoC. This dual approach enables the project to capture both subjective user perceptions and objective performance metrics at the application layer.

The 6G-BRICKS project has deliberately adopted this methodology to ensure a holistic validation framework, one that integrates human-centric evaluation with technical performance insights. Notably, unlike many other initiatives in the 6G domain, 6G-BRICKS does not rely on traditional network-level KPIs (such as latency, throughput, or reliability) as the primary means for deriving or validating OIs. Instead, it emphasizes experience-driven and service-oriented evaluation, aligning more closely with end-user value and real-world applicability.

Table 6. 6G-BRICKS – UC#1-PoC#2 – KVIs OIs

KVI Name	Description	Measurement Method	Survey Questions/Indicators
Fairness	Equal opportunities to access info, events, services	Questionnaires to end-users (live demo) and to stakeholders (demo video)	Extent to which users of diverse genders, ethnicities, and abilities are equitably represented in holograms, roles, and participation across the Metaverse platform
Open Collaboration	How collaboration is improved within geographically distributed stakeholders and party	Questionnaires to end-users (live demo) and to stakeholders (demo video)	Percentage of users actively engaged in collaborative content creation, decision-making, or shared experiences within a metaverse application
Safety	Evaluates how 6G-enabled metaverse applications enhance the physical and psychological safety of users	Application-Related Indicators Questionnaires to end-users (live demo) and to stakeholders (demo video)	Percentage of metaverse user sessions in which no safety-critical incident (e.g., application crash, loss of balance due to latency, unresponsiveness, biometric data loss) occurred during normal operation

Table 7. 6G-BRICKS – UC#2-PoC#1 – KVIs OIs

KVI Name	Description	Measurement Method	Survey Questions/Indicators
Digital Inclusion	Ensure consistent access and processing of sensor data across all system components and users, especially under high-load or dynamic conditions	Application-Related Indicators Questionnaires to end-users (live demo) and to stakeholders (demo video)	Simultaneous Localization and Mapping (SLAM) Data Retention Rate
Trustworthiness	Guarantee accurate reflection of the robot's sensory data and motion state, ensuring trust in system behavior and decision-making	Application-Related Indicators + Questionnaires to end-users (live demo) and to stakeholders (demo video)	Sensor Position Accuracy
Safety	Prevent harm to humans and the environment by detecting failures and minimizing operational risks during unexpected conditions	Application-Related Indicators + Questionnaires to end-users (live demo) and to stakeholders (demo video)	Safety Incident Reduction (SIR) + Connection Stability Rate
Security	Protect system communication from interference, message loss, and cyberattacks, ensuring robust and stable operations	Application-Related Indicators + Questionnaires to end-users (live demo) and to stakeholders (demo video)	Security Incident Reduction (SIR) + System Integrity Rate (SIR)

Table 8. 6G-BRICKS – UC#2-PoC#2 – KVIs OIs

KVI	Description	Measurement Method	Survey Questions/Indicators
Business Value	Business Value is beneficial for operational efficiency, cost reduction, and revenue generation	Questionnaires to end-users (live demo) and to stakeholders (demo video)	Innovation Adoption Rate (IAR)

(*continued*)

Table 8. *(continued)*

KVI	Description	Measurement Method	Survey Questions/Indicators
Economic Growth	Economic Growth is beneficial as Digital Twin adaptation is expected to contribute to the overall development and scaling of the industry	Questionnaires to end-users (live demo) and to stakeholders (demo video)	Productivity Improvement Rate (PIR)
New Value Chain	The New Value Chain Indicator is considered to create collaborative ecosystems, that can revolutionize traditional supply chains by integrating stakeholders from diverse vertical industries	Questionnaires to end-users (live demo) and to stakeholders (demo video)	Objective Indicator Stakeholder Engagement Rate (SER)

At the time of writing, the actual experimental evaluation results are not yet available, as the validation phase is still ongoing. Consequently, current efforts are focused on assessing and refining the proposed evaluation methodologies, with the goal of ensuring their robustness and suitability for accurately measuring KVIs. This includes examining the effectiveness, reliability, and completeness of the selected measurement tools and processes, in order to establish a solid foundation for future quantitative and qualitative analysis.

5 Concluding Remarks

This paper has presented a detailed analysis and review of OIs as a fundamental component in the formulation of KVIs within the context of 6G systems and more particular with focus upon the 6G-BRICKS project. The alignment of technological innovation with broader societal, environmental and economic objectives lies at the forefront of research objectives. Moreover, this work contributes to the ongoing discussion on "how measurable indicators can effectively capture value beyond traditional performance metrics".

A key observation of this study is the classification of OIs into three basic categories (i.e.: network KPIs, application/service-related metrics and questionnaires/surveys-based indicators) enabling a multi-dimensional evaluation framework. The analysis of other pioneer 6G projects (such as ADROIT-6G, TrialsNet, 6G-SANDBOX and Hexa-X II) demonstrates that there are multiple approaches for OI definition. According to the analysis of the present work, projects can adopt hybrid methodologies that combine technical performance with user-centric and societal perspectives, highlighting the evolving and interdisciplinary nature of KVI assessment.

More specifically, 6G-BRICKS introduces a validation approach, emphasizing on application-level metrics and structured feedback, while deliberately limiting the reliance on traditional network KPIs. This choice "reflects" a shift towards experience-driven and service-oriented evaluation, aiming to capture real-world impact and user-perceived value. According to the analysis of the presented PoCs, it is illustrated how this methodology enables the integration of technical performance, usability, inclusiveness and trust-related aspects into a unified evaluation framework.

At the current stage, the evaluation process is still ongoing and limited experimental results are yet available. Nevertheless, the work lays a foundation for the systematic validation of KVIs, while also highlighting the importance of refining methodologies to ensure reliability and scalability.

Conclusively, this paper contributes to the broader effort of embedding societal value in next-generation networks, demonstrating that the evaluation of KVIs requires holistic new evaluation paradigms. Future works will focus on the execution of the validation campaigns, ultimately supporting the establishment of robust, widely accepted frameworks for KVI evaluation in 6G environments.

Acknowledgments. This work has been performed in the scope of the 6G-BRICKS European Research Project and has been supported by the Smart Networks and Services Joint Undertaking (SNS-JU) by receiving funding from the European Union's Horizon Europe (HORIZON) Research and Innovation Programme under Grant AgreementNo.101096954.

References

1. Rockström, J., Gupta, J., Qin, D., et al.: The Global Risks Report 2023 18th Edition – Insight Report. World Economic Forum (WEF), Geneva, Switzerland (2023). https://www3.weforum.org/docs/WEF_Global_Risks_Report_2023.pdf
2. Rantopoulos, M., Chochliouros, I., Verikoukis, C.: Survey on SNS-JU projects evaluation methods towards the assessment of social development goals (SDGs). In: Proceedings of the IEEE 2024 International Workshop on Computer Aided Modeling and Design of Communication Links and Networks (IEEE CAMAD), Athens, Greece, 21–23 October 2024. IEEE (2024), https://doi.org/10.1109/CAMAD62243.2024.10942974
3. Sil, R., Chatterjee, R.: Evolution of next-generation communication technology. In: Bhushan, B., Sharma, S.K., Kumar, R., Priyadarshini, I. (eds.) 5G and Beyond. Springer Tracts in Electrical and Electronics Engineering. Springer, Singapore (2023). https://doi.org/10.1007/978-981-99-3668-7_1
4. United Nations (UN): The 17 Goals. UN, Department of Economic and Social Affairs - Sustainable Development (2020). https://sdgs.un.org/goals
5. Wikström, G., et al.: Key value indicators: a framework for values-driven next-generation ICT solutions. Telecommun. Policy **48**(6), 102778 (2024). https://doi.org/10.1016/j.telpol.2024.102778
6. Osman, H., Bradford, J., Mitchell, S., and Chiavarino, C.: An approach for key value indicator evaluation: enabling consistent assessment of societal impacts. In: Proceedings of the 2025 Joint European Conference on Networks and Communications & 6G Summit (EuCNC/6G Summit), Poznan, Poland, 03–06 June 2025, pp.411–415 (2025). https://doi.org/10.1109/EuCNC/6GSummit63408.2025.11037055

7. 6G4Society ("Towards a sustainable and accepted 6G for Society") Horizon SNS-JU project: Deliverable D1.1: "Societal Aspects in 6G Technology: Concerns, Acceptance Models and Sustainability Indicators" (2024). https://doi.org/10.5281/zenodo.14592217
8. Smart Networks and Services Joint Undertaking (SNS JU): 6G KVIs - SNS Projects Initial Survey Results 2025 – White Paper. SNS JU Test Measurements and Validation Working Group (2025). https://doi.org/10.5281/zenodo.15220945
9. 6G Smart Networks and Services Infrastructure Association (6G SNS IA): 6G-IA White Paper: What societal values will 6G address? – Societal Key Values and Key Value Indicators analysed through 6G use cases (2022). https://doi.org/10.5281/zenodo.6557534
10. 6G Smart Networks and Services Infrastructure Association (6G SNS IA): SNS JU Test, Measurement and KPIs Validation Working Group. https://6g-ia.eu/6g-ia-working-groups/#vision
11. 5G Infrastructure Public Private Partnership (5G PPP): KPIs Measurement Tools. From KPI definition to KPI validation enablement (White Paper) (2023). https://5g-ppp.eu/wp-content/uploads/2023/05/TMV-KPI-Measurement-Tools_1.0-published.pdf
12. 5G Infrastructure Public Private Partnership (5G PPP): White Paper - Beyond 5G/6G KPI Measurement (2023). https://5g-ppp.eu/wp-content/uploads/2023/06/white_paper_b5g-6g_kpi_measurement_FINAL.pdf
13. 6G-BRICKS ("Building Reusable testbed Infrastructures for validating Cloud-to-device breakthrough technologieS") Horizon SNS-JU project, Grant Agreement No.101096954. https://6g-bricks.eu/
14. Park, S.-M., Kim, Y.-G.: A metaverse: taxonomy, components, applications, and open challenges. IEEE Access **10**, 4209–4251 (2022). https://doi.org/10.1109/ACCESS.2021.3140175
15. Ghildiyal, Y., Singh, R., Alkhayyat, A., Gehlot, A., et al.: An imperative role of 6G communication with perspective of industry 4.0: challenges and research directions. Sustain. Energy Technol. Assess. **56**, 103047 (2023). https://doi.org/10.1016/j.seta.2023.103047
16. 6G-BRICKS Project: Deliverable D2.1: Description and definition of targeted PoCs (2014). https://6g-bricks.eu/wp-content/uploads/2024/02/D2.1_Description_and_definition_of_targeted_PoCs_v0.10_for_submission_vFINAL-1–1.pdf
17. Barofsky, I.: The role of objective or subjective indicators. In: Quality. Springer, New York (2012). https://doi.org/10.1007/978-1-4419-9819-4_4
18. Rantopoulos, M., et al.: 6G-BRICKS - an insight into the key value indicators (KVIs) developed. In: Papaleonidas, A., Pimenidis, E., Papadopoulos, H., Chochliouros, I. (eds.) AIAI-2025, AICT, vol.753, pp.21–36. Springer, Cham (2025). https://doi.org/10.1007/978-3-031-97317-8_2
19. Voukelatou, V., Gabrielli, L., Miliou, I., et al.: Measuring objective and subjective well-being: dimensions and data sources. Int. J. Data Sci. Anal. **11**, 279–309 (2021). https://doi.org/10.1007/s41060-020-00224-2
20. International Telecommunication Union Radiocommunication Sector (ITU-R): Framework and overall objectives of the future development of IMT for 2030 and beyond. Recommendation ITU-R M.2160–0. International Telecommunication Union, Geneva, Switzerland (2023)
21. Setiawan, I., Purba, H.H.: A systematic literature review of key performance indicators (KPIs) implementation. J. Ind. Eng. Manag. Res. **1**(3), 200–208 (2020). https://doi.org/10.7777/jiemar.v1i2
22. Chintha, V.R., Kumar, L.: Optimization techniques for 5G NR networks: KPI improvement. Int. J. Creat. Res. Thoughts **9**(9) (2021). https://ijcrt.org/papers/IJCRT2109425.pdf
23. International Telecommunication Union Radiocommunication Sector (ITU-R): IMT towards 2030 and beyond (IMT-2030). International Telecommunication Union, Geneva, Switzerland (2023). https://www.itu.int/en/ITU-R/study-groups/rsg5/rwp5d/imt-2030/Pages/default.aspx

24. Chehade, E.C., Liu, H., Albert, W., Kim, M.: An empirical study of how service designers use metrics. She Ji: J. Des. Econ. Innov. **9**(3), 402–427 (2023). https://doi.org/10.1016/j.sheji.2023.10.001
25. Joshi, L., Kale, S., Chandel, V., Pal, D.: Likert scale: explored and explained. Brit. J. Appl. Sci. Technol. **7**(4), 396–403 (2015). https://doi.org/10.9734/BJAST/2015/14975
26. Dominique, M., Muñoz, D.: A formative measurement validation methodology for survey questionnaires (2025). https://arxiv.org/pdf/2510.14950
27. ADROIT6G ("Distributed Artificial Intelligence-Driven Open & Programmable Architecture for 6G Networks") Horizon SNS-JU project, Grant Agreement No.101095363. https://adroit6g.eu/
28. TrialsNet ("TRials supported by Smart Networks beyond 5G") Horizon SNS-JU project, Grant Agreement No.101095871. https://trialsnet.eu/
29. 6G-SANDBOX ("Supporting Architectural and technological Network evolutions through an intelligent, secureD and twinning enaBled Open eXperimentation facility") Horizon SNS-JU project, Grant Agreement No.101096328. https://6g-sandbox.eu/
30. Hexa-X II ("A holistic flagship towards the 6G network platform and system, to inspire digital transformation, for the world to act together in meeting needs in society and ecosystems with novel 6G services"), Horizon SNS-JU project, Grant Agreement No.101095759. https://hexa-x-ii.eu/
31. ADROIT6G Project: Deliverable 2.3: Requirements, use cases and system architecture. https://adroit6g.eu/wp-content/uploads/2025/01/ADROIT6G_D2.3_Final.pdf
32. TrialsNet Project: Open Call - TrialsNet framework and KPIs/KVIs overview), TrialsNet_Open_Call_TrialsNet_framework_and_KPIs-KVIs_overview.pdf
33. Nielsen, L., et al.: White Paper - Beyond 5G/6G KPIs and Target Values. 5G Public Private Partnership (5G-PPP), Test, Measurement and KPIs Validation Working Group (2022). https://doi.org/10.5281/zenodo.6577506
34. 6G-SANDBOX Project: Deliverable D2.4: Final release of KVI/KPI definition and validation methodology. https://6g-sandbox.eu/wp-content/uploads/2025/05/6G-SANDBOX_D2.4_v1.0.pdf
35. Hexa-X II Project: Deliverable D1.2: 6G Use Cases and Requirements (2023). https://hexa-x-ii.eu/wp-content/uploads/2024/01/Hexa-X-II_D1.2.pdf
36. Hexa-X II Project: KV-KVI Tutorial Webinar (2024). https://hexa-x-ii.eu/wp-content/uploads/2025/01/KV-KVI-Tutorial-Webinar-by-Hexa-X-II_v2.pdf
37. Ahokangas, P., Aagaard, A., Atkova, I., Yrjölä, S., Matinmikko-Blue, M.: Business models in 5G/6G mobile communications. In: Ahokangas, P., Aagard, A. (eds.) The Changing World of Mobile Communications: 5G, 6G and the Future of Digital Services, World of Mobile Communications, pp.137–165. Springer, Heidelberg (2023). https://doi.org/10.1007/978-3-031-33191-6_6
38. International Telecommunication Union - Radiocommunication Sector (ITU-R): Recommendation ITU-T L.1480: Enabling the net zero transition: Assessing how the use of information and communication technology solutions impacts greenhouse gas emissions of other sectors. International Telecommunication Union (2025). https://www.itu.int/rec/T-REC-L.1480-202507-P/en

6G-PATH Experimentation in the B5G/6G Era via a Federated Approach

Ioannis P. Chochliouros[1(✉)], Anastasia S. Spiliopoulou[1], Almudena Díaz Zayas[2], Luís Cordeiro[3], João Fernandes[3], Qi Wang[4], Jose M. Alcaraz Calero[5], Christina Lessi[1], Panayiotis Verrios[6], and Andreea Ancuta Corici[7]

[1] Hellenic Telecommunications Organization (OTE) S.A.,, 99 Kifissias Avenue, 15124 Maroussi-Athens, Greece
ichochliouros@oteresearch.gr

[2] University of Malaga, Malaga, Spain

[3] OneSource Consultoria Informática Lda, Aveiro, Portugal

[4] University of Leicester, Leicester, UK

[5] Aston University, Birmingham, UK

[6] ACTA Ltd., Athens, Greece

[7] Fraunhofer FOKUS Institute, Berlin, Germany

Abstract. The 5G system has the ambition of responding to the widest range of services and applications in the history of mobile and wireless communications. Addressing the question of how a platform can host and integrate verticals and concurrently deal with reconciling their competing and opposing requirements, requires operational 5G/B5G infrastructures that can host various vertical industries' applications. The validation/assessment of use cases via suitable experimentation platforms is fundamental in the development of any new mobile network technology, especially when the corresponding UCs are explicitly correlated to real market needs. After assessing the recent European initiatives in the H2020/5G-PPP and the SNS-JU frameworks, our work focuses upon the innovative ecosystem created by the 6G-PATH project. The 6G-PATH experimentation environment is designed as a distributed, multi-testbed platform that enables coordinated experimentation across geographically dispersed infrastructures while preserving local autonomy and technological diversity. The paper identifies and discusses the corresponding experimentation framework, as it is realized via a federated architectural approach consisting of distinct layers that collectively enable secure access, orchestration, and observability. All involved components, per layer, are discussed as of their specific roles and functionalities.

Keywords: B5G · 6G · Artificial Intelligence (AI) · Federated testbeds · Key Performance Indicators (KPIs) · Key Value Indicators (KVIs) · verticals

1 Introduction

With the fast evolution of communications applications, communications technologies are undergoing revolutionary changes generation after generation. Till today the development of cellular mobile communication systems has undergone five generations. We

Published by Springer Nature Switzerland AG 2027
A. Papaleonidas et al. (Eds.): AIAI 2026 Workshops, IFIP AICT 796, pp. 49–70, 2027.
https://doi.org/10.1007/978-3-032-30507-7_3

are currently experiencing a broad rate of innovative applications offered worldwide within the framework of the fifth generation (5G), covering needs of numerous markets sector and especially emphasizing upon verticals [1]. 5G systems have entered the stage of commercial deployment, providing users with new services, improved user experiences as well as a host of novel opportunities to various industries. 5G is the first mobile telecommunication system generation that holistically considers the seamless delivery of data, services, and applications across all components of the network, from the originating device or application to the receiving device or application. 5G features greater service customisation, paving the way to supporting so-called vertical industries [2].

5G and its recent advancements towards B5G (Beyond 5G) / 6G [3–5] practically aim for industrial communications to help digitize the economy, in a broader scope [6, 7] and also contribute towards a form of global digital transformation [8, 9].

The development of 6G networks and services is underway on a global scale [10]. It is expected that 6G technology will move in commercial phase in 2030 and will open a profound impact worldwide [11]. Many vertical sectors are shifting towards this vision with a data-driven mindset, requiring real-time data collection and analysis, coming from selected trials and tests, being aligned to real market needs. The exponential increase in data speeds and reduced latency provided by 6G will enhance network responsiveness, supporting technical and operational transformations. This shift will accelerate and optimize processes affecting the whole chain management of the corresponding use cases (UCs).

The imminent market launch of B5G services implicates for a solid and extensive basis of prior trials, validation tests and measurements at site facilities which deliver an end-to-end 5G service chain and enable the reproduction of different live network operation conditions. Trials and pilots "address" many different verticals UCs and demonstrate specific features and capabilities [12].

5G technologies clearly deliver on promises to reach the targeted specifications on 5G performance KPIs like data rate, latency, density, coverage, reliability and, as importantly, the benefits that come from flexibility and automation. Most of the initial trials and pilots targeted the demonstration of high data rates and low latency communications performance, focusing on enabling technologies related to: (i) the radio interface like high throughput, millimetre-waves and other new wide spectrum bands, antenna technologies; (ii) the network architecture including virtualization, cloudification, network slicing, edge computing, and; (iii) the introduction of new technologies dedicated to specific UCs (such as, *for example*, technologies for IoT (Internet of Things) and for the automotive sector).

Within this scope, verticals stakeholders are more and more engaged in the different 5G/B5G trials and pilots, both in the pre-commercial and commercial domains and in the EC and national programs. This is well in line with the increased level of engagement by verticals in 3GPP standardization activities on requirements and system architecture level. The clear target is to validate the benefits of 5G/B5G to vertical sectors, proving feasibility of specific use-cases and also de-risking potential specific issues in order to create a path to successful and timely 5G/B5G deployment, passing the break-even points to ensure full adoption of the 5G technology.

The paper is structured around several distinct sections: Sect. 1 serves as an introduction to discuss the current framework with 5G's global deployment and its catalytic presence in numerous sectors, in parallel with appearing challenges for making further evolutionary steps via B5G and 6G. Then, Sect. 2 identifies the critical importance of trials and tests in suitable experimentation platforms aiming to validate paradigms and market-led use cases; in particular, this section discusses the latest European initiatives (from the H2020/5G-PPP and the SNS-JU frameworks) to develop an effective ecosystem consisting of several (federated) testbeds, able to serve innovation via the promotion of KPIs and KVIs. The important role of the ongoing 6G-PATH EU-funded project is recognized. Section 3 presents the architectural structure of the 6G-PATH Experimentation Framework that enables coordinated experimentation across nine geographically distributed testbeds throughout Europe. The architecture employs a federated approach, in which standardised interfaces and common data models "unify" diverse testbed infrastructures into a cohesive experimentation platform while preserving local autonomy and accommodating technological heterogeneity. All components, per distinct layer, are discussed and assessed as of their specific roles and functionalities. Finally, Sect. 4 serves as an overview of the entire paper's scope.

2 Test Experimentation Platforms in the European Ecosystem

B5G/6G experimentation platforms perform a role of critical importance in validating paradigms that, among others, embed intelligence, integrate communication and sensing, and ensure sustainability, security, and resilience by design. Modern experimentation platforms can so enable rigorous testing of enablers like AI-native networks [13, 14], Integrated Sensing and Communication (ISAC) [15], reconfigurable intelligent surfaces (RIS) [16] and cell-free (CF) massive multiple-in, multiple-out (MIMO) radio technologies [17, 18], among others.

2.1 Prior Actions in the H2020/5G-PPP Framework

In the framework of the European research policy towards implementing 5G, there was an initial effort, via the "joint" H2020-5G-PPP context [19], to support the development of a landscape consisting of several testbeds, as defined via three related fundament projects (5G EVE, 5G-VINNI and 5GENESIS) [20].

5G EVE [21] aimed to implement a platform with open, easy-to-use, trustworthy and smart tools, enabling innovative European verticals and SMEs to validate their 5G-ready applications and systems. The project offered to all 5G experimenters a 5G end-to-end facility, allowing them to validate the performance of their 5G-ready solutions, based on standard KPIs, prior to the commercial roll-out 5G networks. 5G EVE enabled experiments with: (i) heterogeneous access, including New Radio (NR), licensed/unlicensed spectrum, advanced spectrum management; (ii) Mobile Edge Computing (MEC), backhaul, core/service technologies, and; (iii) means for site-interworking and multi-site/domain/technology slicing/orchestration.

The 5G-VINNI E2E Facility [22] demonstrated the achievement of 5G KPIs across a range of combinations and permutations of new 5G access technologies and end-user equipment types interconnected by the most advanced 5G core network technologies available. This project provided user friendly zero-touch orchestration, operations and management systems for its corresponding facility, validated 5G KPIs and supported the execution of E2E trial of vertical UCs, creating a viable business and ecosystem model.

The 5GENESIS [71] project has validated 5G KPIs for various 5G UCs, in both controlled set-ups and large-scale events, while supporting further experimentation from vertical markets. More precisely, the 5GENESIS Facility was implemented and was capable of verifying all evolutions of the 5G standard via an iterative integration and testing procedure. In addition, it engaged a wide diversity of technologies and chain innovations that spanned over all domains, achieving full-stack coverage of the 5G landscape. It also unified heterogeneous physical and virtual network elements under a common coordination and openness framework exposed to experimenters from the vertical industries, also enabling end-to-end slicing and experiment automation. Last but not least, it offered the resulting end-to-end 5G facility to developers of services for vertical markets with a fully automated experimentation framework and unified interface for remote uploading, deployment and monitoring of the services under test.

2.2 The Context of the SNS-JU Ecosystem

The ongoing Smart Networks and Services Joint Undertaking (SNS-JU) Framework [23] has also promoted initiatives for trials to support a variety of UCs originating from various verticals, also fostering alignment with EU Member States on 6G Research and Innovation and deployment of advanced 5G networks [24]. An explicit innovative feature of the SNS JU effort was the aim to overpass challenges due to the previous "isolated" testbeds built through the 5G-PPP ecosystem that could hinder large-scale, cross-domain validation, reproducible results, as well as an efficient resource sharing across the participating verticals (such as industry, smart cities and e-health). Thus, the idea was to promote the context of "federated" testbeds, being able to promote interoperability, modularity, and scalability. Several initiatives such as 6G-BRICKS, 6G-SANDBOX, SUNRISE-6G and 6G-PATH have exemplified a "shift" towards pan-European, sustainable federation.

6G-BRICKS [25] is the first open 6G platform that combines cell-free, Open Air Interface (OAI) and RIS, while adopting the proven principles of softwarisation, open Interfaces (O-RAN), and Open Source software stacks, putting future expansion and evolvability at its core [26]. 6G-BRICKS aims to deliver a 6G experimentation facility, building on the baseline of mature ICT-52 platforms [27] that bring breakthrough cell-free and RIS technologies, which have shown promise for growth in B5G networks. Moreover, novel unified control paradigms based on Explainable AI (Artificial Intelligence) and Machine Reasoning are to be explored in detail.

6G-SANDBOX [28] brings a complete and modular facility for the European experimentation ecosystem (in line and under the directions set by SNS JU), which is expected to support for the next decade technology and research validation processes needed in the pathway towards 6G. The target is at technologies and research advances, that span over the entire service provisioning chain, and refer to user/data, control and management planes. In this direction, 6G-SANDBOX introduces the concept of Trial Networks, which refers to fully configurable, manageable and controlled end-to-end networks, composed of both digital and physical nodes. This offers to third parties (including experimenters from open calls) automated experimentation capabilities through a rich and extensible toolbox. Meant to create tangible and long-term impact, the 6G KPIs and KVIs that will be quantified with the facility, will be released to any interested party; while the set of developments and APIs that will be produced, will feed an open repository as an initial step to move the contributions and the lessons learned beyond the project boarders and define a European 6G library.

The SUNRISE-6G [29] approach is inspired by the "network of networks" concept of 6G Networks, aiming to integrate all private and public infrastructures under a massively scalable internet-like architecture. SUNRISE-6G similarly aspires to create a federation of 6G test infrastructures in a pan-European facility that will support converged Testing as a Service (TaaS) workflows and tools, a unified catalogue of 6G enablers publicly accessible by experimenters and cross-domain vertical application onboarding. Experimentation and vertical application onboarding are offered via a Tenant Web Portal that acts as a single-entry point to the facility, serving end-users (e.g., experimenters) and tenants (e.g., vertical developers, infrastructure owners, 6G component manufactures). The project execution is based on 4 pillars, delivering: (i) the Implementation of new 6G enablers, complementary to existing ones being developed in previous SNS projects; (ii) A truly scalable and 3GPP compliant Federation solution that provides access to heterogeneous resources and devices from all Europe; (iii) a Federated AI plane aligned with Artificial Intelligence as a Service (AIaaS) [30] and Machine learning Operations (MLOps) [31] paradigms, which promotes a collaborative approach to AI research that benefits immensely from scaling-up datasets and models and; (iv) a commonly adopted Experimentation Plane, which offers common workflows to experimenters.

2.3 The Approach of the 6G-PATH Project

The EU-funded 6G-PATH project [32] aims to foster the development of advanced technologies supporting deployment towards B5G/6G, via an advanced infrastructure to be available and extended throughout the project duration for broader experimentation purposes. This takes place both in close collaboration with other 6G-IA projects [33] and through the process of Open Calls to engage European companies developing innovations for B5G and 6G systems, as well as bringing new UCs [34] and pilot sites to the ecosystem [35, 36]. Such technologies and pilots will be combined in relevant platforms to be used by a set of applications in UCs corresponding to the four verticals where 6G-PATH will be present, that is: Farming, Education, Health and Smart Cities [37]. Such UCs and their corresponding applications will create demanding requirements from the platforms, thus requiring a proper validation through KPIs [38, 39] and KVIs [40, 41]. The project aims to propose an architecture aiming at providing a unified interaction point for all UCs partners.

The 6G-PATH experimentation framework for the collection of data is built on the OPEN 5GENESIS suite [42], constituting and implementing the framework described in the ETSI TR 103 761 [43]. This is a technical report developed by the European Telecommunication Standards Institute (ETSI) that outlines scenarios and testing frameworks necessary for validating next-generation wireless communication systems, such as 5G and beyond, and ensuring that they "meet" the rigorous requirements of these systems.

Within the context of the 6G-PATH project, the OPEN 5GENESIS suite has been integrated as the engine for the execution of the experiments and has been extended to support the integration of metrics from Prometheus [44], Kafka [45] and Message Queuing Telemetry Transport (MQTT) [46], among other relevant features for experimentation, such as the edition of test cases and the storage of metadata and artefacts related to the experimentation. Figure 1 depicts the framework's functional architecture.

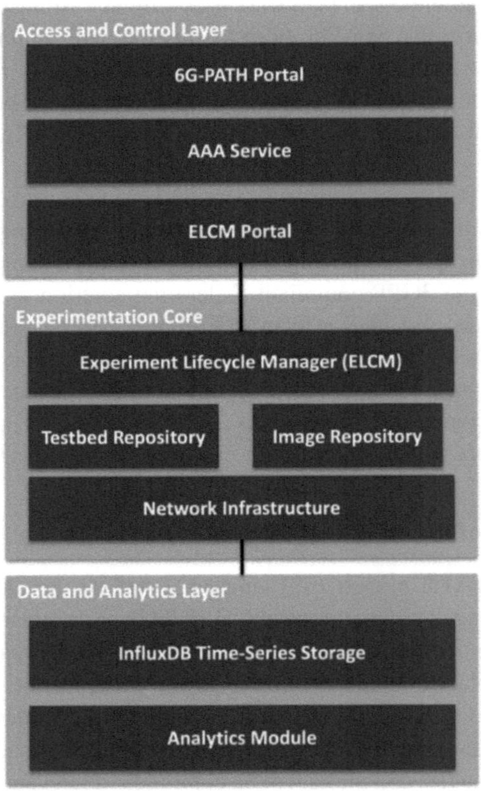

Fig. 1. Functional architecture of the experimentation framework in 6G-PATH

The 6G-PATH framework focuses on delivering core functionalities for supporting experimentation, including experiment formalisation, control, data collection, and result visualization, among others. In particular, the components of the 6G-PATH framework represent the minimum set required to establish an operational experimentation framework across all platforms, allowing the experimentation phase of the project to commence. These components are also designed with a lightweight integration approach to ensure seamless compatibility with the testbeds, facilitating easy deployment and setup.

Several advanced experimentation capabilities have been incorporated into the platforms. The advanced experimentation capabilities refer to the specialised features and functionalities that extend beyond those available in commercial 5G equipment. These capabilities are typically the result of cutting-edge research conducted by specific groups or testbeds, or they may come from the implementation of evolving standards in the telecommunications field. Unlike off-the-shelf 5G solutions, these advanced capabilities often include custom-built network functions, novel hardware or software components, and innovative configurations that "push" the boundaries of current technology. They are designed to support experimental scenarios by integrating new standard features such as CAPIF (Common API Framework) [47], experimental network slicing [48], enhanced Policy Enforcer mechanisms, close-loop configuration solutions, and AI-as-a-Service (AIaaS) features. These capabilities help pave the way for future communication technologies, including developing and validating 6G and beyond.

3 The 6G-PATH Experimentation Framework

Defining and validating use cases is an important step in the development of any new mobile network technology. UCs describe the kind of functionality that needs to be provided and are also used to derive new functional requirements and a sound justification for the targeted performance requirements.

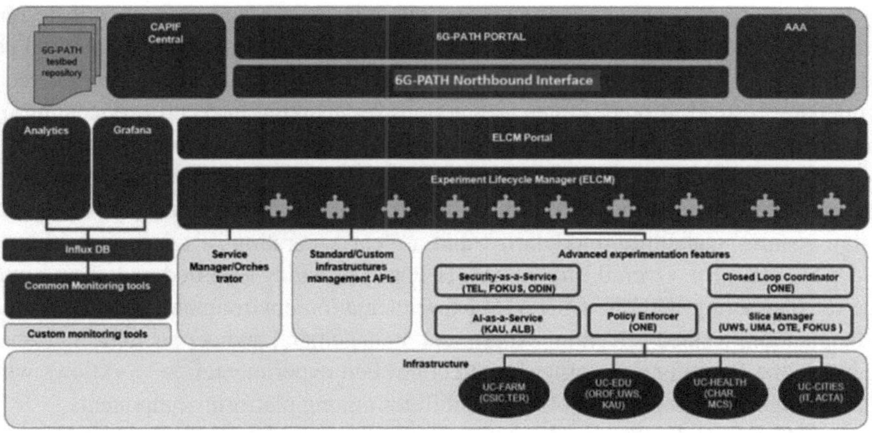

Fig. 2. 6G-PATH Experimentation Framework

Figure 2 presents a comprehensive architectural overview of the 6G-PATH Experimentation Framework, illustrating the layered structure that enables coordinated experimentation across nine geographically distributed testbeds throughout Europe (i.e., the seven project original testbeds and two testbeds coming from the Open Call #1 in "Track A"). The architecture employs a federated approach, in which standardised interfaces and common data models "unify" diverse testbed infrastructures into a cohesive experimentation platform while preserving local autonomy and accommodating technological heterogeneity. The architecture is organised into three distinct horizontal layers, each serving specific functions within the experimentation ecosystem, that is: the upper layer, the middle layer, and the infrastructure layer.

3.1 Uppermost Layer

The uppermost layer provides the primary entry point for experimenters and hosts shared services that operate across all testbeds. This layer implements a unified access model that abstracts the complexity of the underlying distributed infrastructure. This layer is composed of the following components:

The **6G-PATH Portal** serves as the main gateway to the entire experimentation framework. This web-based interface serves as experimenters' first point of contact, providing a graphical environment for discovering available testbeds, understanding their capabilities, and initiating experiments. It provides a unified, web-based interface that enables users to securely access the platform, discover authorised testbeds, manage experimentation activities, and access experiment results, while abstracting the complexity of the underlying multi-testbed infrastructure. The Portal acts as a coordination and interaction layer between users and the core platform services. The 6G-PATH Portal provides a comprehensive set of functionalities designed to support user interaction with the experimentation environment throughout the experiment lifecycle. These include: (i) User authentication and access management; (ii) testbed discovery and selection; (iii) Access to experiment analytics and results, and; (iv) documentation and user support.

The portal implements single sign-on, allowing researchers to authenticate once and access multiple testbeds without re-entering credentials. From an architectural perspective, the Portal does not execute experiments, deploy workloads, or process monitoring data. Instead, it orchestrates user actions by invoking backend services through standardised APIs (Application Programming Interfaces) and by redirecting users to specialised components. The Portal supports the complete experimentation workflow without directly interacting with testbed infrastructures or data collection systems. This design ensures scalability, modularity, and a clear separation of concerns within the 6G-PATH platform. Overall, the 6G-PATH Portal provides a unified and secure interface for interacting with the 6G-PATH experimentation environment. By coordinating authentication, testbed selection, experiment management, and access to decentralised analytics, the Portal enables efficient and controlled experimentation workflows while maintaining a clear separation of responsibilities among platform components.

The **6G-PATH Northbound Interface** operates in parallel with the portal, providing RESTful API access for programmatic interaction. This dual-access pattern (graphical portal for human users, API for automation) enables diverse workflows from manual experiment configuration to fully automated continuous integration pipelines. The 6G-PATH Northbound Interface constitutes the main access layer between user-facing components and the internal services of the 6G-PATH experimentation environment. It provides a secure, standardised, and technology-agnostic interface that enables the 6G-PATH Portal and other authorised external components to interact with the platform's core services, including authentication, testbed discovery, experiment lifecycle management, and monitoring. The Northbound Interface acts as a logical control-plane entry point, decoupling the user-interaction layer from the underlying heterogeneous testbed infrastructure and orchestration mechanisms. Exposing well-defined APIs allows higher-level services to manage experiments without requiring direct knowledge of testbed-specific technologies, protocols, or deployment details. The Northbound Interface/API provides a comprehensive set of functions to support end-to-end experimentation workflows across multiple testbeds and user roles such as: (i) User authentication and access control; (ii) testbed discovery and access management, and; (iii) monitoring, status reporting, and error handling. Standardised error-handling mechanisms ensure that failures are reported in a structured, actionable way, improving troubleshooting and operational robustness. The Northbound Interface is implemented using open, extensible APIs, enabling interoperability with both internal and external components. Overall, the 6G-PATH Northbound Interface provides a secure, scalable access layer that enables seamless interaction between user-facing components and the platform's core experimentation services.

The **AAA** provides centralised Authentication, Authorization, and Accounting (AAA) services. This component maintains user identities, manages role-based access control, enforces permissions determining which testbeds and resources users can access, and logs all authentication events for audit purposes. By centralising identity management, the AAA enables seamless access across the testbed federation with consistent security policies. The AAA component is a core security element of the 6G-PATH platform, responsible for managing user identities, controlling access to platform services and testbeds, and supporting auditing of user activity. The AAA functionality is implemented using Keycloak [49, 50] an open-source Identity and Access Management (IAM) solution that provides a centralised, standards-compliant security framework for the entire 6G-PATH ecosystem. The AAA component ensures that only authenticated and authorised users can access the platform and that their permissions are consistently enforced across all services, including the 6G-PATH Portal, the Experiment Lifecycle Manager (ELCM), the Analytics subsystem, and the Testbed Repository. It also enables Single Sign-On (SSO) [51], allowing users to seamlessly access multiple platform components after a single authentication step.

Keycloak is deployed as a standalone service and acts as the identity provider (IdP) for the 6G-PATH platform. All major platform components are integrated with the AAA service using standard OAuth 2.0 [52] / OpenID Connect (OIDC) [53] mechanisms. Upon successful authentication, Keycloak issues access tokens that are validated by the platform components to enforce authorisation decision. Keycloak's built-in accounting and logging mechanisms support basic auditing and operational monitoring. These include: (i) User authentication and session events, and; (ii) client access and token issuance events. These records provide traceability of platform usage and can be correlated with experiment execution data managed by the ELCM, supporting auditing, troubleshooting, and future extensions toward more advanced usage accounting if required.

The **Image Repository** stores containerised applications and virtual machine (VM) images that experiments deploy. This repository provides version-controlled storage, ensuring experiment reproducibility; the same image version always produces the same deployment. Researchers upload their use case applications to this repository, making them available for deployment across any testbed in the federation.

The Image Repository is a core component of the 6G-PATH experimentation framework, responsible for managing and storing use-case images deployed across the project's testbeds. It ensures that validated and up-to-date images are readily available to the 6G-PATH Experimentation Framework for seamless deployment during experimentation. GitLab serves as the central platform for the full lifecycle of these images and their associated experiments, enabling users to interact through both a web-based interface and the Git command-line for version control. Integrated CI/CD (Continuous Integration /Continuous Deployment) pipelines automate the build, validation, and testing of images, and upon successful checks, publish them to the centralised 6G-PATH Use Case Image Repository. Multiple project-specific repositories can be created within the GitLab environment to support the development of use case images. From this repository, the deployment can be initiated to the appropriate testbeds, while configurable pipeline stages allow for automated execution of test scripts to assess image functionality and performance prior to experimentation. The repository has significantly improved cross-partner collaboration: in fact, teams located at different sites and testbeds can work on shared artefacts in a controlled, transparent manner using standard Git workflows (branches, merge requests, and reviews). This has enabled: (i) Parallel development of use case images by multiple partners; (ii) structured peer review of changes prior to integration; (iii) traceability of modifications over time, supporting reproducibility of experiments, and; (iv) faster onboarding of new contributors through a unified toolchain and process. From an operational perspective, the Image Repository serves as the single source of truth for use-case images within 6G-PATH.

The **6G-PATH Testbed Repository** maintains a comprehensive registry of all participating testbeds. For each testbed, the repository stores technical specifications (available infrastructure, supported features), API endpoints enabling programmatic access, operational status indicating current availability, and capability metadata describing what specific experiments each testbed can support. This registry enables the portal to present accurate, current information about testbed options.

The 6G-PATH Testbed Repository is a centralised service within the 6G-PATH architecture that maintains authoritative information about all registered testbeds. It acts as "the single source of truth" for testbed metadata, access endpoints, and monitoring resources, enabling consistent discovery and controlled access to testbeds across the platform. The repository is accessed programmatically via a REST API and is primarily consumed by the 6G-PATH Portal and other platform components through the Northbound Interface, in coordination with the AAA component. Its role is to ensure that authenticated users are presented only with the testbeds they are authorised to access, together with the necessary technical details to support experiment execution, monitoring, and result visualisation. This Repository supports the centralised registration and maintenance of testbed metadata, controlled exposure of testbed information based on user authorisation, provision of access endpoints required by the Portal to redirect users to testbed-specific services and support for monitoring and analytics by storing references to monitoring databases and dashboards associated with each testbed. By decoupling testbed discovery and metadata management from the Portal and ELCM, the repository improves scalability, simplifies administration, and ensures consistency across multiple testbeds and experimenter entities.

Access to the Testbed Repository is governed by the AAA component. Users must be authenticated and authorised before accessing any testbed information. Authorisation decisions are based on user group membership (e.g., experimenter or testbed groups) and on assigned roles (e.g., experimenter, testbed, and testbed-specific roles). As a result, Testbed operators can view and manage the metadata of the testbeds they own, and Experimenters (consortium partners or third-party users from Open Calls) can view only the testbeds for which they have been granted access and can use these details to run experiments. The Testbed Repository itself does not manage authentication credentials; instead, it relies on validated access tokens issued by the AAA component.

3.2 Middle Layer

The middle layer contains components instantiated per-testbed (purple blocks without background colour), providing customised experimentation capabilities for each facility. This distributed instantiation pattern balances standardisation (i.e., components share common interfaces and data models) with localisation (each instance is optimised for its specific testbed). The components integrating the middle layer are the following:

The **ELCM (Experiment Lifecycle Manager) Portal** provides a web-based unified interface for experiment management within a specific testbed. For experimenters, this interface removes the complexity of creating test cases, limiting the customisation to a pre-defined set of configurable parameters. For platform owners, it separates external users and the testbed capabilities, restricting access to the actual components. Each testbed operates its own ELCM Portal instance, customised to reflect that facility's unique capabilities and configuration options. Through this portal, experimenters define test cases, configure experiment parameters, launch executions, monitor progress in real-time, and access results. Internally, the ELCM Portal makes use of the ELCM APIs for retrieving information about the available test cases and for requesting the execution of experiments, while on the front-end it: (i) Implements user registration and authentication, integrated with the central portal through Keycloak, including access control for specific test cases; (ii) provides a graphical user interface for the definition of experiments; (iii) allows authorised users to modify and customise the test case code directly within the portal, enabling fine-grained adaptation of experimentation logic without requiring external development tools, and; (iv) gives access to execution logs and results and to pre-configured Grafana dashboards for visualisation.

The **Experiment Lifecycle Manager (ELCM)** constitutes the core orchestration engine, managing the complete experiment lifecycle from initial deployment through final collection and aggregation of the collected measurements. Based on the ETSI TR 103 761 standard [43], the ELCM executes test cases defined in the YAML (YAML Ain't Markup Language) format, coordinating complex sequences of operations across infrastructure components. The ELCM is the component that enables the execution and orchestration of experiments across the 6G-PATH testbeds. It enables the execution of concurrent experiments (allowing the isolation of the testbeds' resources). Experiments are defined as a set of test cases which, in turn, are described as the set of actions that must be performed to generate the desired results. These actions (for instance, executing a command, sending a request to an API, retrieving measurements, and delegating to another orchestration solution, among others) correspond to tasks implemented in the

ELCM. The ELCM contains pre-defined tasks for many everyday actions that a testbed owner may need to execute to run a test case. In contrast, new tasks can be easily implemented by following simple guidelines. Once a test case has been defined, it can be exposed to experimenters via the ELCM Portal. At the same time, advanced users and testbed owners can use the ELCM APIs to control experiment execution directly. Each ELCM instance maintains deep integration with its local testbed through the two essential interfaces:

- Service Manager/Orchestrator enables deployment and lifecycle management of network services and functions. The ELCM uses this interface to instantiate Virtual Network Functions (VNFs) and Containerized Network Functions (CNFs) [54] configure network slices [55], deploy MEC (Multi-Access Edge Computing) applications [56, 57] and orchestrate complex multi-component services. The interface abstracts differences between testbed orchestration systems (Open-Source MANO (OSM) [58, 59], Kubernetes [60, 61] proprietary systems).
- Standard/Custom Infrastructure Management APIs provide access to underlying infrastructure resources. Through the APIs exposed by the infrastructure components, the ELCM manages the infrastructure building blocks to execute the tests defined by the experimenter. Custom interfaces accommodate testbed-specific management systems.

The **Analytics component** follows a decentralised approach, where each testbed is responsible for independently deploying the required dashboard modules. Detailed deployment instructions are provided for each testbed owner to ensure consistency. This component collects data and calculates KPIs (and/or KVIs if applicable). It retrieves data from each testbed's 6G-PATH Monitoring Database (e.g., InfluxDB) and calculates KPIs/KVIs based on the Experiment ID provided by the ELCM. The Experiment ID, supplied by the ELCM, allows users to select KPIs associated with specific testbed experiments they are authorised to access. Thus, the Analytics component aggregates monitoring data collected during the tests/experiments, processes it into meaningful insights, and presents results through interactive dashboards:

- Grafana (https://grafana.com/) provides the visualisation platform for creating and displaying dashboards. As an industry-standard open-source tool, Grafana connects to monitoring databases and renders time-series graphs, histograms, statistical summaries, and other visualisations.
- InfluxDB (https://www.influxdata.com/) is a time series database (TSDB) that is used for storage and retrieval of time series data in fields such as operations monitoring, application metrics, Internet of Things (IoT) sensor data, and real-time analytics. Each testbed operates its own InfluxDB instance, but all instances share a common data model, identical schemas and tag structures.
- Common Monitoring Tools include standard measurement utilities deployed across all testbeds: (i) iPerf (https://iperf.fr/) for throughput testing; it is a cross-platform tool that can produce standardised performance measurements for any network. The iperf has client and server functionality and can create data streams to measure the throughput between the two ends in one or both directions; (ii) ping for latency measurement, resource monitoring agents tracking Central processing Unit (CPU)/memory/storage

utilization; The ping tool is used to test whether a particular host is reachable across an IP network. (A ping measures the time it takes for packets to be sent from the local host to a destination computer and back); (iii) protocol analysers capturing network traffic.

- Commercial/Custom Tools accommodate specialised monitoring equipment available at specific testbeds. These might include professional network analysers, Radio Frequency (RF) measurement equipment, or proprietary monitoring systems. The framework supports the collection of data and measurements from these diverse sources and the storage of all of them into the InfluxDB.

The **Advanced Experimentation Features** represent cutting-edge capabilities that differentiate 6G-PATH testbeds from conventional 5G infrastructure.

These features have been classified into five topics, as discussed below. For each topic, different implementations come from different partners. It includes the new advanced features introduced in the 6G-PATH project to extend and enrich the overall technical capabilities available for experimentation. Many of these features build on technologies developed in related projects, research initiatives, and industrial platforms and are incorporated into the 6G-PATH ecosystem to "address" advanced requirements across the cloud, edge, network, data, and AI domains [62]. These features, shown in the darker grey boxes on the right side of the middle layer (as in Fig. 2), include:

- Security-as-a-Service (it is a business model in which a service provider integrates their security services into a corporate infrastructure on a subscription basis more cost-effectively than most individuals or corporations can provide on their own when the total cost of ownership is considered): Implementing Common API Framework- (CAPIF-) compliant API security frameworks [63, 64], these services provide authentication, authorisation, and secure API exposure for experimental applications.
- AI-as-a-Service: Enabling deployment of AI (Artificial Intelligence) / ML (Machine Learning) models at the network edge or core, supporting intelligent network optimisation, predictive analytics, and AI-powered applications [65].
- Close Loop Coordinator: Implementing closed-loop automation where the network monitors its own performance, detects issues or optimisation opportunities, and automatically adjusts configurations without human intervention.
- Policy Enforcer: Enforcing network policies and QoS (Quality of Service) guarantees, ensuring experimental traffic receives configured treatment and validating that policy-based network control operates correctly.
- Slice Manager: Managing the complete lifecycle of network slices – dynamic creation, configuration, monitoring, modification, and deletion of logically isolated network segments with guaranteed characteristics [66].

Not every testbed implements every advanced feature. The testbed repository indicates which facilities offer each capability, reflecting the federation's strength through diversity rather than uniformity.

Table 1 presents an overview of the 6G-PATH complete set of advanced features, with the corresponding testbed and the Technology Readiness Level (TRL).

Table 1. 6G-PATH'S Complete Set of Advance Features per Testbed

Domain	Feature	Testbed	TRL
Security-as-a-Service	CAPIF	UMA	7
	WireGuard Connectivity	FOKUS	6
Policy Enforcer	FOKUS Policy Enforcer	FOKUS	5
	ONEmNEF Policy Enforcer	ALB/IT	6
Slice Manager	FOKUS Slice Manager	FOKUS	5
	UMA Slice Manager	UMA	6
	ALB/IT Slice Manager	ALB/IT	5
	OTE Slice Manager	OTE	5
	AU Slice Manager	AU	5
	ORO Slice Manager	ORO	6
Close Loop Coordinator	MIRO Close Loop Coordinator	FOKUS	5
AI-as-a-Service	KAU AIaaS	KAU	5
	ALB/IT AIaaS	ALB/IT	5
Cloud Native and Edge Computing	Intelligent and Human-Centric Edge-to-Cloud Orchestration	UMA	5
	Advanced Mobility-Aware Edge Computing	IT/ALB	7
	Cloud-Native Health Platform	FOKUS	7
Access and Flow Scheduling	Monty Multi-flow Multi-access Scheduling	KAU	5
Secure data storage, visualisation, and sharing	Secure data storage, visualisation, and sharing	IT/ALB, UMA	5
Network Performance Monitoring	Advanced Network Performance Monitoring	IT/ALB	6
	HPE Aruba Network Observability and Metric Collection	UMA	9
	ORO Network Monitoring Platform	ORO	7
Network orchestration (ZSM)	Network Orchestration across Cloud-Edge-Core Continuum (ZSM)	ORO	6
AI Data Management and Analytics	OmniFabric Cloud-native Data and AI platform	UMA, IT/ALB	7

3.3 Infrastructure Layer

The infrastructure layer represents the actual network infrastructure and the vertical use cases it supports. This layer includes the physical and virtualised components that comprise the testbeds: Radio Access Network elements (base stations, antennas, radio units (RUs) operating in various frequency bands), 5G Core (5GC) Network functions implementing 3GPP-specified components [67, 68] (AMF (Access and Mobility Management Function), SMF (Session Management Function), UPF (User Plane Function), PCF (Policy Control Function), UDM (Unified Data Management), AUSF (Authentication Server Function)), Edge computing platforms hosting applications close to users, and Transport networks connecting all these elements.

Finally, **Use Case Domains** are shown in Fig. 2 as purple ovals at the bottom represent the four vertical sectors that "drive" 6G-PATH experimentation. For each UC we also identify the participating "actors"-members of the 6G-PATH consortium as below:

- UC-FARM (CSIC (Agencia Estatal Consejo Superior de Investigaciones Cientificas), TER (Terraview GmbH), UMA (University of Malaga), HPE (Hewlett-Packard Italiana)): Agricultural use cases validating 5G/6G technologies for precision farming, agricultural robotics, sensor networks, and farm automation.
- UC-EDU (OROF (Fundatia Orange), ORO (Orange Romania S.A.), AU (Aston University), RZ (RedZinc Services Ltd.), KAU (Karlstad University)): Educational use cases exploring immersive learning, remote laboratories, collaborative virtual environments, and educational content delivery.
- UC-HEALTH (CHAR (Charité-UniversitaetsMedizin Berlin), MCS (MCS Data Labs GmbH), FOKUS (Fraunhofer FOKUS Institute)): Healthcare use cases testing telemedicine, remote patient monitoring, and medical device integration.
- UC-CITIES (IT (Instituto de Telecomunicaçoes), ALB (Altice Labs S.A.), ACTA (ACTA Ltd.), OTE (Hellenic Telecommunications Organization S.A.)): Smart city use cases including intelligent transportation and automated logistics.

3.4 Experimentation Workflow

As illustrated in Fig. 3, the experimentation workflow begins at the 6G-PATH Portal, where they authenticate via AAA and select a testbed from the repository. The experimenter can consult the information about the features exposed by the testbeds in the Testbed Repository.

Once the experimenter has chosen a testbed, he/she can decide to deploy a service either before running the experiment or as part of it. The images to be deployed should be stored in the Image Repository, which provides an interface for uploading these images. The experimenter then accesses that testbed's ELCM Portal to configure and launch experiments. The execution of the experiments is oriented towards testing test cases. The 6G-PATH experimentation framework employs YAML as the formal specification language for defining test cases. YAML provides a human-readable format. An experimenter can open a test case file and immediately understand "what it does", without needing to parse complex code. At the same time, the structured nature of YAML ensures that the specification is unambiguous and machine-readable, enabling full automation.

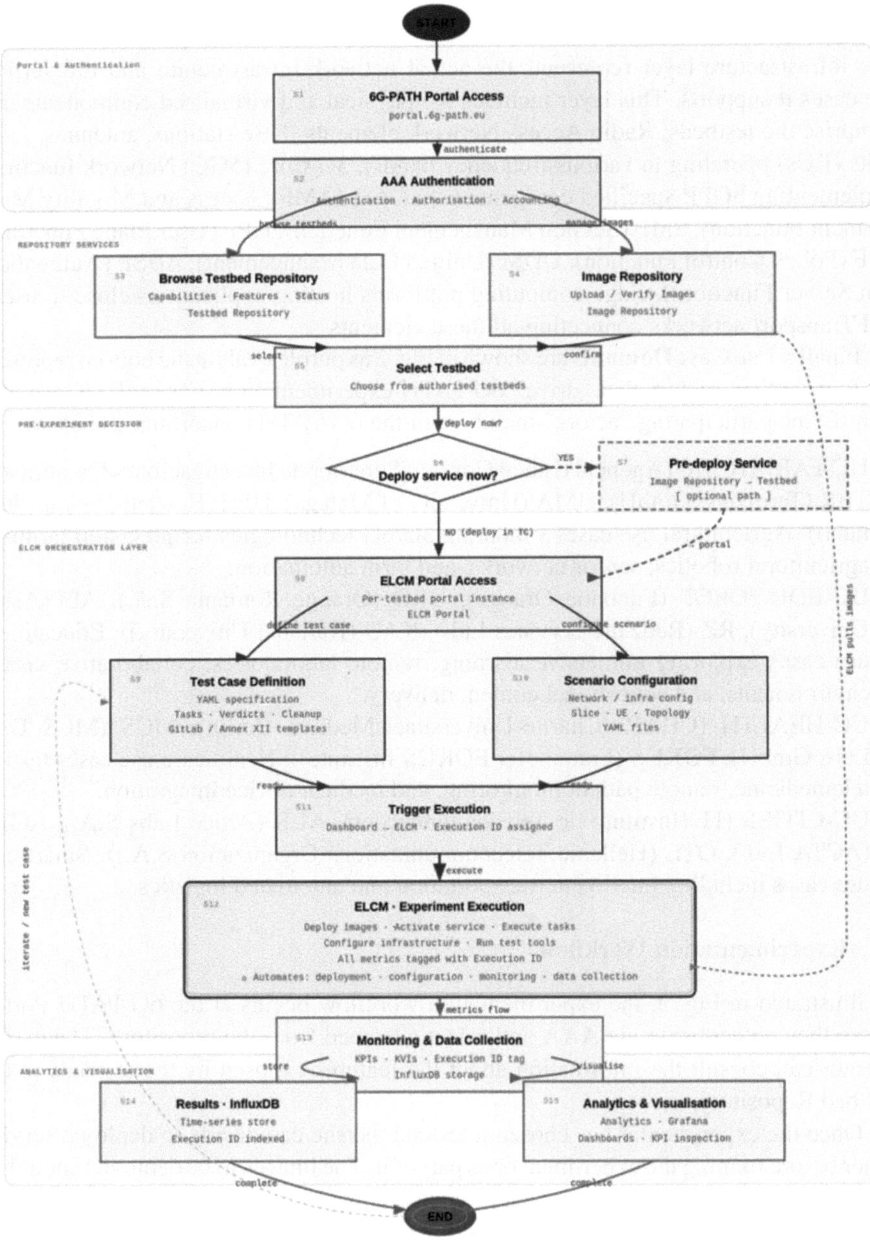

Fig. 3. 6G-PATH Experimentation flow involving layers and components

6G-PATH has predicted for dedicated test cases templates defined to measure the Network KPIs used in the project to characterise the performance provided by the corresponding testbeds. After the textual definition of the test cases, they are implemented using the YAML-based scripting synthesis defined as part of the experimentation framework. The documentation available in the GitLab repository includes examples of test case implementations [69] and the ELCM Portal also includes reference test cases to provide a baseline for experimenters when writing their YAML test cases. At this point, and for experimenters without a technical background, the testbed owners can offer support with programming the executable test cases. Thus, the testbed owners can make available to the experimenter, via the ELCM portal, an implementation of the test cases based on the experimenter's test case description, following the standardised template.

The ELCM Portal includes an editor for writing and checking the syntax of YAML test cases. The ELCM offers a list of tasks [70] which enables a direct translation between the steps defined in the test cases and tasks specified in YAML to implement the cases. Additionally, the ELCM, as an open-source tool, offers the possibility to implement new tasks to control new or proprietary components available in the testbed or that are part of the use case under test. Once the test case is edited, it appears in the experiment dashboard exposed by the ELCM Portal, and the experimenter can create an experiment based on this test case.

The ELCM executes the experiment against the actual network infrastructure. The ELCM is a central component of the experimentation framework, designed to orchestrate and manage the entire lifecycle of 5G experiments. By automating the routine aspects of experimentation (i.e.: deployment, configuration, monitoring, and data collection), the ELCM "frees" researchers to focus upon "what really matters", that is: formulating hypotheses, designing innovative tests, and interpreting results.

The test case includes activating and configuring the service under test and collecting the metrics identified by the experimenter as the "key performance measurements" for the application under test. During the experiment, measurements defined in the test case are collected and tagged with the same execution ID. Once the experiment finishes, all measurements are available in the InfluxDB integrated into the framework. This database is used by the Analytics module to inspect and visualise the measurements recorded.

4 Overview and Concluding Remarks

In the scope of the fast worldwide deployment of 5G, more challenges are now appearing due to innovative use cases originating from diverse vertical sectors of a fully converged market. Such UCs implicate for essential trials in order to be validated and assessed for both technical and business feasibility and beneficial use. In order to allow for proper market implementation but also to support the ongoing transition towards B5G, it is necessary to consider interactive experimentation platforms and availability of modern testbeds to be used for assessing and validating the UCs, especially via appropriate sets of KPIs and KVIs. By bringing UCs to their "operational limits", per separate case, it will be possible not only to evaluate feasibility but also to identify needs and requirements that will "define the path" towards B5G/6G.

In this work we have examined the fundamental "pillars" of the European policy towards promoting the deployment of interactive testbeds within the scope of the previous H2020/5G-PPP framework and then the deployment of federated testbeds within the scope of the ongoing SNS-JU framework. We have so "identified" and discussed the most relevant EU-funded research projects that have served this purpose. Among these we have focused upon the specific context of the ongoing 6G-PATH project that has "core priority" to foster the development of advanced technologies supporting deployment towards B5G/6G, via an advanced infrastructure to be available and extended throughout the project duration for broader experimentation purposes. The collection of data coming from the trials will support the purpose of composing KPIs/KVIs that will be used for the assessment of the involved UC but, mainly, will promote the transition towards B5G/6G.

More specifically, the 6G-PATH experimentation framework for the collection of data is built on the OPEN 5GENESIS suite that has been integrated as an "innovative engine" for the execution of the experiments, in previous works. We have so presented the final status, the architecture, and various capabilities of the 6G-PATH experimentation environment developed within the SNS JU framework under Horizon Europe. This framework: (i) Establishes a federated experimentation framework "ecosystem" enabling coordinated operation across multiple geographically distributed testbeds; (ii) supports consolidation and deployment of advanced experimentation features, including security-as-a-service (SECaaS), slicing, AI-as-a-service (AIaaS), and closed-loop automation; (iii) establishes a standardised experimentation methodology based on YAML-defined test cases, lifecycle automation, and KPI-driven evaluation, and; (iv) validates the platform readiness to support Beyond-5G and emerging 6G trials across Europe.

The 6G-PATH experimentation environment is designed as a distributed, multi-testbed platform that enables coordinated experimentation across geographically dispersed infrastructures while preserving local autonomy and technological diversity. The framework extends the OPEN 5GENESIS suite and aligns with ETSI TR 103 761, ensuring methodological consistency for the definition, orchestration, monitoring, and analysis of experiments in next-generation wireless systems. Core functionalities provided by the platform include experiment formalisation, automated execution, lifecycle management, KPI collection, and analytics-driven visualisation, thereby establishing an operational baseline for large-scale experimentation and validation activities. At the architectural level, the platform is organised into layered components that collectively enable secure access, orchestration, and observability. All these distinct layers have been described in detail.

Overall, the 6G-PATH experimentation environment establishes a mature, interoperable, and extensible platform that serves as the foundation for experimentation activities. By combining federated infrastructures, standardised experimentation methodologies, and cutting-edge features, the platform provides a critical foundation for Europe's transition toward 6G research, innovation, and large-scale deployment and enables the execution of internal trials, open call experiments, and validation activities across the federated testbeds.

Acknowledgements. This work has been performed in the scope of the 6G-PATH European research project and has been supported by the Smart Networks and Services Joint Undertaking (SNS-JU) by receiving funding form the European Union's Horizon Europe (HORIZON) Research and Innovation Programme under Grant Agreement No.101139172.

References

1. Ni, Y., Liang, J., Shi, X., Ban, D.: Research on key technology in 5G mobile communication network. In: Proceedings of the 2019 International Conference on Intelligent Transportation, Big Data & Smart City (ICITBS), January 12–13, 2019, Changsha, China, pp.199–201, (2019). https://doi.org/10.1109/ICITBS.2019.00054
2. Tummala, M., Bekal, P., Kumar, P., Puri, S., Rawat, S., Kumari, A.: A systematic review on current and future prospects of 5G communications. Cogent Eng. **12**(1) (2025), https://doi.org/10.1080/23311916.2025.2547635
3. 5G Public Private Partnership (5G PPP): AI and ML – Enablers for Beyond 5G Networks, version 1.0 (2021). https://zenodo.org/records/4299895
4. Wang, C.-X., et al.: On the road to 6G: visions, requirements, key technologies, and testbeds. IEEE Commun. Surv. Tutorials **25**(2), 905–974. https://doi.org/10.1109/COMST.2023.3249835
5. NTT DOCOMO Inc.: 5G Evolution and 6G, Version 5.0 (White Paper), (2023). https://www.docomo.ne.jp/english/binary/pdf/corporate/technology/whitepaper_6g/DOCOMO_6G_White_PaperEN_v5.0.pdf
6. Viswanathan, H., Mogensen, P.E.: Communications in the 6G era. IEEE Access **8**, 57063–57074 (2020)
7. Saad, W., Bennis, M., Chen, M.: A vision of 6G wireless systems: applications, trends, technologies, and open research problems. IEEE Network **34**(3), 134–142 (2019)
8. Bhat, J.R., Alqahtani, S.A.: 6G ecosystem: current status and future perspective. IEEE Access **9**, 43134–43167 (2021)
9. Trichias, K., Kaloxylos, A., Willcock, C.: 6G global landscape: a comparative analysis of 6G targets and technological trends. In: Proceedings of the 2024 Joint European Conference on Networks and Communications & 6G Summit (EuCNC/6G Summit), June 034–06, 2024, Antwerp, Belgium, pp.1–6 (2024). https://doi.org/10.1109/EuCNC/6GSummit60053.2024.10597064
10. Nayak, S., Patgiri, R.: 6G communications: a vision on the potential applications (2020). http://arxiv.org/abs/2005.07531
11. 6G Flagship: 6G in Logistics. Real-time supply-routing-delivery logistics. Oulu. Finland: University of Oulu (2024). https://oulurepo.oulu.fi/bitstream/handle/10024/54012/nbnfioulu-202502071503.pdf?sequence=1&isAllowed=y
12. The Third Generation Partnership Project (3GPP): 3GPP TR 22.891 V14.2.0: "Feasibility Study on New Services and Markets Technology Enablers; Stage 1 (Release 14)", 3GPP (2016). https://www.3gpp.org/ftp/Specs/archive/22_series/22.891/
13. Hossain, A.R., Liu, W., et al.: AI-native for 6G core network configuration. IEEE Netw. Lett. **5**(4), 255–259 (2023). https://doi.org/10.1109/LNET.2023.3302833
14. Iovene, M., Jonsson, L., et al..: Defining AI native: a key enabler for advanced intelligent telecom networks, Ericsson Whitepaper (2022). https://www.ericsson.com/en/reports-and-papers/white-papers/ai-native
15. Wen, D., Zhou, Y., Li, X., Shi, Y., Huang, K., Letaief, K.B.: A survey on integrated sensing, communication, and computation. IEEE Commun. Surv. Tutorials **27**(5), 3058–3098 (2025). https://doi.org/10.1109/COMST.2024.3521498
16. Jiao, H., Liu, H., Wang, Z.: Reconfigurable intelligent surfaces aided wireless communication: key technologies and challenges. In: Proceedings of the 2022 International Wireless Communications and Mobile Computing (IWCMC), May 30–June 03, 2022, Dubrovnik, Croatia, pp.1364–1368 (2022). https://doi.org/10.1109/IWCMC55113.2022.9824117
17. Chen, S., Zhang, J., Zhang, J., Björnson, E., Ai, B: A survey on user-centric MassiveMIMO systems. Digital Commun. Netw. **8**(5), 695–719 (2022). https://doi.org/10.1016/j.dcan.2021.12.005

18. Zheng, J., et al.: Mobile cell-free massive mimo: challenges, solutions, and future directions. IEEE Wirel. Commun. **31**(3), 140–147 (2024). https://doi.org/10.1109/MWC.004.2300043
19. 5G-PPP ICT-17–2018 call. https://5g-ppp.eu/5g-ppp-phase-3-1-projects/
20. 5G Infrastructure Association (5G-IA): 5G Network Support of Vertical Industries in the 5G Public-Private Partnership Ecosystem, 5G-PPP. https://5g-ppp.eu/wp-content/uploads/2020/02/Vertical-industries-in-the-5G-PPP.pdf
21. 5G EVE ("5G European Validation platform for Extensive trials") Horizon 2020/5G-PPP project, Grant Agreement No.815074. https://www.eurescom.eu/archive/5G-EVE/
22. 5G-VINNI ("5G Verticals INNovation Infrastructure") Horizon 2020/5G-PPP project, Grant Agreement No.815279. https://www.eurescom.eu/archive/5G-VINNI/
23. Smart Networks and Services - Joint Undertaking (SNS-JU), https://smart-networks.europa.eu/
24. 6G Smart Networks and Services Infrastructure Association (6G-IA): European Vision for the 6G Network Ecosystem (White Paper), 6G-IA Vision Working Group (2024). https://doi.org/10.5281/zenodo.13708424
25. 6G-BRICKS (Building Reusable testbed Infrastructures for validating Cloud-to-device breaKthrough technologieS) Horizon SNS JU project, Grant Agreement No.101096954. https://6g-bricks.eu/
26. Chochliouros, I.P., Vardakas, J., Ramantas, K., et al.: 6G-BRICKS: developing a modern experimentation facility for validation, testing and showcasing of 6G breakthrough technologies and devices. In: Maglogiannis, I., Iliadis, L., Papaleonidas, A. and, Chochliouros, I. (eds.) AIAI-2024, AICT, vol.677, pp.17–31. Springer, Cham, (2023), https://doi.org/10.1007/978-3-031-34171-7_1
27. 5G Public Private Infrastructure (5G-PPP): H2020-ICT52–2020: "5G-PPP Smart connectivity beyond 5G". https://5g-ppp.eu/5g-ppp-phase-3-6-projects/
28. 6G-SANDBOX (Supporting Architectural and technological Network evolutions through an intelligent, secureD and twinning enaBled Open eXperimentation facility) Horizon SNS JU project, Grant Agreement No.101096328. https://6g-sandbox.eu/
29. SUNRISE-6G (SUstainable federatioN of Research Infrastructures for Scaling-up Experimentation in 6G) Horizon SNS JU project, Grant Agreement No.101139257. https://sunrise6g.eu/
30. Lins, S., Pandl, K.D., Teigeler, H., et al.: Artificial intelligence as a service. Bus. Inf. Syst. Eng. **63**(4), 441–456 (2021). https://doi.org/10.1007/s12599-021-00708-w
31. Kreuzberger, D., Kühl, N., Hirschl, S.: Machine Learning Operations (MLOps): Overview, Definition, and Architecture (2022). https://arxiv.org/abs/2205.02302
32. Smart Networks and Services – Joint Undertaking (SNS-JU): 6G-PATH ("6G Pilots and TriAls THrough Europe") Project, Grant Agreement No.101139172. https://6gpath.eu
33. The 6G Smart Networks and Services Industry Association (6G-IA). https://6g-ia.eu/
34. Next Generation Mobile Networks (NGMN) Alliance: Use Cases and Analysis v1.0 (2022). https://www.ngmn.org/wp-content/uploads/NGMN-6G-Use-Cases-and-Analysis.pdf
35. 6G-PATH SNS-JU Project: Deliverable 5.1: "Cascade Funding and training to thirdparties – Initial", (2025). https://6gpath.eu/wp-content/uploads/2025/09/6G-PATH-D5.1-August-2025-Final-EC-Version.pdf
36. 6G-PATH SNS-JU Project: Open Call 2 Winners, (2025). https://6gpath.eu/open-call-2-winners/
37. Chochliouros, I.P., Cordeiro, L., Fernandes, J., Díaz Zayas, A., et al.: Promoting deployment of innovative use cases in market verticals for the support of 6G evolution: the 6G-PATH context. In: Maglogiannis, I., Iliadis, L., Karydis, I., Papaleonidas, A and, Chochliouros, I. (eds.) AIAI-2024, AICT, vol.715, pp.154–176. Springer, Cham, (2024). https://doi.org/10.1007/978-3-031-63227-3_11

38. 5G Infrastructure Public Private Partnership (5G PPP): KPIs Measurement Tools. From KPI definition to KPI validation enablement (White Paper) (2023). https://5g-ppp.eu/wp-content/uploads/2023/05/TMV-KPI-Measurement-Tools_1.0-published.pdf
39. 5G Infrastructure Public Private Partnership (5G PPP): White Paper - Beyond 5G/6G KPI Measurement (2023). https://5g-ppp.eu/wp-content/uploads/2023/06/white_paper_b5g-6g_kpi_measurement_FINAL.pdf
40. Fernandes, J., Rosa, L., Chochliouros, I., Cordeiro, L., Díaz Zayas, A., et al.: Paving the path to 6G: the 6G-PATH Project's vision for advanced telecommunications' infrastructure and use cases. In: Proceedings of the 2024 IEEE Future Networks World Forum (FNWF), October 15–17, 2024, Dubai, United Arab Emirates, pp.1–6 (2024)
41. Wikström, G., Bledow, N., et al.: Key value indicators: a framework for values-driven next-generation ICT solutions. Telecommun. Policy, **48**(6), (2024). https://doi.org/10.1016/j.telpol.2024.102778
42. 5GENESIS project: Open 5GENESIS Suite. https://github.com/5genesis
43. European Telecommunications Standards Institute (ETSI): ETSI TR 103 761 V1.1.1 (2022–05): Core Network and Interoperability Testing (INT); Methodologies for E2E Testing & Validation of Vertical Applications over 5G & Beyond networks, (2022). https://cdn.standards.iteh.ai/samples/59575/0f4ec233b75c4f46972e278776e92912/ETSI-TR-103-761-V1-1-1-2022-05-.pdf
44. https://prometheus.io/
45. https://kafka.apache.org/
46. https://mqtt.org/
47. European Telecommunications Standards Institute (ETSI): Open Common API Framework. https://ocf.etsi.org/
48. Martins, J.S.B., Carvalho, T.C., Modeira, R., et al.: Enhancing network slicing architectures with machine learning. Secur. Sustain. Exp. Netw. Integr. (2023). https://arxiv.org/abs/2307.09151
49. Thorgersen, S., Silva, P.I.: Keycloak - Identity and Access Management for Modern Applications: Harness the power of Keycloak, OpenID Connect, and OAuth 2.0 protocols to secure applications. Packt Publishing Ltd., Birmingham, UK (2021)
50. Danquah, D.S., Chunyong, Y.: API security: protecting APIs with keycloak. Int. J. Eng. Res. Technol. (IJERT), **12**(4), 561–564 (2023). https://www.ijert.org/research/api-security-protecting-apis-with-keycloak-IJERTV 12IS04 0284.pdf
51. Pandey, P., Nisha, T,N.: Challenges in single sign-on. J. Phys. Conf. Ser. **1964**(2021), 042016 (2021). https://doi.org/10.1088/1742-6596/1964/4/042016
52. Darwish, M., Ouda, A.: Evaluation of an OAuth 2.0 protocol implementation for web server applications. In: Proceedings of the 2015 International Conference and Workshop on Computing and Communication (IEMCON), October 15–17, 2015, Vancouver, BC, Canada, pp. 1–4, (2015). https://doi.org/10.1109/IEMCON.2015.7344461
53. Dodanduwa, K., Kaluthanthri, I.: Role of trust in OAuth 2.0 and OpenID Connect. In: Proceedings of the 2018 IEEE International Conference on Information and Automation for Sustainability (ICIAfS), December 21–22, 2018, Colombo, Sri Lanka, pp.1–4 (2018). https://doi.org/10.1109/ICIAFS.2018.8913384
54. Red Hat: VNF and CNF, what's the difference? (2022). https://www.redhat.com/en/topics/cloud-native-apps/vnf-and-cnf-whats-the-difference
55. Abdelwahab, S., et al.: Network function virtualization in 5G. IEEE Commun. Mag. **54**(4), 84–91 (2016). https://doi.org/10.1109/MCOM.2016.7452271
56. European Telecommunications Standards Institute (ETSI): Multi-access Edge Computing (MEC). https://www.etsi.org/technologies/multi-access-edge-computing

57. Ahmed, A., Ahmed, E.: A survey on mobile edge computing. In: Proceedings of the 2016 10th International Conference on Intelligent Systems and Control (ISCO), January 07–08, 2016, Coimbatore, India, pp.1–8, (2016). https://doi.org/10.1109/ISCO.2016.7727082
58. Open Source Management and Orechestration. https://osm.etsi.org/
59. Pino, A., et al.: Validation and Benchmarking of CNFs in OSM for pure Cloud Native applications in 5G and beyond. In: Proceedings of the 2021 International Conference on Computer Communications and Networks (ICCCN), July 19–22, 2021, Athens, Greece, pp.1–9 (2021) (2021). https://doi.org/10.1109/ICCCN52240.2021.9522356
60. Kubernetes: Kubernetes API. https://kubernetes.io/docs/reference/kubernetes-api/
61. Ojea, A.: The kubernetes network driver model: a composable architecture for high-performance networking. In: Proceedings of the 2025 IEEE 50th Conference on Local Computer Networks (LCN), October 14–16, 2025, Sydney, Australia, pp.1–7 (2025). https://doi.org/10.1109/LCN65610.2025.11146291
62. 6G-PATH SNS-JU Project: Deliverable 2.2: "Platform architecture and verticals – midterm" (2025). https://6gpath.eu/wp-content/uploads/2025/12/6G-PATH-D2.2-Platform-architecture-and-verticals-midterm-v1.0_Final.pdf
63. Charismiadis, A.-S., Salcines, J.M., Tsolkas, D., Guillen, D.A., Rodrigo, J.G.: The 3GPP common API framework: open-source release and application use cases. In: Proceedings of the 2023 Joint European Conference on Networks and Communications & 6G Summit (EuCNC/6G Summit), June 06–09, 2023, Gothenburg, Sweden, 2023, pp.472–477 (2024). https://doi.org/10.1109/EuCNC/6GSummit58263.2023.10188337
64. Sanchez, A.M., et al.: Offering the 3GPP common API framework as microservice to vertical industries. In: Proceedings of the 2022 Joint European Conference on Networks and Communications & 6G Summit (EuCNC/6G Summit), Grenoble, France, pp.363–368 (2022). https://doi.org/10.1109/EuCNC/6GSummit54941.2022.9815741
65. Zang, H., Alphones, A., Xiong, Z., Niyato, D., Zhao, J., Wu, K.: Artificial-intelligence enabled intelligent 6G networks. IEEE Networks **34**(6), 272–280 (2020)
66. Chochliouros, I.P., Spiliopoulou, A.S., et al.: Dynamic network slicing: challenges and opportunities. In: Maglogiannis, I., Iliadis, L., Pimenidis, E. (eds.) AIAI-2020, AICT, vol.585, pp.47–60. Springer, Cham (2020). https://doi.org/10.1007/978-3-030-49190-1_5
67. The Third Generation Partnership Project (3GPP): 5G System Overview. https://www.3gpp.org/technologies/5g-system-overview
68. Taid, R.: 5G Core network architecture. In: Mobile Communications Systems Development: A Practical Introduction to System Understanding, Implementation and Deployment, Wiley, pp.447–472 (2021). https://doi.org/10.1002/9781119778714.ch20
69. https://gitlab.com/morse-uma/elcm/-/tree/main/Samples?ref_type=heads
70. https://gitlab.com/morse-uma/elcm/-/blob/main/docs/3-2a_GENERAL_TASKS.md
71. 5GENESIS ("5GENESIS: 5th Generation End-to-end Network, Experimentation, System Integration, and Showcasing") H2020/5G-PPP project, Grant Agreement No.815178. https://5g-ppp.eu/5genesis/

6G-PATH: Architecture Validation via Internal and Open-Call Trials

Andreea Ancuta Corici[1(✉)], Hemant Zope[1], Peenal Gupta[4], Martin Hocquel-Hans[2], Banhirup Sengupta[4], Luis Ferreira[5], Marius Corici[1], Leon Roß[3], Mario Lourenço[5], Moritz Ellenberger[3], Andreas Blaeser[3], Luis Cordeiro[5], João Fernandes[5], Luis Rosa[5], Nils Lahmann[2], and Sandra Strube-Lahmann[2]

[1] Fraunhofer FOKUS Institute, Berlin, Germany
{andreea.ancuta.corici,hemant.zope, marius-iulian.corici}@fokus.fraunhofer.de

[2] Clinical Research for Geriatrics, Charité, Berlin, Germany
{martin.hocquel,nils.lahmann,sandra.strube-lahmann}@charite.de

[3] BlackDrop Biodrucker GmbH, Darmstadt, Germany
{ross,ellenberger,ablaeser}@black-drop.de

[4] PinakashieldTech, Tallin, Estonia
{peenal.gupta,banhirup.sengupta}@pinakashield.com

[5] OneSource Consultoria Informática, Coimbra, Portugal
{luis.ferreira,mario.lourenco,cordeiro,joao.fernandes, luis.rosa}@onesource.pt

https://www.fokus.fraunhofer.de, https://pinakashield.com, https://geriatrie.charite.de/en/research, https://onesource.pt, https://black-drop.de

Abstract. This paper presents the 6G-PATH architecture and its validation through internal deployments and open-call trials in a healthcare scenario for chronic wound management. Starting from requirements derived with clinical partners and a survey of nursing personnel ($N = 146$), we identify high availability, security, and seamless access to medical data as primary needs, while "futuristic" ultra-low-latency features rank lower. These findings drive the design of an end-to-end platform that combines a beyond-5G core network with edge capabilities, a secure experimental testbed, and healthcare-specific enablers.

On the network side, the platform integrates Open5GCore, local breakout at the edge, and mechanisms for policy enforcement [9,10,13], Security as a Service, and reliability assurance over terrestrial and satellite backhaul. Healthcare applications are supported by a Kubernetes-native [18] Close Loop Coordinator for Artificial Intelligence (AI) pipeline orchestration across cloud–edge resources, QoS-aware and interoperable bioprinter control, and PATHSHIELD, a 6G-enabled security framework that uses federated learning for malicious device and attack detection and traffic influence for dynamic isolation and mitigation. A realistic testbed with on-premises central and edge nodes and private 5G network on wheels enables trials under strict time and budget constraints. The validation confirms that the proposed architecture

Published by Springer Nature Switzerland AG 2027
A. Papaleonidas et al. (Eds.): AIAI 2026 Workshops, IFIP AICT 796, pp. 71–87, 2027.
https://doi.org/10.1007/978-3-032-30507-7_4

can meet clinical workflow needs while demonstrating how Beyond 5G (B5G) /6G capabilities—network slicing, Multi-access Edge Computing (MEC), federated learning for attack detection and traffic influence for its mitigation—can be concretely exploited in safety-critical healthcare environments.

Keywords: Telehealth · Nomadic Network · Bioprinter · Closed-Loop-Coordinator · Detect-and-Adapt

1 Introduction

The continuous development of Beyond-5G (B5G) and early 6G communication technologies creates new opportunities for strengthening healthcare services, particularly in ageing societies and in rural or otherwise underserved areas. From the perspective of nursing science, these technologies are relevant because they can support continuity of care, improve care quality, and enable more patient-centred service delivery. Digital health infrastructures can facilitate remote consultation, continuous monitoring, clinical decision support, and home-based management of chronic conditions, including chronic wound care [1–3]. At the same time, the successful adoption of such technologies depends on their alignment with the practical needs, expectations, professional responsibilities, and daily workflows of healthcare providers [4,5].

Today, patients suffering from chronic wounds must often travel to specialized wound centers, creating logistical, emotional, and clinical burdens. Wound assessment is frequently manual, painful, and infection-prone, and documentation processes are fragmented across settings. At the same time, demographic change and staff shortages increase pressure on nursing personnel, who need digital tools that genuinely support, rather than complicate, their daily work. Against this backdrop, the 6G-PATH project explores how beyond-5G (B5G) and 6G technologies can be harnessed to enable safe, efficient, and patient-centred care at home.

From the outset, the project was guided by the needs and priorities of nursing staff. Insights stemming from a multi-step survey programme with nursing personnel ($N = 146$) directly inform the design of the 6G-PATH architecture. Advanced testbed features include policy enforcement, reliability assurance across terrestrial and satellite backhaul, Security as a Service. The testbed also integrates a Kubernetes-native Closed Loop Coordinator (CLC) for AI pipeline orchestration across edge–cloud resources, a QoS-aware and interoperable bioprinter control, and PATHSHIELD, a 6G-enabled security framework that leverages federated learning and traffic influence for early detection and mitigation [11,15] of malicious devices and attacks.

The remainder of this paper is structured as follows. Section 2 summarises the nursing personnel survey and the resulting requirements for B5G/6G in healthcare. Section 3 presents the resilient architecture for home-based wound care, including the nomadic Edge Router and hospital-side integration. Section 4 introduces advanced platform features, namely the Closed Loop Coordinator and the PATHSHIELD security framework. Section 5 describes the testbed-based validation setup and reports evaluation results for orchestration, security functions, and QoS-aware bioprinter integration. Section 6 concludes with key lessons learned and an outlook on future work.

2 Nursing Personnel Survey

In 2025 trials and pilots, 120 nursing personnel rated several Key Value Indicator (KVI) dimensions (1–7); all items scored above 5.0. Highest agreement was found for improved healthcare access, quality of life, patient outcomes, and resource optimization, followed by empowerment of healthcare providers, time savings, societal benefits, and cost savings. Nurses thus perceived clear added value in networked solutions, especially for accessibility and outcome-related aspects.

Building on this, the Charité nursing research team conducted a broader online survey (March 2026) to systematize the requirements of healthcare professionals for future B5G/6G applications. The structure of the questionnaire covered the background of the participants (demographics, professional background, Affinity for Technology Interaction) as well as the perception of four B5G/6G technological domains. For a fine granular analysis, a B5G/6G feature prioritization (Force-Choice Task) was introduced (see Fig. 1).

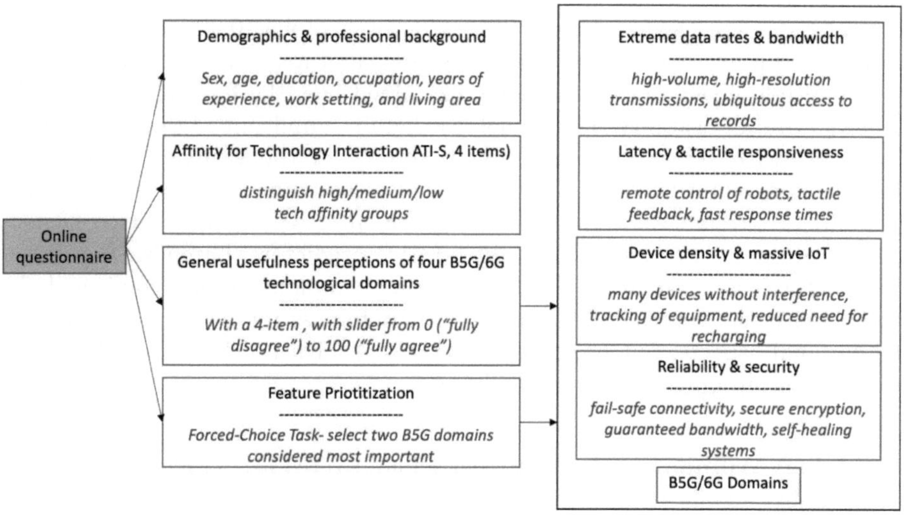

Fig. 1. Structure of the online questionnaire and its components.

The survey was completed by 148 participants, out of 168; after data cleaning, the final sample was 146. Overall, participants held a very positive view of B5G/6G: around three quarters agreed that 6G would improve their work, make processes faster, and be attractive for their field. About 72% agreed that B5G/6G would not only optimize existing workflows but also enable new ways of working.

In terms of specific application domains, participants clearly prioritized foundational infrastructure aspects over "futuristic" functions. Reliability & Security (D4) achieved the highest importance ratings. The top-rated single feature was a fail-safe mobile data connection (mean 91.55), followed by absolutely secure data encryption (90.16). Guaranteed bandwidth (network slicing) and self-healing, predictive network systems were also highly valued. In the Extreme Data Rates & Bandwidth (D1) domain, ubiquitous access to patient records from anywhere was particularly important (84.58). In Device Density & Massive IoT (D3), the elimination of constant recharging of wearables scored very highly (85.71), reflecting a desire for "invisible" technology that reduces day-to-day friction.

By contrast, items involving low-latency, high-tech scenarios received lower importance ratings. Latency-free remote control of applications like tele-surgery robots or wheelchairs (61.58) and photorealistic hologram communication (66.59) were among the least important. This suggests that while such capabilities are often highlighted in 6G visions, they do not reflect the immediate practical needs of nursing staff.

The internal consistency (Cronbach's alpha) was good for most domains: 0.771 (Extreme Data Rates), 0.842 (Latency), 0.855 (Security), and 0.878 for General Usability. Device Density showed a lower alpha (0.29), indicating that the included items may be more heterogeneous and might need refinement.

A multiple linear regression model examined how the four domains predict perceived overall usability. The model was highly significant ($F(4, 134) = 50.29$, $p < .001$) with $R^2 = .600$, meaning that 60% of the variance in perceived usability is explained by the four technological domains. Security ($B = 0.520$, $p < .001$), Extreme Data Rates ($B = 0.286$, $p < .001$), and Device Density ($B = 0.288$, $p = .007$) were significant positive predictors. Latency ($B = 0.009$, $p = .912$) was not significant. The forced-choice ranking results confirmed this pattern with the central role in perceived usefulness for Security and related foundational aspects. Furthermore, a series of Analysis of Variance (ANOVAs) examined group differences were analysed.

Technology Affinity: High-affinity participants rated Device Density, Security, and Usability significantly higher than medium and low affinity groups.

Years of Professional Experience: Nurses with 3–20+ years of experience consistently attributed higher importance and usability to B5G/6G than novices (0–2 years). Significant differences emerged for Extreme Data Rates, Security, and Usability. The authors interpret this as a "reality shock" effect: novices are primarily focused on basic clinical skills and emotional demands, while experienced staff are more aware of systemic inefficiencies that technology could address.

Living Area: Security importance was significantly higher among participants from large metropolitan areas ($>$ 100,000 inhabitants) compared to smaller towns or rural settings ($p = .003$), likely reflecting exposure to more complex and regulated IT environments.

Work Setting: No statistically significant differences at $\alpha = .05$ were found between settings, though descriptive trends suggested that staff in long-term care facilities rated importance and usability somewhat higher.

From a nursing perspective, the main value of B5G/6G is less on ultra-low latency, and more on reliable connectivity, secure data management, and seamless device integration that reduce everyday problems such as outages, documentation burden, and battery issues. Perceived importance and readiness to adopt these systems are strongly influenced by user characteristics like professional experience and technology affinity. Consequently, successful B5G/6G deployment in healthcare requires robust infrastructure combined with user-centric design, careful workflow integration, and tailored training and change management.

3 Resilient Architecture for Care at Home

The 6G-PATH architecture for home-based wound care is aligned with the priorities identified in the nursing survey: reliable connectivity, secure data handling, and seamless access to medical information. Rather than centring on ultra-low latency showcase features, it is designed for robust operation under real-world constraints such as intermittent coverage, limited local infrastructure, and strict data protection requirements (see Fig. 2).

At the patient's home, a nurse uses a portable wound-care kit consisting of a smartphone with the Nurse Care App, a 3D wound scanning tool, and a bioprinter for customized hydrogel patches. The Edge Router combines a local 5G base station providing local coverage to connect the devices, with edge core network functions, creating an on-demand nomadic private network domain at the point of care. The connected devices are authenticated locally, and critical sessions like the ones between the nurse's smartphone and the bioprinter remain on-site reducing the end-to-end communication delay and the dependence on the wide-area backhaul [12].

Regarding integration with hospital information systems (HIS), the German digitalization framework requires support for HL7 Fast Healthcare Interoperability Resources (FHIR) as a data exchange protocol [6]. FHIR defines standardized data structures and interaction patterns for creating, updating, retrieving, and deleting healthcare resources such as Patient, Encounter, and Questionnaire. The next implementation phase of the interface, required by 1 July 2025, extends this

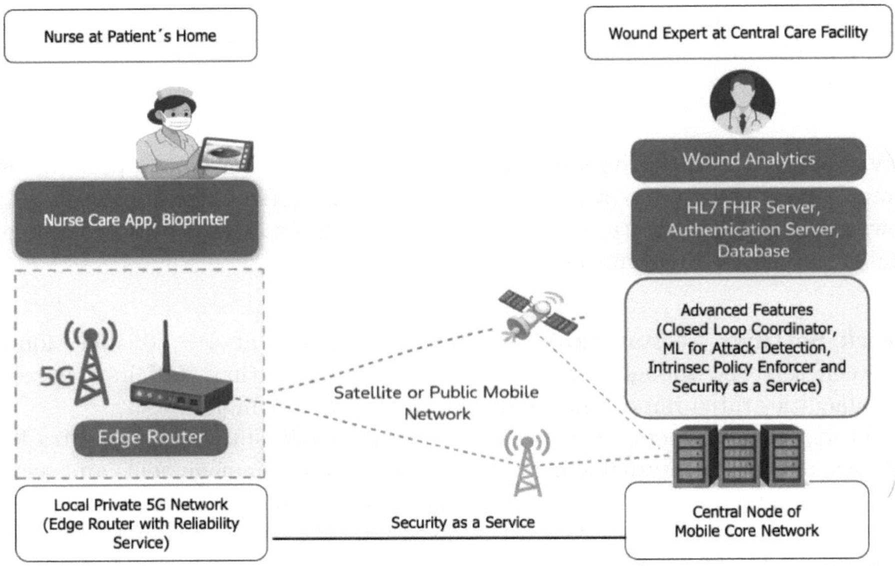

Fig. 2. Topology of the wound care at home using nomadic node (Edge Router).

support to resources for vital parameters, medication, and general data exchange. It also includes type codes for data objects such as scans and videos, as specified by Integrating the Healthcare Enterprise (IHE) Germany [7,8].

To ensure high availability, the Edge Router supports multiple backhaul options and can dynamically select between terrestrial 4G or 5G networks and satellite connectivity. Due to size and energy requirements, the Edge Router is connected to the vehicle the nurse uses. This increases portability and availability at the use case premise. When hospital connectivity is available, medical data and video consultations are transmitted through encrypted Over-The-Top (OTT) tunnels, with Software-Defined Wide Area Network (SD-WAN) steering traffic along the best current path. If terrestrial backhauling degrades due to lack of coverage, the system transparently falls back to satellite backhauling, so wound documentation, remote consultation, and data synchronization remain feasible also in underserved regions.

Within the home-care micro-network, local breakouts keep latency and privacy-sensitive communication at the edge. The Nurse Care App interacts directly with the bioprinter through a local User Plane Function (UPF), avoiding unnecessary round-trips to the central core.

High-resolution 2D and 3D wound data can be processed on the edge to support immediate decisions, whereas more demanding analytics are offloaded to central cloud resources when sufficient connectivity is available.

On the hospital side, all medical information is stored in an FHIR-compliant repository integrated with role-based access control for fine-grained, consent-aware authorization. Nurses, wound experts, and other professionals receive only access appropriate to their role and patient relationship. The Nurse Care App supports secure, interoperable wound documentation, visualization, and multimedia communication with clinical experts. Wound Analytics services generate quantitative measurements and 3D models for personalized hydrogel patches, with results written back to the FHIR store and exposed through existing clinical portals, maintaining continuity of care without disrupting established workflows.

To reduce the implementation and operations complexity, the Edge Router consists of a common of the shelf small-size base station and the Fraunhofer FOKUS Open5GCore toolkit [16], installed on top of a commodity small footprint hardware. On top of the same hardware component, the healthcare applications were also deployed in a containerized manner. Following a pragmatic approach, the Edge Router implements additionally to basic connectivity essential features for nursing staff communication: local breakout and data bearer policy enforcement for the local communication, to enable a secure and reliable data exchange between devices connected to the remote network, secure data handling through securing the local connectivity with specific 5G/6G mechanisms [12] and through an additional encryption across the third party backhauls (4G, 5G or satellite networks) and dependable end-to-end connectivity through automatic backhaul reselection according to momentary network conditions.

4 Second Phase Advanced Features

4.1 Closed Loop Coordinator

The Closed Loop Coordinator (CLC) supports the deployment and lifecycle management of distributed clinical application components across both edge and central environments. Its role is particularly relevant in this use case, as the healthcare workflow combines latency-sensitive services at the point of care, such as wound data acquisition and interaction with local medical devices, with more computationally demanding or coordination-oriented functions that can be executed centrally. The coordinator translates deployment intents into executable workflows and places application components based on infrastructure conditions, inter-component dependencies, latency constraints, and resource requirements. In this way, the CLC enables a healthcare workflow that remains responsive at the edge while still supporting central coordination, secure data handling, and controlled adaptation over time.

In the context of chronic wound management, this means that time-sensitive processing and local service interactions can remain close to the patient. At the same time, services with higher computational demands, such as analytics or AI-driven processing stages, can be assigned to infrastructure offering greater processing capacity, including Graphics Processing Unit (GPU) - enabled resources when necessary. This distinction becomes particularly relevant in trial settings, where connectivity conditions, compute availability, and deployment targets may change over time. By modelling deployment as a dependency-aware workflow, the coordinator ensures that execution steps are carried out in the appropriate order, while allowing independent operations to proceed in parallel where possible. It also provides a structured way to handle failures, enabling the system to react without disrupting the overall workflow. As a result, the orchestration layer contributes to the dependable execution of the digital care process, rather than serving merely as a technical mechanism for application deployment.

4.2 Malicious Device Detection and Traffic Influence

6G-Driven Dynamic Isolation and Mitigation PATHSHIELD utilises an Intrusion Detection and Mitigation Security as a Service (SaaS) platform deployed within the 6G-enabled FOKUS testbed. Upon detecting malicious traffic, mitigation is executed not just via traditional firewalls, but by leveraging 6G dynamic network slicing. This allows the system to instantly quarantine the compromised medical device into an isolated, restricted network slice without disrupting the ultra-reliable required by surrounding critical healthcare infrastructure (see Fig. 3).

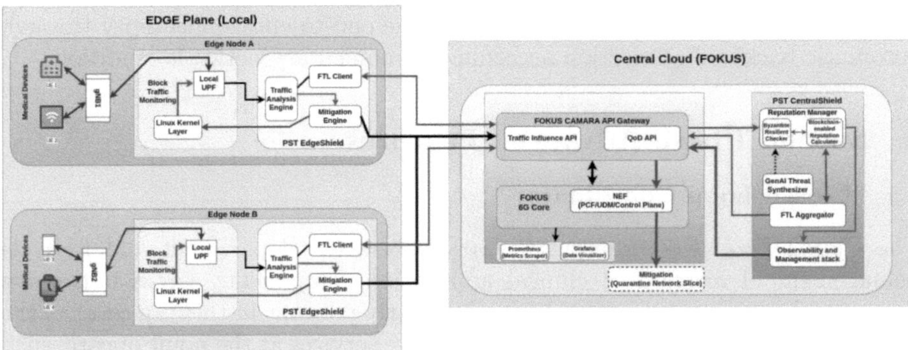

Fig. 3. Distributed architecture of PATHSHIELD AI-based security extension.

Real-Time Federated Transfer Learning (FTL) over 6G. The FTL framework preserves privacy by exchanging only updated model weights instead of raw patient data. 6G support provides massive broadband connectivity, enabling high-frequency, near-instant synchronisation of these weights across aggregation servers and removing latency bottlenecks of legacy networks.

AI-Native Gen-AI Threat Simulation. To outpace attackers and anticipate Zero-Day exploits, the framework incorporates a Gen-AI threat simulator. Capitalising on 6G's natively integrated AI architecture and massive data throughput, the simulator continuously generates and executes highly complex attack scenarios. This allows the primary detection model to rapidly learn mitigation policies and become progressively smarter in real-time.

ZKP Processing at the 6G Edge for Zero-PHI Leakage. Embedding a strict privacy-by-design philosophy, Zero Knowledge Proofs (ZKPs) are used to authenticate devices and validate traffic without exposing sensitive data. Although ZKPs are computationally intensive, offloading these cryptographic tasks to ultra-fast 6G edge-compute nodes prevents PHI leakage while avoiding additional latency for medical devices.

Continuous Zero Trust Enforcement via 6G Software-Defined Networking (SDN). A strict Zero Trust Architecture (ZTA) [21] with the principle "never trust, always verify" replaces perimeter-based security. Using 6G SDN, the network is micro-segmented down to each Internet of Medical Things (IoMT) device, and every internal request is cryptographically authenticated and authorised. Each device receives a real-time behavioural trust score from the FTL model. When anomalies occur, the score is lowered and the 6G SDN controller automatically restricts or revokes the device's lateral access, containing potential zero-day attacks before they spread.

5 Validation and Evaluation Results

5.1 Testbed

The 6G-PATH testbed is a real end-to-end 5G/B5G deployment with two main components: a central node at the Fraunhofer FOKUS on-premises data centre and an edge node at the trial site. The central node runs the 5G core (Open5GCore) and the e-health and platform services on a Kubernetes cluster, providing scalability, high availability, and unified management for components such as the Experiment Lifecycle Manager (ELCM) [26] and analytics dashboards.

The edge node is built on Proxmox virtualisation [19] to isolate services and protect data, and it hosts a 5G User Plane Function (UPF) for local breakout, ensuring low-latency access to locally deployed services. An Amarisoft-based 5G antenna [17] is integrated with the edge node to provide private 5G coverage at the trial site, simplifying deployment while allowing extension with additional radios if needed.

Together, the central and edge nodes form a full operational 5G infrastructure that supports private 5G access, edge–cloud coordination, and containerised healthcare services. This setup enables validation of the 6G-PATH architecture under realistic conditions and serves as the foundation for the internal and open-call trials.

During the trials, the E2E KPIs, involving also the application layer were validated, having sending of the 3D scan towards the FHIR server in less than 2 s. The network KPIs have been measured and analysed, with the diagram displayed in Fig. 4. The average latency of 25 ms and the reliability of 40% at 20 ms are consistent, with the reliability rapidly increasing to 100% for a delay of 50 ms. The jitter of an average of 0.32 ms is keeping the retransmissions on the Transmission Control Protocol (TCP) [28] level, for the applications using Hypertext Transfer Protocol Secure (HTTPS) [29], low enough in order to have a good user experience. The average upload throughput is of 70.36 Mbps, due to using the small 5G cell, for a low cost testbed that can be acquired by community nurses.

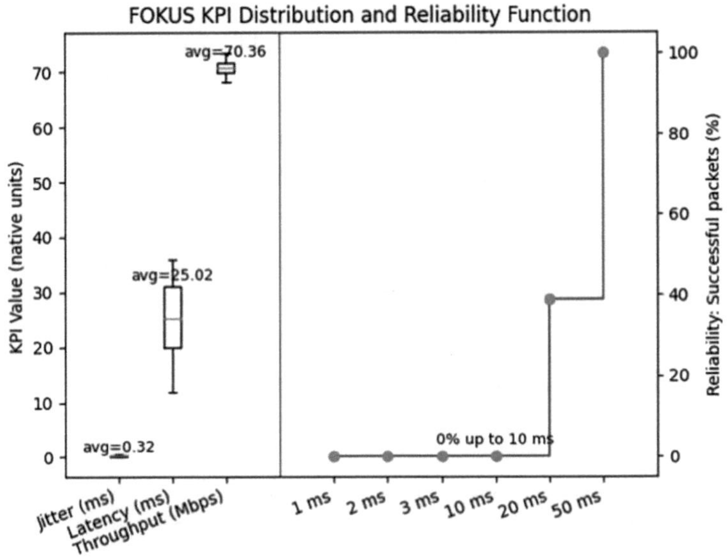

Fig. 4. Network KPIs of the testbed.

5.2 Close Loop Coordinator

To evaluate the role of the Closed Loop Coordinator (CLC) in the 6G-PATH healthcare use case, we consider a deployment scenario aligned with the clinical workflow of the trials. When the Nurse Care App initiates a digital care process, a healthcare application request is submitted to the CLC for deployment (Fig. 5). The CLC interprets this request and decides where to place the application components across edge and central infrastructure: latency-sensitive services are deployed at the edge near the point of care, while computationally intensive analytics are placed on central resources with greater processing and GPU capacity.

The evaluation focuses on whether the CLC can (i) accept a healthcare workflow as an application-level request, (ii) translate it into a placement decision across heterogeneous edge–cloud resources, and (iii) orchestrate deployment that aligns with latency and computational constraints. The emphasis is on feasibility, correctness of placement, and suitability for clinical use.

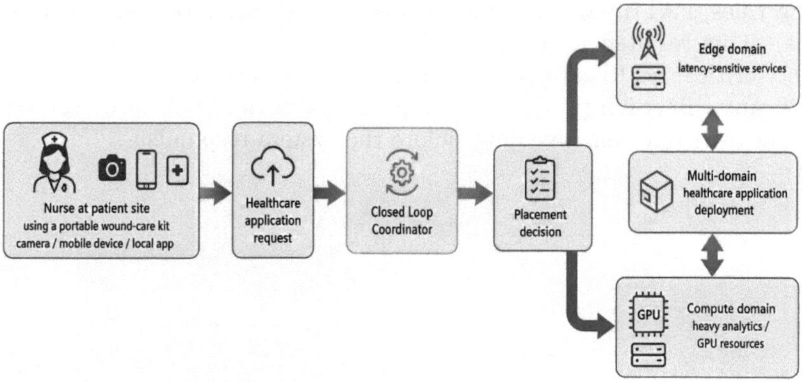

Fig. 5. Representative deployment scenario for the 6G-PATH healthcare use case with the Closed Loop Coordinator to deriving a placement decision.

Qualitatively, the CLC acts as an intermediate decision layer between the healthcare workflow and the infrastructure. Different application components have distinct requirements: some demand proximity to the patient due to interaction and delay sensitivity, while others benefit from powerful central resources. Embedding placement reasoning into orchestration enables coordinated handling of these differences along the edge–cloud continuum. In healthcare, deployment choices directly affect responsiveness, reliability, and usability—dimensions that, according to the nursing requirements analysis, are prioritised over purely latency-driven optimisation.

5.3 Malicious Device Detection and Traffic Influence

The empirical validation of the PATHSHIELD framework within the 6G-PATH testbed was conducted using the *CIC-IoMT2024 dataset* [22], which provides a high-fidelity representation of contemporary cyber-physical threats in medical environments. The evaluation focused on two critical performance dimensions: the temporal agility of the mitigation response and the operational efficiency of the Federated Transfer Learning (FTL) based Intrusion Detection System (IDS) architecture. These results demonstrate that leveraging 6G-native capabilities, such as the Near-Real-Time Radio Access Network (RAN) Intelligent Controller (Near-RT RIC) and software-defined micro-segmentation, provides a definitive advantage over traditional perimeter-based security.

Detection-to-Mitigation Agility Test. The first evaluation phase compared the 6G-driven dynamic isolation of PATHSHIELD against a traditional centralised firewall mitigation strategy.

As illustrated in Fig. 6, the disparity in mitigation latency is profound. While the legacy firewall required a duration of 8 s to search, validate, and apply filtering rules, PATHSHIELD achieved deterministic isolation in a mere 0.015 s (15 ms). This resulted in a measured "Agility Gap" of approximately 7.985 s. In safety-critical healthcare environments, this multi-second window represents a significant vulnerability where a compromised device could propagate lateral threats or exfiltrate sensitive data before the system responds.

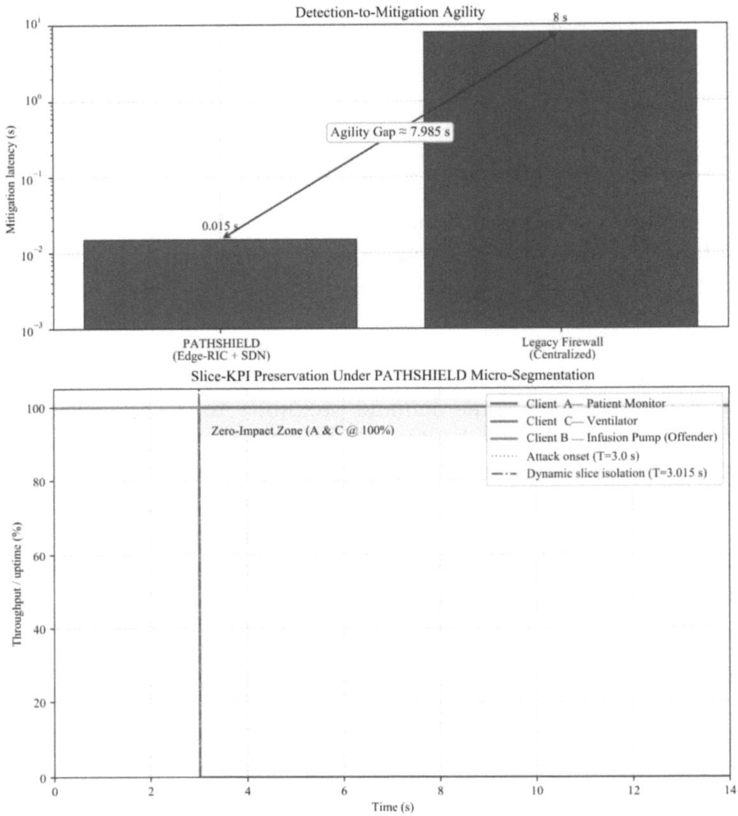

Fig. 6. Detection to Mitigation Agility PATHSHIELD Vs Legacy Firewall.

Furthermore, the "Slice-Key Performance Indicator (KPI) Preservation" analysis highlights the surgical precision of the PATHSHIELD framework. Upon the onset of a malicious attack by Client B (a simulated Infusion Pump) at $T = 3.0$ s, the system initiated dynamic slice isolation at $T = 3.015$ s. As shown in the throughput and uptime traces, Client B was instantly neutralised, with its throughput dropping to 0% to contain the threat. Conversely, Client A (Patient Monitor) and Client C (Ventilator) remained entirely unaffected, maintaining 100% service availability within the "Zero-Impact Zone". This confirms that PATHSHIELD's use of 6G SDN-based micro-segmentation eliminates the collateral damage—such as jitter or throughput degradation—typically associated with the coarse-grained policies of legacy firewalls.

Federated Transfer Learning (FTL) Efficiency and Privacy. The second evaluation phase addressed the trade-offs between detection performance, data privacy, and backhaul resource consumption. The results summarised in Fig. 7 substantiate that the proposed decentralised approach does not sacrifice accuracy for privacy. Both the PATHSHIELD Edge-FTL model and the centralised baseline comfortably exceeded the >98% accuracy target for the detection of known exploits.

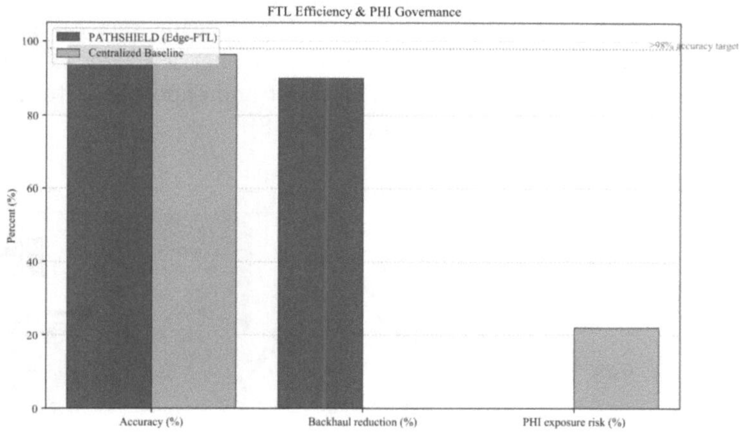

Fig. 7. FTL Efficiency & PHI Governance.

However, the architectural advantages of PATHSHIELD become evident when examining PHI governance and network overhead:

- **Backhaul Reduction:** By exchanging only local model weights rather than raw patient data [20], PATHSHIELD realised a 90% reduction in backhaul bandwidth consumption. This is an essential requirement for 6G networks tasked with supporting massive device densities without creating backhaul bottlenecks.
- **PHI Governance:** Crucially, PATHSHIELD achieved a 0% for the Protected Health Information (PHI) exposure risk. In contrast, the centralised baseline—which necessitates the transmission of raw medical telemetry to a central cloud for analysis—presented a non-negligible exposure risk of approximately 22%.
- **Privacy-by-Design:** By ensuring that sensitive medical data remains at the edge node, the system aligns with the foundational security requirements prioritised by nursing staff and clinical stakeholders, such as secure data encryption and fail-safe connectivity.

In summary, these results validate that the PATHSHIELD framework successfully exploits 6G-native features to provide near-real-time threat mitigation and robust privacy preservation, ensuring that critical healthcare workflows remain resilient even under active cyber-adversity.

5.4 Quality of Service (QoS) Aware Bioprinter Interfacing

The on-site bioprinted personalised patch produced by interfacing the Nurse Care App with the 3D bioprinter. The patch is printed using the STL output of the Wound Analytics while running the pipeline for 2D and 3D segmentation, smoothening and water-tight 3D model generation.

The 5G NR bioprinter interfacing is via a Customer Premises Equipment (CPE) connected to a Raspberry Pi, where Bio-Printing services run. These services include 3D printing slicing, producing Geometric Code (gCode) based on the Stereolithography file format (STL) input and exposing Octoprint based API [25] towards the Nurse Care App (see Fig. 8).

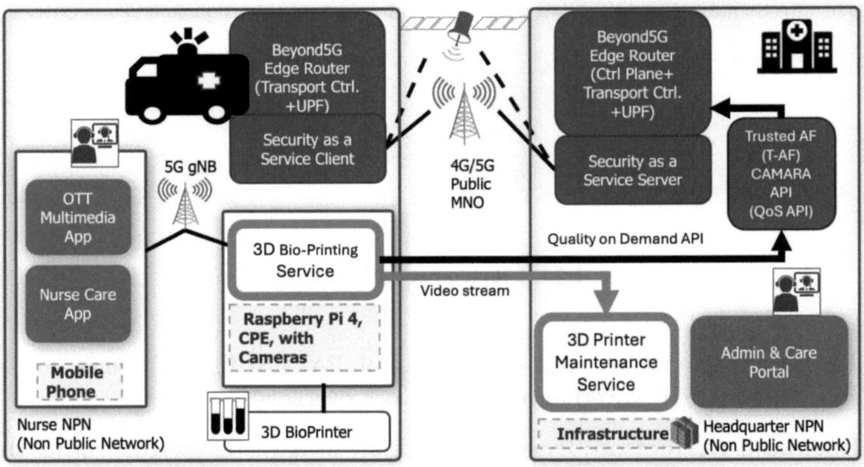

Fig. 8. QoS on Demand for printing quality control and maintenace service integration.

The bioprinting process requires real-time and automatic target/actual comparison, for not overloading the nurse. For this, additional cameras deliver video streams to a cloud-located Maintenance Service. For ensuring that the videos are received by the Maintenance Service with the lowest jitter possible, a Quality on Demand interface towards a Trusted Application Function (T-AF) [27] was implemented using Cloud API Marketplace and Application-Ready (CAMARA) QoS on Demand APIs. The T-AF is requesting the QoS policies enforcement by interfacing with the Network Exposure Function (NEF) and then the Policy Control Function (PCF) [9,11,14] from the Control Plane of Open5GCore.

6 Conclusions and Outlook

This paper presented the 6G-PATH architecture and its validation in a chronic wound care scenario, combining requirements from nursing personnel with an end-to-end beyond-5G/6G-enabled platform. The survey of nursing staff demonstrated that healthcare professionals recognise the transformative potential of B5G/6G, but primarily value reliable connectivity, secure data management, and seamless access to medical information and devices. Flagship low-latency applications, such as tele-robotic surgery, were rated as less relevant for everyday nursing work. These findings underline that successful 6G solutions in healthcare must address concrete infrastructural deficits and workflow frictions before introducing highly complex, high-risk applications.

The proposed architecture responds directly to these needs by providing a resilient, nomadic edge network for the home-care setting, with local breakout, multi-backhaul support (4G/5G and satellite), and secure integration with hospital systems. On top of this network substrate, we deployed healthcare-specific enablers: a Kubernetes-native Closed Loop Coordinator (CLC) for orchestrating distributed workflows across edge and central resources. The open call extensions for i) QoS-aware bioprinter interfacing to support on-site fabrication of personalised wound patches, and ii) the PATHSHIELD security framework, which exploits federated learning, Zero Trust principles, and traffic influence to detect and contain malicious devices, complement the testbed. These extensions continue the effort towards bringing the architecture and prototype of the chronic wound treatment at home towards day-to-day usage. The testbed implementation with real 5G infrastructure and constrained hardware confirms that these mechanisms can be realised under realistic conditions and aligned with clinical workflows.

The validation results indicate that the CLC can translate high-level healthcare workflow intents into consistent placement and deployment decisions across heterogeneous edge–cloud infrastructure, supporting responsiveness at the point of care while leveraging central compute for analytics. The QoS-aware bioprinter integration shows that quality-critical media streams (e.g. maintenance video feeds) can be dynamically prioritised via standardised interfaces, without overburdening nursing staff with technical configuration tasks. PATHSHIELD demonstrates how B5G/6G capabilities such as network slicing and MEC can be used to implement privacy-preserving, AI-driven security functions that are suitable for safety-critical healthcare environments.

Looking ahead, several directions emerge. First, larger-scale and longer-term clinical trials are needed to assess the impact of the 6G-PATH approach on patient outcomes, workload, and acceptance among diverse user groups, including novices and professionals with lower technology affinity. Second, the orchestration and security mechanisms should be extended to support additional medical devices and services, and to integrate with hospital IT governance and certification processes. Third, further automation of monitoring, healing, and reconfiguration processes will be required to maintain reliability as deployments grow in size and complexity. Finally, the strong emphasis of nursing personnel on Key

Value Indicators suggests that future 6G research should systematically combine technical Key Performance Indicator (KPI)s with user-centred KVIs [23, 24] when designing, prioritising, and evaluating networked healthcare solutions.

Acknowledgments. The presented activities are part of the 6G-PATH project, which received funding from the Smart Networks and Services Joint Undertaking (SNS JU) under the European Union's Horizon Europe research and innovation program under Grant Agreement No 101139172.

References

1. World Health Organization: Global Strategy on Digital Health 2020–2025. World Health Organization, Geneva, Switzerland (2021)
2. Bai, X., et al.: Digital health interventions for chronic wound management: a systematic review and meta-analysis. J. Med. Internet Res. **26**, e47904 (2024)
3. Blytt, K.M., et al.: The implementation of telemedicine in wound care: a qualitative study of nurses' and patients' experiences. BMC Health Serv. Res. **24**, 1146 (2024)
4. Gagnon, M.-P., et al.: Systematic review of factors influencing the adoption of information and communication technologies by healthcare professionals. J. Med. Syst. **36**, 241–277 (2012)
5. Kruse, C.S., et al.: Evaluating barriers to adopting telemedicine worldwide: a systematic review. J. Telemed. Telecare **24**, 4–12 (2018)
6. HL7 FHIR protocol. https://www.hl7.org/fhir/overview.html
7. Interoperability via iSIK. https://fachportal.gematik.de/informationen-fuer/isik
8. IHE XDS Classcode, Integrating Healthcare Enterprise (IHE) Germany. https://build.fhir.org/ig/IHE-Germany/ITI.XDS.VS/ValueSet-IHEXDSclassCode.html
9. 3GPP. System Architecture for the 5G System (5GS); Stage 2. 3GPP TS 23.501, Release 17/18
10. 3GPP. Procedures for the 5G System (5GS); Stage 2. 3GPP TS 23.502, Release 17/18
11. 3GPP. 5G System; Network Exposure Function Northbound APIs; Stage 3. 3GPP TS 29.522, Release 17/18
12. 3GPP. Security architecture and procedures for 5G System. 3GPP TS 33.501, Release 17/18
13. ETSI. Multi-access Edge Computing (MEC); Framework and Reference Architecture. ETSI GS MEC 003, V3.2.1 (2024)
14. Linux Foundation CAMARA. Quality on Demand API. Accessed 2026. https://camaraproject.org/quality-on-demand/
15. Linux Foundation CAMARA. Traffic Influence API. Accessed 2026. https://camaraproject.org/traffic-influence/
16. Fraunhofer FOKUS. Open5GCore: 5G Core Network for Research, Testbeds and Trials. Accessed 2026. https://open5gcore.org/
17. Amarisoft. LTE/NR Software gNB Documentation. Accessed 2026. https://tech-academy.amarisoft.com/lteenb.doc
18. The Kubernetes Authors. Kubernetes Documentation. Accessed 2026. https://kubernetes.io/docs/
19. Proxmox Server Solutions GmbH. Proxmox Virtual Environment Documentation. Accessed 2026. https://pve.proxmox.com/pve-docs/

20. Yang, Q., Liu, Y., Chen, T., Tong, Y.: Federated machine learning: concept and applications. ACM Trans. Intell. Syst. Technol. **10**(2), 1–19 (2019)
21. Rose, S., Borchert, O., Mitchell, S., Connelly, S.: Zero trust architecture. National Institute of Standards and Technology, Special Publication 800-207 (2020)
22. Dadkhah, S., et al.: CICIoMT2024: a benchmark dataset for multi-protocol security analysis in Internet of Medical Things. Internet Things **28**, 101396 (2024)
23. Uusitalo, M.A.: Toward 6G: Hexa-X project's key findings. IEEE Commun. Maga. (2025)
24. Wikström, G., et al.: Key value indicators: a framework for values-driven next-generation ICT solutions. Telecommun. Policy **48**(3), 102778 (2024)
25. OctoPrint. OctoPrint documentation. Accessed 2026. https://docs.octoprint.org/en/main/index.html
26. Experiment Life-Cycle Management platform. https://github.com/6G-SANDBOX/ELCM
27. SliceFinity. Network API Platform for Telecom Monetisation. Accessed 2026. https://slicefinity.com/platform/
28. Eddy, W. (Ed.): Transmission Control Protocol (TCP). IETF RFC 9293 (2022). https://www.rfc-editor.org/rfc/rfc9293
29. Rescorla, E.: HTTP Over TLS. IETF RFC 2818 (2000). https://www.rfc-editor.org/rfc/rfc2818

A Business Blueprint for Data Monetization

Udo Bub[1,2(✉)], Christos Gizelis[3], Rob Schneider[4], Eduardo Vyhmeister[5], and Andrea Visentin[5]

[1] Eötvös Loránd University (ELTE), Budapest, Hungary
udobub@inf.elte.hu
[2] 1001 Lakes Oy, Helsinki, Finland
[3] OTE Group, Athens, Greece
[4] FIR E. V. an Der RWTH, Aachen, Aachen, Germany
[5] University College Cork, Cork, Ireland

Abstract. This paper presents a novel action blueprint for data monetization for commercial use. It consists of three modules that were developed as self-contained work packages, namely the Data Monetization Maturity Model (DMMM), a set of strategy archetypes for data monetization including a corresponding business canvas tool, and a novel data valuation model. Together, these elements form a coherent framework that enables companies to assess their readiness for data monetization, quantify the value of their data assets, and design viable, value-based business models. We present these three components and report the results of a pilot deployment with practical use cases in an industrial setting. The paper summarizes key results of the DATAMITE project and adds further transfer insights.

Keywords: Data Monetization · Maturity Model · Monetization Strategies · Monetization Canvas · Data Valuation Model

1 Introduction

Companies increasingly recognize data as a strategic asset but still face major challenges in turning this potential into measurable economic value. Many organizations lack clear structures, valuation methods, and business models to monetize data responsibly and profitably [7]. This work addresses this gap by providing a practical, evidence-based framework for transforming data into sustainable business value.

This paper introduces a comprehensive approach, combining three key components to form a blueprint: a Data Monetization Maturity Model (DMMM) [4] to assess an organization's readiness and define improvement paths; a Data Valuation Model [15] to quantify the value of data assets through measurable indicators and KPIs; and a Strategy Canvas with twelve actionable templates based on strategy archetypes to translate analytical insights into concrete business model designs and pricing mechanisms [5], which itself is applied to a set of twelve data monetization strategy archetypes [9]. Thus, we summarize original work results of the DATAMITE project that have been partially

Published by Springer Nature Switzerland AG 2027
A. Papaleonidas et al. (Eds.): AIAI 2026 Workshops, IFIP AICT 796, pp. 88–101, 2027.
https://doi.org/10.1007/978-3-032-30507-7_5

pre-published in a comprehensive project report [5, 9] and augment it with novel results and insights of practical deployment in an industrial setting.

Together, these tools guide companies from strategic orientation to economic execution, enabling them to design and evaluate value-based data offerings tailored to their context.

The applied research followed a design science research (DSR) methodology [11, 12]. Extensive literature research [5, 9] yields that no blueprint artefact exists, yet, to cover the practical problem of data monetization. The resulting framework that forms the blueprint has been validated iteratively through pilot testing with European companies across different sectors, confirming its usability and adaptability.

The paper is organized as follows: the conceptual foundations for maturity models, monetization strategies, and data valuation modeling, as well as the applied design science research (DSR) approach are laid out in Sect. 0. The three individual components of the blueprint, namely the DMMM, the data strategies and their monetization canvas, as well as the data valuation model are presented in Sect. 0. Evaluation based on pilot tests are presented in Sect. 1, whereas Sect. 2 shows results of a first practice test in an industrial setting. The paper closes with a discussion and an outline of the next steps in Sect. 3.

2 Conceptual Foundations

2.1 Maturity Models

The DMMM was the first model to assess an organization's maturity for data monetization. Please refer to [4] for detailed background information.

Maturity models are a well-established management tool for executives [1]. With their help awareness for the design of relevant areas of action can be created and a progressing development path be structured. Improvements of capabilities, processes and structures can be systematically addressed.

A maturity model consists of maturity criteria whose degree of fulfillment is the baseline for the calculation of aggregated maturity indicators. To build a maturity model, adequate criteria must be found and formulated in a way that allows for consistent grading. For continuous maturity models the answers are self-assessments on a Likert scale, e.g. on a scale of five ranging from "not at all" to "fully" applicable. Typically, the criteria are grouped to dimensions that represent a thematic cluster, such as "strategy", "culture", or "technology" [1]. Needed are also well-tuned descriptions of five to seven maturity levels. A maturity model requires also a technique that determines which capabilities should be fulfilled for the respective maturity level and a description of how the grading is calculated.

In the context of data monetization, we want to focus on the type of continuous maturity models: In continuous maturity models, all criteria are assigned to all maturity levels, including different characteristics per level to outline the maturation path along all stages. The degree of fulfillment has to be calculated, for example by deriving an average value from the answers to all criteria.

2.2 Data Monetization Strategies and Business Canvasses

We developed twelve distinct archetypes for data monetization strategies. These have been derived from an extensive literature analysis and subsequent expert reflection in the DATAMITE project [9]. It follows the distinction of main approaches: direct and indirect data monetization, e.g. [10, 16].

Direct data monetization aims to generate revenue by selling data as a product or service. In this approach, data is treated as a tradable asset. Examples include selling raw data, exchanging data for services or benefits (data bartering), or creating added value by bundling data-based services with existing offerings ("wrapping") [2, 9, 16].

Indirect data monetization focuses on enhancing existing products or services through data usage rather than selling the data itself. Here, data creates additional value within conventional products, for example through targeted advertising, personalized recommendations, or the development of data-driven products and services [6].

Data value creation is defined in [2] as the process of transforming the potential value of data into tangible benefits. Closely related is the data–information–knowledge hierarchy [3], where raw data represents unprocessed facts, information emerges through contextual analysis and interpretation [8], and knowledge is created through application and understanding.

Based on a literature review, [8] identifies twelve organizational approaches to data value creation, which form the basis for the data monetization strategies described in [9]:

- Increasing the value of an organization's data assets through data preparation.
- Enhancing the value of an organization's information assets by creating new insights.
- Optimizing or innovating products and services based on data-driven insights.
- Fine-tuning pricing strategies through data analytics.
- Improving customer interaction and company perception using data-driven approaches.
- Streamlining organizational processes through data-driven optimization.
- Exchanging raw data with external entities.
- Exchanging prepared data in any modified form to meet specific needs.
- Sharing insights derived from data analysis with external stakeholders.
- Exchanging data models or components used in analytical processes.
- Wrapping core products or services with additional information derived from data.
- Delivering services grounded in information to take proactive actions for customers.

Motivated by the success of the Business Model Canvas [14], various canvas-based tools have been developed to simplify complex interdependencies into visual decision frameworks. For example, the VDMA platform economy expert group introduced a canvas for monetizing platform-based products and services in machinery and production contexts [6]. This model was adapted and successfully applied as a tool for developing data monetization strategies.

2.3 Data Valuation Modeling

Due to its immaterial nature, it is very difficult to determine the absolute value of data. Thus, organizations still lack a consistent and actionable way to calculate the economic worth of their data. To overcome this, we have developed a data valuation model to make a structured and operational approach for data valuation possible. The model has been pre-published in [15] and been integrated into the data monetization blueprint as in [5]. In the following, we summarize and cite from these references. Data valuation models can be categorized in three different types.

Qualitative Scoring: these approaches assign datasets a score reflecting their quality, compliance, and strategic significance, but not their production cost or potential price on the *market.*

Cost- and Income-Based Valuation: this approach calculates a baseline proxy value by aggregating historical and ongoing costs related to data acquisition, cleaning, storage, and maintenance. These measures align well with established accounting principles, and they provide a quantifiable foundation for linking data management efforts with financial reporting and cost control mechanisms.

Utility-Oriented Estimates: This category focuses on projecting the economic benefits through the use of data, i.e. utility. Models in this group quantify the impact of data on factors such as operational efficiency, risk mitigation, or competitive advantage.

Different examples of these three categories are exhibited referenced in [15]. Hybrid frameworks aim at integration of multiple valuation logics into unified models. Also, our approach targets a combination of these categories by quantifying the quality of data and subsequently their relevance, and if applicable, their utility. In this context it is necessary to differentiate between these attributes of data [15]:

Quality: Data quality represents the extent to which data accurately and comprehensively reflects real-world conditions while adhering to defined standards and expectations. High-quality data forms the foundation for trustworthy analytics, enables accurate valuation or pricing, and sustains confidence among both external buyers and internal stakeholders.

Relevance: Relevance refers to the usefulness of a dataset within a specific context, task, or decision process. It captures the degree to which the data contributes to achieving a defined organizational goal, such as informing a particular decision, supporting a workflow, or enabling a targeted optimization effort. Relevance is therefore context-dependent: the same dataset may be highly relevant to one user or use case but of limited value to another.

Utility: By contrast, Utility reflects the broader functional potential of a dataset across multiple scenarios, tasks, or domains. Whereas relevance describes usefulness in a specific context, utility represents the intrinsic capacity of data to generate value in a wide range of applications. Utility therefore captures cross-domain applicability.

The Data Valuation Model developed in DATAMITE is decision-based: a series of questions need to be answered and based on the chosen path of the underlying decision tree, weighted values are calculated and aggregated into a normalized summation (Decision-Based Valuation) which results in a final scalar that needs to be interpreted as proportional to its data value [15].

3 The Components of the DATAMITE Business Blueprint

3.1 Component 1: The Data Monetization Maturity Model (DMMM)

The dimensions of the DMMM were developed and adapted as described in [4], focusing on the dimensions most relevant for data monetization. The model comprises seven dimensions:

Culture & Skills: Organizational culture, employee mindset, and competencies related to data sharing and monetization.

Customer: Understanding of data consumers and integration of customer feedback into data product development.

Data Business Product: Degree to which data services are packaged into understandable, usable, and billable products.

Data Strategy: Integration of data-related aspects into business strategy.

Information Technology (IT): Technical capabilities and agility required to deliver data business products.

Organization: Organizational readiness, agility, governance structures, and KPIs supporting data monetization.

Processes: Readiness of business processes, including legal and regulatory aspects.

The criteria catalog is structured according to these dimensions, which can be visualized as axes in a spider chart (see in Fig. 3). Scores per dimension are calculated as the average Likert-scale rating across all associated criteria. The spider chart enables intuitive gap analysis between the current and target state, helping derive targeted actions and maturity improvement measures. Further details are provided in [4].

3.2 Component 2: The Strategy Archetypes and Monetization Canvas

A thorough literature review was carried out within the DATAMITE project [9]. In an iterative approach, we have clustered and structured the identified strategies to the twelve archetypes depicted in Fig. 1. As a result, twelve individual DATAMITE Monetization Canvases were developed, each representing one of the twelve strategic archetypes defined in the project. Every canvas template illustrates how a particular data monetization strategy can be operationalized by combining the relevant organizational capabilities from the DMMM, the KPIs from [5], and the qualitative and quantitative logic of the VDMA structure.

This approach provides companies with an intuitive and comparable reference for designing and assessing strategy-specific data-driven business models (Fig. 2). By presenting all fields in a pre-filled example format, users gain a tangible impression of which activities, resources, and competencies are required to implement a chosen strategy successfully.

For the blueprint, a model canvas was pre-filled for each of the twelve strategy archetypes and documented in the appendix of [5]. Two adaptations were introduced to tailor the framework. First, the original "Pricing Model" field was replaced with organizational capabilities derived from the Data Monetization Maturity Model (DMMM). For each monetization strategy, the most relevant capability set was assigned to highlight the organizational prerequisites for successful implementation.

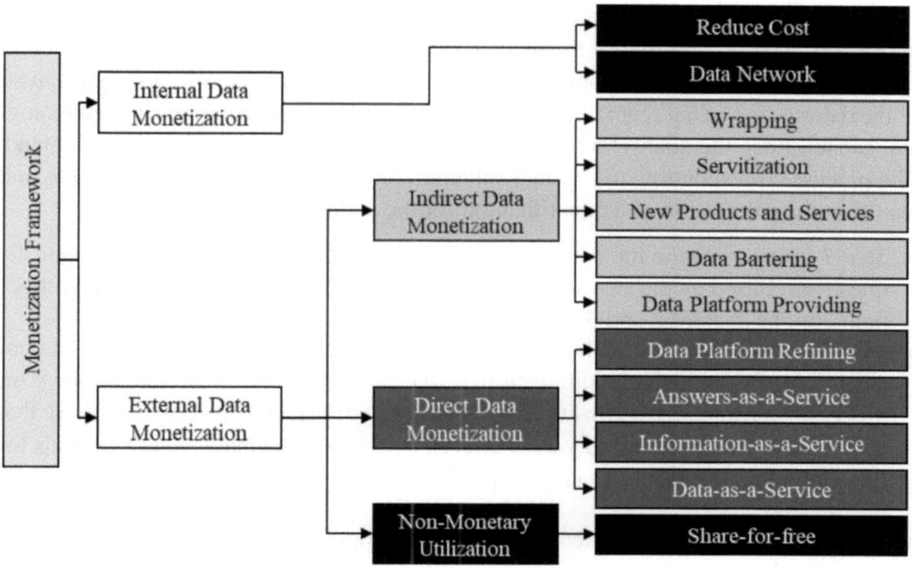

Fig. 1. The twelve strategy archetypes.

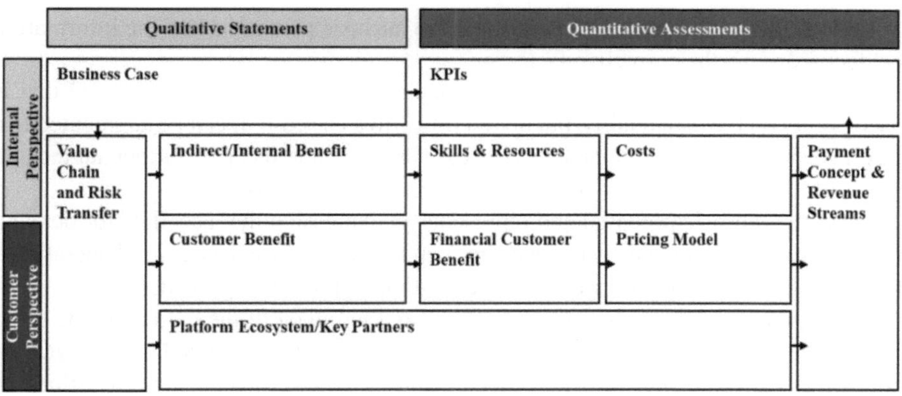

Fig. 2. Data Monetization Canvas, based on [6].

Second, the remaining Canvas fields were systematically completed to provide a comprehensive overview of each strategy. This enables users to identify the most relevant KPIs for assessing the performance and financial impact of a specific data monetization approach.

3.3 Component 3: The Data Valuation Model

In this section, we give an overview of the DATAMITE data valuation model, focusing on applicability for pilot use cases and real-world scenarios. Thus, we can only exhibit a summary and excerpts, while we refer to a description of the full model to [15].

As mentioned in Sect. 0, the data valuation model is based on decision-based valuation, giving high importance to answers to questionnaires which determine different calculation paths and tailoring options. The answers inform about the operational context of the dataset (including regulatory constraints, competitive positioning, and technological capabilities), the quality of the data as well as the fitness of the dataset to demand. The process corresponding to the data valuation model is performed in three steps and results in the calculation of a quantification for the value of the dataset:

- *Step 1* is to determine the context of the dataset by means of a series of diagnostic questions. Based on the answers, a series of recommendations is given for the further path options in steps 2 and 3.
- *Step 2* is to determine which of the following dataset quality factors are to be considered for further calculation: *accuracy*, *age*, *completeness*, *legal compliance cost*, *processing cost*, *return on investment*, *timeliness*, *variety*, *volume*. For all of those that are considered, a normalized value between 0 and 1 is calculated, where 1 stands for the maximum achievable quality. A quality index Q is calculated from an arithmetic mean value.
- The final value V is calculated in *Step 3* as follows. First a normalized QRU factor has to be determined

$$V = \frac{QRU \times \sum(Val \times ICF)}{V_P}$$

QRU is the main valuation driver. *Val* is the intrinsic potential, *ICF* the information cost factor and V_p the corrective factor.

QRU is an index value that is either calculated only as a Quality index Q that is based purely on the data quality, but not on fitting to a use case. It can be augmented to a relevance index R that takes match to a use case into account. It can be further augmented to a Utility index U when match to a series of use cases is possible.

Val is the intrinsic potential and represents an expression that accounts for demand and costs. Costs are modeled using one-time capital expenditure (Capex) and operational expenditure (Opex) that are involved in generating and producing the data set.

ICF stands for *Information Cost Fraction* and is linked to the data strategy. For a one-time data sale, $ICF = 1$. In subscription-based or service-oriented models, $ICF < 1$ is typically used to account for retained rights or repeated data usage over time. In certain multi-utility scenarios *ICF* can exceed 1 to capture multi-utility scenarios such as in indirect monetization cases where the same dataset supports multiple applications or revenue streams. This adjustment is introduced only when Utility is not the primary valuation metric, as the Utility dimension inherently reflects the dataset's multi-use potential. is set to 1 in all experiments related to this paper. *ICF* is set to 1 for all tests related to this paper.

The corrective factor V_p adjusts the estimated dataset value according to acquisition and processing times. Depending on the dataset type, two cases are distinguished:

For datasets requiring significant processing time(t_p), $V_p = 1 + T_p/T_a$. For datasets that are purchased or involve negligible processing, a constant adjustment is applied: $V_p = 1 + 0.05$ down to $V_p = 1 + 0.01$.

V, as the final value of the dataset, is a scalar. To receive a final value in a currency, concrete market situations have to be included, which is not possible for a theoretic framework. As such, V can merely be used for comparative purposes, for example for comparing the value of one dataset to another. When market experience for one dataset has resulted in a concrete price tag of one dataset, then price tag of the other can be calculated by rule of proportion.

The DATAMITE Data Valuation Model can consider many parameters that might only be relevant for specific use cases. It is a first attempt to mirror the complexity of quantifying data value, and it is not possible to present all details in this workshop paper. The model is highly tailorable and offers consistently opportunities to replace calculation by expert estimates when analytical information of the dataset is not available. Please refer to [15] for a complete exposure of questionnaires and formulae with a thorough discussion and calculation of concrete examples.

4 Pilot Testing for the DATAMITE Business Blueprint

We evaluated the three components of the blueprint with representatives of six partner organizations in the DATAMITE project. In the following we will talk about pilot use cases where a company has the leadership and determines the dataset.

Pilot A is lead by a smart cities service provider, Pilot B by an incumbent telecommunications company, Pilot C by a Distribution Network Operator (DNO), Pilot D likewise of a DNO, but from a different country. Pilot E is lead by a high performance computing center (HPC) and Pilot F likewise by an HPC, but from a different country.

The test of the DMMM is for a whole organization (Sect. 1.1), whereas the monetization strategies and the dataset valuation refers to a concrete dataset owned by this organization and the results bundled together in Sect. 1.2.

4.1 Pilot Test on Organizational Level: Monetization Maturity Model DMMM

The DMMM evaluation was conducted in one-hour interview sessions led by the principal investigator, who guided participants through the criteria catalog and provided clarifications where necessary. Interviewees included DATAMITE project members and experts from innovation, data engineering, and technology departments, assessing data monetization readiness from the perspective of their organizations.

Responses were recorded on a five-point Likert scale, ranging from 1 ("does not apply at all") to 5 ("fully applies"). Participants were encouraged to answer intuitively, with only semantic clarifications and calibration hints provided. A score of 3.5 per dimension was defined as the threshold for engaging in data monetization without major additional readiness measures.

Table 1 depicts the overall maturity scores for the six pilot organizations. The overall score itself is the arithmetic average of the score of the seven dimensions, i.e. all dimensions are equally weighted.

All interviewees were asked at the end of their session if they considered the results as giving a realistic picture of the maturity of their organization and if they would suggest further questions. The qualitative answers were convincingly positive about the accuracy of the overall picture and the completeness of the catalog. However, need for calibration of the answers for comparison becomes evident.

Table 1. Results of the DMMM assessment for the pilot evaluation

	Pilot A	Pilot B	Pilot C	Pilot D	Pilot E	Pilot F
Overall Score	*3.33*	*2.88*	*2.47*	*3.33*	*3.74*	*3.00*

Along with further adjustments from the tests (reformulations, merger of criteria, new criteria), this led to the release of the criteria list with 61 entries exhibited in [4].

4.2 Pilot Tests on Dataset Level: Monetization Strategies and Valuation

Tests were carried out with the lead organizations of the DATAMITE pilots to determine usefulness and fitness of the data monetization strategy archetypes from Sect. 0 and the valuation model from 0. The respective organization representative was asked in an interview to describe their dataset and choose a fitting strategy archetype. The interviewees were also asked to select the determinants of the dataset valuation model using the questionnaires of the data valuation model that are listed in [15]. Steps 1 through 3 from Sect. 0 have been processed per interview. In step 2, the interviewees were required to select and quantify the quality factors in order to calculate the quality index Q. For this, it is necessary to calculate a percentage value in relative relationship to the maximum within the range of possible values which yields case specific weights. When applicable, a relevance index R was calculated, however, no utility index U was applicable to the discussed datasets. The following collection summarizes the dataset description, the applicable monetization strategy, the selection of the quality metrics and the result of the dataset valuation. Please refer to [5] for further background of the quantitative results.

Dataset Pilot A (Smart Cities Service Provider)
The lead organization for Pilot A provided a dataset from continuous industrial process monitoring. It includes heterogeneous parameters such as substance concentrations, flow rates, pressure and thermal profiles, as well as operational data like batch IDs, machine settings, energy consumption, runtime states, and maintenance logs. The data supports predictive maintenance, process optimization, anomaly detection, and compliance. It is used to develop forecasting models, analyze process behavior, and assess system performance. Additional value can be generated through derived indicators, quality metrics, and digital-twin-ready datasets.

The dataset is most aligned with **Information-as-a-Service (IaaS)** or internal optimization strategies. Determining quality metrics for the dataset value are *Age, Timeliness, RoI, Processing Cost.* Calculated value of dataset, including relevance (demand side) considerations: 13.38.

Dataset Pilot B (Incumbent Telecommunications Company)
The lead organization for Pilot B selected a dataset based on anonymized mobile network traffic and mobility indicators. It includes aggregated metrics such as signaling activity, movement patterns, traffic volumes, temporal usage profiles, and population density flows. The dataset supports applications in urban planning, smart mobility, tourism analytics, transport optimization, event management, and retail site assessment.

Because the dataset consists of processed, privacy-preserving aggregates that can be delivered directly as insights, the appropriate monetization strategy is **Information-as-a-Service (IaaS).** Determining quality metrics for the dataset value are *Variety, Volume, Processing Cost.* Calculated value of dataset, including relevance (demand side) considerations: 6.13.

Dataset Pilot C (Energy Distribution Network Operator)
The lead organization for Pilot C, a Greek electricity distribution operator, defined a dataset consisting of smart-meter telemetry, medium-voltage monitoring data, and digital network model files. The data includes voltage, current, load patterns, power flows, operational events, and grid topology information. The dataset is used to analyze grid performance, detect anomalies, optimize network operations, improve maintenance planning, and support long-term infrastructure planning.

Because the primary benefits arise internally—through reduced operational costs, fewer service interruptions, and improved asset management, the dataset fits best into a **Reduce Cost** strategy. Determining quality metrics for the dataset value are *Accuracy, Processing Cost.* Calculated value of dataset, including relevance (demand side) considerations: 20.70.

Dataset Pilot D (Energy Distribution Network Operator)
The lead organization for Pilot D, the main operator of Portugal's electricity distribution network, defined a dataset containing operational measurements from medium- and low-voltage infrastructure. It includes telemetry such as voltage and current levels, transformer loading, switching events, asset states, and load profiles.The dataset supports grid monitoring, anomaly detection, maintenance planning, and demand forecasting, as well as applications such as fault localization, overload prediction, and distribution optimization.

Due to its operational relevance and its direct impact on efficiency, the dataset is most strongly associated with internal value creation through cost reduction, thus a **Reduce Cost** strategy. Determining quality metrics for the dataset value are *Age, Accuracy, Volume, Completeness RoI.* Calculated value of dataset, including relevance (demand side) considerations: 7.69.

Dataset Pilot E (High Performance Computing Center)
The lead organization for Pilot E selected a dataset from environmental monitoring stations across Poland. It includes weather and agriculture-related parameters such as temperature, humidity, precipitation, soil conditions, and other environmental indicators. The dataset supports agricultural decision-making, including irrigation and crop management, as well as research applications such as simulation models, forecasting tools, and early-warning systems. It also enables automated alerts for events like frost, heat, and soil moisture anomalies.

Because the HPC provides not only raw observations but also interpreted signals and alerts, the dataset aligns with **an Information-as-a-Service (IaaS)** strategy. Determining quality metrics for the dataset value are *Age, Volume, Completeness.* Calculated value of dataset, including relevance (demand side) considerations: 7.94.

Dataset Pilot F (High Performance Computing Center)

The lead organization for Pilot F provided a dataset from meteorological weather stations across Italy. It includes temperature, humidity, atmospheric pressure, wind conditions, precipitation, and related environmental parameters. The dataset is high-resolution, continuously updated, and calibrated for modeling purposes. It is used for climate analysis, weather prediction, hydrological simulations, and environmental forecasting. Additional value can be created through derived products such as GRIB files, analytical indicators, and machine-learning-ready features.

Because users benefit most from flexible access to high-quality raw measurements, the appropriate strategy is **Data-as-a-Service (DaaS)**. Determining quality metrics for the dataset value are *Age, Timeliness, RoI, Processing Cost:* 6. Calculated value of dataset, including relevance (demand side) considerations: 19.60.

Throughout all interviews, it was straightforward to map a strategy archetype to the described dataset. The corresponding pre-filled canvasses from [5] were unanimously welcomed as a starting point to develop the concrete business model.

The application of the Valuation Model was carried out successfully across all participating organizations. As expected, the diversity of datasets, contexts, and assumptions led to differing valuation outcomes, reflecting the distinct characteristics of each case. Across all interviews, the participating companies expressed strong interest in the methodology and viewed the practical application of the model as highly insightful and relevant for understanding the economic potential of their data, e.g. for a sensibility analysis of contributing determinants, such as quality metrics. It is important to emphasize that the primary value of the model lies in its application for comparing values across cases rather than in producing absolute results. More experience needs to be built up to further empirical evidence to make better sense of the results.

It is important to emphasize that the value estimations produced within the use cases were conducted for the purpose of evaluating and validating the methodology, rather than providing definitive or market-based valuations of the datasets. The numerical results generated by the model should therefore not be interpreted as direct measures, proxies, or certified assessments of dataset market value. Instead, the valuation approach is intended to support relative comparison across datasets, highlight differences in value-driving characteristics, and enable organizations to reason about their assets in a structured manner. When used together with external reference points or benchmarks, the model can also serve as a basis for linear approximations or rule-of-three-type estimations, assisting organizations in forming indicative price ranges while acknowledging that final market valuations depend on broader commercial and contextual factors. The primary purpose is to demonstrate the methodology, support structured comparison across use cases, and facilitate informed discussion within a defined application context.

5 Practice Test

As a next step the viability of the blueprint is to be tested in real world environments. For this, the organization from Pilot B was addressed, interviewing staff outside of the DATAMITE project on emerging real monetization cases. It should be noted that these use cases and roles have not yet existed at the beginning of the DATAMITE project but have emerged within its runtime.

Fig. 3. Organizational development over time, assessed by the DMMM. The same organization was interviewed within 18 months. The threshold for a meaningful engagement in data monetization in the DMMM is a value of 3.5 out of 5.

The practice test of the DMMM was conducted with the same organization over a time of 18 months. The interview was conducted with the same company representative. Figure 3 depicts a spider chart of the assessment for the lead organization of Pilot B. (The left-hand side reflects the detailed values of the entry for Pilot B in Table 1.)

As can be seen, the organizational maturity has increased during the period of observation. Especially, new roles and positions around the data business have been created and staffed during this period, including data business product managers. Processes have been set up to execute this business. Thus, mainly the dimensions Data Business Product, Organization, Processes, and Data Strategy have been assessed above the threshold of 3.5. It would be far-fetched to interpret the improvement to be inherently caused by the DATAMITE project. On the other hand, the fact that the organization was a main driver of this project reflects the fact, that it was seriously on the path for boosting its capability towards data monetization and the DMMM was able to assess these ongoing improvements accordingly.

Further, the valuation model was tried out to compare two real-world data sets together with the responsible data business product manager of the same organization. For simplicity, the comparison was conducted purely on quality considerations, omitting the demand-side with relevance or utility considerations. The first dataset (*A*) forms the basis for a data product to predict the probability of churn of a specific telecommunications customer. The second dataset (*B*) contains all of the telecommunication services ordered by a customer. The value of dataset *A* has the determining quality metrics of *Age, Timeliness, Accuracy, Variety, Completeness,* and *Legal Compliance Costs* and was calculated as 0.29 whereas the dataset *B* with *Age, Accuracy,* and *Completeness* was calculated to be 0.31. Dataset *A* is the basis for a sophisticated and targeted prediction algorithm whereas dataset *B* can be used for many broad customer analytics considerations. While their value based on pure quality metrics is comparable, a difference can be anticipated on the modeling of the demand side (*Relevance*, *Utility*) which proved to be too difficult to carry out precisely enough at the time of discussion.

6 Discussion and Next Steps

The three components of the DATAMITE business blueprint, namely the DMMM, the strategy archetypes with pre-filled canvasses, and the data valuation model have been successfully tested in pilot environments. A transfer into real world environments has already been successfully validated with the DMMM and the archetypical strategy canvas templates which are tested as ready for productization. The valuation model still needs to be refined to reach relevance in practice. The remarkable contribution here is that it is the first data valuation model of its kind and thus a promising starting point for reaching higher readiness levels. Please refer to the context-specific discussion of the limitations of the valuation model in Sect. 1.2 and Sect. 2. Further, we will start the formal formulation of an overarching method [13] of the corresponding process for applying the blueprint will be started next.

Acknowledgments. The research leading to these results has received funding from the European Commission under the Horizon Europe Programme's project DATAMITE (grant agreement No. 101092989). Special thanks to Finn Bacher for his support in writing the project reports that are cited in this paper.

References

1. Back, A., Bub, U., Wagner, D.: Organisationale Ambidextrie für Dgitale Transformation gezielt entwickeln – Konzeption des CDO-CIO Do-it Kit auf Basis eines Reifegradansatzes. J. HMD, **59** (2022). https://doi.org/10.1365/s40702-022-00874-9
2. Baecker, J., Engert, M., Pfaff, M., Krcmar, H.: Business strategies for data monetization: deriving insights from practice. In: Potsdam, 15th International Conference on Wirtschaftsinformatik (2020)
3. Braganza, A.: Rethinking the data-information-knowledge hierarchy: towards a case-based model. Int. J. Inf. Manage. **24**(4) (2004)
4. Bub, U., Gizelis, C., Schneider, R.: Towards a data monetization maturity model. In: International Conference on Artificial Intelligence Applications and Innovations - AIAI 2025 IFIP WG 12.5 International Workshops, Limassol (2025)
5. Bub, U., Schneider, R., Bacher, F., Vyhmeister, E.: Mechanisms and Action Blueprints for Data Monetisation in European Companies. Deliverable Report D4.3, DATAMITE Project (2025) https://zenodo.org/records/17987536. Accessed 17 Apr 2026
6. Fischer, S., et al.: Monetarisierung plattformbasierter Produkte und Services. VDMA, Frankfurt (2023)
7. Gizelis, C.A. et al.: Data monetization opportunities and challenges: the European landscape by DATAMITE. In: Maglogiannis, I., Iliadis, L., Karydis, I., Papaleonidas, A., Chochliouros, I. (eds) Artificial Intelligence Applications and Innovations. WG 12.5 International Workshops. AIAI (2024). IFIP Advances in Information and Communication Technology, vol. 715. Springer, Cham. https://doi.org/10.1007/978-3-031-63227-3_5
8. Kakuschke, N.: Data Value Creation Matrix – Options for Organizations to Create Value from Data, Proc. European Conference on Information Systems, Paphos (2024)
9. Layhem, I., Loers, M., Roye, D.: Strategies for Improving Data Monetisation, Deliverable Report D4.1, DATAMITE Project (2024). https://zenodo.org/records/14882174. Accessed 17 Apr 2026

10. Parvinen, P., et al.: Advancing data monetization and the creation of data based. Commun. Assoc. Inf. Syst. **47**(2), 25–49 (2020)
11. Offermann, P., Levina, O., Schönherr, M., Bub, U.: Outline of a design science research process. In: Proceedings of Internernational Conference on DESRIST, Malvern, PA (2009)
12. Offermann, P., Blom, S., Schönherr, M., Bub, U.: Design range and research strategies in design science publications. In: Proceedings of 6th ACM International Conference on Design Science Research in Information Systems and Technology (DESRIST), Springer Lecture Notes in Computer Science (LNCS 6629), Milwaukee WI (2011)
13. Offermann, P., Blom, S., Levina, O., Bub, U.: Vorschlag für Komponenten von Methodendesigntheorien. Int. J. WIRTSCHAFTSINFORMATIK **52**(5) (2010)
14. Osterwalder, A., Pigneur, Y.: Business Model Creation. Wiley, Hoboken (2010)
15. Vyhmeister, E., Pietropaoli, B., Bub, U., Schneider, R., Visentin A.: A Framework for Data Valuation and Monetisation (2025).https://doi.org/10.48550/arXiv.2512.07664
16. Wixom, B.H. Ross, J.W.: How to monetize your data. MIT Sloan, **58**(3), 10–13 (2017)

A Methodology for the Technoeconomic Assessment of ISAC-Enabled Network Deployments

Ioanna Mesogiti[1(✉)], Eleni Theodoropoulou[1], George Lyberopoulos[1], Foteini Setaki[1], Markos Anastasopoulos[2], Anna Tzanakaki[2], Jesus Guttierez[3], German Castellanos[4], Eduard Jorswieck[5], Luis Diez[6], Valerio Frascolla[7], and Navid Nikaein[8]

[1] OTE Hellenic Telecommunications Organisation S.A.Greece,, Athens, Greece
imesogiti@ote.gr

[2] Institute of Accelerating Systems and Applications, University of Athens, Athens, Greece

[3] IHP GmbH – Leibniz Institute for High Performance Microelectronics/Leibniz-Institut für innovative Mikroelektronik, Frankfurt Oder, Germany

[4] Accelleran, Antwerpen, Belgium

[5] Technische Universität Braunschweig, Braunschweig, Germany

[6] Universidad de Cantabria, Santander, Spain

[7] Intel Deutschland GmbH, Feldkirchen, Germany

[8] Bubbleran, Biot, France

Abstract. 6G networks will rely on highly heterogeneous and disaggregated infrastructures, while access networks must meet stringent coverage and performance requirements while incorporating Integrated Sensing and Communication (ISAC) as a native capability, introducing challenges in sensing performance, coverage, and resource requirements. AI/ML techniques are expected to play a key role in enabling adaptive and efficient network operation. To this end, transport networks will need to support diverse deployments, including macro and dense micro radio units as well as distributed and cloud-based RAN architectures (D-RAN, O-RAN), while converging fronthaul, backhaul, and sensing traffic over multi-technology wireless and optical infrastructures. Such complex deployments depend on geography, feasibility, traffic demand, technologies' availability and scalability, and cost. Therefore, early-stage techno-economic evaluation of alternative deployment options is essential to identify cost drivers, optimize design choices, and assess sensing-related architectural options, enabling sustainable and economically viable 6G network planning. This paper proposes a methodology to perform technoeconomic analysis of ISAC-enabled 6G networks and provides insights on technoeconomic factors affecting deployment options of network sensing in 6G networks.

Keywords: 6G Network · ISAC · Transport network · Techno-economic

Published by Springer Nature Switzerland AG 2027
A. Papaleonidas et al. (Eds.): AIAI 2026 Workshops, IFIP AICT 796, pp. 102–115, 2027.
https://doi.org/10.1007/978-3-032-30507-7_6

1 Introduction

It is a fact that 6G network services will pose stringent coverage and data rate requirements to access network segments. In parallel, the inclusion of Integrated Sensing and Communication (ISAC) as a main capability of 6G access networks [1, 2] can pose new challenges in the deployment of the networks – related to sensing performance, sensing coverage, capacity requirements for sensing, etc. On the other hand, AI/ML (Artificial Intelligence/ Machine Learning) techniques can play a key role in operational network deployments. This landscape of 6G requirements on one hand and enablers on the other, can lead to very dissimilar network deployments in terms of technologies used, performance achieved and capabilities that are enabled. 6G-SENSES [3, 16] and MULTI-X [4] projects are investigating various technology and deployment options for the support of ISAC in 6G networks.

To this end, for transport network segments it will be necessary to support high-capacity macro-coverage Radio Units (RUs), dense layers of high capacity micro-coverage RUs, or/and versatile Distributed- and Cloud-based Radio Access Network (D- and C-RAN), or Open-RAN (O-RAN) setups, while transporting sensing alongside communication services. For this purpose, the transport network shall be equipped with mechanisms to support flexible and scalable access network deployments, to converge fronthaul (FH) and backhaul (BH) traffic of various functional splits (FS) alongside sensing-related channels over a single infrastructure consisting of various wireless and optical technologies.

In this context, the delivery of radio access and transport network deployments that are capable to serve the 6G service requirements is not a straightforward task. In practice, many factors shall be considered, such as area specifics, deployment feasibility, long-term service roadmaps, traffic demand and growth patterns/forecasts, as well as infrastructure availability, scaling capabilities and the implicated costs. The scaling capabilities and the identification of the implicated costs shall take into consideration the various deployment phases (over time), in order to pre-estimate the critical, high cost factors and to extract deployment guidelines at network pre-planning stages – prior to the definition of the specific network deployments to be realized. In this context, the techno-economic evaluation of large-scale alternative network deployments is necessary to identify cost optimizations and to investigate various technological aspects and critical parameters (e.g., sensing technologies, sensing functions placement, sensing-related performance parameters) at early stages towards delivering economically viable and sustainable deployments.

This paper proposes a methodology for the techno-economic evaluation of ISAC -enabled mobile network deployments, aiming to identify cost optimizations and to investigate various technological aspects and critical parameters at early stages towards delivering economically viable and sustainable deployments. The methodology is based on previous studies' fully parameterized expandable techno-economic analysis tools [5–7] that reflect the concepts of 5G and beyond network deployments. The tool has been applied in the case of a typical dense urban area and the results confirm its usage potential in identifying critical ISAC cost factors, and applying in similar contexts.

The paper is organized as follows: Sect. 2 presents a methodology and a tool for performing techno-economic analyses of 6G ISAC-enabled networks. In Sect. 3, the network modelling, dimensioning and deployment aspects are discussed, along with relevant operator principles that need to be considered. The next section presents an application of the tool in modeling and dimensioning an indicative ISAC-enabled network deployment, followed by cost assessment of various deployment scenarios. A number of network deployment alternative scenarios are identified and evaluated from a techno-economic perspective. Finally, conclusions are drawn in Sect. 5.

2 Techno-Economic Analysis Methodology and Tool

In general, performing techno-economic analysis is seldom a straightforward task, the underlying reasons being many and versatile. Some of these reasons are related to the scope and goal of the analysis, the level of detail of input information in terms of deployment area specifics, the network segment and the technologies in focus, the scale of the system and so on. Therefore, there are various types of analysis applied at different stages of a solution commercialization, with different focuses depending also on the entity performing the analysis (external or internal department, strategy/financial or technical department, etc.).

In the context of 6G-SENSES and MULTI-X, the methodology proposed in [6] and [7] is adjusted to ISAC-enabled deployments, and comprises the following steps:

Step 1. Definition of the area/vertical premises under study. This step aims to define the coverage area and model the physical/vertical premises environment specifics. 6G-SENSES analysis focused on a medium-to-large scale dense urban deployment.

Step 2. Definition of the service scenarios in terms of coverage area, traffic demand, sensing coverage area, sensing performance etc., and their scaling over years.

Step 3. Definition of the access and transport deployment blueprint, providing a general model of alternative RAN, BH/ FH and Edge/5G Core Network (CN) options that can co-exist in a deployment. At this point, alternative placement options of sensing function options are modelled.

Step 4. Definition of the scaling rules for each technology and the dimensioning rules for each segment. In practice this includes:

- RAN dimensioning: access network nodes' elements calculation based on capacity and coverage over years; including access RUs/ Baseband Units (BBUs)/ Distributed Units (DU)/ Central Units (CU) capacity, gNBs disaggregation model, existence or not of RAN sensing and elements calculation based on sensing coverage.
- Transport dimensioning: capacity and required links calculation considering the adoption of various FS options, sensing channel requirements, transport aggregation levels, transport technologies link capacity/range/hops, etc.
- Edge dimensioning: compute resources calculation considering the application services and Network Functions requirements, loading factors, etc.
- Core segment placement and dimensioning of User Plane Functions (UPFs) to serve the Edges.

Step 5. Definition of the cost information and its scaling rules for all elements that are modelled/analyzed.

Step 6. Setting of analysis timeframe; commonly 5–10 years for telecom networks.

Step 7. Definition of the deployment scenario in terms of technologies mix, including selection of FS, wireless/optical technologies, sensing options, etc.

Step 8. Application of common Cash Flow Model, which leads to automatically calculated Capital /Operational Expenses (CAPEX/OPEX) breakdown, as well as the Total Cost of Ownership (TCO) estimation, on per technology/equipment/segment basis. In practice, CAPEX/OPEX and TCO are calculated considering equipment- and fiber deployment- specific costs, labor costs, operations and maintenance, as well as additional financial figures such as Weighted Average Cost of Capital (WACC) and Tax Deduction (% of equipment cost). The Yearly Total Cost (YTC) has been calculated by harmonizing the sum - each CAPEX has to be annualized, splitting the investment by the appropriate *amortization period* (*AP*)- as follows:

$$YTC = \sum_{j=1}^{N} \frac{CAPEX_i}{AP_i} + \sum_{j=1}^{M} OPEX_j$$

where $CAPEX_i$ and $OPEX_j$ are the i-th component and j-th component of CAPEX and OPEX respectively.

Step 9. Iteration of all steps for various deployment scenarios and collection of analytical comparative cost results of the different scenarios, in order to identify key factors influencing cost and extract deployment recommendations.

The main inputs and outputs of the technoeconomic analysis model focusing on ISAC-enabled network deployments are presented in Fig. 1 below.

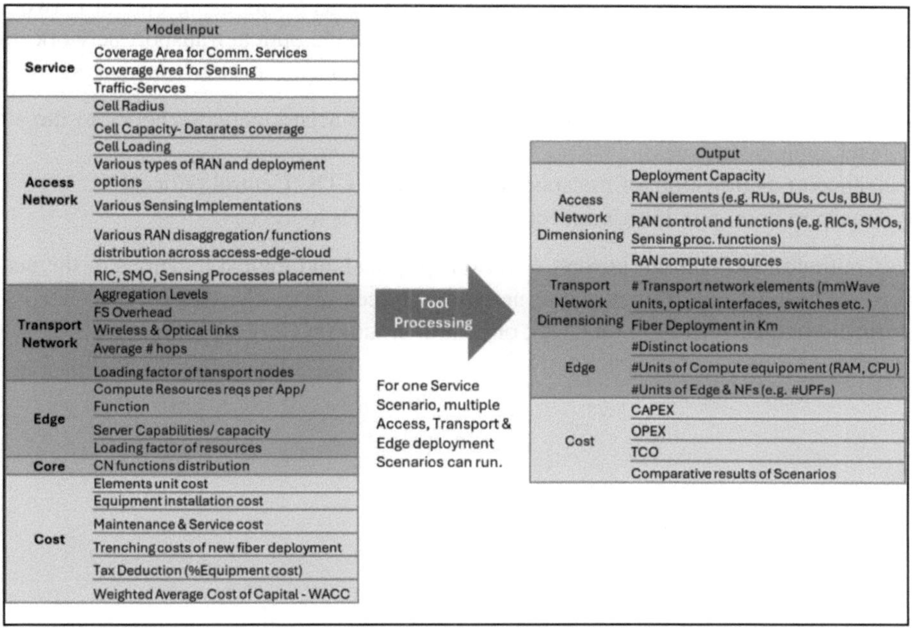

Fig. 1. Techno-economic Analysis Inputs/Outputs for ISAC-enabled Deployments

3 Deployment Blueprint and Modelling Aspects

3.1 ISAC-Enabled Mobile Network Deployment Blueprint

The techno-economic approach outlined in Steps 3 and 4 of Sect. 2 involves modelling the physical architecture of a 6G network, which includes the essential RAN with or without sensing capabilities, various transport network segments (access, aggregation and core), as well as edge and core components. The foundational principles guiding 6G network architectures assume multiple network and computing infrastructure configurations at a highly granular level, incorporating disaggregated pools of networking, computing, and storage resources. The baseline principles for both physical and logical/functional architectures adhere to those in [8–11] and [13]. The deployment options implementing the high-level architecture can be many. The principles and these deployment options are reflected in a general deployment model/blueprint.

More specifically, the model encompasses a wide range of RAN configurations to support advanced deployment scenarios. These include non-3GPP access using IEEE 802.11ad as a RU integrated into the 6G network via N3 Interworking Function (N3IWF), traditional gNB or D-RAN setups with or without sensing capabilities, sub-6 GHz RUs with integrated sensing, and O-RAN architectures enhanced with sensing functionality.

The model also reflects the widely adopted network roll-out principle of transport networks being deployed as multiple hierarchical transport network segments. In general, considering the current trend of minimizing the number of segments from the access to the CN, the transport network model comprises three levels/segments: the access transport segment, the aggregation transport segment and the core transport segment.

The access transport links are aggregated at various levels using optical network technologies and the traffic is forwarded to the backbone optical transport network. In particular, we distinguish the following hierarchical transport network segments:

- Transport access, providing connectivity from the access network nodes to the 1st level aggregation sites;
- Transport aggregation, of transport access links at COs (Central Offices);
- Transport core, providing connectivity between COs to the CN.

Compute resources are present at various physical and logical locations of the network for hosting applications and/or network services such as Virtual BBUs (vBBUs). These are indicated as edge (at COs), or central clouds (at CN).

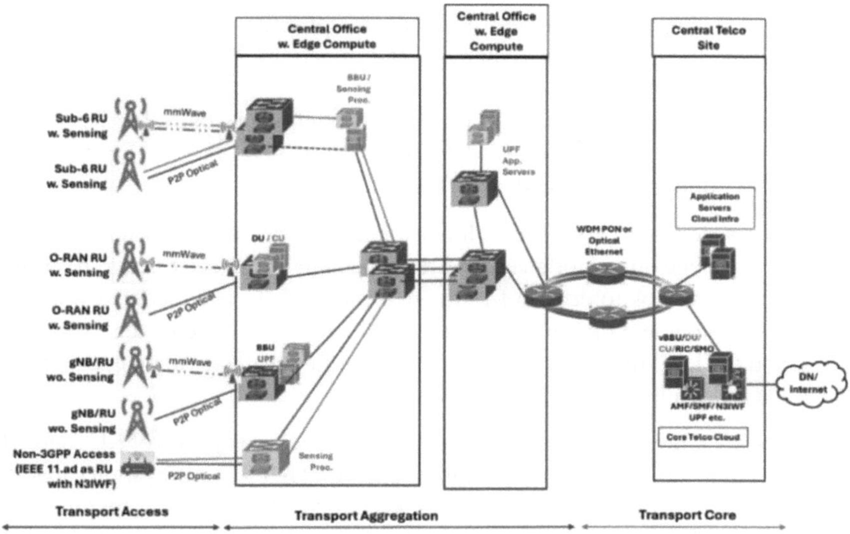

Fig. 2. Physical Architecture Blueprint

The overall blueprint that has been used in 6G-SENSES techno-economic analysis is presented in Fig. 2. The techno-economic tool essentially constitutes a mathematical model of the deployment blueprint in terms of components, segments, elements dimensioning and scaling.

3.2 Network Modeling, Dimensioning and Deployment Aspects

Access Network Deployment and Dimensioning. Especially, considering only the provisioning of communication services, the 6G access network comprises a dense layer of short-range access network nodes Remote RUs (RRUs) connected to BBUs deployed at edge or cloud, and gNBs to serve the high traffic demand at specific hotspot areas and vertical premises. This layer is complemented by a macro layer of longer-range access network nodes (RRUs or gNBs) for maximizing coverage over the wider area. It shall be noted that the discrimination between RRUs and gNBs is modelled with the transport network modelling where various FSs are considered. The access nodes' radio coverage characteristics are modelled at the radio network modelling. Considering the provisioning of sensing capabilities, multiple technology options can be considered (as in 6G-SENSES) namely: O-RAN gNBs with sensing capabilities, non-3GPP access network nodes with sensing capabilities (based on IEEE 11.ad) integrated to the 6G network via N3IWF, and standard 3GPP RAN nodes (sub-6 based) with sensing capabilities (mostly considered in MULTI-X).

The key technical characteristics of the RAN nodes that have been modelled are related to:

- Capacity of RUs – vendor specific input.
- Data rates achieved at cell-edge and range of cell-edge - Operator specific constraint deriving from communication service-driven radio network planning.

- Maximum loading factor of RUs – Network Operator specific constraint.
- Scalability of various Radio elements and functions (i.e. ratios of: RU:BBU, RU:DU:CU, etc.)
- Scalability of Radio Control functions, i.e. RAN Intelligent Controller (RIC), Service Management and Orchestration (SMO), etc.
- Various FS options (referring to eCPRI A to E options).

The access network deployment dimensioning is performed considering generic radio-coverage calculations for a certain area especially given a service to be provided at cell edges, as well as forecasts of traffic demand density. The model also considers mixed RAN deployment options depending on the level of usage of the various types of RAN, and the level of support of sensing (ISAC). In the deployment under study we consider the following options (RAN scenarios):

- Type A RAN represents a standard 3GPP gNBs model (composed of RUs and BBUs or silo gNBs) with no sensing capabilities, but with high RU aggregation capabilities reflecting the commercial large vendor trends in B5G RAN. We consider this type of RAN to serve the high traffic demand at specific hotspot areas and vertical premises.
- Type B RAN represents an O-RAN gNB model composed of RUs/DUs/CUs, with sensing capabilities but with less aggregation capabilities.
- Type C represents an ISAC-enabled (3GPP or ORAN) RAN node. [14]
- Type D is a non-3GPP (based on IEEE 11.ad) ISAC-enabled node connected to the CN via N3IWF, while communicating sensing information to the O-RAN RIC.

5G Transport Network Deployment and Dimensioning. In general, the data-plane architecture considers an integrated optical (Point-to-Point (P2P) or Passive Optical Network (PON) based) and wireless (millimeter Wave (mmWave), Sub-6) network topology and infrastructure to support jointly backhauling of gNBs, and fronthauling of various FS of RRUs to BBUs or O-RAN RUs/DUs. The transport access deployment options are related to the incorporation of sensing capabilities at RAN (at various sensing service/availability levels), to the usage of different FSs, to the usage of various wireless and optical technologies and to other deployment specificities [8, 9, 15].

More specifically, it is necessary to consider the FSs, architecture and functionality support for the coexistence of them over the same infrastructure, namely eCPRI A, eCPRI B, eCPRI C, eCPRI D, eCPRI Id, eCPRI IID/IU, eCPRI E. In turn, it implies that the throughput overhead of each FS needs to be considered in the dimensioning of the transport links between the access network node and the BBU [12].

Considering the general mobile networks' deployment models and the most widely considered technologies, the network deployment options and technologies scaling rules for the transport access are:

- mmWave links for BH and/or FH providing ~ 10 Gbps average data rates per link, being highly dependent on the spectrum (frequency, bandwidth), the distance between the two nodes and the radio environment. mmWave links are implemented by pairs of transceivers, while links' capacity scales by adding new pairs of transceivers. The wireless transport connections may consist of one or multiple hops, defined as deployment options in the techno-economic analysis. Moreover, multiple links per connection/hop may be considered, in case the traffic to be served exceeds the capacity limits of the equipment.

- P2P optical or Wavelength Division Multiplexing-PON (WDM PON) connections for BH/FH links at 10 or 25 Gbps, given the wide penetration of this technology in the market, and the availability of the relevant information. Scaling of these links is performed by adding connections interfaces and connecting them to optical switches. The latter vary depending on the transport segment that are placed. To this end, at transport aggregation level (Leaf Type) switches can be used aggregating 18 P2P interfaces of 10 or 25 Gbps to up to 6 aggregate interfaces of 40 Gbps. At transport core level, Spine type switches are considered switching/aggregating 32 interfaces of 40 or 100 Gbps.

The scenarios can differ in the grade at which each of these technologies is used.

The access transport links are aggregated at 1st level at COs (edge sites), and then at 2nd level towards the Central Telco Site where also the CN resides. At 1st aggregation level we consider 18 mmWave or P2P links aggregated to Leaf type optical switches. Spine type switches are considered to be used at transport core segments to aggregate, at 2nd level, optical interfaces with flexible degrees of aggregation (reaching 32×40 Gbps or 100Gbps optical interfaces).

For all the transport segments other deployment specifics are modelled, such as the maximum link utilization (usually set to 80%) for the access transport links, the maximum loading factor for the aggregation nodes connected interfaces, etc.

Usage and Placement of vBBUs and Edge Computing. Compute resources are considered at various physical and logical locations of the network for hosting applications and/or network services such as vBBUs and UPFs. These are indicated as Edge Compute located at COs. Similarly, to large scale deployments' common practice, it is assumed that COs host the transport aggregation equipment.

By modifying the deployment options and the relevant model parameters, different access network, access transport and aggregation transport deployment scenarios can be defined, dimensioned and evaluated.

4 Techno-Economic Evaluation of 5G Network Deployments

The stepwise methodology implemented by a technoeconomic analysis tool was used to perform a techno-economic assessment for a 5-year timeframe of the various network deployments. The first step for the evaluation is the definition of the area of deployment. The definition refers to the total surface (km^2) that needs to be covered. Based on the area definition and the assumed equipment used in the access network nodes, the radio coverage parameters (i.e. coverage radius of access network nodes) can be evaluated as average pre-planning assumptions. Although the tool provides this option, given the fact that in the 6G era dense urban areas traffic demand will drive network planning, in the area under study we extract the RAN deployment on traffic demand basis. In particular, in the example case, as area under coverage/study we consider a dense urban area, over which a peak aggregate traffic demand data rate will reach 1Tbps at peak hour. RAN and transport network dimensioning is performed on this basis, while auxiliary information such as the current or tentative deployment of cabinets as COs is also defined at this point. In the case of the area under study, the assumed radio network characteristics are summarized in Table 1.

Table 1. Radio Network related assumptions

Radio network related assumptions	
Dense Urban Area	100%
Total Traffic Demand (Peak Hour) Gbps	1000
Average Cell Range Type A	500
Average Cell Range Type B	200
Average Cell Range Type C	200
Average Cell Range Type D	70
Average Distance to CO (m)	500
#1st Level COs	15
#2nd Level COs	2

4.1 Techno-Economic Analysis Scenarios

The evaluation covered multiple deployment scenarios, varying by RAN type composition, transport network options, and sensing capability. Table 2 summarizes the considered scenarios, which include single-type deployments such as Type A (Typical RAN) and Type B (O-RAN), as well as mixed-type configurations like Type CD (50% Type C and 50% Type D), Type BCD (50% Type B, 30% Type C, 20% Type D), and Type ABCD (35% Type A, 15% Type B, 20% Type C, 20% Type D). For each scenario, two transport options were considered— GF (Greenfield) and BF (Brownfield). The GF scenarios refer to no existing fiber deployment in the area and while the BF scenarios refer to the existence of fiber deployment in 50% of the locations of the RAN. Also, for each RAN and transport deployment option, both sensing-enabled and non-sensing configurations were evaluated, providing a comprehensive view of performance across diverse network compositions and capabilities. The tool was used to model the network deployment parameters and the results extracted by the tool provided absolute cost numbers of CAPEX, OPEX, TCO, RAN/Transport/CN deployment costs.

Table 2. Indicative Deployment Scenarios under study.

Deployment Scenarios			No
Type A: Only Typical RAN in service	GF	With Sensing	#1
		No Sensing	#2
	BF - 50%	With Sensing	#3
		No Sensing	#4

(continued)

Table 2. (*continued*)

Deployment Scenarios			No
Type B: Only O-RAN in service	GF	With Sensing	#5
		No Sensing	#6
	BF - 50%	With Sensing	#7
		No Sensing	#8
Type CD: In service: Type C RAN - 50%; Type D RAN - 50%	GF	With Sensing	#9
		No Sensing	#10
	BF - 50%	With Sensing	#11
		No Sensing	#12
Type BCD: In service: Type B RAN 50%; Type C RAN - 30%; Type D RAN - 20%	GF	With Sensing	#13
		No Sensing	#14
	BF - 50%	With Sensing	#15
		No Sensing	#16
Type ABCD: In service: Type A RAN 35%; Type B RAN 15%; Type C RAN - 20%; Type D RAN - 20%	GF	With Sensing	#17
		No Sensing	#18
	BF - 50%	With Sensing	#19
		No Sensing	#20

Using the aforementioned list of scenarios, operators can run comparative studies between the various scenarios sets to evaluate the impact of the different cost factors on the network deployment. Indicatively, a first set of scenarios (Scenarios Set 1 (Optical network deployment GF vs BF)) can focus on the evaluation of all GF optical transport compared to various BF options. Another set of scenarios (Scenarios Set 2 (Impact of Sensing on Cost)) can be used to focus on the evaluation of the cost of sensing for various RAN deployment options. Additional set of scenarios can focus on the evaluation of various RAN deployment options compared to the commercially available highly aggregated RAN options, on the evaluation of various sensing data traffic patterns and so on.

4.2 Analysing Techno-Economic Results

In general, the scenarios analysed reflect the complexity and diversity of future 6G ecosystems that can vary in RAN, sensing and transport network technology choices, and the architectural configurations in terms of RAN, network FS, mix of 3GPP RAN, O-RAN and non-3GPP access, centralised versus distributed deployments and so on. Through the comparative evaluation of costs, broken down per network segment, critical network deployment factors can be revealed. Focusing on the cost implications of integrating sensing capabilities into communication networks, the cost impact apparently varies depending on the mix of sensing technologies and their placement within the network. The results highlight the importance of carefully selecting sensing solutions and deployment strategies, enabling operators to balance performance benefits with economic sustainability in future 6G networks.

Before analysing the extracted results for the case study deployments, it must be highlighted that techno-economic outcomes are inherently sensitive to dynamic market factors. Equipment prices, vendor competition, procurement volumes, and bilateral agreements can significantly influence both CAPEX and OPEX per case. As a result, conclusions drawn from one context may not be directly transferable to another, particularly as market conditions evolve and new technologies mature. For these reasons, each operator's investment strategy should be assessed individually using tailored techno-economic analysis tools, such as the one presented in this study.

The results of the 1st scenarios set can be used to study the impact of the cost of fiber on TCO. For instance, in the deployment under study, the additional cost fiber transport ranges between 2%–7% as percentage over all network deployment TCO (comparing BF vs. GF deployments). The additional capacity required to support the extra transport network traffic incurred by sensing capabilities leads only to an additional 1%-2% cost increase – expressed as percentage over all network deployment TCO. Thus, it becomes obvious that, unlike the results of previous generation mobile networks [6, 7], the cost of fiber deployment is no longer a critical cost factor, compared to the complete network deployment TCO. The reason lies both in the large capacities provided by fiber links and in the low cost of fiber equipment, as well as in the comparatively high cost of the RAN. Apparently, the extra capacity required for sensing impacts the cost of the transport deployment, that's why we observed a slightly higher impact of fiber transport on TCO in the case of sensing-enabled deployment (Fig. 3).

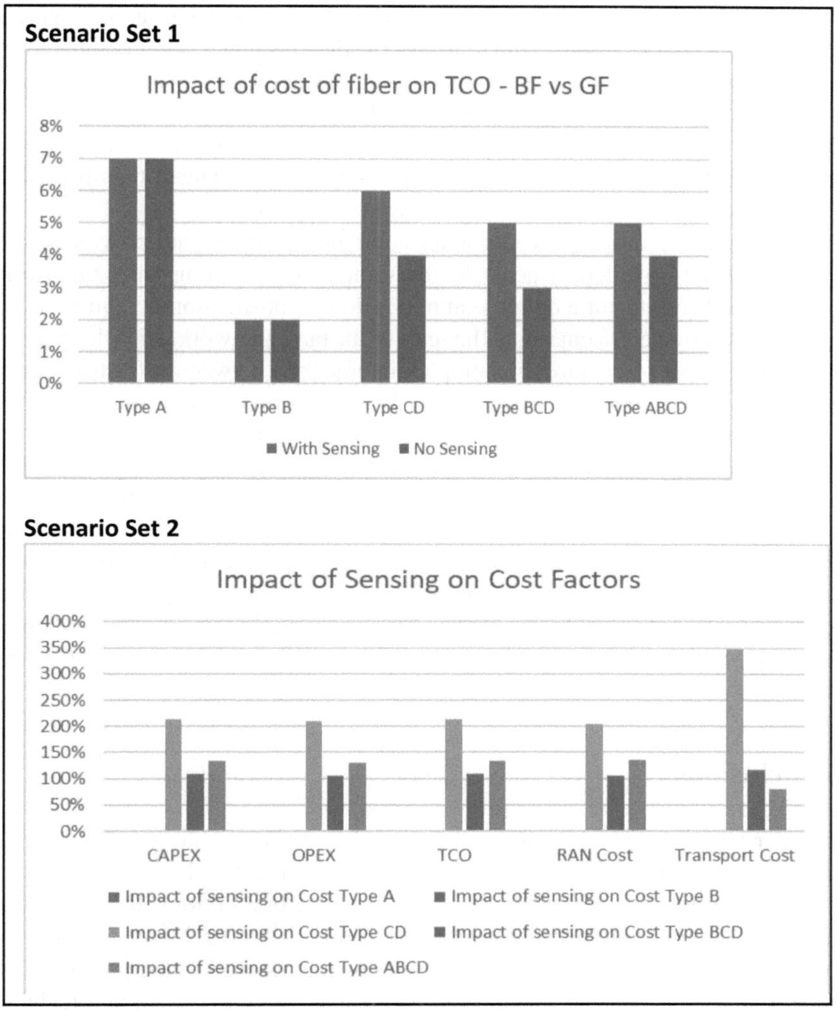

Fig. 3. Indicative Results driven from proposed Techno-economic analysis methodology

The results of the 2nd scenarios set can be used to study the additional cost incurred in total, and per network segment, when sensing is introduced in the various RAN deployment options (given BF deployment) compared to the non-sensing deployment. For instance, for the RAN technology options under study, for Type A (Typical RAN) and Type B (O-RAN), introducing sensing is almost cost-neutral as there is ~ 0% overhead across CAPEX, OPEX, TCO, RAN, and Transport. For Type CD, sensing introduces additional costs, driven primarily by transport and substantial increases in the total deployment CAPEX, OPEX and TCO. This is due to the significant infrastructure augmentation needed to support sensing. For Type BCD sensing incurs cost increase across all factors with transport still being a key cost increase factor, although less extreme than in the Type CD scenarios. Finally, for Type ABCD, while sensing drives high RAN-side and CAPEX/TCO overhead, the transport overhead is much lower compared to the BCD and CD scenarios. This suggests that diversified RAN mixes can reduce transport pressure but shift incremental cost to the RAN domain.

Additional scenarios can be used to evaluate the cost effectiveness of aggregated vs. highly disaggregated RAN options across all segments, to evaluate the dimensioning and thus impact of sensing data traffic patterns on TCO, etc.

As a general conclusion drawn, unitary equipment costs cannot provide safe conclusions about network deployment. At the same time, selecting an optimal mix of technologies and architectural options cannot be done in abstraction; it requires detailed modelling of deployment scenarios at the scale of the target network. High-level assumptions are insufficient to capture the complex interactions between infrastructure components, performance requirements, and cost drivers. Instead, accurate decision-making depends on scenario-specific evaluations that reflect real deployment conditions, including network topology, traffic evolution, and technology integration choices. To this end, techno-economic analysis based on technoeconomic tools including network modelling and dimensioning is useful for quick and coarse evaluation of a large number of scenarios. Analysis of longer-term scenarios can also provide insights related to future-proofness of deployment and to securing investments. The more accurate the pricing information, the more accurate and valuable the results of the analysis. To this end, the cost and cost models of the equipment are critical factors, making analysis highly sensitive to the cost assumptions.

5 Conclusions

In this paper, we propose a methodology framework and an associated tool for the techno-economic analysis of ISAC-enabled 6G network deployments. The proposed approach facilitates the systematic evaluation of diverse architectural options, including heterogeneous RAN configurations and converged transport networks, by modelling, dimensioning, and cost-analyzing individual network segments while incorporating critical parameters related to sensing integration, performance requirements, and technology choices. The application of the methodology to representative deployment scenarios highlights key cost drivers and trade-offs, offering valuable insights into the selection of cost-efficient and scalable 6G solutions. Owing to its flexible design, the tool can be extended to accommodate additional technologies, more complex deployment strategies, and evolving market conditions, thereby supporting comprehensive assessment and informed decision-making for sustainable, high-performance 6G network planning.

Acknowledgements. The research leading to these results has received funding from the European Commission's Horizon Europe, Smart Networks and Services Joint Undertaking, research and innovation program under grant agreement #101139282, 6G-SENSES "SEamless integratioN of efficient 6G wireleSs tEchnologies for communication and Sensing", and under #101192521, MULTI-X "Advancing 6G-RAN through multi-technology, multi-sensor fusion, multi-band and multi-static perception".

References

1. ITU-R IMT towards 2030 and beyond, "New Recommendation ITU-R M.2160 on the "IMT-2030 Framework" (November 2023)". https://www.itu.int/en/ITU-R/study-groups/rsg5/rwp5d/imt-2030/Pages/default.aspx
2. 3GPP TR 22.837 V19.4.0 (2024-06) Feasibility Study on Integrated Sensing and Communication (Release 19)
3. SNS JU Project 6G-SENSES. https://6g-senses.eu/. Accessed April 2026
4. SNS JU Project MULTI-X. https://multix-6g.eu/. Accessed April 2026
5. Oughton, E.J., Lehr, W.: Surveying 5G techno-economic research to inform the evaluation of 6G wireless technologies. IEEE Access **10**, 25237–25257 (2022). https://doi.org/10.1109/ACCESS.2022.3153046
6. Mesogiti, I., et al.: Macroscopic and microscopic techno-economic analyses highlighting aspects of 5G transport network deployments. Photon Netw. Commun. **40**, 256–268 (2020). https://doi.org/10.1007/s11107-020-00912-w
7. Mesogiti, I., et al.: Techno-Economic Aspects of 5G Transport Network Deployments. Optical Network Design and Modeling. ONDM 2019. LNCS, vol. 11616, pp. 118–129. Springer, Cham (2019). https://doi.org/10.1007/978-3-030-38085-4_11
8. Tzanakaki, A., Anastasopoulos, M.: Optical transport networks supporting integrated communications and sensing in 6G. In: 2025 European Conference on Optical Communications (ECOC), Copenhagen, Denmark, pp. 1–4, 2025. https://doi.org/10.1109/ECOC66593.2025.11263441
9. Anastasopoulos, M., Gutiérrez, J., Tzanakaki, A.: Optical transport network optimization supporting integrated sensing and communication services. In: Optical Fiber Communications Conference and Exhibition (OFC), San Francisco, CA, USA, pp. 1–3, 2025
10. Li, X., et al.: MultiX: advancing 6G-RAN through multi-technology, multi-sensor fusion, multi-band and multi-static perception. IEEE Wirel. Commun. https://doi.org/10.1109/MWC.2025.3629589
11. Robitzsch, S., et al.: Architecture considerations for ISAC in 6G. In: 2025 IEEE Conference on Standards for Communications and Networking (CSCN), Bologna, Italy, pp. 1–5, 2025. https://doi.org/10.1109/CSCN67557.2025.11230762
12. Larsen, L.M.P., Checko, A., Christiansen, H.L.: A survey of the functional splits proposed for 5G mobile crosshaul networks. IEEE Commun. Surv. Tutor. **21**(1), 146–172 (2019). Firstquarter, https://doi.org/10.1109/COMST.2018.2868805
13. Gramaglia, M., et al.: Towards 6G Architecture: Key Concepts, Challenges, and Building Blocks. Zenodo (2025). https://doi.org/10.5281/zenodo.17540520
14. Khan, F., Diez, L., Maletic, N., Petri, M., Gutiérrez Terán, J., Agüero, R.: ISAC meets O-RAN: a RIC service to ensure sensing delay requirements (2025). https://doi.org/10.5281/zenodo.18594949
15. Anastasopoulos, M., et al.: Demonstration of a multi-technology 6G transport network integrating THz and optical network technologies empowered by federated learning. J. Opt. Commun. Netw. **17**, C156–C169 (2025)
16. Gutiérrez, J., et al.: Seamless integration of efficient 6G wireless technologies for communication and sensing enabling ecosystems. In: Maglogiannis, I., Iliadis, L., Karydis, I., Papaleonidas, A., Chochliouros, I. (eds.) Artificial Intelligence Applications and Innovations. AIAI 2024 IFIP WG 12.5 International Workshops. AIAI 2024. IFIP AICT, vol. 715. Springer, Cham (2024). https://doi.org/10.1007/978-3-031-63227-3_13

AI-Powered Wildfire Detection

Alexandros Kostopoulos[1(✉)], Ioannis P. Chochliouros[1], George Lyberopoulos[1], Dimitris Salmatanis[1], Jason Diakoumakos[1], Ioannis Panaretou[2], Alexandros Patsias[2], Christos Zaroliagis[3], Spyros Kontogiannis[3], and Dimitris Tzempelikos[4]

[1] Hellenic Telecommunications Organization (OTE) S.A., 99 Kifissias Avenue, 15124 Maroussi, Athens, Greece
alexkosto@oteresearch.gr
[2] Sammy IKE, Patras, Greece
[3] University of Patras, Patras, Greece
[4] Municipality of Egaleo, Egaleo - Attica, Attica, Greece

Abstract. The AMBITIOUS EU-funded project aims at providing a fundamental technological infrastructure, which will offer advanced data aggregation and clean-up, analytics, AI-enabled forecasting and secure information exchange mechanisms, via a transparent computing continuum infrastructure, to be integrated with existing, mature services of SMEs, unleashing for them yet unforeseen functionalities and opening up new pathways of commercial exploitation. In this paper, we focus upon the surveillance and monitoring use case, employing an AI-based framework for data driven applications. We present the overall architecture and pilot setup and we also investigate our AI-based wildfire detection system together with the pilot evaluation process.

Keywords: 5G; AI; Real-Time Monitoring · Surveillance · Wildfire Detection

1 Introduction

The AMBITIOUS EU-funded project [1, 2] targets three primary goals: (i) Boosting the digital capabilities and international competitiveness of European businesses; (ii) advancing innovation through tech solutions that tackle security, sustainability, and well-being issues, and; (iii) encouraging cooperation among industry, academia, and the public sector to achieve a shared impact.

Large segments of today's economy are going digital with new services and novel solutions [3]. The transformative impact of digitalisation on economies is demonstrated by how digital technologies reshape markets, industries, and labour dynamics in a globalised context [4, 5]. For the European Union to be able to cope with a wide range of challenges (e.g., combat climate change, urbanization, energy production, workers' safety and many other issues), it is vital that European companies, especially the SMEs, are at the forefront of digitalization [6, 7]. New digital solutions offer possibilities to reduce the carbon footprint [8] while improving the life of millions of people with

Published by Springer Nature Switzerland AG 2027
A. Papaleonidas et al. (Eds.): AIAI 2026 Workshops, IFIP AICT 796, pp. 116–130, 2027.
https://doi.org/10.1007/978-3-032-30507-7_7

increased safety and security, and better comfort, thus drastically enhancing living standards [9, 10]. By being in the forefront of the digital era, European companies will also be able to export solutions and services, being competitive in a world market framework [11].

Towards being aligned with the above strategic policy, AMBITIOUS aims at developing a foundational technological framework characterized by cutting-edge data aggregation, analytics, Artificial Intelligence- (AI-) powered forecasting and secure data exchange, all of which are supported by a transparent computing continuum. This framework meshes with existing mature services (at Technology Readiness Level 6 (TRL6) or higher) to "unlock" new functions and business prospects. Central technological "pillars" intend to deliver standardized utilities, thereby reducing duplication and expenses. These pillars underpin a variety of services and enable third-party entities to employ the framework for developing and upgrading their own services. The pillars tackle significant practical challenges like real-time observation, hazard forecasting, and health protection, pushing forward innovations in fields like data analytics, AI [12], 5G [13], computing continuum [14] and IoT sensing capabilities [15]. Demonstrations will cover sectors like safety, smart water management, precision agriculture, and digital health and well-being. Additionally, AMBITIOUS reinforces regional tech cooperation across Europe, aligning with the smart specialization priorities of the involved regions.

In this paper, we extend our work presented in [16]. In particular, we address urban surveillance needs through real-time incident detection [17, 18] with the urban monitoring module delivered in Egaleo's Municipal Public Park, in the wider Athens-Attica area in Greece. The use case is further enhanced via complementary capabilities in areas such as on-demand image data annotation, data annotation customisation, Unmanned Aerial Vehicle- (UAV-) assisted monitoring in case of emergencies and system interoperability. The combined provided outputs are used in the pilot's deployments, for demonstrating the applicability of the use case solution across both maritime and urban domains under real-world testing and validation conditions.

The current landscape in the urban surveillance domain reveals significant gaps that create opportunities for advanced AI-enabled and IoT-driven solutions such as those demonstrated in AMBITIOUS. The legacy surveillance systems provide limited predictive analysis capabilities; they mainly integrate modules that enable cloud storage of the data and data monitoring dashboards. Systems that incorporate "smart" characteristics in the surveillance for incident detection areas are still in a premature stage [19]. Systems that incorporate real-time IoT data processed on the edge for feeding custom AI-enabled algorithms to create dynamic services [20] (e.g. incident notifications) have not been validated in a market-ready level yet.

Public spaces today rely heavily on CCTV and manual monitoring, which provide limited real-time situational awareness [21]. Video surveillance is an integral part of the contemporary world and its use increases the sense of security but also generates certain risks. While AI-based incident detection systems are gradually being introduced [22] (e.g. for fire detection, intrusion monitoring or crowd analytics), their integration with autonomous UAV platforms is still rare. AMBITIOUS combines AI-based object detection and segmentation with autonomous UAVs [23] capable of operating in both

Global Positioning System- (GPS-) enabled and GPS-denied environments. Complemented with the existing IoT and cloud infrastructure, these technologies enable real-time monitoring and data processing, offering a scalable solution for municipalities and urban authorities. Our effort leads the global trend for the urban surveillance market which is the introduction of fusion data models on the edge, integrated in various IoT sensors and AI-powered analytics for UAVs, able to deliver comprehensive situational awareness while ensuring compliance with European data protection standards [24, 25].

This paper focuses on the surveillance and monitoring use case in AMBITIOUS, employing an AI-based framework for data driven applications. The paper is organized as follows: Sect. 2 presents the overall architecture and pilot setup. Section 3 presents our AI-based wildfire detection system. The pilot evaluation process is investigated in Sect. 4. We conclude our remarks, the technical challenges and future steps in Sect. 5.

2 Overall Architecture and Pilot Setup

In this section, we present the overall architecture of the use case focused on AI-enabled surveillance and monitoring of controlled areas.

Fig. 1. AMBITIOUS Smart Surveillance Use Case Pilot Area

Egaleo Municipal Public Park stands as the largest green space in Western Attica, and includes various educational institutions, along with sports and food service facilities, and the open-air "Alexis Minotis" theater. The areas of focus for the particular pilot are the green spaces of the grove mainly for early detection of fire and prevention of malicious activities (cf. Fig. 1).

The figure below (Fig. 2) depicts the overall architecture and the main components for the pilot setup. In the pilot area, we deployed the Virtual Private Network (VPN) client for the secure connection with the OTE's (Hellenic Telecommunications Organization S.A.) Research Laboratories, we ensured 5G WAN (Wide Area Network) connectivity, as well as we setup cameras for video streaming and snapshots. On the research laboratories site, we use the VPN server for secure connectivity, the SFTP (Secure File Transfer Protocol) [26] Server for hosting the video and image files, as well as the GPU (Graphics Processing Unit) Server for video and image AI processing. Last but not least, a wide range of data is collected, either via sensors or from external libraries.

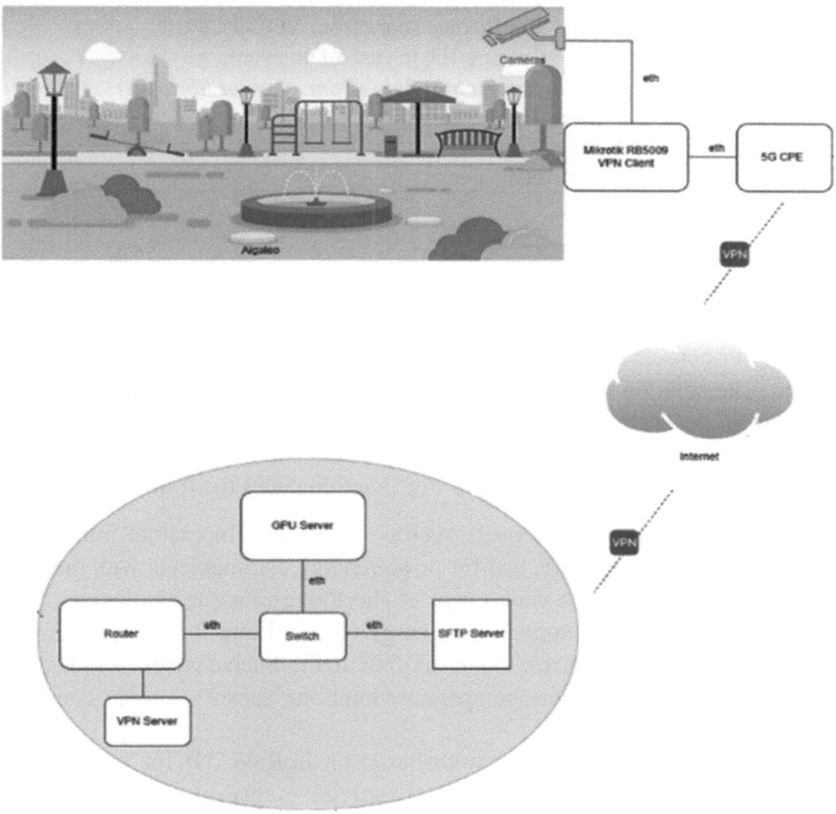

Fig. 2. Overall architecture and pilot setup

Table 1 summarizes the main components for the AMBITIOUS surveillance use case setup.

Table 1. Main components for the use case setup.

Activity	Description
Pilot Area	• VPN Client • 5G WAN Connectivity • Cameras
Research Laboratories	• VPN Serer • SFTP Server • GPU Server, AI process
Data Collection	• ***Camera snapshots & videos*** • ***Meta-data*** ▪ Timestamp. ▪ Camera geolocation. ▪ Confidence score from YOLO [27]. ▪ Camera ID, in case of an event. • ***Environmental data*** *(from external libraries)* ▪ Temperature ▪ Humidity ▪ etc.

3 AI-Based Wildfire Detection System

An entirely "in-house", an end-to-end platform/solution for smart applications has been developed. The solution is based entirely on open-source technologies, and it is modular by design. As such, it is vendor- and technology-agnostic, capable of integrating numerous and heterogeneous sensors, modules and devices into a common ecosystem.

The IoT testbed layout is depicted in Fig. 3 and includes the following:

- A wide range of end-devices/sensors, such as air-quality, temperature, humidity, pressure, activity, luminance, fire, and for power/energy communicate with the backend cloud infrastructure over a wide range of short/long range technologies (5G, Ethernet, WiFi, z-wave, Bluetooth Low Energy (BLE), Long Range Wide Area Network (LoRaWAN) and Narrow-Band IoT (NB-IoT)). Such devices include cameras, microphones, motion sensors, temperature/humidity sensors, energy consumption monitoring devices, etc.
- IoT hubs/gateways (local and remote–based on LoRaWAN) for facility automation and energy management/control (based on events/rules) supporting multiple HAN (Home Area Network)/BAN (Body Area Network)/LAN (Local Area Network)/WAN technologies/interfaces; over 150 technologies and protocols are currently supported.
- A common backend infrastructure (including storage, monitoring/data visualization, command exchange, etc.).

Additionally, the end-users can connect remotely to the back-end system to have access to their data, as well as control their end-devices. For example, switching on/off lights, monitoring temperature and humidity, detecting motion, tracking power and energy consumption, etc.

The back-end system is also enabled to provide data analytics, as well as real-time data visualisation to the end-users. The end-users are also enabled to create customised figures and data visualisation. For example, users are enabled to select the starting/ending point of the requested data, the duration (on an hourly/daily/monthly basis), etc.

Hence, the considered IoT platform supports the following capabilities:

- *Monitoring (power/energy/voltage/cameras);*
- *Energy management and control (remotely, on-demand);*
- *Facility automation (based on predefined events/rules;*
- *Push notifications at end-users' mobile devices;*
- *Enhanced security and data privacy (VPN, SSL (Secure Socket Layer) Certificates);*
- *Data visualisation.*

The underlying operating systems used are:

- *Analytics server:* Linux (Ubuntu/CentOS [28])
- *Gateway:* Rasbian
- *IoT devices:* Custom versions that vary.

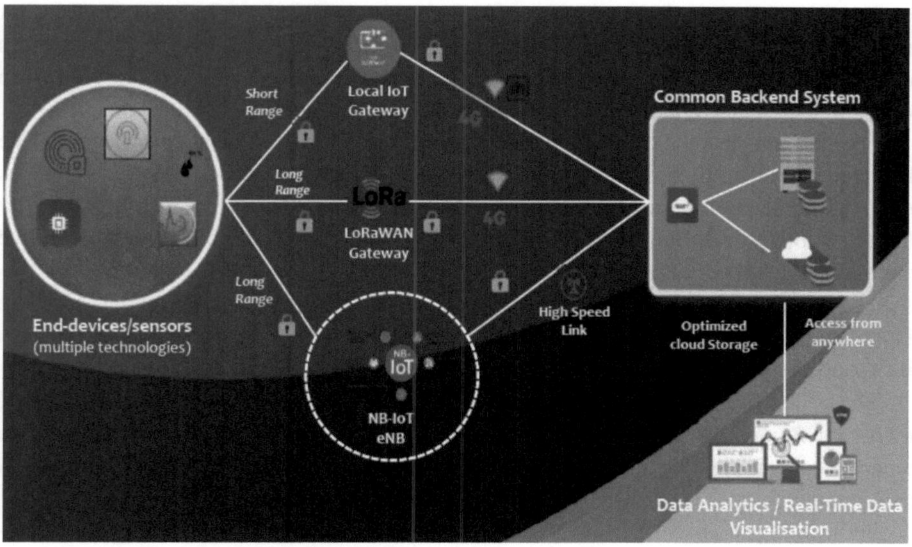

Fig. 3. IoT Testbed Layout

Within the envisioned AI-based framework, we intend to develop, validate, maintain and enhance an AI/ML-based end-to-end (E2E) solution for early wildfire detection and alerting. In particular, the following services will be provided:

- **AI-based Detection**: Early smoke/wildfire, in (near) real-time, in long distances, with high accuracy, based on video footage from cameras and/or drones.

- **Portal:** WebGUI at Control Room (e.g., cameras on map, live feed, historical "detection" events, coverage area, alerts, etc.).
- **Alerting Upon Event:**
- *Visual at smartphones:* enriched push notification messages to closed user groups incl., snapshot and direct (RSTP) link to camera's feed.
- *Visual at WebGUI:* pop-up windows showing snapshots.
- *Audio and visual alerts at Control-Room:* strobe, siren, voice announcement.

A set of cameras is setup in the context of the surveillance use case. Within the context of the AMBITIOUS project, enhanced AI mechanisms for image and object recognition and alerting are being deployed and tested (e.g., AI object recognition [29], smart cameras, augmented information and alerting, etc.) [30, 31]. To train the AI-based detection algorithms, we use real-time data from the surveillance area, as well as open datasets.

The platform also supports the use of VR glasses [32] by the administrator, being enabled to monitor several camera inputs on a virtual multi-windowed environment. Moreover, the platform users could receive alerts for emergency events (e.g., fire, harsh weather conditions, etc.) to inform the involved stakeholders. All the data received by the cameras and sensors is sent via a gateway to a 5G router, using the commercial mobile network.

The IoT service is accessible via any end-device (e.g. phone tablet, laptop, Virtual Reality (VR) glasses), from any network. Two user interfaces are available: The first interface is via a mobile application installed in end-users' devices, which enables users to access their IoT devices. The second interface communicates with web server via http requests, which also enables users to define specific automations for their devices.

Figure 4 presents the overall AI-based framework for wildfire detection service. The developed wildfire detection system is designed to identify smoke in its early stages using artificial intelligence and camera networks. The system combines high-quality datasets, object detection models, and a custom software pipeline that processes live camera feeds and delivers alerts to users in real time.

The process begins with data collection. High-resolution images and videos are gathered from available sources on the internet. Videos are broken down into still images to expand the dataset and capture a wider variety of smoke conditions.

The collected images then go through annotation, where tools such as LabelImg [33] are used to manually mark smoke regions by drawing bounding boxes. These annotations generate coordinate files that tell the training algorithm exactly where smoke appears in each image.

For training, we use YOLOv8 (You Only Look Once, version 8) [27, 34, 35], a state-of-the-art object detection model. The dataset is split into training, validation, and test sets. Training updates the model's weights, validation ensures it is not overfitting, and the test set provides a final performance measure. During training, the system monitors metrics such as precision, recall, and mean average precision (mAP). The best-performing version of the model is automatically selected and exported for deployment.

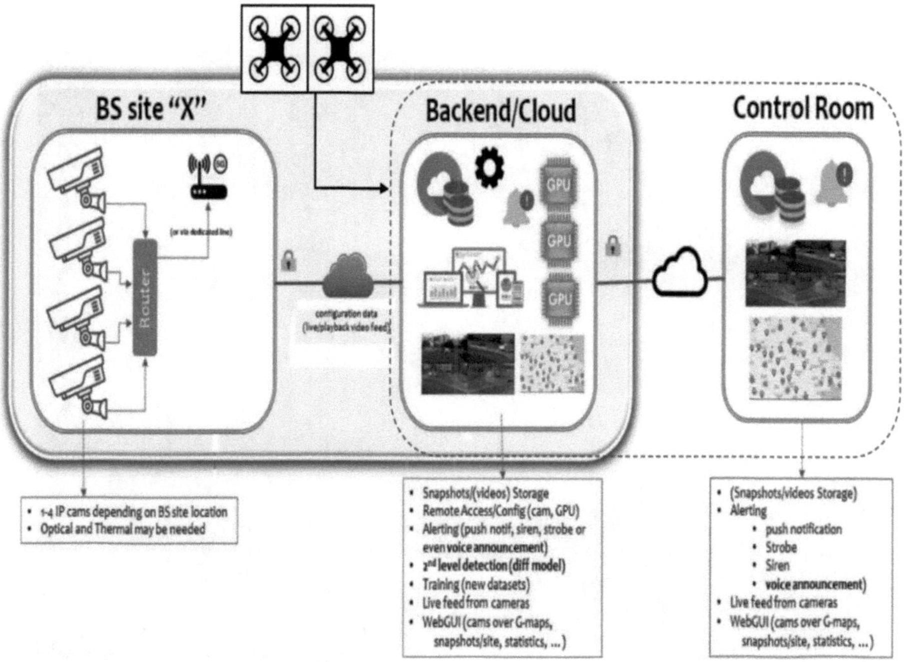

Fig. 4. AI-based framework for wildfire detection service

Once trained, the model is deployed in a real-time inference pipeline. A custom Python script connects to RTSP (Real Time Streaming Protocol) camera feeds and processes each frame with the trained YOLOv8 model. When smoke is detected, the system highlights it with a bounding box, saves a short video clip of the event and immediately sends an alert to users via pushover notifications. To support operations and monitoring, we have built a web-based graphical interface.

From the interface, all cameras are visible on a map, and each camera has its own library where all detection videos are stored. Users can access live camera feeds, review past detections, and check the status of all deployed cameras. System health monitoring ensures that if a camera goes offline, a notification is sent automatically.

In practice, the full workflow is: *cameras capture the environment*, *the AI model processes the video feed*, *detections trigger notifications and are stored*, and *the web interface gives users full access to both live and historical data.*

This end-to-end pipeline creates a practical and scalable wildfire monitoring solution, enabling early detection and timely alerts while providing transparency and traceability through the management interface. Figure 5 depicts the developed graphical user interface with the snapshots from wildfire detection incidents.

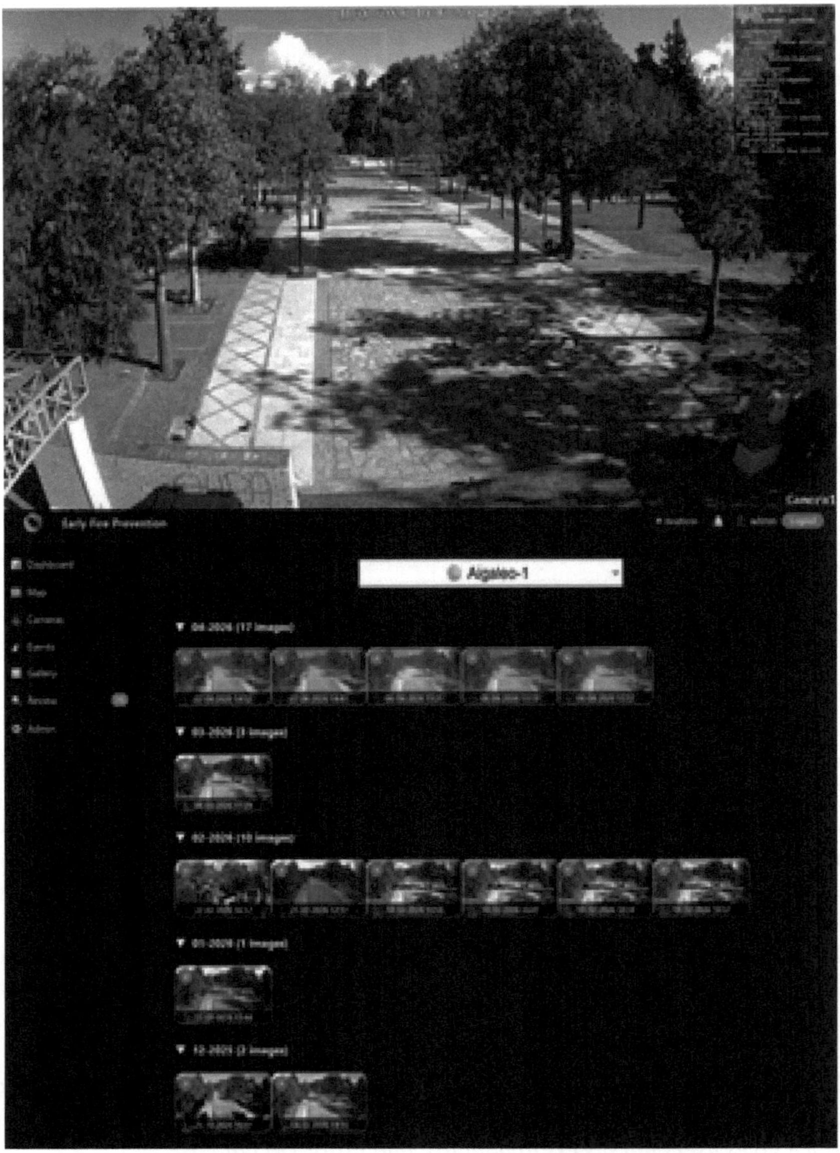

Fig. 5. Snapshots from wildfire detection incidents

4 Pilot Evaluation Process

In this section, we present of evaluation process for the smart surveillance pilot of the AMBITIOUS project. In particular, it consists of two cycles. The first one took place in the middle of the project, while the second one will take place before the project ends.

The main domains we consider for both cycles are: The *necessary infrastructure*, the *main functional/non-functional requirements*, the *focus groups* for determination and training of the end-users, the *provided functionalities*, as well as the *new services and tools*.

Table 2 present activities that are taking place in the framework of cycle 1, while Table 3 corresponds to cycle 2.

Table 2. Cycle 1 Setup for evaluation

Activity	Description
Infrastructure	• Internet protocol (IP) cameras for presence/incident detection • 5G Router for secure network access & data upload to the cloud • VPN Server • SFTP Server • GPU Server/AI processing
Main Functional/Non-Functional Requirements	• Connect IoT devices • Data feed mechanisms • Data storing mechanism • Secure data transmission Ensure cross-platform compatibility (web, mobile), VPN and FTP (File Transfer Protocol) access, periodical snapshots saving for dataset creation, enable AI-based algorithms for fire detection, 5G connectivity
Focus group: determination & training	Egaleo Municipality Officers • Municipal Authority fully supportive • Qualified personnel available for training • Availability for use case validation
Provided functionalities	• On-demand image retrieval API • IoT Management Dashboard • Image/object/activity recognition
New services & tools	• Incident detection algorithm • Early warning/notification mechanism • Real-time streaming-monitoring User Interface (UI)

Table 3. Cycle 2 Setup for evaluation

Activity	Description
Infrastructure	• UAVs

(*continued*)

Table 3. (*continued*)

Activity	Description
Functional/Non-Functional Requirements	• Incident/Alert Mechanisms • History page • Continuous network availability • Low system latency • Confirmed message delivery Ensure cross-platform compatibility with UAV platform provider, VPN and FTP access, periodical snapshots saving for dataset creation, enable AI-based algorithms for fire detection, 5G connectivity
Focus group: determination & training	Egaleo Municipality Officers • Municipal Authority fully supportive • Qualified personnel available for training focused on the new features • Availability for use case validation (cycle 2)
Provided functionalities	• Image/Video Streaming Service • Live streaming backend software (SW) module(s) • Image/video feed from UAVs, Image/object/activity recognition
New services & tools	• Training Datasets & Application Programming Interfaces (APIs) • Image/Video streaming User Experience (UX) • Fire detection/alarming & UAV support • Data Annotation mechanisms and training datasets • UAV live streaming service

5 Discussion and Future Work

5G is not only a new radio access technology offering higher data rates and lower latencies, but it is considered as an enabler for supporting cutting edge tools and applications [36, 37] in the new era of computing continuum, mixing cloud, edge and Internet of Things (IoT) resources [38, 39]. To provide capability to industrial applications, the 5G network uses dedicated technologies like "slicing" [40] and "Edge computing" [41]. The resulting new technology platform enables developers to deploy their software not only centrally in the cloud and distributed in the end-users' laptops and mobile phones, but also at the network edge. This new architecture paves the way for new business models, value chains and deployment models offering Small- and Medium-sized Enterprises (SMEs) to serve their clients even better with highly responsive applications and services. Systems could be designed to be more fault tolerant and robust using a combination of backend components deployed centrally and closer to the end-users.

Several activities for the development of digital solutions based on 5G technology are currently taking off in many parts of Europe, giving businesses and consumers many opportunities for connecting and efficiently interacting with other business partners, service providers and social networks. New ecosystems and value networks will evolve and many business opportunities will occur [42].

The main goal of AMBITIOUS [1] is to deliver a fundamental technological infrastructure, providing advanced data aggregation and clean-up, analytics, Artificial Intelligence- (AI-) enabled forecasting and secure information exchange mechanisms, via a transparent computing continuum infrastructure, integrated with existing, mature services (of at least Technology Readiness Level 6 (TRL6)) of the relevant stakeholders (i.e., SMEs), unleashing for them yet unforeseen functionalities and opening up new pathways of commercial exploitation. The envisaged fundamental infrastructure is provided via the deployment of technological pillars, which interact with existing services towards supporting the envisioned functionalities. The purpose of a "pillar" is to provide the same generic functionalities to diverse services (demonstrated by a diverse set of specific use cases) as a concrete processing chain, aiming at avoiding unnecessary redundancy of resources and budget.

In this paper, we focused on the surveillance and monitoring use case, employing an AI-based framework for data driven applications. We presented the overall architecture and pilot setup, we investigated the implemented AI-based wildfire detection system, as well as the pilot evaluation process.

We plan to enrich our existing dataset for smoke and fire detection via continuous training for fine-tuning the applied AI algorithms. As a next step, we will focus on UAV stand-alone platform setup along with a mobile application for live-streaming. After performing a set of testing UAV flights, we will integrate the operation of the UAV with our platform, so as to automatically trigger the UAV upon fire-detection incident. The pilot execution results will be consolidated and evaluated against the new AI models and algorithms.

Acknowledgments. The paper has been based on the context of the *AMBITIOUS* ("*Advanced CoMputing Continuum Solutions for Boosting DigITalization across European RegionS*") European research project. This work has received funding from the European Union's Interregional Innovation Investments Instrument (I3) under Grant Agreement No. 101115116.

References

1. AMBITIOUS ("Advanced CoMputing Continuum Solutions for Boosting DigITalization across European RegionS") I3-2021-INV1 Project, Grant Agreement No. 101115116. https://ambitious-project.eu/
2. Kostopoulos, A., Chochliouros, I.P., et al.: Boosting digitalization across European regions: the AMBITIOUS approach. In: Maglogiannis, I., Iliadis, L., Karydis, I., Papaleonidas, A., Chochliouros, I. (eds.) Artificial Intelligence Applications and Innovations. AIAI 2024 IFIP WG 12.5 International Workshops. AIAI 2024. IFIP, AICT, vol. 715, pp. 47–61. Springer, Cham (2024). https://doi.org/10.1007/978-3-031-63227-3_4

3. Foreman-Peck, J., Zhou, P.: Digitalisation and the Digital Economy. In: Applied Economics in Globalised Economies. Palgrave Macmillan, Cham (2025). https://doi.org/10.1007/978-3-031-85621-1_12
4. Gawer, A.: Digital platforms and ecosystems: remarks on the dominant organizational forms of the digital age. Innovation **24**(1), 110–124 (2022). https://doi.org/10.1080/14479338.2021.1965888
5. Constantinides, P., Henfridsson, O., Parker, G.G.: Introduction - platforms and infrastructures in the digital age. Inf. Syst. Res. **29**(2), 381–400. https://doi.org/10.1287/isre.2018.0794
6. Skare, M., de las Mercedes de Obesso, M., Ribeiro-Navarrete, S.: Digital transformation and European small and medium enterprises (SMEs): a comparative study using digital economy and society index data. Int. J. Inf. Manag. **68**, 102594 (2023), https://doi.org/10.1016/j.ijinfomgt.2022.102594
7. Bouwman, H., Nikou, S., de Reuver, M.: Digitalization, business models, and SMEs: how do business model innovation practices improve performance of digitalizing SMEs? Telecommunications Policy **43**(9), 101828 (2019). https://doi.org/10.1016/j.telpol.2019.101828
8. European Commission: Measuring the impact of digital solutions on the climate (2024). https://digital-strategy.ec.europa.eu/en/news/measuring-impact-digital-solutions-climate
9. McKinsey Global Institute: Smart cities: Digital solutions for a more livable future (2018). https://www.mckinsey.com/capabilities/operations/our-insights/smart-cities-digital-solutions-for-a-more-livable-future
10. Silva, B.N., Khan, M., Han, K.: Towards sustainable smart cities: a review of trends, architectures, components, and open challenges in smart cities. Sustain. Cities Soc. **38**, 697–713 (2018). https://doi.org/10.1016/j.scs.2018.01.053
11. Giordano, M., Hieronimus, S., Smit, S., et al.: Accelerating Europe: Competitiveness for a new era. McKinsey Global Institute (2024). https://www.mckinsey.com/mgi/our-research/accelerating-europe-competitiveness-for-a-new-era
12. Arjoune, Y., Faruque, S.: Artificial Intelligence for 5G Wireless Systems: Opportunities, Challenges, and Future Research Directions. Cornell University (2020). https://arxiv.org/pdf/2009.04943
13. Chen, W., Lin, X., Lee, J., et al.: 5G-Advanced Towards 6G: Past, Present, and Future. Cornell University (2023). https://arxiv.org/abs/2303.07456
14. Bittencourt, L.F., Rodrigues-Filho, R., Spillner, J., De Turck, F., Santos, J., et al.: The computing continuum: past, present, and future. Comput. Sci. Rev. **58**, 100782 (2025). https://doi.org/10.1016/j.cosrev.2025.100782
15. Agarwal, K., Agarwal, K., Jha, A.K., Joshi, I.: Intelligence and internet of things with 5G technology: application and development. In: Proceedings of the 2022 International Conference on Electronics and Renewable Systems (ICEARS), 16–18 March 2022, Tuticorin, India, pp.762–766. IEEE (2022). https://doi.org/10.1109/ICEARS53579.2022.9752190
16. Kostopoulos, A., Chochliouros, I.P., Lyberopoulos, G., Panaretou, I., et al.: An IoT framework for AI-based surveillance applications. In: Papaleonidas, A., Pimenidis, E., Papadopoulos, H., Chochliouros I.P. (eds.), AIAI-2025, AICT, vol. 753, pp.45–55. Springer, Switzerland (2025). https://doi.org/10.1007/978-3-031-97317-8_4
17. Zhang, H., Zhang, R., Sun, J.: Developing real-time IoT-based public safety alert and emergency response systems. Sci. Rep. **15**, 29056 (2025). https://doi.org/10.1038/s41598-025-13465-7
18. Ali, K., Nguyen, H.X., Vien, Q.T., et al.: Review and implementation of resilient public safety networks: 5G, IoT and emerging technologies. IEEE Network **35**(2), 18–25 (2021). https://doi.org/10.1109/MNET.011.2000418

19. Joglekar, P., Jha, D., Dhorage, P., Thakkar, D., Dhumal, O.: Intelligent public surveillance system. In: Proceedings of the 2025 3rd International Conference on Intelligent Systems, Advanced Computing and Communication (ISACC), 27–28 February 2025, Silchar, India, pp. 323–328 (2025). https://doi.org/10.1109/ISACC65211.2025.10969367
20. Baliyar Singh, R.K., Dash, J.K., Reddy, K.H.K: The role of Edge-AI in edge enabled IoT systems: a comprehensive performance analysis. Peer-to-Peer Netw. Appl. **19**, 35 (2026). https://doi.org/10.1007/s12083-025-02182-7
21. Socha, R., Kogut, B.: Urban video surveillance as a tool to improve security in public spaces. Sustainability **12**(15), 6210. https://doi.org/10.3390/su12156210
22. Wiz Experts Team: What is AI Incident Response? Benefits and Use Cases (2026). https://www.wiz.io/academy/detection-and-response/ai-for-incident-response
23. Demir, A.H., Yavas, B., Yazici, M., Aksu, D., Aydin, M.A.: Object Detection and Tracking with Autonomous UAV. Cornell University (2022). https://arxiv.org/pdf/2206.12941
24. Kumar, S., Tiwari, A., Ahirwar, Y., Kumar, G., Arafat, M.Y.: The rise of UAV-based smart surveillance: a systematic review of trends and technologies. IEEE Access **13**, 181553–181575 (2025). https://doi.org/10.1109/ACCESS.2025.3621736
25. Ham, Y., Han, K.K., Lin, J.J., Golparvar-Fard, M.: Visual monitoring of civil infrastructure systems via camera-equipped unmanned aerial vehicles (UAVs): a review of related works. Vis. Eng. **4**(1), 1–8 (2016). https://doi.org/10.1186/s40327-015-0029-z
26. Jumpcloud: What is SFTP (Secure File Transfer Protocol)? (2025). https://jumpcloud.com/it-index/what-is-sftp-secure-file-transfer-protocol
27. YOLOv8. https://yolov8.com/
28. Hostinger: CentOS vs Ubuntu: which one to choose for your web server? (2025). https://www.hostinger.com/tutorials/centos-vs-ubuntu
29. Tsirtsakis, P., Zacharis, G., et al.: Deep learning for object recognition: a comprehensive review of models and algorithms. Int. J. Cogn. Comput. Eng. **6**, 298–312 (2025). https://doi.org/10.1016/j.ijcce.2025.01.004
30. Eenaja, A., Gunda, R., et al.: Improving public safety through AI and machine learning-driven CCTV surveillance systems. Int. J. Progress. Res. Eng. Manag. Sci. **5**(6), 2627–2635 (2025)
31. Jacob, T.P., Pravin, A., Rajakumar, R.: An AI-powered smart camera for object detection. In: Proceedings of the 2021 6th International Conference on Communication and Electronics Systems (ICCES), 08–10 July 2021, Coimbatre, India, 2021, pp.1701–1703 (2021). https://doi.org/10.1109/ICCES51350.2021.9489064
32. Koutromanos, G., Kazakou, G.: Augmented reality smart glasses use and acceptance: a literature review. Comput. Educ.: X Reality **2**, 100028 (2023). https://doi.org/10.1016/j.cexr.2023.100028
33. LabelImg Website. https://labelimg.org/
34. Ferreira, D., Basiri, M.: Dynamic target tracking and following with UAVs using multi-target information: leveraging YOLOv8 and MOT algorithms. Drones **8**(9), 488 (2024). https://doi.org/10.3390/drones8090488
35. Hussain, M.: YOLO-v1 to YOLO-v8, the rise of YOLO and its complementary nature toward digital manufacturing and industrial defect detection. Machines **11**(7), 677 (2023). https://doi.org/10.3390/machines11070677
36. Altowaijri, S.M., Ayari, M.: The synergistic impact of 5G on cloud-to-edge computing and the evolution of digital applications. Mathematics **13**(16), 2634 (2025). https://doi.org/10.3390/math13162634
37. Ma, X., Xu, M., Li, Q., Li, Y., Zhou, A., and Wang, S.: 5G Edge Computing – Technologies, Applications and Future Visions. Springer, Cham (2024). https://doi.org/10.1007/978-981-97-0213-8
38. The 5G Infrastructure Association (5G-IA): European Vision for the 6G Network Ecosystem (2021). https://doi.org/10.5281/zenodo.5007671

39. Schaeffer, D., Drake, S., Olson, P.C.: A taxonomy of 5G stakeholders. In: Proceedings of the 2021 IEEE 4th 5G World Forum (5GWF), 13–15 October 2021, Montreal, QC, Canada, 2021, 13–15 October 2021, pp. 358–361. IEEE (2021)
40. Chochliouros, I.P., Spiliopoulou, A.S., Lazaridis, P., et al.: Dynamic network slicing: challenges and opportunities. In: Maglogiannis, I., Iliadis, L., Pimenidis, E. (eds.) AIAI-2020, AICT, vol.585, pp.47–60. Springer, Cham (2020). https://doi.org/10.1007/978-3-030-49190-1_5
41. The Third Generation Partnership Project (3GPP): 5G System Overview (2022). https://www.3gpp.org/technologies/5g-system-overview
42. Barletta, F., Massimiani, F. Pierangeli, F., Spada, M.R., et al.: 5G networks. an overall perspective for the innovation management. In: Proceedings of the 2018 IEEE 4th International Forum on Research and Technology for Society and Industry (RTSI), 10–13 September 2018, Palermo, Italy, pp.1–4. IEEE (2018). https://doi.org/10.1109/RTSI.2018.8548354

Applying Trustful APIs for Quality on-Demand and Traffic Influence

Andreea Ancuta Corici[1](✉), Rohit Sengupta[2], Hemant Zope[1], Marius Corici[1], and Adela Sescu[2]

[1] Fraunhofer FOKUS Institute, Berlin, Germany
{andreea.ancuta.corici,hemant.zope, marius-iulian.corici}@fokus.fraunhofer.de
[2] Slicefinity, London, UK
{rohit.sengupta,adela.sescu}@slicefinity.com
https://fokus.fraunhofer.de, https://slicefinity.com/

Abstract. Network APIs remain largely unfamiliar to the application development community, which results in limited commercialization of exposed mobile network capabilities despite the significant progress achieved in recent standardization efforts. Recent 3GPP releases and open industry initiatives such as CAMARA aim to simplify the exposure and consumption of network functionalities through standardized and developer-friendly interfaces. However, the lack of a trusted execution and validation environment still prevents application developers from efficiently testing, validating, and refining innovative service concepts.

This paper proposes a Trusted Application Function that bridges the gap between programmable network exposure and practical application experimentation. The solution provides controlled access to CAMARA-aligned Network APIs, integrates authorization and policy enforcement, and enables end-to-end validation within a real testbed environment. The approach is validated through healthcare and automotive traffic-influence scenarios, demonstrating measurable improvements in latency, prioritization, and service reliability. The results underline the importance of trusted middleware for accelerating Network API adoption toward 6G programmable and intent-driven networks.

Keywords: Beyond 5G · CAMARA APIs · Quality on Demand

1 Introduction

The exposure of mobile network capabilities through standardized Network APIs marks a key shift toward programmable communication systems. 3GPP and CAMARA simplify capability access, yet adoption remains limited due to the lack of trusted environments for controlled experimentation across heterogeneous operators. Meanwhile, verticals like healthcare and automotive require deterministic connectivity that best-effort networks cannot ensure, making trusted,

Published by Springer Nature Switzerland AG 2027
A. Papaleonidas et al. (Eds.): AIAI 2026 Workshops, IFIP AICT 796, pp. 131–142, 2027.
https://doi.org/10.1007/978-3-032-30507-7_8

policy-driven use of Quality on Demand and Traffic Influence essential. To address this limitation, this paper introduces the concept and implementation of a Trusted Application Function that mediates secure and policy-compliant access to CAMARA-aligned Network APIs while providing orchestration, abstraction, and validation capabilities within a controlled experimental environment. The proposed approach enables application developers to interact with programmable connectivity features under realistic network conditions and supports measurable evaluation in representative vertical scenarios. The remainder of this paper presents the relevant background and standardization context, derives requirements from healthcare and automotive use cases, details the proposed solution architecture, and reports validation results obtained within a 5G testbed deployment.

2 Background

The background section positions the proposed Trusted Application Function within the evolving landscape of standardized capability exposure and developer-facing Network APIs.

2.1 Relevant Standards and Initiatives

Programmable network exposure is driven by complementary standardization and ecosystem efforts that turn mobile networks into service platforms. In 3GPP, the Network Exposure Function and TS29.522 enable secure interaction between applications and core services [1]. GSMA Open Gateway, CAMARA, and TMForum Open APIs jointly define interoperable, commercially scalable Network APIs [5–7,12], yet integration across diverse implementations remains complex [13]. Within the SNS-JU landscape, most projects focus on 6G architecture, experimentation, AI, sustainability, and security [14–16], while governance frameworks such as CAPIF [8] emphasize discovery and access control [2]. Orchestration and validation of Network API use by verticals are still only partially addressed, motivating the Trusted Application Function proposed in this paper as a complementary orchestration, authorization, and validation layer for scalable, trustworthy Network API consumption in enterprise scenarios.

2.2 CAMARA APIs Deep Dive

CAMARA is a global open-source initiative that defines standardized telecom Network APIs to expose mobile network capabilities through simple, consistent, and developer-oriented interfaces. Hosted by the Linux Foundation and supported by collaboration among operators, the GSMA, cloud providers, and the developer ecosystem, it aligns standardized exposure models with operational deployment realities. By translating underlying 3GPP exposure mechanisms into consumable service interfaces, CAMARA abstracts operator-specific complexity and enables application portability across heterogeneous network environments [7].

A key characteristic of CAMARA is the structured grouping of exposed capabilities into functional API domains reflecting concrete application needs. The principal capability groups include:

- **Identity and security APIs**, enabling number verification without Short Message Service (SMS)-based authentication, SIM-swap detection for fraud prevention, and device reachability validation.
- **Quality-of-service APIs**, allowing applications to request guaranteed latency, bandwidth, or prioritization for specific sessions, thereby supporting latency-sensitive services such as cloud gaming, immersive media, and remote control.
- **Location APIs**, exposing network-derived device positioning with appropriate consent handling to support logistics optimization, regulatory compliance, and anomaly detection.
- **Connectivity and network-information APIs**, providing visibility into access technology, roaming status, and coverage conditions.
- **Messaging and event APIs**, delivering network-triggered notifications and lifecycle callbacks associated with device or session state.

From an implementation perspective, CAMARA APIs are typically realized as RESTful services described using OpenAPI specifications and secured through OAuth 2.0 [19] and OpenID-based authorization frameworks [4,20]. This design enables deployment through operator API gateways, federation via aggregators, and exposure through hyperscaler marketplaces, thereby supporting multi-operator reach and cloud-native integration patterns. In addition, the separation between CAMARA technical API definition and the GSMA Open Gateway commercial exposure establishes a layered ecosystem in which interoperability, scalability, and monetization can evolve independently while remaining technically aligned [5].

Beyond immediate 5G applicability, the CAMARA abstraction model anticipates future service exposure paradigms in which programmable connectivity, edge compute interaction, contextual awareness, and trust mechanisms converge into unified developer-consumable interfaces. As such, CAMARA constitutes a foundational step toward intent-driven and application-aware networking envisioned for 6G systems, where network behavior becomes dynamically controllable through standardized service APIs [9,10].

3 Requirements Analysis

This section derives functional and operational requirements for the trusted mediation of Network API usage by vertical applications, focusing on healthcare and automotive scenarios needing deterministic connectivity and controlled traffic steering.

In the SNS JU 6G-PATH chronic wound management prototype, a community nurse uses a mobile app to create 3D wound models while consulting a remote expert via multimedia communication. Reliable connectivity is required for model upload, interactive sessions, and access to historical 3D models and analytics (depth, surface, volume). Under congestion, traffic prioritization is needed to ensure timely upload of models and download of analytical results. CAMARA-based Quality on Demand [9] and Traffic Influence [10] allow the healthcare application to request bounded latency, sufficient bandwidth, and prioritized transmission for the duration of critical sessions; the mobile network enforces these requirements and releases resources when the session ends (see Fig. 1). This mechanism was validated in this paper over public mobile infrastructures, demonstrating healthcare-grade on-demand connectivity with operator-agnostic interoperability and improved safety and responsiveness for chronic wound documentation.

Similarly, connected transport systems (e.g., unmanned aerial vehicles and road vehicles) depend on predictable, reliable mobile connectivity with bounded latency, adequate bandwidth, and traffic prioritization for safety-critical, latency-sensitive functions such as navigation assistance, hazard signaling, emergency communication, remote control, and over-the-air updates, which cannot be consistently supported by best-effort networking.

4 Integrated Prototype Solution Design

The architecture of the integrated prototype that used to validate and evaluate the healthcare use case requirements relating to Quality on Demand and Traffic Influence is depicted in Fig. 2. On the application exposure side, the Trusted Application Function (T-AF) environment comprised dedicated services implementing Traffic Influence, Quality on Demand, and Network Slice Booking functionalities.

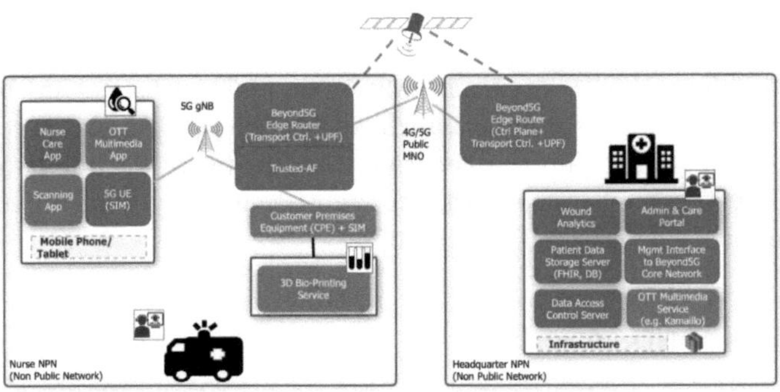

Fig. 1. Topology of the chronic wound management use case.

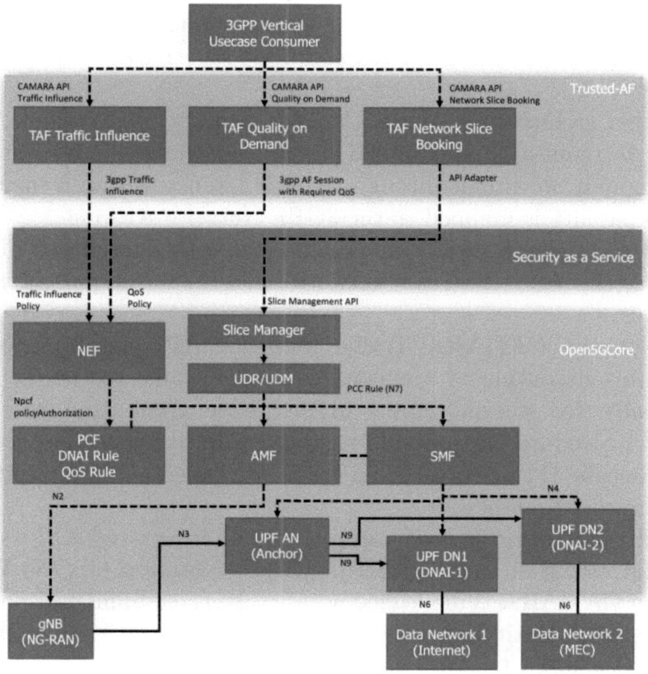

Fig. 2. Prototype architecture.

4.1 Mobile Core Network

The mobile core network of the testbed is based on the Open5GCore implementation, which provides a research-oriented realization of 5G core control and user-plane functions suitable for experimentation, validation, and integration with external service exposure components [17].

Within the testbed mobile core network, enforcement of programmable connectivity relied on the Network Exposure Function (NEF) and Policy Control Function (PCF), complemented by additional elements including Access and Mobility Management (AMF), Session Management (SMF), User Data Management (UDM), and multiple User Plane Functions (UPF) serving distinct data network instances.

4.2 Trusted AF

Network APIs are exposed to enterprise consumers through a Trusted Application Function (T-AF), which provides authorization, control, and policy enforcement required for secure and reliable service consumption. The T-AF authorizes third-party applications, such as healthcare sensors or drone controllers, while fulfilling CAMARA API procedures inside the telecom network via southbound integration and applying service-level agreement policies including capacity control, admission control, and service assurance to ensure predictable operational behavior.

Within this architecture, the CAMARA Quality on Demand API enables applications to request time-bounded prioritized quality of service in terms of uplink throughput, downlink throughput, and latency within a specified service area. This capability is mapped to the 3GPP Network API defined in TS 29.522 Release 17 for an Application Function session with guaranteed bit rate quality of service, through which the network enforces the requested performance characteristics.

In parallel, the CAMARA Traffic Influence API enables applications to request optimized routing of application-specific traffic to reduce latency and jitter, typically by steering flows toward edge computing resources. This time-limited procedure corresponds to the Traffic Influence service defined in TS 29.522 Release 17, where selected traffic is routed along an optimized path to achieve improved latency.

Secure exposure of these mechanisms relies on integrated API security based on OAuth authorization and JavaScript Object Notation (JSON) Web Tokens, together with CAMARA three-legged access tokens enabling user-consent-aware authorization and identity propagation across administrative domains [11]. This security model enables trustworthy interaction between enterprise applications and telecom network functions while preserving identity control, authorization integrity, and regulatory compliance.

5 Validation and Evaluation

The proposed Trusted Application Function solution was validated within the FOKUS 6G-PATH testbed environment in order to assess its capability to provide measurable value for vertical application scenarios consuming CAMARA-based Network APIs. The evaluation focused on demonstrating controlled traffic steering, temporary quality prioritization, and secure policy enforcement under realistic deployment conditions representative of enterprise service consumption.

The validation methodology combined functional verification with quantitative performance assessment. Functional validation ensured correct authorization, API invocation, and policy enforcement across the interaction between the Trusted Application Function, the Network Exposure Function, and the Policy Control Function. Quantitative evaluation analyzed latency reduction, throughput prioritization, and service differentiation achieved through Traffic Influence and Quality on Demand procedures, comparing baseline best-effort connectivity with policy-driven programmable connectivity.

All experiments were executed using an environment composed of real gNB and mobile phones, software mobile network core and trusted Application Function, as described in the previous section, and application-side services. This setup enabled reproducible experimentation while preserving deployment realism, thereby supporting credible assessment of the operational benefits introduced by programmable Network API exposure.

5.1 Testbed Setup

The deployment combined containerized application-side elements, native 5G core network functions, radio access infrastructure, including an Amarisoft software - based NG-RAN gNB implementation enabling configurable radio access experimentation and controlled QoS validation [18], and measurement tooling, thereby enabling controlled end-to-end experimentation of CAMARA-based Network API procedures. The T-AF service suite was deployed as Kubernetes containers, together with database service and database administration containers, as well as a web-based graphical user interface supporting API invocation and operational testing. These components collectively provided authorization, orchestration, lifecycle management, and persistent state handling for enterprise interaction with telecom network capabilities.

Secure connectivity between the external Trusted Application Function sandbox and the protected testbed environment was established using encrypted WireGuard tunneling [21], combined with policy-controlled authorization and slice-management interfaces to ensure isolation between trusted and non-trusted domains. Experimental tooling included Swagger-based interfaces for CAMARA API testing, web servers deployed within target data networks for reachability validation, *iperf*-based traffic generation and measurement, and controlled latency and packet-loss injection for Key Value Indicators (KPI) evaluation. This configuration enabled direct comparison between baseline best-effort connectivity and policy-driven programmable connectivity, thereby supporting quantitative validation of Traffic Influence and Quality on Demand behavior.

The following test scenarios were used for evaluating the value (KVI) created for vertical use case consumers.

5.2 Traffic Influence Test Scenario

The Traffic Influence capability was evaluated in a vertical application context where programmable edge steering is required to reduce end-to-end latency for latency-sensitive services. In this scenario, an application hosted on a multi-access edge computing platform, representative of healthcare or automotive workloads, invokes the CAMARA Traffic Influence API in order to steer application-specific traffic from the default mobile data path toward an optimized edge path. This steering operation is achieved through modification of the Data Network Access Identifier, enabling selective routing of the application flow while preserving standard routing for all other traffic.

Within the FOKUS testbed, controlled latency was intentionally introduced (see Fig. 3) along the default Data Network (DN) path associated with DN1, resulting in an observed end-to-end latency of approximately 80 ms. Following activation of the Traffic Influence procedure, application traffic was redirected toward the optimized edge path, where the measured latency decreased to approximately 20 ms, thereby demonstrating the quantitative performance improvement enabled by programmable traffic steering.

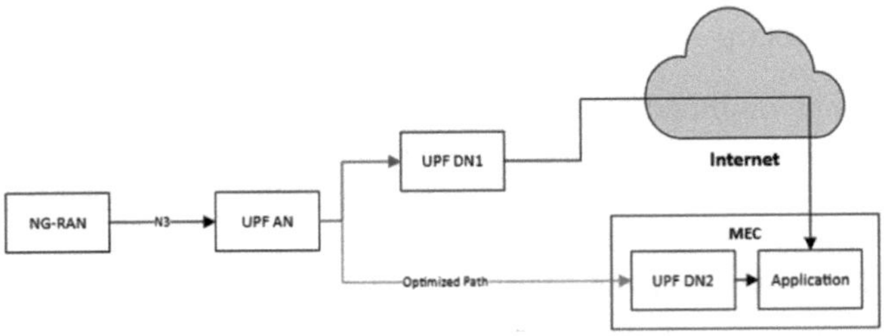

Fig. 3. Testbed setup - edge compute steering.

Finding: An additional validation aspect concerned selective traffic filtering. During Traffic Influence activation, it was validated that only flows matching the application-specific traffic filter were redirected toward the optimized path, while unrelated traffic, exemplified by external connectivity such as public Domain Name System (DNS) access, continued to traverse the default data network without interruption. This behavior confirms that Traffic Influence enables deterministic latency optimization for targeted application flows without impacting concurrent best-effort traffic.

The latency measurements summarized in Table 1 confirm the existence of two clearly separated performance regimes associated with default routing and Traffic Influence steering. Under baseline conditions, the red regime exhibits a mean round-trip latency of approximately 89 ms, while the steered green regime reduces the latency to approximately 21 ms, corresponding to a reduction of more than 70%. The reported 95% confidence intervals demonstrate statistical stability of both regimes across the evaluated samples.

The empirical latency distributions are further illustrated in Fig. 4, where the Cumulative Distribution Functions (DNF) show a distinct horizontal separation between the default and steered paths. This separation confirms deterministic path steering rather than stochastic fluctuation and provides quantitative evidence that programmable Traffic Influence enables predictable latency improvement for latency-sensitive application flows.

Table 1. Latency statistics for the three regimes (20 samples each).

Regime	Mean (ms)	Std (ms)	n	95% CI (± ms)
Red (before)	89.33	6.35	20	2.97
Green (steered)	20.58	5.77	20	2.70
Red (after)	89.33	6.35	20	2.97

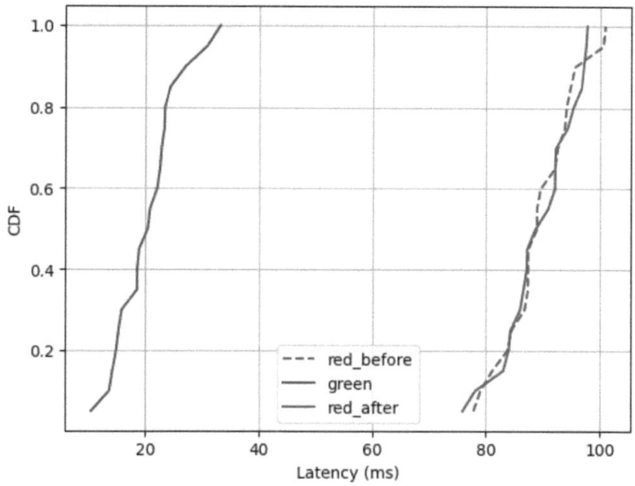

Fig. 4. Empirical CDF of round-trip latency for the three regimes (red-before, green-steered, red-after), each based on 20 samples. (Color figure online)

5.3 Quality on Demand Test Scenario

The Quality on Demand capability was evaluated in a vertical application scenario requiring temporary prioritization of network resources for mission-critical communication. In this scenario, the application specifies the device identity, flow description associated with the target application endpoint, and a QoS profile including uplink and downlink bitrate together with latency constraints. A representative use case considers an unmanned aerial vehicle delivering emergency medical supplies, where reliable and prioritized connectivity toward the backend control application is required during mission execution. The prioritization request is initiated through invocation of the CAMARA Quality on Demand API.

Within the FOKUS testbed, prioritization behavior was validated using a guaranteed bit rate QoS configuration corresponding to the expression $5QI = 1$, see [3]. The maximum uplink capacity provided by the radio access infrastructure was approximately 10 Mbps. Under baseline conditions, two user devices generating uplink traffic shared the available capacity equally, each achieving approximately 5 Mbps. After activation of the Quality on Demand procedure with the QoS profile `GBR_5QI1_Pri1_8Mbps`, the prioritized device achieved approximately 8 Mbps while the non-prioritized device was limited to approximately 2 Mbps, thereby confirming effective traffic prioritization.

From an operational perspective, practical deployments avoid the strict guaranteed bit rate enforcement and instead implement customized QoS policies within the next-generation radio access network that provide prioritization without absolute guarantees. As illustrated in Fig. 5, the prioritized end-to-end application flow is represented in green, the non-prioritized standard flow in grey, and unrelated background traffic not matching the QoD traffic filter in black, demonstrating selective prioritization without disruption of concurrent services.

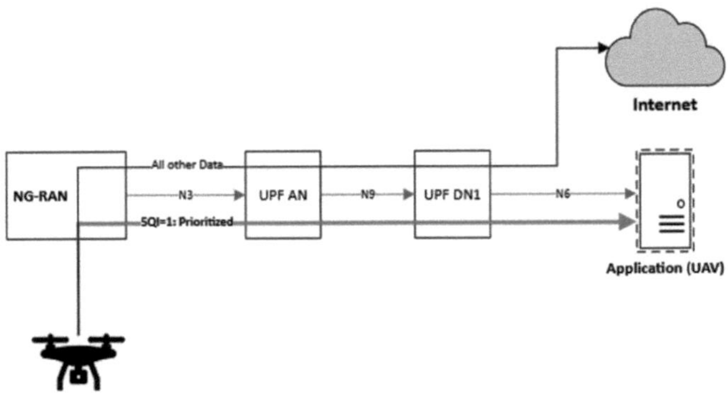

Fig. 5. Testbed setup - prioritization via Quality on Demand.

5.4 Lessons Learned

The experimental validation confirms that programmable Network API exposure enables measurable service differentiation for vertical applications, particularly in scenarios requiring latency steering and temporary quality prioritization. Traffic Influence demonstrated deterministic latency reduction through selective edge steering, while Quality on Demand validated controlled bandwidth prioritization without disrupting concurrent best-effort traffic. These results highlight the practical feasibility of policy-driven, application-aware connectivity over public mobile infrastructures.

At the same time, the evaluation reveals structural challenges that limit large-scale adoption of Network APIs in current deployments. Architectural diversity across operator environments, fragmented backend data sources, heterogeneous radio technologies, and regulatory constraints related to identity and data protection introduce integration complexity and increase operational cost. Consequently, standardized APIs alone are insufficient to guarantee seamless interoperability or rapid commercialization.

The Trusted Application Function emerges as a necessary middleware abstraction that consolidates authorization, orchestration, data normalization, and policy enforcement across heterogeneous network domains. By integrating security mechanisms, multi-source data handling, and service assurance procedures, the Trusted Application Function enables scalable and trustworthy exposure of capabilities to enterprise consumers using APIs alligned with the CAMARA standard specifications. This architectural role is expected to become increasingly relevant in the transition toward 6G systems, where intent-driven control, AI-assisted automation, and cross-domain programmability will require dependable mediation between applications and network intelligence.

6 Conclusion and Outlook

Network exposure is becoming strategically important as mobile systems evolve from pure connectivity to programmable service platforms. Market trends and standards point to Service Level Agreement (SLA) -driven connectivity where enterprises request performance aligned with application needs. The proposed Trusted Application Function enables controlled exposure and validation of the CAMARA - aligned Network APIs, demonstrated in a 5G testbed using Traffic Influence for deterministic latency reduction and Quality on Demand for temporary prioritization in mission-critical healthcare and automotive scenarios. These capabilities extend to domains such as media, industrial automation, and remote control, proving operational value when combined with trusted orchestration, policy enforcement, and secure authorization. However, architectural diversity, fragmented data, heterogeneous access, and regulatory constraints create integration complexity, highlighting the need for middleware that harmonizes data, protocols, and policies across domains. The Trusted Application Function provides this abstraction and is expected to be essential as 6G extends Network APIs toward compute, sensing, analytics, and AI-driven intent. CAMARA-aligned exposure with trusted orchestration is thus a key enabler for intelligent, service-driven 6G platforms, motivating further work on interoperability, AI-based policy automation, and cross-domain orchestration.

Acknowledgment. The presented activities are part of the 6G-PATH project, which received funding from the Smart Networks and Services Joint Undertaking (SNS JU) under the European Union's Horizon Europe research and innovation program under Grant Agreement Number 101139172. Fraunhofer FOKUS has the role of one of the testbeds and Slicefinity is engaged in the project through an accepted open call project.

References

1. 3GPP.5G System; Network Exposure Function Northbound APIs; Stage 3, 3GPP TS 29, vol. 522. Release 17/18 (2023)
2. 3GPP. Common API Framework for 3GPP Northbound APIs; Stage 2, 3GPP TS 23, vol. 222. Release 17/18 (2023)
3. 3GPP. System Architecture for the 5G System (5GS); Stage 2, 3GPP TS 23, vol. 501. Release 17/18 (2023)
4. 3GPP. Security architecture and procedures for 5G System, 3GPP TS 33, vol. 501. Release 17/18 (2023)
5. GSMA. GSMA Open Gateway Initiative: Exposing Network Capabilities via Common APIs, White Paper (2023)
6. GSMA. GSMA Open Gateway: Unlocking the Power of Network APIs. Accessed 2026. https://www.gsma.com/solutions-and-impact/gsma-open-gateway/open-gateway-unlocking-the-power-of-network-apis/
7. Linux Foundation. CAMARA Project Open Source Network API Framework. Accessed 2026. https://camaraproject.org/

8. Kulczak, F.: EVOLVED-5G announces the first release (Release 1.0) of the 3GPP CAPIF Core Function. 5G-PPP (2022). https://5g-ppp.eu/evolved-5g-announces-the-first-release-release-1-0-of-the-3gpp-capif-core-function/
9. Linux Foundation CAMARA. Quality on Demand API. Accessed 2026. https://camaraproject.org/quality-on-demand/
10. Linux Foundation CAMARA. Traffic Influence API. Accessed 2026. https://camaraproject.org/traffic-influence/
11. Linux Foundation CAMARA. CAMARA API access and user consent management. Accessed 2026. https://github.com/camaraproject/IdentityAndConsentManagement/blob/main/documentation/CAMARA-API-access-and-user-consent.md
12. TM Forum. TM Forum Open APIs and Interoperability Framework. Technical Overview (2023)
13. Yrjölä, S., Ahokangas, M., Matinmikko-Blue, D.: Platform-based business models for 5G and beyond. Telecommun. Policy **44**(9) (2020)
14. SNS JU. European Smart Networks and Services Strategic Research and Innovation Agenda for 6G. Smart Networks and Services Joint Undertaking (2023)
15. Hexa-X-II Consortium. Hexa-X-II Vision and Architectural Framework for 6G Networks. European SNS JU Project Deliverable (2024)
16. 6G-SANDBOX Consortium. 6G-SANDBOX: Experimental Platform for Future 6G Technologies. European SNS JU Project Deliverable (2023)
17. Fraunhofer FOKUS. Open5GCore: 5G Core Network for Research, Testbeds and Trials. Accessed 2026. https://open5gcore.org/
18. Amarisoft. LTE/NR Software gNB Documentation (LTEENB). Accessed 2026. https://tech-academy.amarisoft.com/lteenb.doc
19. Hardt, D.: The OAuth 2.0 Authorization Framework. IETF RFC 6749 (2012)
20. Sakimura, N., Bradley, J., Jones, M., de Medeiros, B., Mortimore, C.: OpenID Connect Core 1.0. OpenID Foundation (2014)
21. Donenfeld, J.A.: WireGuard: next generation kernel network tunnel. In: Proceedings of Network and Distributed System Security Symposium (NDSS) (2017)

Bridging the Adoption Gap: A Techno-Economic and Strategic Commercialisation Framework for 6G Across European Verticals

Imesha D. Premarathne[1](✉), Vishanth Weerakkody[1], Jing Li[1], Uthayasankar Sivarajah[2], Ioannis Chochliouros[3], and Luís Cordeiro[4]

[1] University of Bradford, Bradford, Richmond Road, Bradford, West Yorkshire BD7 1DP, UK
idpwedik@bradford.ac.uk

[2] Kingston Business School, Kingston Hill Campus, Kingston upon Thames, Surrey KT2 7LB, UK

[3] Hellenic Telecommunications Organization S.A. (OTE), 99 Kifissias Avenue, 151 24 Maroussi, Athens, Greece

[4] One Source, Consultoria Informática Lda., Lote 12, 3030 Coimbra, Portugal

Abstract. The transition of sixth-generation (6G) mobile networks from research excellence to market deployment depends not only on technological maturity, but also on techno-economic design, regulatory harmonisation, and ecosystem alignment. This paper draws on early findings from the Horizon Europe SNS JU 6G-PATH project, which studies ten use cases across Smart Farming, Education, Healthcare, and Smart Cities verticals. The use cases are positioned on the Technology Readiness Level (TRL) and Technology Adoption Life Cycle (TALC) scales on the basis of secondary market analysis, refined through expert panel review. All use cases occupy TRL 4–6, constrained by rural connectivity gaps, regulatory fragmentation, skills deficits, and uncertain return on investment. Six recurrent commercialisation pathways are then comparatively assessed, and a Transformative Commercialisation Model (TCM) is proposed. The TCM builds on existing European telecom policy tools; universal service obligations, spectrum coverage requirements, and co-investment rules, and adds a new mechanism in which funding and access are linked to verified real-world outcomes measured through Key Value Indicators (KVIs). The paper maps the key policy instruments and responsible regulators required for scale, and outlines validation steps for later phases of 6G-PATH.

Keywords: 6G · Techno-economics · Commercialisation · TALC · TRL

1 Introduction

Sixth-generation (6G) networks are emerging as a foundational infrastructure for Europe's digital economy, extending beyond capacity improvements to an AI-native platform integrating ultra-low latency, terahertz spectrum, massive machine-type communications, and sensing capabilities [13, 25]. Supported by the Smart Networks and

Published by Springer Nature Switzerland AG 2027
A. Papaleonidas et al. (Eds.): AIAI 2026 Workshops, IFIP AICT 796, pp. 143–157, 2027.
https://doi.org/10.1007/978-3-032-30507-7_9

Services Joint Undertaking (SNS JU) under Horizon Europe, with over €900 million allocated for 2021–2027, 6G is central to Europe's technological sovereignty ambitions, with deployment expected by 2030 [16, 25].

Despite strong public investment, the transition from proof-of-concept to sustainable deployment remains uncertain. Existing European telecom policy instruments, such as universal service obligations, spectrum coverage conditions, European Electronic Communications Code (EECC)-based co-investment, and state-aid broadband schemes, have not achieved balanced sectoral diffusion, leaving gaps in areas like farming, rural education, and healthcare [4, 11, 15, 18, 30]. This highlights the need to reassess policy tools for alignment with vertical, outcome-oriented services.

Current research has primarily focused on technological and architectural aspects of 6G, with limited integration of techno-economic, commercialisation, and policy dimensions into a unified framework [19, 24, 28]. To address this gap, the 6G-PATH project analyses ten use cases across four verticals, combining technology validation with business model development. This paper synthesises these insights and contributes in three ways: by positioning all use cases along TRL and TALC scales using a structured consortium-driven process; by comparatively analysing six commercialisation pathways; and by proposing a Transformative Commercialisation Model (TCM) aligned with telecom policy instruments rather than generic business frameworks. Accordingly, the study aims to address three research questions (RQ) as follows.

RQ1. How technologically and market-ready are the 6G-PATH use cases as measured jointly by the TRL scale and the TALC model?

RQ2. Which commercialisation pathways are emerging across these four verticals, and how do they compare in terms of core logic, vertical-specific suitability, and exposure to the structural barriers constraining 6G diffusion?

RQ3. How can established European electronic-communications instruments such as universal service obligations under the EECC, spectrum-auction coverage conditions, and EECC Article 76 co-investment be extended to support outcome-conditioned, inclusive 6G commercialisation that reaches Late-Majority and Laggard adopter segments?

RQ1 is addressed in Sect. 4, RQ2 in Sect. 5, and RQ3 in Sects. 6 and 7. Rest of the chapter organization is as follows. Section 2 reviews the theoretical and policy foundations. Section 3 describes the methodology followed by Sect. 4 which presents the cross-vertical readiness analysis. Section 5 presents the commercialisation pathway comparison. Section 6 introduces the TCM and Sect. 7 provides the barrier-instrument-regulator mapping. Section 8 concludes with limitations and future work.

2 Background and Related Work

2.1 European 6G Policy Context

The European 6G agenda rests on three interlocking instruments. The SNS JU under Horizon Europe Cluster 4 coordinates pre-commercial 6G research, of which 6G-PATH belongs to Stream [31]. The Gigabit Infrastructure Act (Regulation (EU) 2024/1309) establishes gigabit-connectivity targets and legal frameworks for rapid rural deployment

[6]. The Digital Decade Policy Programme (Decision (EU) 2022/2481) sets measurable 2030 targets including gigabit coverage for all European households and, per its statutory text, "at least 75% of Union enterprises" using cloud, big data, and AI [9]. The harmonisation of spectrum allocation, data-sovereignty frameworks (including the GDPR, Data Act, and Data Governance Act), and sector-specific compliance regimes (such as the Medical Device Regulation [MDR] and the Radio Equipment Directive [RED] Class III delegated acts) remains significantly uneven across EU Member States [5, 20]. This fragmentation is driven by delayed national designation of competent authorities, divergent enforcement of penalty regimes, and critical capacity bottlenecks within national notified bodies.

2.2 Telecoms-Native Reference Points

For a techno-economics audience, a vertical connectivity commercialisation framework should be grounded in established European electronic-communications policy instruments rather than generic Business Model Canvas derivatives. Four instruments are particularly relevant: universal service obligations under the EECC, which require minimum adequate broadband availability from designated operators, historically supported through universal service funds [8]; spectrum-auction coverage obligations for bands such as 700 MHz, 3.4–3.8 GHz and 26 GHz, aligned with RSPG strategic opinions and CEPT/ECC technical frameworks, requiring population, geographic or indoor-connectivity targets [7]; FTTH and high-capacity co-investment under EECC Article 76, allowing dominant operators to offer regulated co-investment access in exchange for regulatory relief [1]; and state-aid-cleared public-private schemes under the 2023 Gigabit State-Aid Guidelines [10]. These instruments share a common logic: exchanging regulatory relief or public subsidy for accelerated deployment where market forces alone are insufficient. However, they remain calibrated to connectivity outputs, such as lines passed or population covered, rather than vertical outcomes. The TCM proposed in Sect. 6 therefore extends this toolkit by replacing coverage conditions with an outcome-based, KVI-triggered revenue-share mechanism.

2.3 Technology Readiness, TALC, and Ecosystem Frameworks

The TRL framework defines nine stages from basic principles (TRL 1) to operational deployment (TRL 9) [14]. Current 6G research is generally positioned at TRL 3–4, with advanced pilots at TRL 5–6 and commercial deployment expected around 2030. The TALC model, based on Rogers' Diffusion of Innovations [29] and Moore's "crossing the chasm" [21], classifies adopters as Innovators, Early Adopters, Early Majority, Late Majority, and Laggards. However, TALC was developed for consumer-technology diffusion and does not fully reflect institutional procurement cycles in sectors such as healthcare, education, and agriculture; its adopter proportions are also descriptive rather than predictive. Accordingly, this paper uses TALC as a segmentation framework, not a forecasting model, and combines it with TRL and policy analysis to capture technological maturity and deployment context. Techno-economic analysis is widely used in telecommunications to assess deployment feasibility, cost structures, and adoption dynamics, especially across 4G, 5G, and emerging 6G transitions. It typically combines technical performance, cost, demand, and policy variables to evaluate commercial viability under uncertainty. Business-model theory is considered as a supporting lens, including Osterwalder's Business Model Canvas [23], the Triple Layered Canvas [17], the Ecosystem Pie Model [32], and Hexa-X-II's ecosystem approach [35]; however, this study grounds its commercialisation pathway typology in telecoms-native practice. Overall, prior work has examined 6G policy, techno-economic readiness, and business models largely separately. Limited research integrates technology maturity, market adoption dynamics, and telecom regulatory instruments into a single framework, particularly for vertical-specific deployments requiring outcome-oriented service models beyond existing connectivity-focused policy tools. This study addresses this gap by combining TRL–TALC readiness assessment, cross-vertical commercialisation pathways, and telecom policy instruments within one analytical framework.

3 Methodology

This study employs a mixed-method research design combining secondary market analysis with a structured, multi-stage consortium elicitation process of expert panel review. The empirical basis consists of ten 6G-PATH use-case business-model analyses and their consortium-validated assessments, drawing on early-phase techno-economic insights from an active Horizon Europe pilot rather than post-deployment data.

In Stage 1, a systematic review of secondary sources, including industry reports, EU policy documents, OECD and UNESCO materials, and academic literature was conducted. This informed the development of an initial analytical framework comprising cross-vertical readiness assessment (based on TRL and TALC), a typology of six commercialisation pathways, a preliminary Transformative Commercialisation Model (TCM), and an initial mapping of regulatory barriers.

Stage 2 involved a structured workshop with six commercialisation experts from the 6G-PATH consortium and affiliated organisations. The workshop evaluated the completeness of the commercialisation pathways and the coherence of the TCM with European telecom policy instruments, leading to targeted refinements of the framework.

In Stage 3, the revised framework was validated through a workshop with 31expert consortium partners including vertical champions representing the ten use cases. The detailed discussions with these expert review panel confirmed TRL and TALC classifications and contributed to refining barrier-instrument-regulator mappings. Where uncertainty persisted, TRL values were expressed as ranges, with conservative estimates adopted. The final framework was subsequently endorsed by the full consortium as the consolidated cross-vertical commercialisation position.

Three limitations were identified. First, the absence of large-scale primary end-user data limits quantitative validation, which is planned for Phase 2 trials. Second, industry projections may reflect optimism bias and are treated as indicative. Third, while expert and champion validation ensures strong triangulation, it does not provide statistical robustness. Future work will address this through large-scale adopter surveys across the four verticals.

4 Cross-Vertical 6G Adoption Readiness

4.1 Vertical-Level Market Signals

The four 6G-PATH verticals display distinct demand dynamics but converge within a similar maturity range. Smart Farming is expected to grow steadily, supported by European policy frameworks, though constrained by rural connectivity gaps, fragmented interoperability, and uneven digital adoption [12]. Healthcare shows strong growth potential, with expanding 5G-enabled use cases such as teleconsultation, remote monitoring, and AI-driven clinical workflows, alongside increasing maturity of enabling technologies such as network slicing [26, 33]. In contrast, the Education sector faces persistent structural challenges in digital readiness and infrastructure, with disparities linked more to institutional resources than student demographics [3, 34]. Smart Cities represent the fastest-growing vertical in Europe, with significant projected investment, driving increased focus on complex, multi-stakeholder business-model design for urban digital infrastructure [27].

4.2 TRL and TALC Positioning

Table 1 consolidates the TRL and TALC assessment produced through the consortium process described in Sect. 3.

Two key patterns emerge from the cross-vertical analysis in Table 1. First, the 6G-specific integration layer is consistently positioned within the TRL 4–6 range, indicating a shared intermediate level of technological maturity across all use cases. Second, most use cases are situated at the transition between Innovators and Early Adopters in the TALC, with the exception of UC-CITIES-3. It represents a structural outlier, despite relatively advanced technical maturity (TRL 6), its market adoption remains limited to Late Majority or Laggard segments. This divergence is largely due to the continued reliance on legacy TETRA/TETRAPOL systems in public-safety contexts, where adoption is shaped by stringent reliability requirements, regulatory embedding, institutional inertia, and professional alignment, leading to increased resistance to technological substitution. Overall, this heterogeneity highlights the need for a commercialisation framework that addresses not only early-stage adoption but also the structural barriers present in later TALC segments.

4.3 Structural Barriers

Four structural barriers emerge consistently across the analysed verticals, shaping both technology adoption and commercial viability. First, rural connectivity gaps, where persistent rural-urban infrastructure divides in smart farming [12], limited rural 5G coverage in healthcare relative to urban areas [26], and uneven digital readiness of schools [34]. At the European level, harmonisation of terahertz (THz) spectrum bands for emerging 6G applications remains limited [5, 20]. At the national level, implementation of digital strategies such as those under the Common Agricultural Policy (CAP) Strategic Plans varies considerably across Member States [12]. In addition, sector-specific regulatory frameworks, including the General Data Protection Regulation (GDPR), are

Table 1. TRL and TALC positioning of 6G-PATH use cases.

Vertical	Use Case	TRL	TALC	Condensed Rationale
Smart Farming	UC-FARM-1 Water Saving	**5–6**	Early Adopters	Precision irrigation commercially mature; 6G real-time phenological processing and drone orchestration in relevant-environment validation
	UC-FARM-2 Smart Vineyards	**4–5**	Innovators-Early Adopters	Multi-source data fusion lab-validated; Automated Guided Vehicle (AGV)/ Autonomous Aerial Vehicle (AAV) integration with 5G/6G networks in initial trial
Education	UC-EDU-1 Extended Reality (XR) Rural School	**5**	Early Adopters	Mobile XR (XR Caravan) validated in lab; budget and rural-connectivity constraints limit field expansion
	UC-EDU-2 Classroom of the Future	**5–6**	Early Adopters	XR prototypes demonstrated; haptic/wearable integration in live teaching still controlled
	UC-EDU-3 XR Health Training	**5**	Early Adopters	Medical simulation validated in controlled environments; professional-training market offers higher willingness-to-pay
Healthcare	UC-HEALTH-1 3D Hydrogel Patches	**5–6**	Innovators-Early Adopters	3D medical printing lab-validated; nomadic micro-networks experimental; novel-device regulatory pathways add friction

(continued)

Table 1. (*continued*)

Vertical	Use Case	TRL	TALC	Condensed Rationale
	UC-HEALTH-2 Elderly Monitoring	**6**	Early Adopters-Early Majority	Wearable monitoring commercially available; AI predictive analytics validated; demographics drive demand
Smart Cities	UC-CITIES-1 Connected & Sensing City	**5–6**	Early Adopters	High-distribution video leverages 5G; predictive traffic orchestration demonstrated in controlled settings
	UC-CITIES-2 Automated Logistics	**6**	Early Adopters-Early Majority	AGV tech mature (components TRL 7–8); 6G-specific integration at demonstration level
	UC-CITIES-3 Security Coordination	**6**	Late Majority / Laggard (entrenched legacy)	Mission-critical comms established; Terrestrial Trunked Radio (TETRA)/TETRAPOL (brand name of a digital professional mobile radio standard developed by Airbus Defence and Space), competing with TETRA) entrenchment creates displacement barriers despite technical maturity

interpreted and applied inconsistently in education and healthcare contexts, creating further barriers to scalable service deployment [5]. Third, digital literacy and skills deficits constrain effective adoption across multiple sectors. End users in farming, education, and healthcare often lack the technical competencies required to integrate advanced digital solutions into existing workflows, thereby slowing diffusion even where infrastructure is available. Fourth, uncertain return on investment (ROI) presents a critical economic barrier. Potential adopters frequently face substantial upfront costs, while the long-term economic benefits of 6G-enabled services remain insufficiently demonstrated, particularly in early-stage deployments. This uncertainty reduces investment incentives and contributes to delayed adoption across all verticals.

5 Commercialisation Pathways

From the ten use-case analyses, six commercialisation pathways emerge as dominant (Table 2).

Table 2. Commercialisation pathways across 6G-PATH use cases.

Pathway	Core Logic	Key Strengths	High-Suitability Verticals
Platform as a Service (PaaS) / Platform	Subscription or pay-per-use access to integrated 6G services	Low upfront CAPEX; scalable; fits resource-constrained adopters	All four verticals; especially Education, Healthcare, Smart Cities
Data as a Service (DaaS)	Monetisation of aggregated datasets for insurers, policymakers, researchers	Recurring revenue independent of end-user willingness-to-pay	Smart Farming (phenological); Smart Cities (mobility/environmental)
Direct Sales & Licensing	Outright sale of hardware and licensing of software IP	Clear revenue recognition; fits conventional procurement	Healthcare devices; Smart Farming (agribusinesses); municipal
Private-Public-Partnership (PPP)	Co-financing between public authorities, operators, and vendors	De-risks deployment; aligns with EU funding; enables scale pilots	All verticals; central to Education and Smart Cities
Open Innovation	Open calls, APIs, community-driven content	Accelerates innovation; broadens ecosystem	Education (content co-creation); Smart Cities (third-party apps)
Hybrid	Deliberate combination of the above	Maximum market reach; accommodates heterogeneous buyers	Healthcare (hospital + rural clinic); Smart Cities (metro vs. town)

Three key observations emerge from the comparative analysis. First, no single commercialisation pathway dominates across verticals; instead, effective deployment requires a context-sensitive and often hybridised approach. Second, public-private partnerships (PPPs) play a structurally significant role, as the public-good characteristics of agricultural sustainability, rural education, public health, and urban resilience justify public co-financing. This aligns with established European funding frameworks, including Horizon Europe, the Recovery and Resilience Facility, and the 2023 Gigabit State Aid Guidelines [10]. Third, commercialisation pathways that rely primarily on individual end-user willingness to pay encounter the most pronounced adoption barriers, particularly in segments where the societal value proposition is strongest but private incentives are weakest. This misalignment between private incentives and societal value constitutes the central challenge that the TCM seeks to address.

6 The Transformative Commercialisation Model (TCM)

6.1 Rationale and Architecture

Conventional commercialisation follows the TALC, where vendors initially target Innovators and Early Adopters before gradually reaching the Early and Late Majority, with Laggards adopting last. This diffusion pattern is represented in Fig. 1, which maps the five adopter segments, their standard population shares, and the differentiated role the TCM plays at each stage, from enabling experimental innovation at the Innovator end, through use-case validation and scaling, to partnership-based de-risking and inclusive transitions at the Late Majority and Laggard end. While effective, this staged diffusion creates a time lag, often up to a decade, between market entry and broad societal impact. This delay disproportionately affects underserved groups, including rural communities, small municipalities, and vulnerable populations, reflecting structural inequalities in access to digital infrastructure and services. In the context of 6G, such gradual diffusion is misaligned with European Union strategic priorities, including the Digital Decade, the Green Deal, and the Digital Single Market, which require faster and more inclusive adoption across all segments.

To address this, a two-phase TCM is proposed. In Phase 1 (Barrier Reduction), adoption among Late Majority and Laggard segments is accelerated through public-sector support mechanisms such as government subsidies, EU-funded programmes, NGO-led training, shared infrastructure, and consortium-backed pilot access. During this stage, ecosystem actors are funded primarily through public procurement and programme-based financing (e.g., Horizon Europe), rather than end-user payments, with the aim of reducing financial, informational, and capability barriers.

In Phase 2 (Threshold Commercialisation), the model transitions to a sustainable commercial structure once predefined adoption thresholds are met. These thresholds are assessed using Key Performance Indicators (KPIs) and Key Value Indicators (KVIs), capturing measurable outcomes such as efficiency gains or service improvements. At this stage, adopters begin to pay for services, while ecosystem partners derive value through mechanisms such as revenue sharing, licensing, or service agreements, with all terms defined ex ante to ensure transparency and incentive alignment.

Conceptually, the TCM extends established telecom policy instruments (Sect. 2.2) into an outcome-oriented framework. While Universal Service Obligation (USOs) ensure the availability of connectivity, the TCM ensures delivery of measurable value. Similarly, whereas spectrum-auction coverage conditions link license obligations to population coverage targets, the TCM links them to verified outcome-based metrics. Finally, while Article 76 of the EECC facilitates risk-sharing in infrastructure deployment through co-investment, the TCM extends this de-risking logic to the service and outcome layer. From a regulatory perspective, the TCM is, in principle, compatible with the 2023 Gigabit State Aid Guidelines, as Phase 1 support is conditional, outcome-audited, and time-limited.

6.2 Role by TALC Segment

The TCM does not replace conventional pathways for Innovators and Early Adopters; it layers on top of them to address downstream segments (Table 3).

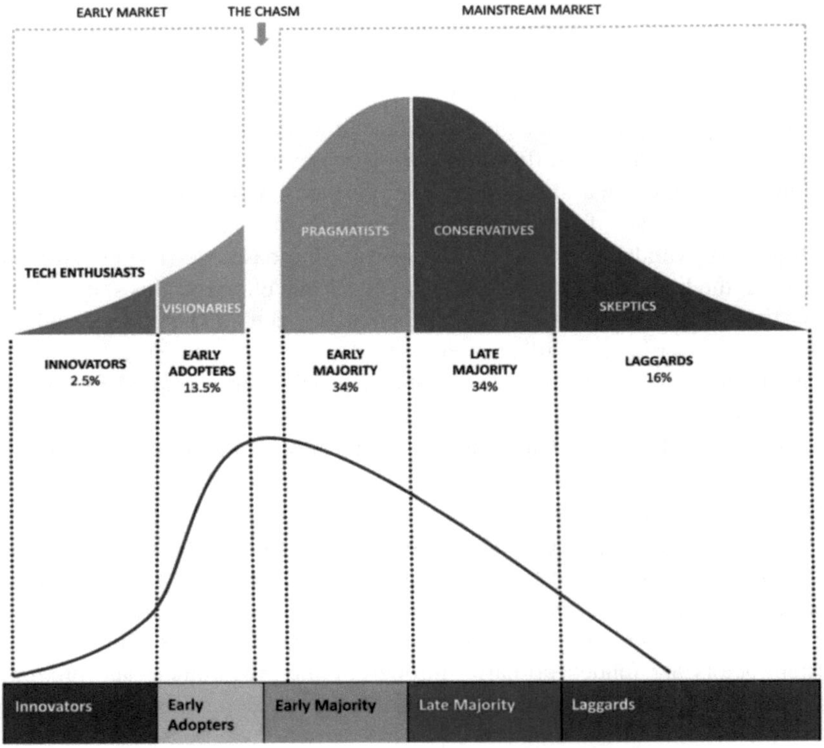

Fig. 1. *TALC and differentiated TCM strategies by adopter segment.*

Table 3. Transformative Commercialisation strategy by TALC segment.

TALC Stage	Strategy	Key Instruments	Lead Stakeholders
Innovators	Sandboxing and testbed access; minimal commercial pressure	6G testbeds, simulators, pre-commercial pilots, research grants	Research institutions, deep-tech start-ups, R&D labs
Early Adopters	Amplify impact by aligning outcomes with KVIs	Co-design; impact measurement via KVIs; funding matchmaking	Digital-first SMEs, tech-forward municipalities, public innovators
Early Majority	Bridge the trust gap with replicable demonstrators and toolkits	Sector-specific demonstration hubs; standardised "adoption blueprints"; interoperability certification	Sectoral SMEs, technology vendors, industry clusters

(continued)

Table 3. (*continued*)

TALC Stage	Strategy	Key Instruments	Lead Stakeholders
Late Majority	TCM Phase 1: bundled access, training, and policy support as turnkey service	6G Inclusion Grants; shared-infrastructure cooperatives; consortium-based procurement	Ministries, regional development agencies, local government alliances
Laggards	TCM Phase 1 extended: transitional models backed by regulatory mechanisms and subsidies	"6G Readiness Incubators"; digital-service minimums; phased transition to Phase 2 once KPIs/KVIs achieved	National regulators, EU digital-inclusion programmes, NGOs, training bodies

6.3 Theoretical Contribution

The TCM makes three contributions. First, it extends Moore's "crossing the chasm" by identifying a second, less-studied chasm between the Early and Late Majority in infrastructure markets and proposing a non-market bridging mechanism. Second, it operationalises inclusive digital transformation by linking commercialisation design to KVIs [22, 35], a 6G-native concept rarely integrated with telecom policy instruments. Third, by tying monetisation to validated outcome thresholds, it aligns incentives among vendors, adopters, and public funders, rewarding real-world impact rather than installed-base growth alone. This aligns with the broader 6G-PATH approach to market-vertical use-case deployment [2].

7 Policy and Regulatory Implications

7.1 Barrier-Instrument-Regulator Mapping

Regulatory fragmentation is a binding constraint on 6G commercialisation. For the TCM to function, harmonisation of spectrum, certification, and data-governance regimes is not desirable but required. Table 4 maps the Sect. 4.3 barriers to specific European instruments and lead regulators, moving the analysis beyond high-level framing.

Table 4. Barrier-Instrument-Regulator mapping for 6G commercialisation at EU level.

Barrier	Specific Instrument	Lead Regulator	Horizon

(*continued*)

Table 4. (*continued*)

Barrier	Specific Instrument	Lead Regulator	Horizon
THz/mmWave pioneer-band fragmentation (100–330 GHz)	RSPG Opinion on 6G Spectrum + CEPT ECC Decision/Report on upper 6 GHz and sub-THz; consistent national licensing	RSPG; CEPT ECC; National Regulatory Authorities (NRA)s	2026–2028
Medical 6G device conformity (UC-HEALTH-1)	Delegated Acts under RED 2014/53/EU, Arts. 3(3)(a) and 3(3)(i); MDR (EU) 2017/745 Class III	European Commission; European Telecommunications Standards Institute (ETSI) / European Committee for Standardization (CEN)	2026–2027
Public-safety 6G vs. TETRA/TETRAPOL entrenchment (UC-CITIES-3)	RSPG Opinion on PPDR; CEPT ECC Report on broadband-PPDR migration; national interoperability mandates aligned with 3GPP MCX	RSPG; CEPT ECC; national Public Protection and Disaster Relief (PPDR) authorities	2026–2030
Vertical interoperability and KVI standardisation	3GPP Release 19/20 normative work on 6G enablers; ETSI ISG on KVIs; SNS JU Test, Measurement and Validation (TMV) KVI harmonisation outputs	3GPP; ETSI; SNS JU TMV WG	2026–2028
THz/mmWave pioneer-band fragmentation (100–330 GHz)	RSPG Opinion on 6G Spectrum + CEPT ECC Decision/Report on upper 6 GHz and sub-THz; consistent national licensing	RSPG; CEPT ECC; national NRAs	2026–2028

7.2 Sustainability Integration

6G networks are highly energy-intensive, with early testbeds showing around 40% higher power consumption than 5G, posing risks to European Green Deal objectives if sustainability is not explicitly addressed. The 6G-PATH analysis identifies five integrated sustainability dimensions, technological, operational, social, economic, and environmental, that must be embedded within commercialisation strategies. TCM incorporates these dimensions by linking progression between phases to both performance and sustainability outcomes. For example, in smart farming, transition to Phase 2 monetisation depends not only on achieving connectivity KPIs but also on meeting sustainability-focused KVIs. Workforce readiness is treated as a critical cross-cutting factor, with training and capacity-building integrated into Phase 1 to ensure adopters can realise both technological and sustainability benefits.

8 Limitations, Future Work, and Conclusion

This study has three main limitations. First, it relies on secondary data and early-stage consortium elicitation, with empirical validation of the TCM deferred to Phase 2 pilots. Future work will include quantitative modelling of threshold parameters, revenue-sharing mechanisms, and public-private risk allocation using approaches such as Social Return on Investment (SROI) and Total Public Good Value, linking KPIs to Key Value Enablers (KVEs) and validated KVIs. Second, TALC positioning is based on structured but judgement-driven elicitation, with large-scale surveys planned for further validation. Third, the framework is grounded in the European regulatory context, limiting direct transferability to other regions, though partial alignment exists with initiatives in Japan and South Korea.

Future research within 6G-PATH will focus on longitudinal KVI tracking during Phase 2 trials, integrated financial modelling incorporating KPI thresholds, KVE activation and attribution, and monetised public value. Comparative evaluation with other SNS JU projects (e.g., Hexa-X-II, TrialsNet, 6G-VERSUS) and third-party experimentation is also planned.

In conclusion, the paper presents a techno-economic commercialisation framework for 6G based on ten 6G-PATH use cases, aligned with telecom policy instruments. All use cases are positioned within TRL 4–6 and the Innovators-to-Early-Adopters transition, except UC-CITIES-3, which remains a Late-Majority/Laggard outlier due to legacy system entrenchment. Four cross-cutting barriers, rural connectivity, regulatory fragmentation, skills gaps, and uncertain return on investment, are identified. The main contribution is the TCM, a two-phase model combining Barrier Reduction and threshold-based commercialisation, where monetisation is tied to validated KVI outcomes. By extending existing European policy instruments rather than introducing a standalone construct, the framework emphasises that the success of Europe's 6G agenda depends not only on technological advances but also on effective alignment of commercial models, regulatory frameworks, and inclusive adoption mechanisms.

References

1. BEREC. (2020). | BEREC. In https://www.berec.europa.eu
2. Chochliouros, I. P., et al.: Promoting deployment of innovative use cases in market verticals for the support of 6G evolution: the 6G-PATH context. IFIP Adv. Inf. Commun. Technol., 154-176 (2024). https://doi.org/10.1007/978-3-031-63227-3_11
3. European Commission. Digital Economy and Society Index (DESI) 2022 Thematic chapters (2022a). https://ec.europa.eu/newsroom/dae/redirection/document/88764
4. European Commission. Path to the Digital Decade Policy Programme Decision (EU) 2022/2481 (2022b)

5. European Commission. Commission calls on 18 Member States to comply with the EU Data Governance Act. Shaping Europe's Digital Future (2024a). https://digital-strategy.ec.eu
6. European Commission. Gigabit Infrastructure Act- Regulation - EU - 2024/1309. Europa.eu (2024b). http://data.europa.eu/eli/reg/2024/1309/oj
7. European Conference of Postal and Telecommunications Administrations (CEPT). ECO Documentation. Cept.org (2026). https://docdb.cept.org
8. European Parliament and Council of the European Union. Directive (EU) 2018/1972 of the European Parliament and of the Council of 11 December 2018 establishing the European Electronic Communications Code (Recast). Official Journal of the European Union, L 321, 36–214 (2018). https://eur-lex.europa.eu/eli/dir/2018/1972/oj
9. European Parliament and Council of the European Union. Decision (EU) 2022/2481 of the European Parliament and of the Council of 14 December 2022 establishing the Digital Decade Policy Programme 2030. Official Journal of the European Union, L 323, 4–26 (2022). https://eur-lex.europa.eu/eli/dec/2022/2481/oj
10. European Commission. Communication from the Commission: Guidelines on State aid for broadband networks 2023/C 36/01. Official Journal of the European Union, C 36, 1–42 (2023). https://eur-lex.europa.eu/legal-content/EN/TXT/?uri=CELEX:52023XC0131(01)
11. Ferrandis, J., Ramos, S., Feijóo, C.: An assessment of estimation models and investment gaps for the deployment of high-speed broadband networks in NUTS3 regions to meet the objectives of the European Gigabit Society. Telecommun. Policy **45**(7) (2021)
12. Finger, R.: Digital innovations for sustainable and resilient agricultural systems. Eur. Rev. Agric. Econ. **50**(4) (2023). https://doi.org/10.1093/erae/jbad021
13. González-Prelcic, N., et al.: The integrated sensing and communication revolution for 6G: vision, techniques, and applications. Proc. IEEE (2024)
14. Héder, M.: From NASA to EU: the evolution of the TRL scale in public sector innovation. Innov. J. **22**(1) (2017)
15. Jape, S.D., Mungase, K.V., Thite, V.B., Jadhav, D.: A comprehensive analysis on 5G, IoT and its impact on agriculture and healthcare. In: Proceedings of the 2023 2nd International Conference on Augmented Intelligence and Sustainable Systems (ICAISS), Trichy, India, 23–25 Aug. 2023, pp. 1599–1605 (2023)
16. Jiang, W., Han, B., Habibi, M.A., Schotten, H.D.: The road towards 6G: a comprehensive survey. IEEE Open J. Commun. Soc. **2**, 334–366 (2021)
17. Joyce, A., Paquin, R.L.: The triple layered business model canvas: a tool to design more sustainable business models. J. Clean. Prod. **135**(1), 1474–1486 (2016)
18. Kakizawa, H.: The value of public service broadcasting in Japan during COVID-19 pandemic: an analysis of WTP by Blinder-Oaxaca decomposition. Telecommunications Policy **47**(3), 102523 (2023). https://doi.org/10.1016/j.telpol.2023.102523
19. Matinmikko-Blue, M., Yrjölä, S., Ahokangas, P.: Multi-perspective approach for developing sustainable 6G mobile communications. Telecommun. Policy 102640–102640 (2023)
20. Mildebrath, H., Faucheu, T.: Author: Hendrik Mildebrath with Titouan Faucheux. In Members' Research Service PE, vol. 762, p. 475 (2024). https://www.europarl.europa.eu
21. Moore, G.A., McKenna, R.: Crossing the chasm (1991). https://api.semanticscholar.org/CorpusID:106549889
22. Osman, H., Bradford, J., Mitchell, S.: Bridging the gap between 6G technologies and societal values: a comprehensive analysis of key value indicators (KVIs) and business models. In: 2022 IEEE Wireless Communications and Networking Conference (WCNC), pp. 1–5 (2024). https://doi.org/10.1109/wcnc57260.2024.10570540
23. Osterwalder, A., Pigneur, Y.: Business Model Generation. Wiley, Hoboken (2010)
24. Oughton, E.J., Lehr, W.: Surveying 5G techno-economic research to inform the evaluation of 6G wireless technologies. IEEE Access **10**, 25237–25257 (2022)

25. Pennanen, H., Hänninen, T., Tervo, O., Tölli, A., Latva-Aho, M.: 6G: the intelligent network of everything. IEEE Access **13**, 1319–1421 (2025)
26. Peralta-Ochoa, A.M., Chaca-Asmal, P.A., Guerrero-Vásquez, L.F., Ordoñez-Ordoñez, J.O., Coronel-González, E.J.: Smart healthcare applications over 5G networks: a systematic review. Appl. Sci. **13**(3), 1469 (2023). https://doi.org/10.3390/app13031469
27. Perätalo, S., Ahokangas, P., Iivari, M.: Smart city business model approach: the role of opportunities, values, and advantages. Innov.: Eur. J. Soc. Sci. Res., 1–25 (2023). https://doi.org/10.1080/13511610.2023.2286439
28. Quy, V.K., Chehri, A., Quy, N.M., Han, N.D., Ban, N.T.: Innovative trends in the 6G era: a comprehensive survey of architecture, applications, technologies, and challenges. IEEE Access **11**, 39824–39844 (2023). https://doi.org/10.1109/access.2023.3269297
29. Rogers, E.M.: Diffusion on Innovations. The Free Press (1983)
30. Salemink, K., Strijker, D., Bosworth, G.: Rural development in the digital age: a systematic literature review on unequal ICT availability, adoption, and use in rural areas. J. Rural. Stud. **54**(54), 360–371 (2017). https://doi.org/10.1016/j.jrurstud.2015.09.001
31. Smart Networks and Services Joint Undertaking (SNS JU). Strategic Research and Innovation Agenda (2023). https://smart-networks.europa.eu/wp-content/uploads/2023/12/sns-ju-sria-2021-2027-second-edition-2023.pdf
32. Talmar, M., Walrave, B., Podoynitsyna, K.S., Holmström, J., Romme, A.G.L.: Mapping, analyzing and designing innovation ecosystems: the ecosystem pie model. Long Range Plan. **53**(4), 101850 (2020). https://doi.org/10.1016/j.lrp.2018.09.002
33. Tian, C., Cao, H., Garg, S., Kaddoum, G., Hassan, M.M., Xie, J.: 5G in healthcare: matching game-empowered intelligent medical network slicing. Alex. Eng. J. **77**, 95–107 (2023). https://doi.org/10.1016/j.aej.2023.06.041
34. Van-de-Werfhorst, H.G., Kessenich, E., Geven, S.: The digital divide in online education: inequality in digital readiness of students and schools. Comput. Educ. Open **3**(3), 100100 (2022). https://doi.org/10.1016/j.caeo.2022.100100
35. Wikström, G., et al.: Key value indicators: a framework for values-driven next-generation ICT solutions. Telecommun. Policy 102778–102778 (2024)

Designing the Future of Secure Intelligence: A Vision for AI-Enabled Cyber-Resilient Ecosystems

Christos A. Gizelis[1(✉)], Achilleas Marinakis[1], Stavros Papamokos[1], Mihalis Kefalogiannis[1], Ioanna Mesogiti[1], Giorgos Liberopoulos[1], Elina Theodoropoulou[1], Maria Poulimenou[2], Louiza Kachrimani[2], Anna Tzanakaki[3], Markos Anastassopoulos[3], Thomas Azrak[4], Maria-Eleni Dimitrakopoulou[5], Odysseas Kokkinos[5], Luca Bianconi[6], and Giulia Clerici[6]

[1] OTE Group of Companies, Athens, Greece
{cgkizelis,amarinaki,spapamokos,mkefalogiannis,imesogiti,glimperop, etheodorop}@ote.gr
[2] UBITECH LTD, Athens, Greece
{mpoulimenou,lkachrimani}@ubitech.eu
[3] National Kapodistrian University of Athens, Athens, Greece
atzanakaki@uoa.gr, maanast@phys.uoa.gr
[4] EBOS, Nicosia, Cyprus
Thomasa@ebos.com.cy
[5] INNOV-ACTS, Limassol, Cyprus
{mdimitrakopoulou,okokkinos}@innov-acts.com
[6] STAM SRL, Genova, Italy
{l.bianconi,g.clerici}@stamtech.com

Abstract. In the accelerated evolution of digital ecosystems, there is a demand for a new synthesis of Artificial Intelligence (AI), cybersecurity-by-design, and autonomous decision-making in diverse settings. This vision paper provides a consolidated view, formulated by six European initiatives, VIGILANCE, CyberAId, ENFORCE, ACT4FOOD, CTIS4NIS, and 5G-TACTIC, that contribute jointly to the evolution of intelligent, cyber-resilient, and trustworthy next-generation systems. Employing common methodologies, prototypes, immense pilot deployments, and trials, the EU initiatives through the collective, present in this paper, a coherent roadmap to install these components into future large-scale digital infrastructures: automation driven by AI, proactive threat detection, zero-touch operational paradigm, and any type of trustworthy data flow. Also, the vision engulfs related topics like federated and collaborative AI, guarding all the cyber-physical continuum, secure and interoperable data spaces, and after that application-driven intelligence, forwards the range across the domains from critical infrastructures to the food systems guaranteeing a mechanism to bring what has been described to the physical world. The paper concludes by presenting a common architectural blueprint and starts highlighting open research issues and policy considerations that could build an environment where

Published by Springer Nature Switzerland AG 2027
A. Papaleonidas et al. (Eds.): AIAI 2026 Workshops, IFIP AICT 796, pp. 158–178, 2027.
https://doi.org/10.1007/978-3-032-30507-7_10

AI-driven cyber resilience intelligence would become a rudder of European digital autonomy and societal resilience in forthcoming decades.

Keywords: AI · Cybersecurity · Resilience

1 Introduction

Digital transformation drives rapid progress in contemporary societies which results in increased exposure to cyber-attacks against critical services, industrial operations and infrastructures. The development of new cyber threats exhibits an increasing complexity and geographic expansion that require cybersecurity systems to evolve beyond their existing reactive defense strategies. Artificial Intelligence (AI) empowers organizations to build their future cybersecurity systems through its ability to deliver real-time threat detection and predictive analysis and autonomous threat handling systems.

Research and innovation programs develop AI technologies which will improve cybersecurity protection. The projects VIGILANCE and CyberAId work on developing threat detection systems that use AI for establishing situational awareness while ENFORCE investigates security systems that use automated processes to enforce security protocols through defined policies. The sector-specific programs ACT4FOOD, 5G-TACTIC and CTIS4NIS, demonstrate how organizations can use AI-based cybersecurity solutions to protect their critical infrastructure in the agri-food sector and next-generation communication systems.

The implementation of AI technology brings fresh dangers to organizations which encompass model-based adversarial assaults and the difficulty in understanding AI systems and the establishment of trustworthiness. Organizations to create complete security designs which should focus on developing dependable and trustworthy AI systems that can withstand cybersecurity attacks.

The current cyber threat landscape requires organizations to use intelligence-based security instead of their existing traditional defense methods. Organizations need to build cyber resilience by developing systems that can both stop attacks and detect and respond to new security threats as they appear. The system needs to support ongoing learning processes while handling information needs and enabling teamwork between different organizations and technologies.

Intelligence in cybersecurity exists because data collection creates actionable information. CyberAId and VIGILANCE develop predictive threat intelligence through their systems, while ENFORCE and CTIS4NIS provide security solutions that operate according to policies and compliance requirements. The 5G-TACTIC and ACT4FOOD projects show that specific fields require their own unique solutions. Cyber threats now operate across multiple industries and international boundaries, which makes it necessary to establish protected information sharing systems that use federated learning and interoperable platforms to create shared intelligence for effective cyber defense.

The joint vision of the projects centers on secure intelligence identifying AI systems as defenders against attacks. They allow organizations to establish secure data-sharing environments which operate through automated security management and interoperable architectural frameworks that use federated and collaborative AI systems to protect user data. The initiatives implement security processes throughout the system lifecycle while their cybersecurity design framework undergoes testing through extensive pilots in critical infrastructure and telecommunications and agri-food sectors. The collaborative program enhances digital sovereignty by connecting technological advancements to European policy goals while establishing a base for upcoming research activities and standard development and trustworthy AI-driven cybersecurity system implementation.

2 Cyber-Resilience-Synergy-Network

The Cyber-Resilience-Synergy-Network (CRSN) is a Security Alliance, formed by a portfolio of interconnected projects (including 5G-TACTIC, CTIS4NIS, VIGILANCE, ACT4FOOD, ENFORCE, and CyberAId), addresses the growing complexity and cross-border nature of cybersecurity threats that impact European critical infrastructure systems while fulfilling new compliance requirements established by NIS2 and the Cyber Resilience Act. The alliance creates a standardized operational framework through its combination of multiple initiatives which establish a structured system for sharing threat intelligence and automating security operations while using AI technologies to improve detection and response capabilities. Its scope includes telecom and critical infrastructure and food supply chains and security operations as it utilizes common AI/ML technology and threat intelligence and automated orchestration to create a complete cybersecurity system which protects all defense phases while enabling international cooperation and enhancing operational performance throughout Europe. Details about the interconnected projects are presented in the following section.

3 Projects Landscape and Contributions

3.1 Overview of VIGILANCE

The aim of VIGILANCE [33] (Versatile Intelligent aGents for Interconnected Ledgers and Autonomous Next-gen Cybersecurity Ecosystems) is a European initiative devoted to altering the safeguarding of Critical Infrastructures, government sector establishments, and private corporations. The primary goal is reducing the engineering effort and deployment cost of intelligent cyber defense strategies supported by a Zero Trust Architecture by means of a contemporary, scalable self-adjusting five-level platform. What the project does is coupling many advanced technologies, which are: Adversarial AI, Generative AI, Blockchain and Quantum Computing thereby, allowing continuous checking; real-time anomaly detection; and risk and vulnerability assessments to grow accordingly to adapt in meeting its promise to shift from reactive cybersecurity approaches towards a sustainable and proactive security ecosystem.

3.2 Overview of CyberAId

CyberAId [7] will significantly enhance the cyber-resilience of European Critical Infrastructures (CIs) in the finance and other industrial sectors based on the development and deployment of a novel agentic AI infrastructure that will be used to autonomously and intelligently coordinate and orchestrate a pool of state-of-the-art cybersecurity tools and services for key digital technologies. The CyberAId infrastructure will leverage cutting edge cybersecurity technologies in order to address the entire cyber-resilience lifecycle of financial CI assets and processes including incidents and attacks' prediction, monitoring, reporting and response. At the same time, the Agentic AI-based orchestration of CyberAId's cybersecurity capabilities will enable the project to address common and emerging cybersecurity challenges for financial CIs in an integrated, coordinated, scalable and intelligent way that is nowadays hardly possible.

Overall, the project will deliver cybersecurity innovations in the following areas that address key digital technologies:

1. CyberAId-BLUEPRINTS: CyberAId will deliver a Reference Architecture and detailed cybersecurity blueprints tailored to the security needs of financial CIs.
2. CyberAId-PROACTIVE: CyberAId will provide solutions for advanced proactive vulnerability management, which will incorporate automated AI-driven penetration testing, quantum-resistant cryptography, privacy-preserving analytics, and secure coding practices to effectively prevent cyber threats.
3. CyberAId-MONITOR: The project will develop and deliver real-time monitoring solutions for cybersecurity, which will leverage network-level monitoring tools enhanced by eBPF (extended Berkeley Packet Filter) technology, anomaly detection capabilities, and data-level analytics.
4. CyberAId-REPORT: CyberAId will develop innovative incident response capabilities, which will integrate AI-driven contextual analysis and automated regulatory reporting.

3.3 Overview of ENFORCE

The ENFORCE project [8] (Enforcing End-User-Driven Secure Services Across Diverse Domains in the Computing Continuum) is a European cybersecurity initiative launched in January 2026. The project's core objective is to deliver a standards-driven orchestration platform that secures critical digital infrastructures across the "unified compute continuum," which spans from cloud environments to hardware-assisted IoT devices at the far-edge. ENFORCE integrates advanced 5G connectivity, AI-driven behavioral analytics, and edge networking to provide continuous, real-time vulnerability checks and automated response mechanisms. Key innovations include automated Trusted Execution Environment (TEE) migrations to ensure data confidentiality during attacks and dynamic intervention in service function chains to meet strict Service Level Agreements (SLAs).

3.4 Overview of ACT4FOOD

ACT4FOOD [2] is an innovative EU project that strengthens the cybersecurity, safety, and resilience of food supply chains in response to the growing risks introduced by digital transformation. Recognising that food security and safety are fundamental rights, the project develops advanced cybersecurity technologies, secure data-sharing frameworks, and AI-driven risk assessment models to protect the integrity and availability of food systems. ACT4FOOD delivers an AI-powered cybersecurity system capable of threat detection, anomaly monitoring, intrusion prevention, and incident response across Industrial Control Systems (ICS), IoT networks, and supply chain operations. It integrates a blockchain-based Information Exchange Platform for secure, tamper-proof data exchange, alongside privacy-preserving techniques such as anonymisation and secure aggregation. The project further extends the Rapid Alert System for Food and Feed (RASFF) with a Cyber Threat Intelligence feed, enabling coordinated responses to cyber threats. At its core, ACT4FOOD introduces TACCP 4.0, an advanced framework combining AI-driven risk ranking, cyber-physical threat detection, and food defence strategies to address threats such as ransomware, IoT vulnerabilities, industrial sabotage, and fraud. Validated across real-world use cases in aquaculture, dairy, and retail, ACT4FOOD enhances regulatory alignment and positions Europe at the forefront of food cybersecurity and digital trust.

3.5 Overview of 5G-TACTIC and CTIS4NIS

Acknowledging the rapidly evolving cybersecurity threat landscape and the critical need to ensure robust protection mechanisms within 5G infrastructures, the 5G-TACTIC project [1,4] addresses foundational challenges associated with the secure design, deployment, and operation of next-generation mobile networks. In particular, it targets the complexities introduced by open, disaggregated, and multi-vendor 5G ecosystems–especially within Open RAN (O-RAN) environments–where interoperability and supply chain diversification may expand the attack surface. To mitigate these risks, 5G-TACTIC develops a comprehensive framework of Critical Security Controls aligned with emerging European regulatory requirements, focusing on secure software development lifecycles, protection of data confidentiality and integrity through trusted mechanisms, and automated lifecycle management [9,22]. Advanced threat detection and response capabilities are also incorporated by integrating technologies such as Security Information and Event Management (SIEM), Security Orchestration, Automation and Response (SOAR), Software Bill of Materials (SBOM) analyzers, and AI-driven analytics for anomaly detection and predictive threat intelligence. Complemented by cross-border information exchange mechanisms among telecom operators, regulators, and CSIRTs, as well as the extension of established security assurance methodologies e.g. 3GPP Security Assurance Specifications (SCAS) / 3GPP Security Assurance Methodology (SECAM), 5G-TACTIC establishes a baseline for secure, interoperable, and resilient 5G deployments validated in real-world operational environments.

Building upon this foundation, the CTIS4NIS project advances the state of the art by focusing on the operationalization and large-scale validation of cybersecurity solutions in alignment with the Network and Information Security Directive (NIS2) and the Cyber Resilience Act (CRA). Extending the technological and methodological work of 5G-TACTIC, CTIS4NIS emphasizes the creation of a cohesive European cybersecurity ecosystem that integrates diverse stakeholders and enables coordinated incident detection, response, mitigation, and recovery across national boundaries. The project aims to design and deploy integrated IT-based solutions that combine Zero Trust Networking principles, Cyber Threat Intelligence platforms, and tightly coupled SIEM and SOAR capabilities enhanced with AI-based analytics and vulnerability scoring. Furthermore, CTIS4NIS introduces structured processes and workflows aimed at strengthening both technical and regulatory capacities, ensuring that cybersecurity practices are consistently applied across heterogeneous 5G environments. In this way, CTIS4NIS not only extends but also operationalizes the security-by-design principles of 5G-TACTIC, contributing to a more resilient, compliant, and scalable cybersecurity posture for European 5G infrastructures.

4 Joint Impact of the Six EU Projects

The six EU projects in Cyber-Resilience-Synergy-Network have a big effect on the EU's digital landscape by using novel technologies to switch from reactive to proactive cybersecurity models. The primary objective of these projects is to make critical infrastructure more resilient and strengthen Europe's technological independence.

4.1 Deployment of Breakthrough Technologies

The strategic integration of breakthrough technologies represents a key pillar of the projects that are part of the synergy. It is directing a fundamental shift toward proactive defense within European digital infrastructures. These initiatives automate challenging tasks involving real-time pattern recognition, log analysis, and continuous vulnerability scanning by incorporating Artificial Intelligence (AI), including Large Language Models (LLMs) and generative AI, alongside Big Data Analytics and Software-Defined Networking (SDN) into operational environments. This automation improves operational resilience by facilitating automated response mechanisms to work almost instantly, which significantly reduces the "window of opportunity" for malicious actors to take advantage of system weaknesses. Also, the adoption of future-proof technologies, including quantum-resistant cryptography and secure Trusted Execution Environment (TEE) migrations, will maintain long-term data confidentiality and service continuity even if emerging computational threats arise. Together, these developments empower organizations to manage environments that are becoming more complex while maintaining high standards of cybersecurity.

4.2 Reinforcement of EU Strategic Autonomy

One of the main objectives of all six projects in the synergy is to significantly decrease the dependency on non-EU cybersecurity technologies. This will assist in keeping critical European infrastructure secure from potential foreign influence. All six initiatives focus on the development of EU-based tools, like European AI models and open-standard orchestration layers, to establish and maintain technological sovereignty by prioritizing indigenous innovation. Zero-Trust architectures and standardized service function chaining constitute two ways to secure the digital supply chain. These advancements guarantee that only validated components and services operate within the network, which makes the EU's digital technology ecosystem more robust and reliable.

4.3 National and Cross-Border Collaborative Ecosystems

All six projects are designed to facilitate the transition of National Security Operation Centers (SOCs) into interoperable, cross-border platforms that are capable of handling large-scale cybersecurity incidents. The main focus of this change is the emphasis on intelligence pooling. This is achieved through the creation of original Cyber Threat Information (CTI) feeds that enable EU Member Countries to share useful intelligence on a large scale. The projects empower a coordinated response to complex, cross-border cyber incidents by creating collaborative frameworks and standardized APIs, including those based on ETSI and TM Forum specifications. This unified approach ensures that new threats are rapidly communicated across different domains and infrastructures. This results in a collective EU-wide defense mechanism that improves situational awareness and reduces overall operational risks.

4.4 Regulatory Alignment and Capacity Building

The collective impact of these initiatives extends to the practical implementation of key EU legislation, guaranteeing that technological innovation remains both compliant and scalable across the Union. All projects directly support the NIS2 Directive, the Cyber Resilience Act (CRA), and the Cybersecurity Act by including regulatory requirements into their architectural designs. The initiatives stress the need for specialized capacity building through the establishment of Cybersecurity Learning Centers and dedicated upskilling programs in order to address the critical workforce shortage of approximately 500,000 unfilled cybersecurity positions in Europe. Additionally, the economic impact is optimized when Small and Medium-sized Enterprises (SMEs) have access to cost-effective, scalable security solutions that lower adoption barriers for them. By combining regulatory alignment with professional development and accessible technology, synergy's projects foster a secure digital ecosystem that strengthens the competitiveness of European industries.

5 Methodologies and Technical Approaches

5.1 Cybersecurity and Threat Intelligence for Critical Environments

Critical environments across Europe, such as energy, transport, healthcare, telecoms, and food systems, are increasingly interconnected through IT, OT, IoT, and advanced communication networks, significantly expanding their attack surface. Reports from ENISA [22] highlight the growing sophistication of cyber threats, including ransomware and DDoS attacks, as well as the reuse of tools across sectors. This evolution makes traditional perimeter-based security insufficient, driving a shift toward intelligence-driven and proactive cybersecurity strategies. A key component of this approach is structured cyber threat intelligence (CTI), supported by frameworks like ENISA's [19,20] six-step CTL methodology and regulatory requirements under the NIS2 Directive. These create both the need and the opportunity for coordinated, cross-sector collaboration, as seen in initiatives like VIGILANCE, CyberAId, ENFORCE, ACT4FOOD, CTIS4NIS, and 5G-TACTIC, which aim to align CTI processes and enable interoperable threat intelligence across domains.

These initiatives combine AI-driven detection, shared data models, and advanced security architectures to make threat intelligence operational. Machine learning enhances intrusion detection but introduces challenges such as limited data, interpretability, and adversarial risks, emphasizing the need for explainable and well-governed systems. Projects like ACT4FOOD extend CTI into cyber-physical domains, while CTIS4NIS and 5G-TACTIC focus on telecom security and DevSecOps practices. Integration into real-world systems is achieved through SOC platforms, zero-trust architectures, and automated orchestration, often supported by technologies like blockchain for secure information sharing. Together, these efforts contribute to a federated, AI-enabled threat intelligence ecosystem, capable of addressing interconnected risks and strengthening resilience across critical infrastructures.

5.2 Trustworthy AI, Ethics, and Compliance

Increasing integration of AI within cybersecurity systems introduces significant systemic risks together with new technological capabilities. These risks challenge existing governance models. In parallel, AI-driven decision-making processes gained a more and more central role for threat detection, incident response, and resilience strategies towards critical domains such as digital infrastructures, telecommunications, energy distribution, financial services and other critical systems. Thus, reliance on AI increases every day and together with it those concerns related to trust, accountability, and control, particularly now that autonomous or semi-autonomous mechanisms are deployed at scale and globally. Recent European policy developments highlighted the pressing need to ensure AI systems operate in a secure, transparent, and human-centric manner. These European regulatory initiatives, namely NIS2 Directive and the Cybersecurity Act, emphasise the need for enhanced resilience, risk management, and certification mechanisms across digital ecosystems. These policies state clearly and undeniably this necessity is no longer optional. It is a prerequisite for their adoption within the European digital ecosystem. As such, Trustworthy AI emerges as a foundational paradigm to align technological innovation with European values, regulatory requirements, and cybersecurity objectives.

Ethical principles, regulatory obligations, and operational instruments integrate into a multi-layered framework for Trustworthy AI as guiding principles for the European approach to AI governance. The European Commission in 2019 established the High-Level Expert Group on AI (also known as HLEG [11,12]) that produced foundational Ethics Guidelines for Trustworthy AI. They require systems in the EU to be lawful, ethical, and robust throughout their lifecycle and establish a human-centric vision of AI. This vision is grounded in the protection of fundamental rights and the promotion of societal well-being, in full agreement with EU (and UN) principles. Building upon this foundation, the more recent AI Act was released and adopted. It introduces a binding, risk-based regulatory framework classifying AI systems according to their potential impact. According to that, it distinguishes, among others, between prohibited practices and high-risk applications subject to strict obligations. Operationalisation of Trustworthy AI within the European Union steps in significantly thanks to this transition from soft-law initiatives to enforceable regulation. A set of assessment and governance instruments - such as the Assessment List for Trustworthy AI (ALTAI [10]), Fundamental Rights Impact Assessments (also known as FRIA), and human oversight mechanisms - complement this EU regulatory layer with practical means to translate requirements into actionable processes. All these elements create European continuity in initiatives for an approach to AI governance tout court from ethical guidance to technical and organizational implementation.

Even though this European governance framework provides a comprehensive foundation for addressing ethical, legal, and societal concerns about Trustworthy AI, the cybersecurity dimension of AI systems emerged as a critical policy priority on its own [13–15]. The attack surface offered by the internet and pervasive connectivity of systems and devices reached a huge size. Upon all this, AI systems introduce a novel and expanded attack surface. Exploiting this latter, vulnerabilities may affect not only traditional software components but also data, models, and decision-making processes. As highlighted by ENISA [19], threats such as data poisoning, adversarial manipulation, and model exploitation can compromise the integrity, reliability, and trustworthiness of AI systems across their lifecycle. Moreover, complex distributed systems - where AI solutions operate across cloud, edge, and interconnected infrastructures - exacerbate these risks more. Furthermore, emerging paradigms such as federated AI and collaborative cyber defence - implying multiple actors contribute to shared intelligence and distributed model training - make this challenge even more pronounced. Linked to these paradigms, additional layers of complexity regarding trust, data governance, and interoperability are also introduced by mechanisms for cyber threat intelligence sharing and cross-organisational cooperation - such as those envisioned in CRSN. In this sense, the assurance of security and integrity of shared models, data pipelines, and decision outputs becomes essential to prevent the propagation of compromised information across the network.

Responding to all these challenges, besides regulatory activities, the cybersecurity of AI was the focus of European standardisation efforts. They promoted a lifecycle-based approach integrating security requirements from design to deployment and maintenance. In particular, recent work by ETSI on Securing Artificial Intelligence defines baseline cybersecurity principles for AI systems, emphasising secure-by-design, risk management, and continuous monitoring practices. Cybersecurity as an essential component of Trustworthy AI is then recognised by broader policy developments, bridging the gap between regulatory requirements and technical implementation.

The necessity of going beyond traditional cybersecurity paradigms and adopting integrated governance models that jointly address AI-specific risks and system-level resilience is highlighted by this convergence between policy and standardization efforts. It is an indication for European policy activity. Under this perspective, cybersecurity becomes a foundational enabler for the trustworthy deployment of AI and its secure deployment in any system and domain.

The emphasis on human-centric governance, ensuring AI systems support, rather than replace, human decision-making processes, is a central pillar of the European approach to Trustworthy AI. Safeguarding fundamental rights and maintaining meaningful human control over AI-driven systems plays a key role for the principle of human agency and oversight. This finds a parallel in the Ethics Guidelines for Trustworthy AI that indicates that AI systems should be designed to empower users, enabling informed decision-making while preserving individual autonomy and accountability.

EU AI Act reinforces this principle. It explicitly requires appropriate human oversight for high-risk AI systems. It ensures automated decisions can be effectively monitored, interpreted, and, where necessary, overridden. For AI-driven actions may have significant operational and societal implications making this requirement particularly relevant in domains such as cybersecurity. Under this perspective, human oversight is a crucial and central aspect. This can be implemented through different governance mechanisms, namely: human-in-the-loop (HITL), human-on-the-loop (HOTL), and human-in-command (HIC) approaches. Each of these mechanisms provides varying degrees of human intervention and control. The choice on what should be adopted is made considering context and level of risk. Relying on these models human actors are ensured to retain the ability to supervise system behaviour, intervene in decision processes, and - maybe most important - maintain ultimate responsibility for outcomes. In this sense, to ensure accountability, transparency, and compliance with fundamental rights, including the right not to be subject solely to automated decision-making processes - a principle core for European regulations [23] on AI-based systems - such mechanisms are essential from a policy perspective. The necessity of the role of human actors in overseeing decision-making processes is even more critical in complex cybersecurity environments where AI systems are increasingly used to support threat detection, incident response, and strategic activities. As a consequence, the enablement of human operators to oversee AI in mission-critical scenarios is key: training environments and simulation-based decision support systems can play a crucial role since they can be used to validate system behaviour, test response strategies, and strengthen human-AI collaboration before deployment in real-world operations. The European projects referenced in this article often go in this direction. This perspective challenges the notion of fully autonomous cyber defence systems, from a policy and operational standpoint. The contrasted balance between efficiency (or speed) and control (or accountability) is a central topic for the reflections on trustworthiness of AI and compliance with contexts and ethics. To make it clearer, while automation can significantly enhance speed and efficiency of actions, fully removing the human from the decision loop introduces often unacceptable risks if talking about accountability, unpredictability, and loss of control. A potentially compliant strategy for AI is to be leveraged to augment human capability and expertise in decision-support, enabling more informed, timely, and context-aware responses. Following this reflection, across critical and distributed digital ecosystems Trustworthy AI implies embedding human-centric governance as part of cybersecurity systems integrating AI-based features. This is essential to foster trust, ensure accountability, and enable the responsible deployment of AI. At European level, the above-mentioned integration between compliant trustworthiness of AI and cyber-security systems has meaningful implications for the development of cyber-resilient ecosystems.

As proposed in this article by highlighting the CRSN concept, the approaches for future cyber-defence are increasingly characterised as distributed, collaborative and intelligence-driven. They see multiple stakeholders contributing to shared situational awareness and coordinated response capabilities and establishing trust across those elements in the defence-chain becomes fundamental for effective cooperation overcoming organisational, sectoral, and national boundaries. As such, AI must be trustworthy and this is a necessary foundation to enable secure and reliable information sharing, particularly in relation to CTI and federated AI models. Interoperability among systems is facilitated by the adoption of a common governance framework and alignment with EU regulatory and standardization initiatives, paving the way for Trustworthy AI. It ensures that shared data, models, and insights can be trusted and effectively leveraged across different elements and actors of this defence-chain. This is even more challenging and relevant in cross-border scenarios - as those present and core for the EU - where heterogeneous infrastructures, regulatory contexts and human activities (not only economic ones) must be harmonised to support cyber-resilience strategies.

Furthermore, the emergence of integrated policy-driven ecosystems - where trust, compliance, and security are embedded by design - is fostered by the mentioned convergence of AI governance, cybersecurity regulation, and technical standardisation. Under this perspective, Trustworthy AI acts on one side as a compliance requirement and on the other one as an enabler of scalability, collaboration, and innovation with the goal of supporting the deployment of cross-sectorial and cross-domain cyber defence capabilities.

Ultimately, it is necessary to derive that the large-scale adoption of AI-enabled cybersecurity solutions remains limited without robust mechanisms to ensure trust, transparency, and accountability.

On the contrary, embedding Trustworthy AI principles - within the design and operation of cyber defence systems - makes possible fostering resilient, interoperable, and human-centric digital ecosystems with the capability of addressing the evolving threat landscape in a coordinated and sustainable manner - and in line with EU ethics concerns [3,6,27,29–31].

6 Pilots Across Domains

6.1 Pilots of VIGILANCE

The VIGILANCE project is testing and validating its Framework for Autonomous Cybersecurity across the four distinctive pilots in critical sectors. The telecommunications pilot is geared towards enhancing SOCs by automating threat detection, correlation, and root cause analysis, in order to reduce the alert fatigue for the analysts and boost incident response efficiency. The maritime and logistics pilot located at the Port of Rotterdam focuses on cyber-physical resilience, securing the juncture between digital control systems and the physical operations of the port to mitigate disruption to global supply chains. For the financial sector, the pilot seeks to implement AI-driven intelligence to protect the value of money and customer reputation with secure data and transaction environments that enables threat information to circulate securely yet independently across borders and institutions. The Industry 4.0 pilot, developed at Siemens, emphasizes smart manufacturing environments integrating the Zero Trust Architecture and digital twin technologies to predict, simulate, and eliminate cyber threats in real-time and enable continuous and secure industrial production.

6.2 Pilots of CyberAId

In the financial sector, CyberAId solutions based on AI that bundle giant language models, federated learning, advanced monitoring, and digital twin technologies aim to increase the detection of fraud, anti-money laundering (AML) processes, and cyber resilience. Elements enhanced are improved detection accuracy, reduced false positives, and the monitoring overload to ensure compliance, whereas the methodology, examined in pilot settings, remains scalable for all sizes of institutions. Within client impersonation detection in banking and trading systems, CyberAId employs AI to examine email communications, zeroing in on linguistic, structural, and metadata anomalies which might imply fraudulent behavior. This ability is being further complemented through federated learning-allowing multiple institutions to enhance detection models in a collaborative manner without sharing sensitive data. Alternatively, adaptive monitoring follows a paradigm where security rules and thresholds are continually updated in tune with attack patterns to guarantee the relevance of defenses. When it comes to payments, CyberAId carries the multi-staged AML framework. This includes transaction network analysis to reveal latent structure and portray patterns of surprise, such as that concerning structuring or layering, as well as advanced log correlation, which stitches together the data points of transactions, customers, and systems to get a deeper insight into behavior that is considered suspicious. LLM-assisted analysis forms the cornerstone, where also digital twin simulations are being utilized in order to peruse any complex scenarios automatically and come out with full and compliant reports. This results in more accurate detection and a few, if not zero, false alerts. CyberAId in banking security is a potential integrated solution that thrives concurrently for anomaly detection and incident response. It is designed to monitor activities generated on many channels, linking behavioral analysis with network visibility to increase the insight into identifying possible cyber activity. Shark-like triacylg. The response mechanism will help automatically forward the triage, investigation, and mitigation reactions or operations via AI support, judging almost instantly to enable a 360-degree wall-to-wall view of organizational security posture. Together, these capabilities will bring swifter help to incidents and overall improved decision-making and risk control. CyberAId also increases cyber-resilience in high-frequency trading settings without degrading the system's performance. It protects proprietary trading algorithms by monitoring for unauthorized access or manipulation, ensures market data feed integrity through real-time anomaly detection and automated failover mechanisms, and drives regulatory compliance by automating incident resolution and reporting in line with EU requirements. In broader terms, CyberAId enables financial institutions to enhance fraud and AML detection, mitigate operational overhead, increase regulatory compliance, and maintain strong, adaptive security in a growingly complex and high-risk environment.

6.3 Pilots of ENFORCE

The ENFORCE project introduces a comprehensive framework for validation intended for assuring the effectiveness, durability, and adaptability of a security orchestration platform across the computing continuum from edge to cloud. Validation is pursued in a dual manner, combining controlled experimentation in an extended blueprint infrastructure with real-world testing in carrier environments. This way, both repeatable testing conditions and realistic pre-commercial validation are enabled, including SOC-capable operations and cross-border collaboration that are in line with EU cybersecurity objectives. Under this context, ENFORCE defines three main validation cases to focus on secure service orchestration. The first case is all about secure domain registration and service provisioning. It addresses how the infrastructure's domain is onboarded, how trusted connections are to be established, and what assurance levels have to be extended by way of attestation and risk analysis. The platform supports both automated and self-registration of domains, generates security recommendations, and deploys monitoring mechanisms to improve visibility. The validation of security controls for service onboarding is also performed as it conducts vulnerability assessments of deployment artefacts and aligns the service assurance to SLA and security requirements. This also holds good for multidomain environments, where ENFORCE enforces security policies across heterogeneous infrastructures and coordinates compliance with performance and security constraints. The second validation case validates runtime security and adaptive protection. The validation focused on measuring the platform against continuous monitoring of infrastructure and services by assessing risks and dynamically adapting security mechanisms. Anything that changes in the environment (like for instances, adding new nodes) should trigger dynamic re-evaluation processes and mitigation actions, an example being access control, traffic redirection, or standing up additional monitoring functions. The platform is capable of integrating threat data from SIEM and databases on vulnerabilities to use artificial intelligence (AI)-based analytics for predicting risks and optimizing responses. The credentials are interoperable across different services, with security decisions orchestrated on the basis of domain-specific constraints aimed at keeping service integrity and ensuring compliance. The third validation case emphasizes the identification and mitigation properties of ENFORCE. The platform is capable of foraging into both commonplace and advanced cyber-villain threats, thereby providing for immediate response actions such as traffic filters for blocking or directing malicious traffic. For advanced threats, AI-based decision mechanisms determine the best course of action for hostipable mitigation systems, which may include host reconfiguration, migration, or rejuvenation in order to minimize service fractures. Additionally, ENFORCE implements cross-domain collaborative protection, wherein an attack in one domain can trigger cooperative responses in other domains, hence strengthening resilience across distributed environments. Thus, ENFORCE gives assurance towards secure, responsive, and coordinated service orchestration across heterogeneous multi-domain infrastructures while building in resilience, guaranteeing ceaseless security, and meeting today's intricate and shifting cybersecurity needs within next-generation telecom and other cloud ecosystems.

6.4 Pilots of ACT4FOOD

Providing secure data handling at each level of the supply chain is a priority area of ACT4FOOD. Such secure handling of operational, compliance-related data includes denial management, storage, and exchange that is supported by AI-driven anomaly detection, secure data aggregation, and SIEM monitoring, allowing for a general categorization of its means of data protection. Instantly visible, these results offer a point of verification of trust in which threat intelligence sharing better syncs the mechanisms of early cyber threat detection and, through a collaborative effort, ultimately strengthens harmlessness equilibriums across different sectors. Being proactive is a core part of the ACT4FOOD philosophy about vulnerability management-which is identifying and mitigating risks in advance of exploitation. Automated vulnerability scanning, penetration testing, risk modeling driven by AI, etc., are fundamental strategies in this identification of vulnerabilities around the IT and OT ecosystems, including IoT devices and industrial systems. The help of Continuous Cyber Threat Intelligence feeds to monitor, together with compliance tools that follow well-established standards like NIS2 and GDPR, provides assurance to one's security posturing. Cross-test collaboration in terms of risk assessment and cross-supply chain testing also reinforces the organization's systems overall. In the domain of aquaculture, ACT4FOOD secures IoT sensor data within cold chain logistics. Maintenance of the environmental conditions is crucial for food security. The solution detects threats like data tampering, GPS spoofing, and network intrusions using AI-based anomaly detection, intrusion detection systems, and data integrity mechanisms supported by blockchain. In this respect, automated response capabilities are put in place to isolate compromised elements and reinstate the conduct of a trusted system. The compromise response ensures reliable, tamper-proof monitoring without the need for changing existing infrastructure. Among dairy processing environments, the initiative seeks to ensure the operational technology involving ICSs and associated devices. Artificial intelligence-enabled monitoring, IPS with DLP logging, and threat intelligence work as the three lines of defense on behalf of the system being threatened from system manipulation and cyber-physical assaults. By utilizing advanced threat intelligence, penetration testing-cum-real-time decision support, other IT capabilities, the system ensures the detection and rapid response to any breach or possible breaches to system operations, data integrity, and so forth, as per defined standards. Finally, while in the retail environment, ACT4FOOD helps ensure secure and fictionalized deals or inventory maintenance processes that rely on smart and automatic technologies; it integrates mechanisms like anomaly detection, intrusion detection systems, and blockchain-secured records to mitigate security threats like POS malware, tampering with data, and IoT exploitations. Automated mitigation mechanisms and privacy-enhancing analytics shall fast-track real-time response and situational awareness, thus ensuring that retail operations are secure, trustworthy, reliable, and resilient. Generally put, ACT4FOOD addresses food chain cybersecurity concerns through secure data sharing, proactive risk management, and resilient digital operation support for trust, compliance, and sustainability in modern food systems.

6.5 Pilots of 5G-TACTIC and CTIS4NIS

The 5G-TACTIC testing and evaluation activities focus on validating security requirements derived from its use cases, aiming to assess how effectively its security toolbox mitigates vulnerabilities across diverse 5G environments. These include open-source, virtualized, and multi-vendor deployments, ensuring interoperability and resilience under realistic conditions. Key areas of evaluation include vulnerabilities in the Radio Access Network (RAN), Open RAN (O-RAN), and 5G Core Network, with emphasis on secure operation in complex, disaggregated infrastructures. Test scenarios address issues such as slice isolation, denial-of-service attacks, secure authentication, and protection of communication interfaces. Additional assessments target Software-Defined Networking (SDN) components, examining their configuration, resilience, and ability to maintain performance under stress. Overall, the methodology integrates planning, execution, and evaluation into a unified framework, delivering a comprehensive validation of secure and reliable 5G operations across multiple European testbeds.

Building on these infrastructures, the CTIS4NIS project extends testing to integrated, multi-technology telecom environments combining RAN, core networks, cloud resources, AI/ML systems, and cybersecurity tools. Pilots in Greece and Romania focus on detecting and mitigating cyber threats under realistic conditions, including vulnerability management and coordinated responses to attacks on critical components. A key objective is enabling cross-border collaboration between telecom operators, supporting real-time information sharing and synchronized incident response. Through extensive testing of cybersecurity, interoperability, and performance, the project ensures that results are repeatable and transferable, contributing to resilient and coordinated protection of next-generation telecom infrastructures.

7 Integration with European Data, AI, and Cybersecurity Regulations

The European Union regulates AI through a complex and interconnected ecosystem of legal frameworks, including the AI Act [5], GDPR [17,24], NIS2 Directive [16], Cybersecurity Act [18], Cyber Resilience Act, and Data Act. Rather than relying on a single law, the EU has adopted a multi-layered governance approach where each instrument addresses specific objectives such as data protection, cybersecurity, and digital services. These regulations interact and sometimes overlap, creating both opportunities and challenges in terms of coherence, legal certainty, and implementation. As a result, organizations must navigate multiple regulatory domains simultaneously, ensuring that AI systems align not only with AI-specific rules but also with broader requirements related to data governance, security, and societal values.

At the core of this framework, the AI Act introduces a risk-based approach with strict obligations for high-risk systems, emphasizing transparency, accountability, and human oversight, while the GDPR sets fundamental constraints on how personal data can be used in AI systems. In parallel, cybersecurity regulations such as NIS2 and the Cybersecurity Act impose requirements for risk management, incident reporting, and system robustness. This overlapping regulatory landscape makes compliance a continuous, integrated process across the entire AI lifecycle, encouraging a "compliance-by-design" approach where legal requirements are embedded from the earliest stages of system development. Ultimately, the EU model promotes trustworthy AI by aligning technological innovation with regulatory, ethical, and security principles, ensuring resilient and compliant digital systems.

8 Open Challenges and Research Directions

The three fields of AI, cybersecurity-by-design, and autonomous operations show promising signs of convergence yet face multiple unresolved problems that research must tackle in the upcoming years. The primary challenge requires researchers to develop AI security systems which maintain robustness and explainability and trustworthiness while operating in environments which require continuous model updates without generating security flaws.

The combination of federated and collaborative AI systems creates new issues which require organizations to establish data governance protocols and methods for protecting user privacy while enabling secure model distribution across different systems that operate in various domains. The development of standardized architectural frameworks and operational protocols which enable seamless large-scale system operations while maintaining sovereignty rights constitutes the fundamental requirement for achieving genuine system interoperability between cyber-physical technologies and data space environments. The implementation of zero-touch autonomous systems creates new problems which require organizations to establish effective accountability systems and human monitoring procedures and emergency security protocols for all critical sectors including energy and telecommunications and food systems.

The process of making experimental pilots operational requires organizations to develop new methods for validating results and new rules for governance and new methods to gain public acceptance of technological changes. The achievement of these objectives will enable organizations to implement AI-driven cyber resilience solutions which create a secure and trustworthy digital ecosystem for autonomous operations throughout Europe.

9 Scalability and Distributed Learning

The rapid expansion of digital infrastructures across cloud, edge, and IoT environments creates major challenges for scaling AI-driven cybersecurity systems, particularly in managing computational, storage, and network resources. As data volumes grow and architectures become more decentralized, efficient resource utilization becomes essential. Scalability refers to a system's ability to handle increasing workloads while maintaining performance, and it is critical for enabling machine learning across millions of distributed devices where data cannot be centrally aggregated. Unlike traditional software, ML scalability involves handling continuously growing datasets, longer training times, and higher computational demands, often leading to increased costs. To address this, modern systems rely on distributed training techniques that parallelize computations across multiple machines or GPUs, making large-scale AI deployment feasible.

However, scalability in distributed learning introduces additional complexities, including communication overhead, heterogeneous device capabilities, and uneven data distributions. These challenges are particularly evident in real-world environments and are further compounded in cybersecurity contexts, where expanding infrastructures also increase the attack surface. As highlighted by ENISA [21], scalable AI systems are more exposed to threats such as adversarial attacks, data poisoning, and model manipulation. Addressing these risks requires the development of secure, interoperable, and scalable AI frameworks that integrate distributed learning with strong cybersecurity principles. Such approaches are essential for building resilient, autonomous, and trustworthy systems capable of supporting next-generation critical infrastructures [25,28,32].

10 Next-Generation Cybersecurity Challenges

The transition toward intelligent, automated, and interconnected digital environments is creating a new generation of cybersecurity challenges that go beyond traditional, isolated defenses. Security is shifting from static, perimeter-based models to dynamic, integrated systems spanning the entire compute continuum–from edge devices to cloud infrastructures–where workloads constantly move and the attack surface becomes fluid. This requires unified orchestration capable of enforcing consistent security policies across heterogeneous environments while maintaining performance. At the same time, Zero-Trust Architectures redefine security by placing identity at the center, applying continuous risk assessment to both human and non-human entities, and enforcing least-privilege access in real time. In parallel, real-time "zero-touch" vulnerability management aims to eliminate delays between detection and remediation through AI-driven automation, transforming cybersecurity into a continuous, embedded process within digital operations.

Alongside these shifts, resilience and trustworthiness become critical design goals. Advanced resilience focuses on systems that can maintain functionality even under active attack, using techniques like dynamic reconfiguration and self-healing architectures to ensure continuity. The rise of adversarial AI introduces new risks, requiring robust model hardening methods to defend against manipulation, data poisoning, and privacy breaches. At a broader level, regulatory compliance and strategic autonomy add another layer of complexity, as organizations must align with evolving legal frameworks while reducing dependence on external technologies. Together, these challenges define a cybersecurity paradigm where automation, adaptability, and human oversight are tightly integrated to ensure secure, resilient, and sovereign digital ecosystems.

11 Human-AI Collaboration and User Trust in Autonomous Systems

As AI capabilities mature, Security Operations Centres and critical infrastructure operators increasingly deploy AI for alert triage, anomaly detection, incident investigation, and reporting. In practice, analysts use AI mainly as a decision-support tool–interpreting data, generating hypotheses, and drafting outputs–while retaining control over critical decisions. Over time, AI becomes a routine cognitive aid that reduces workload rather than replacing human judgement. Research shows that effective humanAI collaboration depends on trust, which is shaped by perceived performance, reliability, explainability, and fairness. Crucially, trust must be calibrated to avoid both over-reliance and underuse. These principles are reflected in the EU AI Act, which requires human oversight, transparency, and the ability to intervene or override AI systems, especially in high-risk domains like critical infrastructure.

Operational experience in SOCs confirms that AI works best for repetitive, time-sensitive tasks, while humans handle interpretation, exceptions, and high-impact decisions. Design approaches such as human-in-the-loop systems, explainability tools, and moderate levels of automation improve accuracy and reduce workload without eroding human expertise. The CRSN initiatives apply these principles across sectors by combining AI-driven insights with human oversight, training, and governance frameworks. Projects like ACT4FOOD and CyberAId emphasize explainability, user training, and collaborative decision-making, ensuring AI systems remain transparent and accountable. Overall, the emerging model for trustworthy autonomy integrates AI capabilities with human expertise, supported by regulation, auditability, and continuous skill development to maintain resilience and alignment with human values [26].

12 Conclusion and Future Work

The vision paper presents the combined research work of Cyber-Resilience-Synergy-Network (CRSN) which merges research from VIGILANCE, CyberAId, ENFORCE, ACT4FOOD, CTIS4NIS, and 5G-TACTIC to create cyber-resilient ecosystems that use artificial intelligence for European digital transformation. The CRSN Alliance shows how intelligent automation and secure data spaces and proactive cybersecurity can be used to build next-generation infrastructure through its large-scale pilot projects and their ability to work across different domains. The alliance will achieve its future objectives through additional partnerships with EU-funded projects, which will expand its operational reach and build stronger connections between different project teams. CRSN will focus on three main objectives which include expanding its existing projects, developing new technologies that meet upcoming standards and regulations, and promoting the use of reliable AI-based systems for cybersecurity protection in essential industries.

Acknowledgment. This work has received funding from the European Commission under the Digital Europe Programme and the European Cybersecurity Competence Centre (ECCC). The research leading to these results was supported by the following projects: 5G-TACTIC (Grant Agreement No. 101127973), CTIS4NIS (Grant Agreement No. 101249584), VIGILANCE (Grant Agreement No. 101249737), ENFORCE (Grant Agreement No. 101249431), CyberAId (Grant Agreement No. 101249596), and Act4Food (Grant Agreement No. 101249720).

References

1. 5G-TACTIC EU project. https://www.5g-tactic.eu/. Accessed 31 Mar 2026
2. ACT4FOOD EU project. https://act4food.eu/. Accessed 31 Mar 2026
3. Alic, D.: The role of data protection and cybersecurity regulations in artificial intelligence global governance: a comparative analysis of the European union, the united states, and China regulatory framework. Search in (2021)
4. Anastasopoulos, M., et al.: 5G trusted and secure network deployments and services: the 5G-tactic approach. In: 2024 IEEE 29th International Workshop on Computer Aided Modeling and Design of Communication Links and Networks (CAMAD), pp. 1–6. IEEE (2024)
5. Bird & Bird: European union artificial intelligence act: A guide. https://tinyurl.com/7s7fksxs. Accessed 31 Mar 2026
6. Canavese, D., Ferreira, A., Kamm, L., Rodriguez, A.Q.: Uncovering challenges of cybersecurity cross-regulation in EU legislation. Inf. Softw. Technol. 108033 (2026)
7. CyberAId EU project. https://cyberaidproject.eu/. Accessed 31 Mar 2026
8. ENFORCE EU project. https://enforceproject.eu/. Accessed 31 Mar 2026
9. European Commission, Directorate-General for Communications Networks, Content and Technology: Cybersecurity of 5g networks - eu toolbox of risk mitigating measures. https://digital-strategy.ec.europa.eu/en/library/cybersecurity-5g-networks-eu-toolbox-risk-mitigating-measures. Accessed 31 Mar 2026
10. European Commission – High-Level Expert Group on Artificial Intelligence: Assessment list for trustworthy artificial intelligence (altai). https://ec.europa.eu/newsroom/dae/document.cfm?doc_id=68342. Accessed 31 Mar 2026
11. European Commission – High-Level Expert Group on Artificial Intelligence: A definition of artificial intelligence: Main capabilities and disciplines. https://tinyurl.com/3f5zvce3. Accessed 31 Mar 2026
12. European Commission – High-Level Expert Group on Artificial Intelligence: Ethics guidelines for trustworthy ai. https://ec.europa.eu/newsroom/dae/document.cfm?doc_id=60419. Accessed 31 Mar 2026
13. European Parliament - Policy Department for Transformation, Innovation and Health (ITRE Committee): Interplay between the ai act and the eu digital legislative framework. https://tinyurl.com/mr46cay3. Accessed 31 Mar 2026
14. European Parliamentary Research Service (EPRS): Artificial intelligence and cybersecurity. https://tinyurl.com/4pemtu9w. Accessed 31 Mar 2026
15. European Parliamentary Research Service (EPRS): The impact of the general data protection regulation (gdpr) on artificial intelligence. https://tinyurl.com/yx8nfbyp. Accessed 31 Mar 2026
16. European Union: Directive (eu) 2022/2555 on measures for a high common level of cybersecurity across the union (nis 2 directive). https://eur-lex.europa.eu/eli/dir/2022/2555/oj/eng. Accessed 31 Mar 2026
17. European Union: Regulation (eu) 2016/679 (general data protection regulation – gdpr, https://eur-lex.europa.eu/eli/reg/2016/679/oj/eng, [Online; accessed 31-March-2026]
18. European Union: Regulation (eu) 2019/881 (cybersecurity act). https://eur-lex.europa.eu/eli/reg/2019/881/oj/eng. Accessed 31 Mar 2026
19. European Union Agency for Cybersecurity (ENISA): Artificial intelligence cybersecurity challenges. https://www.enisa.europa.eu/publications/artificial-intelligence-cybersecurity-challenges. Accessed 31 Mar 2026

20. European Union Agency for Cybersecurity (ENISA): Cybersecurity of ai and standardisation. https://www.enisa.europa.eu/publications/cybersecurity-of-ai-and-standardisation. Accessed 31 Mar 2026
21. European Union Agency for Cybersecurity (ENISA): Securing machine learning algorithms. https://www.enisa.europa.eu/publications/securing-machine-learning-algorithms. Accessed 31 Mar 2026
22. European Union Agency for Cybersecurity (ENISA): Threat landscape for 5g networks report, https://www.enisa.europa.eu/publications/enisa-threat-landscape-report-for-5g-networks, [Online; accessed 31-March-2026]
23. Falce, V.: Data regulations and fundamental rights. https://tinyurl.com/2pymj9bp Accessed 31 Mar 2026
24. Hervé, A.: Data protection and artificial intelligence: the European union's internal approach and its possible promotion through trade agreements. Artificial Intelligence and International Economic Law: Disruption, Regulation, and Reconfiguration, p. 193 (2021)
25. Kairouz, P., McMahan, H.B.: Advances and open problems in federated learning. Found. Trends Mach. Learn. **14**(1–2), 1–210 (2021)
26. Lee, J.D., See, K.A.: Trust in automation: designing for appropriate reliance. Hum. Factors **46**(1), 50–80 (2004)
27. Lodder, A.R., Toet, J.J.: Towards cyber security regulation of software in the european union. In: Legal Developments on Cybersecurity and Related Fields, pp. 131–144. Springer, Cham (2024)
28. McMahan, B., Moore, E., Ramage, D., Hampson, S., y Arcas, B.A.: Communication-efficient learning of deep networks from decentralized data. In: Artificial Intelligence and Statistics, pp. 1273–1282. PMLR (2017)
29. Novelli, C., Casolari, F., Hacker, P., Spedicato, G., Floridi, L.: Generative ai in EU law: liability, privacy, intellectual property, and cybersecurity. Comput. Law Secur. Rev. **55**, 106066 (2024)
30. Saqib, H.M., Amin, H.: Comparative analysis of ai regulation for fintech cybersecurity and privacy in the European union and Qatar. Discov. Artif. Intell. (2025)
31. Sharkov, G.: European standardization landscape for trustworthy ai & cybersecurity. https://www.enisa.europa.eu/sites/default/files/all_files/42%20-%20sharkov.pdf. Accessed 31 Mar 2026
32. Shivashankar, K., Hajj, G.S.A., Martini, A.: Scalability and maintainability challenges and solutions in machine learning: systematic literature review. arXiv preprint arXiv:2504.11079 (2025)
33. VIGILANCE EU project. https://vigilance-project.eu/. Accessed 31 Mar 2026

Energy Data Sharing Through Data Spaces with DATAMITE: Supporting Digital Transformation

Konstantinos Kontodimas[1(✉)], Iason-Ioannis Panagos[1], Savvas Manikas[1], and Vasileios Siopidis[2]

[1] Hellenic Electricity Distribution Network Operator (HEDNO) S.A., 20 Perraivou & 5 Kallirois Street, 117 43 Athens, Greece
{k.kontodimas,i.panagos,s.manikas}@deddie.gr
[2] Centre for Research and Technology Hellas (CERTH), 6th km Charilaou - Thermi Rd, 570 01 Thermi, Thessaloniki, Greece
vasisiop@iti.gr

Abstract. Europe's transition toward interoperable and sovereign data ecosystems drives the digital transformation of several sectors and requires practical solutions for automated and efficient cross-sector data sharing. Especially in the energy sector, such ecosystems can contribute to innovation and resource optimisation by facilitating collaboration between organisations and researchers. This paper evaluates the DATAMITE framework as an enabler for automated, secure, and standardised energy data exchange within the context of an energy Distribution System Operator's (DSO) network operations. Through a pilot involving a DSO and an intelligence service provider, we demonstrate how DATAMITE supports end-to-end processes, from data ingestion and quality validation to anonymisation, harmonisation, policy definition, and publication to an Energy Data Space catalogue. Eight validation scenarios are implemented to test the framework's capabilities to support the process of preparation and sharing of data products through an Energy Data Space. The results showcase substantial reductions in manual effort and time-to-consumption, while improving data product compatibility and governance, compared to previous workflows and underscore the DATAMITE framework's role in enabling scalable, trustworthy data exchange and supporting the improvement of energy efficiency in the sector.

Keywords: Data spaces · Data products · Digital transformation · Digital circular economy

1 Introduction

Europe's data economy is currently lagging behind that of the United States and risks falling further behind as China accelerates its growth [19]. In 2024, the U.S.

Published by Springer Nature Switzerland AG 2027
A. Papaleonidas et al. (Eds.): AIAI 2026 Workshops, IFIP AICT 796, pp. 179–192, 2027.
https://doi.org/10.1007/978-3-032-30507-7_11

data market reaches 404 M€ with an 18.7% growth rate, while Europe stands at 90 M€ with 9.7% growth, and China records 68 M€ but expands rapidly at 37.9%. This gap is particularly critical in the context of Europe's ongoing digital transformation, where data acts as a key enabler for resource optimisation, energy efficiency, and the transition toward a circular economy.

To address this challenge, Europe has introduced a comprehensive data strategy [16] aimed at strengthening its position in a data-driven society while unlocking the value of data for sustainable and efficient resource use. Central to this effort is the creation of a unified data ecosystem that supports cross-sector data sharing, enabling smarter energy systems, optimised industrial processes, and circular value chains. Initiatives such as the Common European Data Space [15] (CEEDS), Gaia-X [17], and SIMPL [18] play a pivotal role in advancing interoperable and trustworthy data infrastructures.

Within this context, Data Spaces, coordinated by organisations such as the International Data Spaces Association (IDSA) and initiatives like the Data Spaces Support Centre (DSSC), represent a key enabler of scalable and trustworthy data sharing. However, their large-scale adoption is hindered by the limited maturity of core technologies, particularly data space connectors such as the Eclipse Dataspace Components [14] (EDC) and FIWARE [7] solutions, which are not yet fully production-ready. Current implementations also fall short in enabling advanced data sovereignty, as they primarily support basic access policies and rely on data transfer or service-based consumption, without allowing data processing within the provider's infrastructure, an important capability for reducing data movement and improving energy efficiency. In addition, the lack of standardised authentication and trust mechanisms, including full alignment with the Gaia-X framework, further limits interoperability and slows the development of scalable, cross-sector data ecosystems.

Effective data sharing requires a structured process encompassing data collection, handling, validation, and governance to ensure availability, accessibility, and quality. This involves capabilities such as data discovery, format harmonisation, and the incorporation of semantic layers to enhance interoperability and reduce system friction. At the same time, compliance with regulatory requirements must be ensured, including anonymisation procedures and the definition and enforcement of data access and usage policies.

In the energy sector, data sharing plays a critical role in enabling advanced planning and decision-making processes. Intelligence service providers rely on high-quality data to optimise system operation and investment strategies, particularly in the context of increasing penetration of Renewable Energy Sources (RES) and stochastic loads. Distribution System Operators (DSOs), such as HEDNO [8], currently provide such data mainly through manual or offline procedures. The lack of automation in data preparation and sharing, combined with insufficient mechanisms to enforce data quality criteria, not only hampers efficient data exchange but also limits opportunities for collaboration and revenue generation. Although several solutions exist for data governance, quality, and security, both proprietary [2–4,9] and open source [1,10,11], these are primarily focused on internal data management and rarely support interoperable data sharing. For example, OpenMetadata [11] includes some data sharing considerations but lacks integration with suitable data space connectors.

The European Commission has also recognised the importance of data sharing for the energy sector, emphasising the need for a dedicated and interoperable infrastructure to support efficient data exchange among energy stakeholders. This objective is being advanced through the development of the CEEDS [15], which aims to establish a secure and federated data ecosystem. By enabling improved data accessibility, interoperability, and governance, CEEDS supports key functionalities such as the integration of distributed energy resources, optimisation of system operations, and enhanced energy efficiency, while facilitating cross-sector collaboration and contributing to the broader goals of digital transformation and sustainable resource management.

DATAMITE [6,13] is an open-source modular and multi-domain framework that focuses on exploiting data value through interoperability and data exchange. Its modules offer tools for enhancing data governance, quality and security, and it also incorporates the appropriate connectors for data sharing to a collection of ecosystems, including Energy Data Spaces, through a plugin-based approach. Data discovery, ingestion, harmonisation and fairness evaluation are also supported through its various tools.

2 Methodology

2.1 Problem Definition

System planning is a critical task for Distribution System Operators (DSOs) like HEDNO [20]. It implies developing toolsets for the distribution network planning, aimed at delivering optimal decision support, optimising investments, and minimising CAPEX & OPEX, taking under consideration the projected penetration of Renewable Energy Sources (RES) and stochastic loads (e.g., eletrical vehicles) – considering smart charging services availability, grid constraints regarding losses, power factor, or voltage magnitudes. The following three modules aid a DSO to plan better its system:

a) optimal sizing/siting methodology to select and size the relevant assets (including RES, voltage regulators, etc.),
b) AI-based load and Distributed Energy Resources (DERs) generation forecasts module; and
c) AI-based state estimation algorithms to identify the state variables of the power system, while tackling low real-time data availability.

To perform these tasks, an external intelligence provider may be engaged by the DSO, and an Energy Data Space can serve as the appropriate medium through which the provider can discover and consume the DSO's data.

For testing and demonstration, HEDNO cooperated with CERTH who acted as the intelligence provider partner, consuming the provided data to deliver its intelligence services back to the data provider, HEDNO. Specifically, HEDNO provided a complex data product to CERTH, enabling it to simulate the operation of a section of HEDNO's medium-voltage (MV) network and propose optimisation measures.

The Energy Data Space utilised for the data exchange is DATA CELLAR [5], a data space project that contributes to the int:net *Blueprint of the Common European Energy Data Space* (CEEDS) [21], which outlines a comprehensive roadmap aimed at realising a common framework for energy data exchange and innovation. The CEEDS blueprint aims to accelerate the adoption of data spaces and enable innovative intelligence services through improved interoperability.

Currently, HEDNO collects and certifies measurements from its system, ensuring the availability and statistical analysis of metering data in accordance with data transparency principles and the protection of consumers' personal information. HEDNO uses SCADA[1] system for monitoring the grid, and AMI[2] Meter Data Management (MDM) systems to collect energy measurements. Sharing data with service providers is far from being an easy or automated process. Automation requires services to better find and manage data; to homogenise it; including semantic layers to minimise frictions between systems and increase data interoperability; to guarantee that sensitive and personal data is handled according to laws and regulations, including (pseudo-) anonymisation processes; or to define and enforce global data access control policies. This lack of automation not only complicates sharing data with intelligence service providers but also exploring monetisation or collaboration options like the exploitation of data markets or data spaces.

2.2 Pilot Description

HEDNO has integrated DATAMITE to test and validate streamlining the data sharing process using its various modules, ensuring that all data meets the required quality standards.

Initially, the framework discovers data either from HEDNO's databases, or through manual upload, and securely stores it in its storage service. Next, the data quality is assessed by applying built-in key performance indicators (KPIs) and user-defined quality rules, ensuring that the data meets the necessary quality criteria for sharing with third parties. The framework manages the metadata, data lineage and data versioning, and, most importantly, ensures seamless intra-corporate findability and accessibility of the data with access-control mechanisms. Any sensitive information is anonymised and the data is harmonised, using the framework's support tools. Following this, DATAMITE facilitates data sharing capabilities for the creation of data products, the assignment and enforcement of precise usage policies to them, and for publishing data to (energy) data spaces for broader dissemination. A potential data consumer finds the products of interest in the data space's data catalogue, and, using the data space's connector negotiates a contract and consumes the products. Figure 1 illustrates the high-level architecture of HEDNO's pilot deployment of DATAMITE.

---

[1] Supervisory Control and Data Acquisition.

[2] Advanced Metering Infrastructure.

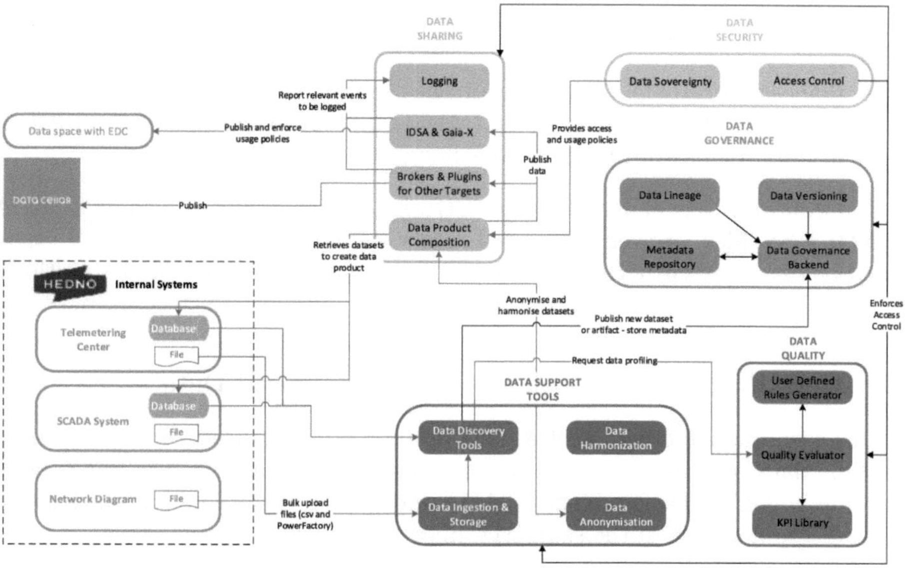

Fig. 1. HEDNO's pilot setup. The diagram depicts the DATAMITE modules and components and the data and metadata flow.

In order to implement pilot's objectives, a thorough demonstration and validation plan was designed that employed all previously mentioned DATAMITE capabilities. The test scenarios are described in Sect. 3, while the business impact is showcased in Sect. 4.

3 Platform Validation and Testing

Eight test scenarios were defined to evaluate the platform, each leveraging capabilities across the full set of software modules. These scenarios are summarised as follows:

1. Dataset creation from multiple data sources
2. Data product composition with anonymised data
3. Data quality assessment with user-defined rules
4. Definition of access and usage policies
5. Data product composition with harmonised data
6. Onboarding procedure to DATA CELLAR
7. Data product publishing to DATA CELLAR Catalogue
8. Data product search and consumption via an Energy Data Space

3.1 Dataset Creation from Multiple Data Sources

In this scenario, the process of discovering and ingesting data from multiple data sources was demonstrated. Specifically, the connectors provided by the DATAMITE framework enable direct integration with the following systems:

- A replica PostgreSQL database that collects measurement data from the SCADA system.
- A replica PostgreSQL database of the Advanced Metering Infrastructure (AMI) Meter Data Management (MDM) system, which contains measurement data for medium-voltage consumers.

In addition to the above, the demonstration included bulk uploading SCADA & AMI CSV files, as well as PowerFactory network model files. In all cases, datasets were created with their corresponding metadata, such as descriptions, domains, glossary terms.

3.2 Data Product Composition with Anonymised Data

In this scenario the creation of a data product from datasets originating from multiple data sources was demonstrated. A synthetic data product was created by combining CSV files from the SCADA and AMI systems, and a PowerFactory network topology file of the same MV lines.

The composition process included anonymising sensitive data columns contained in the AMI datasets, removing columns that were not mandatory for the final data product, analysing and merging structured files that can be unified, and bundling the composite data product with the inclusion of the binary semi-structured PowerFactory files.

Additionally, a data product was created directly from the AMI PostgreSQL database. This involved executing queries on the database using the Trino SQL query engine [12], and applying anonymisation techniques to sensitive data, as is done for the composite data product.

The anonymisation techniques applied were value hashing, masking, suppression, generalisation and pseudo-anonymisation with format preservation. Of these techniques, suppression is the only one that removes the selected column from the dataset, while the others preserve the column but replace the values.

3.3 Data Quality Assessment with User-Defined Rules

In this scenario, a set of data quality rules was defined and applied to SCADA and AMI datasets. The DATAMITE platform evaluated these rules alongside predefined key performance indicators (KPIs), producing quantitative quality scores and ensuring that the datasets conformed to modern data standards and were suitable for use.

DATAMITE supports the assessment of multiple quality dimensions, including *accuracy*, *completeness*, and *validity*. Each rule comprises one or more logical clauses applied to dataset attributes. Users can define rules by selecting fields, specifying comparison operators, and combining clauses using logical operators.

In total, 11 rules were defined and grouped into five categories: (i) timeliness of SCADA measurements, ensuring that the delay between source and recording timestamps does not exceed two minutes; (ii) completeness, verifying that key metadata fields are populated; (iii) validity, ensuring that selected columns contain acceptable values; (iv) consistency, confirming correct measurement units (megawatts –MW– for active power and megavolt-amperes reactive –MVAr– for reactive power); and (v) AMI data conformance, validating accepted values in the data class field.

The platform produced rule-level indicators, expressed as the percentage of records satisfying each rule, which were then aggregated into overall dataset quality scores. All rules achieved 100% except the timeliness rule (99.17%), with minor deviations likely caused by communication delays between the Remote Terminal Unit (RTU) and the SCADA server. This demonstrates the capability of the approach to identify anomalies in measurement recording.

3.4 Definition of Access/Usage Policies

This scenario evaluated the DATAMITE platform's ability to define access/usage policies for data products through policy-based controls integrated with the Eclipse Data Space Components (EDC) connector.

Three data products were considered, all derived from HEDNO's distribution network operations: (i) SCADA-based voltage measurements from HV/MV substations (from year 2022), (ii) AMI metering data with 15-minute active and reactive power measurements, and (iii) a bundled product combining SCADA and metering data with a network model of the corresponding medium-voltage line.

Each publication was associated to a usage policy defining permitted actions and constraints. Three policies were applied: the first allowed use of SCADA data only between 1/3/2026 and 30/4/2026, the second applied the same temporal restriction to metering data and additionally limited usage to the European Union and the third was applied to the bundled dataset, restricting use to the same period, within the EU, and exclusively for research purposes, explicitly prohibiting commercial use.

A summary of the applied policies is provided in Table 1.

Table 1. The access/usage policies used for data publications.

Data Publication	Description
SCADA Voltage Measurements	Allows the action use for the time interval from 1/3/2026 to 30/4/2026.
AMI Measurements	Allows the action use for the time interval from 1/3/2026 to 30/4/2026 and only within the EU region.
Bundled Energy Data Product	Allows the action use from 1/3/2026 to 30/4/2026, within the EU region, and only for research activities, while explicitly prohibiting commercial use.

Once the policies were defined and associated with the data product publications, and after all relevant metadata had been reviewed, the platform was able to expose them to the DATAMITE data space catalogue.

3.5 Data Product Composition with Harmonised Data

This scenario demonstrated the creation of a data product containing load measurements from HEDNO's SCADA system. The measurements were retrieved in separate files per medium-voltage feeder and could not be directly merged due to structural inconsistencies. Data harmonisation was used to align the datasets to a common format, enabling their integration.

A reference model and associated vocabularies were defined to guide the transformation process. For each dataset, metadata (e.g., field names and data types) was extracted and used to derive mapping rules, which were then applied to transform the data into a harmonised structure.

Two data artifacts extracted from the same SCADA system by different operators exhibited slight format variations. One artifact already conformed to the desired structure, while the other required harmonisation to align with it. Table 2 presents the reference format, while Table 3 shows the artifact requiring harmonisation (the shaded cells depict the values that need to be harmonised).

Table 2. Artifact having the desired format.

SCADA time	Source time	Label	Description	Corrected Value	Unit
1/1/2022 0:00	1/1/2022 0:00	`MS-Location1_1-16`	LINE 1–16 CURRENT	21.87	A
1/1/2022 0:30	1/1/2022 0:30	`MS-Location1_1-16`	LINE 1–16 CURRENT	20.31	A

Table 3. Artifact in need of harmonisation. Fields and headers that need harmonisation are depicted in shaded cells.

Scada	**Source**	Label	Description	**Value**	Unit
1/1/2022 0:00	1/1/2022 0:00	`MS-Location1_1-19`	LINE 1-19 CURRENT (REVERSE FLOW)	**9,18**	**Ampere**
1/1/2022 0:15	1/1/2022 0:15	`MS-Location1_1-19`	LINE 1-19 CURRENT (REVERSE FLOW)	**8,99**	**Ampere**

A dataset was created and both CSV files were uploaded as artifacts, with appropriate delimiter settings. The harmonisation workflow was then applied:

metadata was extracted, mappings were defined, and the transformation was executed to produce a harmonised file.

Finally, a data product was composed by combining the harmonised datasets from feeders 1–16 and 1–19 into a single artifact. The aggregation was performed and the result was the final output file.

3.6 Onboarding Procedure to DATA CELLAR

As outlined in previous sections, the pilot aimed to demonstrate the provision of energy data to an intelligence service provider through an Energy Data Space. In this context, integration with the DATA CELLAR project was established. A data portal plugin was developed within the DATAMITE framework to enable interaction with the DATA CELLAR connector, subject to the required onboarding prerequisites.

Following infrastructure deployment, the onboarding process proceeded with wallet provisioning and the creation of the Legal Participant identity using the DATA CELLAR built-in scripts. These steps registered the participant in the DATA CELLAR ecosystem by creating and verifying its Decentralised Identifier (DID) within the catalogue and registry services.

During this process, the participant received a set of Verifiable Credentials[3] issued by DATA CELLAR, including:

- Gaia-X Terms and Conditions Credential (`gx:GaiaXTermsAndConditions`)
- Legal Registration Number Credential (`gx:legalRegistrationNumber`)
- Legal Participant Credential (`gx:LegalParticipant`)

These credentials confirmed compliance with data space governance rules and established a verified legal identity within the ecosystem. They were stored in the participant wallet and made accessible through the DATA CELLAR wallet interface. Once issued and verified, the participant was registered in the data space catalogue, completing the onboarding process. At this stage, HEDNO was able to publish assets, register service offerings, and interact with other connectors via the EDC-based connector API, using the integrated DATAMITE data portal plugin.

3.7 Data Product Publishing to DATA CELLAR Catalogue

This test scenario evaluated the DATAMITE platform's capability to create publications through the DATA CELLAR connector and its ability to leverage third-party data space ecosystems for distributing energy data to external stakeholders.

Before interacting with the DATA CELLAR connector, HEDNO was required to obtain Verifiable Credentials (VCs) through the onboarding process (described in Sect. 3.6). These credentials established a trusted identity within the data space ecosystem and were mandatory to enable secure data exchange.

[3] https://gaia-x.eu/gaia-x-and-verifiable-credentials-presentations/.

The scenario considered a bundled data product derived from HEDNO's energy distribution network, consisting of SCADA measurements, AMI metering data, and a network topology model. In particular, it included voltage measurements from HV/MV substations (from year 2022), active and reactive power measurements at 15-minute intervals, and a medium-voltage network topology file.

To create a publication, the data product and the target portal were selected, i.e. the DATA CELLAR connector. The publication metadata was then defined and reviewed, after which the platform exposed the datasets to the portal's catalogue. The resulting publication appeared in DATAMITE's interface and was made available in HEDNO's data catalogue as a service offering. Verified DATA CELLAR consumers operating compatible connectors were then able to discover the publication through the federated catalogue and access the associated assets.

3.8 Data Product Search and Consumption via Energy Data Space

This scenario explored two approaches for data discovery and consumption through data space technologies: (i) the DATA CELLAR connector and (ii) the DATAMITE-integrated EDC connector. In both cases, CERTH, acting as an intelligence service provider, discovered and consumed datasets published by HEDNO for use in intelligence service simulations. The DATAMITE environment provided plugins enabling publication compatibility with both connectors.

DATAMITE EDC Connector. CERTH accessed the DATAMITE front-end and selected the remote HEDNO connector. The catalogue was retrieved, exposing available publication assets, each identified by a unique asset ID, and datasets belonging to the same data product were represented as individual assets. For each selected asset, the corresponding usage policy was retrieved in machine-readable ODRL[4] format, allowing inspection of constraints such as geographic restrictions. CERTH selected HEDNO's *Telemetry Center* dataset, which had been anonymised prior to publication.

Contract negotiation was then initiated, resulting in a formal agreement and a contract identifier confirming acceptance of the usage conditions. A transfer process was subsequently established to prepare data access. The platform then retrieved the Endpoint Data Reference (EDR), including the endpoint and authorisation token, which enabled secure access to the dataset. The data was returned in structured form corresponding to the selected asset.

By repeating this process for the remaining required datasets, CERTH accessed HEDNO's electricity grid data through an automated workflow covering discovery, policy inspection, contract negotiation, and secure retrieval under defined conditions.

[4] Open Digital Rights Language.

DATA CELLAR Connector. CERTH provided the HEDNO endpoint address in the corresponding field of the catalogue fetch endpoint and retrieved the provider's federated catalogue. The catalogue exposed all available datasets, each described through metadata, and data access was granted solely based on valid Verifiable Credentials. CERTH then selected the relevant asset identifier and invoked the consume asset endpoint to retrieve the dataset. It should be noted that the current DATA CELLAR connector implementation does not support advanced usage policy definitions and as a result, constraints such as temporal, geographic, or purpose-based restrictions, which were available in the DATAMITE EDC-based approach, were not applicable. By repeating the asset consume request for the remaining datasets, CERTH retrieved all required data to support intelligence service simulation workflows.

4 Performance Evaluation and Business Impact

The effectiveness of the DATAMITE framework was assessed in the context of the pilot comparing its data-management and data-sharing workflows with previously established manual and offline procedures used within HEDNO. Measurements collected during the pilot demonstrated substantial improvements across multiple operational dimensions, including workflow duration, manual effort, interoperability, data quality management, and storage efficiency. The following key performance indicators, presented in Table 4, summarise the most significant outcomes observed during the evaluation, reflecting the impact of automation, standardisation, and centralised governance introduced by the framework.

Table 4. Key Performance Indicators for business impact.

Key Performance Indicator	Value
Reduction in time required to share data via data portals and data spaces compared to manual or hard-coded methods	65%
Reduction in effort required to share data via data portals and data spaces compared to manual or hard-coded methods	65%
Reduction in time to reach target data consumers	80%
Increase in the percentage of data products that are technically compatible with external platforms	70%
Reduction in the number and diversity of roles involved in data quality evaluation processes	50%
Reduction in data duplication	50%

DATAMITE contributes to HEDNO's business objectives by accelerating internal organisational processes and enhancing overall operational efficiency.

Data sharing constitutes a core component of HEDNO's strategic outlook, as the sole DSO in Greece, holds an advantageous position in data collection. Providing access to this data for external stakeholders (research institutions, universities, and private-sector entities) is important to HEDNO. Such exchanges enable HEDNO to obtain research results and specialised intelligence services, thereby strengthening its infrastructure, supporting more effective system planning, improving resource management, and ultimately reducing operational expenditures. Furthermore, these collaborations improve service offerings and cultivate an environment conducive to innovation and create additional incentives for investment in green energy technologies. The resulting advancements not only enhance value for end consumers but also generate broader societal benefits.

An essential consideration in data sharing is the time and effort required to deliver the data. Although internal protocols for data dissemination are already in place, they necessitate substantial preparation, negotiation, and coordination across departments and personnel, resulting in delays. In contrast, DATAMITE offers a suite of advanced tools accessible through a user interface, reducing data preparation and publication time. These tools streamline the entire data-sharing workflow, encompassing all steps required for preparing and publishing data to a portal or data space, such as DATA CELLAR, by consolidating these actions within a single platform. Moreover, DATAMITE automates multiple tasks within the data preparation phase, including data ingestion, harmonisation, anonymisation, and quality assurance, which traditionally required extensive manual effort for editing, reviewing, and validating data, and were prone to human error. Empirical observations from the pilot demonstrated that the components integrated into the DATAMITE platform execute these functions automatically with minimal human intervention, reducing the overall time and effort associated with data sharing by approximately 65% compared to previous methods.

The use of data spaces and similar portals significantly accelerates data exchange between HEDNO and external stakeholders through automation. For data consumers, obtaining access to datasets through a data space involves: completing the onboarding process, browsing the catalog of available offerings, and selecting the desired data product. Connectors then automatically manage the data-sharing procedure and enforce usage and access policies, thereby reducing the time required for data acquisition. These automated mechanisms yield a measurable improvement in data-sharing efficiency, up to 80% based on the time elapsed from the initial data request to final acquisition, when compared to previous workflows that relied on traditional sharing protocols and mutual trust between partners to ensure appropriate data use.

Data interoperability is simultaneously ensured through adherence to international standards and frameworks, enhancing dataset compatibility with external platforms. The architecture of DATAMITE facilitates interoperability and the integration of heterogeneous data sources by automating regulatory tagging, metadata standardisation, and interoperability validation, enabling organisations to generate compliant data products efficiently. The resulting datasets conform to established ontologies and vocabularies during the preparation phase, improving compatibility with existing frameworks and standards by approximately 70%, and ensuring seamless integration and exchange with current infrastructures. DATAMITE mitigates inefficiencies in traditional data review through automation.

The evaluation showed that another significant improvement introduced by the DATAMITE framework is the reduction of data duplication for each data source by 50%. Under previous practices, multiple copies of the same dataset were frequently stored across different platforms and internal systems, resulting in increased storage costs, inconsistencies in data quality and completeness, and challenges related to version control, all of which contributed to increased administrative overhead for HEDNO. DATAMITE enforces centralised metadata governance and incorporates robust deduplication mechanisms, ensuring that each dataset is maintained as a single authoritative source. This approach enhances data integrity while simultaneously reducing infrastructure-related costs.

In a similar manner, the data quality assessment tools integrated into the framework have substantially improved the workflows of personnel responsible for preparing data prior to dissemination. DATAMITE incorporates multiple components dedicated to data quality management, offering functionality for defining, applying, and evaluating quality rules across datasets. The rule-definition interface provides considerable flexibility in constructing quality constraints and supports the evaluation of multiple dimensions within each dataset (e.g., applying rules to individual columns), thereby ensuring high-quality outputs and alignment with contemporary data standards. By consolidating all relevant components within a single interface, the framework simplifies and accelerates the entire quality-assessment process.

The performance evaluation showcases that HEDNO realises a broad set of strategic, operational, and economic advantages through the adoption of the DATAMITE framework and its associated data-sharing infrastructure by improving its workflows, lowering associated costs and promoting efficient collaboration with external stakeholders. These capabilities strengthen HEDNO's position as a key data provider and enhance HEDNO's strategic value, contributing to more effective planning and service delivery across the energy ecosystem. Furthermore, these results reflect the performance of the framework within the scope of the pilot and its potential for broader operational deployment, while underscoring its impact regarding resource optimisation.

5 Conclusion

This paper evaluates how the DATAMITE framework supports Distribution System Operators (DSOs) to efficiently exchange data through interoperable, policy-driven data-space technologies. The framework was evaluated through a pilot application over eight test scenarios involving dataset creation, data product composition, onboarding to an Energy Data Space, and cross-connector data consumption. The results show significant improvements in workflow efficiency, reductions in effort and time required for data preparation, sharing, and quality management. These improvements translate into faster access to intelligence services, more efficient planning processes, and reduced operational overhead, highlighting DATAMITE's potential to enable digital circular economies within and beyond a data-driven energy ecosystem.

Acknowledgments. This study was funded by the European Union (GA: 101092989).

Disclosure of Interests. The authors have no competing interests to declare that are relevant to the content of this article.

References

1. Amundsen. https://www.amundsen.io/. Accessed 15 Apr 2026
2. Ataccama. https://www.ataccama.com/. Accessed 15 Apr 2026
3. Atlan. https://atlan.com/. Accessed 15 Apr 2026
4. Collibra. https://www.collibra.com/. Accessed 17 Sept 2025
5. DATA CELLAR. https://datacellarproject.eu/. Accessed 15 Apr 2026
6. DATAMITE. https://datamite-horizon.eu/. Accessed 15 Apr 2026
7. FIWARE. https://www.fiware.org/. Accessed 15 Apr 2026
8. HEDNO. https://www.deddie.gr/. Accessed 15 Apr 2026
9. Informatica. https://www.informatica.com/platform.html. Accessed 15 Apr 2026
10. LinkedIn DataHub. https://datahubproject.io/. Accessed 15 Apr 2026
11. OpenMetaData. http://open-metadata.org. Accessed 15 Apr 2026
12. Trino — Distributed SQL query engine for big data. https://trino.io/. Accessed 15 Apr 2026
13. Aroca, J.A., et al.: Boosting data monetisation with datamite. In: IFIP International Conference on Artificial Intelligence Applications and Innovations, pp. 33–46. Springer, Cham (2024)
14. Eclipse Foundation: Eclipse Dataspace Components Project. https://projects.eclipse.org/projects/technology.edc. Accessed 15 Apr 2026
15. European Commission: CEEDS. https://www.ceeds.energy/. Accessed 15 Apr 2026
16. European Commission: European Data Strategy. https://commission.europa.eu/strategy-and-policy/priorities-2019-2024/europe-fit-digital-age/european-data-strategy_en. Accessed 15 Apr 2026
17. European Commission: Gaia-X Trust Framework. https://gaia-x.eu/. Accessed 15 Apr 2026
18. European Commission: SIMPL Programme. https://simpl-programme.ec.europa.eu/dashboard/home. Accessed 15 Apr 2026
19. European Commission: The European Data Market Study. https://ec.europa.eu/newsroom/repository/document/2025-13/EDM_2024__2026__First_Report_on_Facts_and_Figures_9cU0iIjcuSZhjmwI9TchwqenidQ_114043.pdf. Accessed 15 Apr 2026
20. Henriques, R.A., et al.: Sharing electricity distribution data via energy data spaces with datamite. In: IET Conference Proceedings CP922, vol. 2025, pp. 1660–1664. IET (2025)
21. int:net: Blueprint of the Common European Energy Data Space (2024). https://intnet.eu/images/resources/Blueprint_CEEDS_v2.pdf. Accessed 15 Apr 2026

Harmful Content Moderation in e-Participation Platforms

Rui Vidal[2], Marco Neto[2], Tomas Dias[2], Pedro Tomas[1,2(✉)], Luis Rosa[2], and Luis Cordeiro[2]

[1] University of Coimbra, CISUC, DEI, Coimbra, Portugal
[2] OneSource, Coimbra, Portugal
{rui.vidal,marco.neto,tomas.dias,pedro.tomas,luis.rosa, cordeiro}@onesource.pt

Abstract. Moderating harmful textual content in e-participation platforms requires balancing user safety with the protection of legitimate democratic expression, procedural fairness, and deliberative quality. This paper reviews the evolution of automated moderation approaches, from rule-based and classical machine learning methods to transformers and large language models, while highlighting the contextual, explainability, bias, and governance challenges that are especially salient in civic settings. Building on this review, the paper presents a multi-LLM moderation workflow with council-based consolidation and human oversight. Experimental results using a test set of 150 examples show that while individual model accuracy peaked at 0.6267 with Llama 3.2, an oracle accuracy of 0.9467 highlights the potential for improved results. Aggregating judgments through a council yielded 0.5733 accuracy, suggesting that refining consolidation rules is a key path forward for robust decisions. The proposed workflow is further situated as a possible moderation component within the broader Co-Participation platform. The study positions harmful content moderation in e-participation as a socio-technical governance challenge rather than a conventional text classification task, and emphasises the need for evaluation methods aligned with deliberative and institutional goals.

Keywords: e-Participation · Harmful Content Moderation · Large Language Models · Civic AI

1 Introduction

Digital e-participation platforms have become vital tools for fostering citizen engagement, public consultation, and democratic deliberation, as illustrated by platforms such as vTaiwan [16], Consul [4], and Decidim [7]. These platforms demonstrate that civic moderation is embedded in institutional settings where deliberative quality, fairness, transparency, and accountability are central, and in which harmful content must be interpreted in light of workflows, roles, and the boundary between abuse and legitimate democratic disagreement. Within

Published by Springer Nature Switzerland AG 2027
A. Papaleonidas et al. (Eds.): AIAI 2026 Workshops, IFIP AICT 796, pp. 193–206, 2027.
https://doi.org/10.1007/978-3-032-30507-7_12

this context, however, such platforms are increasingly confronted with harmful textual content, including hate speech, harassment, toxic rhetoric, implicit aggression, and misinformation, with consequences for participation, institutional trust, and the integrity of deliberative processes.

Early efforts relied on rule-based systems and traditional Machine Learning (ML) techniques focused on surface-level patterns, which were easily circumvented by paraphrasing and coded language. Deep Learning (DL), a branch of neural-network-based ML, enabled richer semantic representation but remained limited in long-range dependencies, implicit intent, and discourse-level interpretation. Transformer architectures and Large Language Models (LLMs) have advanced moderation by capturing contextual meaning, tone, and pragmatic cues, which is especially relevant in e-participation environments, where message interpretation depends on dialogue structure, institutional framing, and socio-political context. Moderating participatory discourse remains particularly challenging because harm is inherently contextual, since in policy debates and multi-turn discussions, meaning depends on conversational history, community norms, and the boundary between harmful discourse and legitimate democratic expression.

In contrast to broader surveys of abusive language detection, this review is organised around the governance and interpretive requirements of e-participation platforms, where moderation must address democratic dissent, procedural fairness, institutional accountability, and deliberative quality rather than toxicity alone. It synthesises moderation paradigms from rule-based systems and classical ML to Transformers and LLMs, examining their strengths, limitations, and challenges in contextual modelling, bias, explainability, governance, and evaluation. Specifically, it traces their evolution, analyses their use in e-participation, compares their civic trade-offs, and outlines a multi-LLM workflow with council-based consolidation and human oversight.

This research was conducted within the scope of the CoParticipation project [8], as an experimental phase aimed at exploring and validating approaches for the moderation of malicious content in e-participation platforms. CoParticipation aims to be a next-generation digital participation platform designed to support more inclusive, collaborative, and safe participatory processes through digital engagement tools and AI-based assistance. Within that broader context, the present study focuses on one specific component of the project, namely the moderation of harmful content in e-participation settings.

2 Harmful Content in e-Participation Platforms

Harmful content in e-participation platforms includes textual contributions that may cause psychological, social, or institutional harm to individuals, groups, or the participatory process itself [31], such as hate speech, harassment, offensive language, implicit threats, intimidation, and misinformation. These behaviours can undermine deliberation, discourage civic engagement, marginalise vulnerable participants, and erode trust in democratic institutions.

In contrast to generic social media, e-participation platforms operate within institutional frameworks, emphasising procedural fairness and reasoned dialogue. Harmfulness depends on intent, target, and context [6], with seemingly benign statements becoming harmful through sarcasm, implicit hostility, or coded language [20]. Moderation must balance harm prevention with the protection of legitimate political expression, as overtly "toxic" content may constitute democratic dissent, while subtle exclusion, intimidation, or misinformation can have outsized institutional effects [31,35]. This broader literature has been synthesised in survey work such as Fortuna and Nunes [12] and Kiritchenko et al. [20], which provide important methodological and ethical background for the present discussion.

Socially grounded taxonomies classify harmful content along type, target, intent, and pragmatics, and severity [6]. Types include identity-based hate, non-identity insults, harassment, sexual aggression, threats, and misinformation. Targets may be individuals, groups, or institutions. Intent and pragmatics capture whether language is malicious, sarcastic, satirical, or legitimate, while severity ranges from mild incivility to explicit violence or sustained intimidation. This multidimensional perspective highlights the limits of lexical methods and the need to consider discourse structure, conversational dynamics, and community norms, as misclassification may suppress legitimate expression or miss subtle harms [27,35].

Such taxonomies are central to automated moderation, guiding annotation, evaluation, and context-aware interpretation. Across platforms, intent, context, and severity are essential for analysing harmful discourse and form the conceptual basis for modern automated approaches, including language models [6].

Overall, effective moderation in e-participation thus requires context-aware models that engage with conversational history, institutional norms, and pragmatic intent. The next section examines the evolution of moderation technologies in response to these requirements.

3 Evolution of Text Moderation Models

Automated harmful text detection has advanced rapidly over the past decade, driven by advances in Natural Language Processing (NLP), which is the study of computational methods for analysing human language, and ML. This section reviews the transition from classical ML to modern LLMs, highlighting their capabilities, limitations, and relevance for e-participation moderation. Rather than aiming for exhaustive coverage of the broader abusive-language literature, the discussion focuses on the main methodological paradigms and on the properties that matter most in participatory settings, namely contextual interpretation, transparency, robustness across domains, and civic governance requirements.

3.1 Classical and Deep Learning Approaches

Early harmful content detection relied on rule-based systems and classical supervised ML classifiers. Rule-based approaches, using keyword blacklists and manual heuristics, were simple and interpretable but highly sensitive to lexical variation and easily bypassed through misspellings or character substitutions. They also produced frequent false positives in legitimate contexts such as quotations, academic writing, and journalism [18,29]. While still used for transparency and low computational cost, they were insufficient for capturing the complexity of socially harmful language.

Supervised ML models, including Support Vector Machines (SVM), Logistic Regression (LR), and Naïve Bayes, framed harmful content detection as a text classification problem [12]. Although efficient and interpretable, these models struggled with implicit or sarcastic harms and generalised poorly across platforms due to dataset-specific vocabulary and annotation conventions [30].

Early DL approaches shifted toward end-to-end representation learning. Convolutional Neural Networks (CNNs) and Recurrent Neural Networks (RNNs) could extract semantic patterns directly from raw text, reducing dependence on handcrafted features [12]. Pre-trained word embeddings improved robustness to paraphrasing, spelling variation, and informal language, enhancing performance across diverse online contexts [5].

However, first-generation DL models retained limitations: they struggled with long-range dependencies, required large annotated datasets, and remained vulnerable to dataset imbalance and annotation bias [30]. Critically, they lacked mechanisms to incorporate conversational context, discourse structure, or pragmatic intent, which are essential for detecting harmful behaviour in deliberative and participatory environments. In e-participation settings, these limitations are especially restrictive because harm may emerge through reply structure, sustained incivility, or indirect intimidation rather than isolated lexical cues.

3.2 Transformer-Based Moderation Models

The introduction of Transformer architectures marked a major transition in text modelling. By replacing sequential processing with self-attention mechanisms, Transformers enable models to capture global dependencies within text, allowing each token to attend to contextually relevant elements regardless of positional distance [32]. This capability substantially improved the representation of semantic meaning and discourse structure, making Transformer-based models particularly effective for text classification tasks.

Encoder-based Transformer architectures became the dominant paradigm for harmful content detection, as they generate contextualised embeddings capable of capturing nuanced linguistic patterns and supporting improved cross-domain generalisation [10]. These models demonstrated strong performance in identifying both explicit and implicit forms of abusive language, consistently outperforming earlier DL architectures across a range of moderation benchmarks [34].

However, the adoption of Transformer-based moderation models also introduced new challenges. Their increased architectural complexity reduces interpretability relative to classical approaches, complicating the explanation and justification of moderation decisions in high-stakes environments. Although attention visualisation and post-hoc explainability methods have been proposed, the opacity of deep contextual representations remains a significant concern, particularly in participatory settings that require transparency and accountability. In addition, Transformer models continue to rely heavily on annotated datasets and may reproduce social, cultural, or demographic biases present in training data [37]. These properties make Transformer-based models more suitable than earlier approaches for e-participation platforms, where distinguishing legitimate democratic disagreement from harassment often depends on conversational context, although their opacity remains a serious challenge for accountable deployment.

3.3 Large Language Models for Moderation

Building on Transformer architectures, recent LLMs trained on web-scale corpora exhibit advanced reasoning, dialogue, and instruction-following capabilities [24]. Prominent examples include OpenAI's GPT series [3], Meta's LLaMA [2], and Google DeepMind's Gemma [1]. Large-scale self-supervised pre-training equips these models with broad linguistic, semantic, and pragmatic abilities, enabling generalisation across tasks and domains [24]. In contrast to earlier supervised systems, LLMs can classify harmful content in zero or few-shot settings, reducing reliance on task-specific retraining [22].

LLMs support both zero-shot and few-shot moderation, enabling adaptation through instructions or a small set of annotated examples without retraining. This is especially useful in e-participation contexts, where policies change over time, and labelled datasets are often limited [35].

Recent work also explores moderation-oriented LLM variants, instruction-tuned on safety-labelled corpora and structured risk taxonomies. These models support policy-aware classification and structured risk assessment within moderation pipelines [17], illustrating the feasibility of using LLMs as central tools for automated e-participation moderation, though institutional oversight remains essential [13,21]. This is especially important in civic platforms, where moderation must remain aligned with institutional rules while still preserving legitimate democratic expression.

Modelling Tone, Intent, and Implicit Harm. A persistent challenge in harmful content detection is that abusive or manipulative intent is often expressed indirectly. Sarcasm, coded language, polite hostility, indirect threats, and context-dependent meanings complicate annotation and automated analysis. Classical ML and first-generation DL models struggled with these subtleties due to limited contextual modeling [20].

LLMs improve contextual representation by capturing long-range dependencies, discourse-level signals, and pragmatic patterns. Self-attention allows tokens to condition on distant context, embeddings encode meaning relative to surrounding discourse, and pre-training on diverse communicative settings enables modelling of pragmatic language use. Consequently, LLMs can better distinguish reclaimed language from abuse, humour from harassment, or neutral facts from harmful misinformation [6], a distinction critical in participatory environments where political critique and exclusionary discourse may coexist.

Nevertheless, modelling tone and intent remains challenging. LLMs can struggle with culturally specific norms, community codes, or highly local references. Linguistic analysis alone may be insufficient, as conversational structure, temporal dynamics, and interactional context heavily influence perceived harm [20]. In e-participation settings, this means that even strong LLMs are most reliable when moderation decisions are supported by surrounding context and, where needed, human review.

Prompt-Based Moderation and Its Implications. Contemporary LLMs are controlled through prompts (i.e., natural-language instructions) that define task objectives, decision criteria, and output structures at inference time. In moderation, prompts allow models to act as classifiers, policy interpreters, or explanation generators without parameter updates or task-specific retraining. They can encode category definitions, normative guidelines, and structured response formats, promoting consistency and supporting evaluation [22].

This instruction-based paradigm offers a flexible way to align model behaviour with institution-specific moderation frameworks by operationalising policy directly at inference time rather than only through retraining [26]. Prompts can explicitly encode moderation criteria, enabling systems to reflect the procedural and normative requirements of participatory environments. For example, they may instruct a model to distinguish legitimate political criticism from identity-based attacks, assign policy-defined risk levels, and account for deliberative criteria such as respectfulness, evidence-based argumentation, relevance to policy discussion, and multilingual or context-sensitive norms [26].

However, prompt-based moderation also introduces methodological and operational challenges. Model outputs can be highly sensitive to prompt design, producing variability across semantically equivalent inputs [22]. This also creates exposure to prompt injection, in which adversarial or strategically crafted inputs attempt to override, redirect, or confuse moderation instructions, either explicitly or implicitly. Such vulnerabilities can reduce policy adherence, weaken reliability and robustness, and enable safety-bypass strategies. These risks highlight the need for systematic prompt design, prompt versioning, evaluation protocols, and governance oversight in high-stakes civic moderation contexts.

3.4 Comparative Perspective on Modelling Approaches

Considered collectively, the evolution from classical feature-based models to LLM-driven moderation reflects a shift from surface-level pattern detection to context-aware, pragmatically grounded, and increasingly policy-aware language understanding. Rule-based systems and traditional ML classifiers remain useful as interpretable baselines and lightweight filters, although their reliance on lexical features limits their ability to detect implicit, context-dependent, or discourse-level harm [29].

Early DL models improved robustness to linguistic variation, paraphrasing, and informal language through distributed semantic representations. Although their sequential architectures constrained long-range dependency modelling, conversational structure, and pragmatic intent detection, these remained central challenges in deliberative moderation [30]. Transformer-based encoders advanced moderation by enabling contextualised representations via self-attention, improving performance and cross-domain transfer. However, they raised concerns about interpretability, data dependency, and biases in training corpora [32]. LLMs extend these capabilities with instruction-following, in-context learning, and natural-language reasoning, supporting dynamic moderation, policy-aware classification, and explanation generation. These features are particularly relevant for governance-focused environments like e-participation, where moderation criteria may be institution-specific and contestable. Challenges remain, including sensitivity to prompt design, high computational costs, and susceptibility to manipulation or policy misalignment [22].

In e-participation, harmfulness often depends on intent, discourse function, and conversational context rather than keywords alone. As summarised in Table 1, rule-based and classical models remain useful as lightweight baselines, whereas transformers and LLMs provide stronger contextual reasoning but introduce challenges in transparency, bias, and robustness, reinforcing the need for human oversight.

Table 1. Trade-offs of moderation approaches in e-participation settings

Approach	Strengths	Context	Interpretability	Limitations
Rule-based	Simple, transparent filtering	Low	High	Obfuscation, sarcasm, false positives
Classical ML	Data-efficient baselines	Low	Medium	Domain shift, weak implicit harm
Early DL	Local semantics	Medium	Low	Long-range limits, weak discourse cues
Transformers	Global context	High	Low-Medium	Bias, limited transparency
LLMs	Policy-aware reasoning	Very High	Variable	Prompt attacks, instability

Table 1 summarises these complementary trade-offs across interpretability, contextual understanding, and key limitations. Rather than representing a linear replacement of earlier approaches, this progression reveals distinct strengths and failure modes that contemporary research seeks to evaluate and combine within socio-technical moderation frameworks, particularly in participatory environments where transparency, accountability, and normative alignment, and the protection of legitimate democratic expression are critical [6].

4 Conceptual Perspectives on LLM-Based Moderation in e-Participation

Building on recent literature, this section complements broader surveys of abusive-language detection by synthesising conceptual perspectives on LLMs in civic moderation, highlighting functional roles, design considerations, and governance principles in e-participation rather than proposing a new technical framework [12,20]. In contrast to recent civic-platform analyses such as [35], the emphasis here is on a broader conceptual synthesis of moderation paradigms, governance requirements, and workflow implications for e-participation platforms.

Moderation can be viewed as a multi-stage interpretive process. Contributions are analysed for semantic content, tone, and pragmatic intent, followed by an assessment of potential harm relative to participatory norms and institutional rules. LLMs increasingly serve as components for semantic and pragmatic reasoning, enabling contextual classification, policy-aware interpretation, and structured moderation rationales [17,23]. Their ability to consider extended discourse context is particularly valuable in deliberative environments, where meaning emerges through interaction [28].

Human oversight remains central. Automated outputs serve as decision-support rather than autonomous judgments, with moderators and institutions handling escalation, accountability, and normative alignment to mitigate model error and bias. Transparency and policy explicitness are also critical. LLMs can map content to policy categories and generate natural-language explanations, supporting interpretability, contestability, and institutional trust [11,25]. In civic settings, this also requires preserving the conditions under which a decision was made, including the applicable policy and prompt formulation.

Finally, research emphasises adaptability across participatory infrastructures. Conceptual approaches focus on interpretive challenges and the evolving role of language models, enabling insights to transfer across platforms, institutional arrangements, and governance contexts [35].

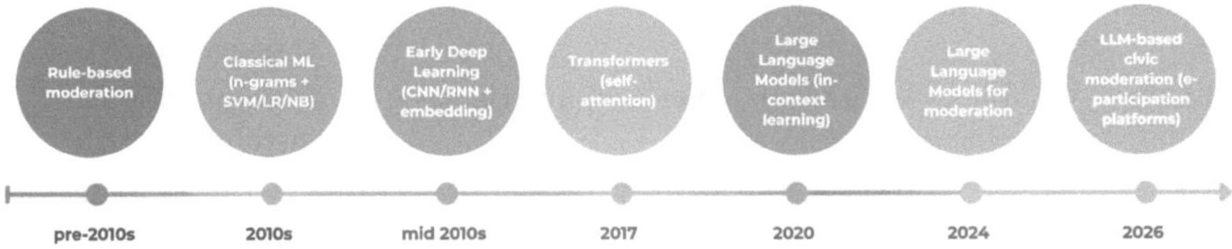

Fig. 1. Timeline of modelling paradigms for harmful content detection in civic settings.

Figure 1 summarises the progression of modelling approaches discussed in this section, from **rule-based moderation** and **classical ML** classifiers to **early DL** models, **Transformers**, and **LLM-based moderation**. This evolution reflects a shift from surface-level pattern matching to increasingly contextual and semantically grounded representations that better capture paraphrase, implicit intent, and discourse-level phenomena. More recently, **LLM-based civic moderation** extends these capabilities to e-participation platforms through in-context learning, instruction-following, and policy-conditioned moderation, while also raising governance and operational concerns such as prompt sensitivity, computational cost, and the need for stronger oversight to ensure consistency, transparency, and normative alignment.

4.1 Council-Based Moderation Workflow

This subsection presents a moderation workflow for e-participation platforms, integrating automated analysis with structured human oversight. As shown in Fig. 2, the workflow follows a risk-based process that balances scalability, governance, traceability, and disagreement handling. Rather than treating moderation as a single classification step, the workflow separates low-cost filtering, policy-based analysis, disagreement assessment, and final human validation.

Fig. 2. Illustrative multi-LLM moderation workflow with council-based decision

Incoming messages first pass through a lightweight pre-processing layer that filters spam, flooding, and clearly disallowed patterns while performing basic normalisation. For reproducibility and auditing, messages may be logged with clear delimiters, enabling deterministic replay and post-hoc inspection. Messages that pass pre-filtering are then evaluated by a small group of LLMs configured with the platform's moderation policy. To improve consistency and auditability, inference may be run with the temperature set to 0, reducing stochastic variation. The prompting setup may also support multilingual inputs and instructions, allowing the same policy structure to be applied across different languages. Each model produces a structured record containing a binary decision, a severity score (0–10), and a brief rationale grounded in the message and policy. When available, conversational context can be included to clarify intent, such as criticism versus harassment, and to reduce false positives from quotations or counter-speech. At this stage, the system may also support standard moderation metrics, including accuracy, cohen's kappa, and F1 score, particularly when comparing context-aware and context-free predictions.

The resulting structured outputs are then passed to a council stage, where candidate model decisions are compared and aggregated under a shared evaluation protocol. Depending on the implementation, this may be done pairwise or pointwise against a common rubric. Recent work on council-based and mutual LLM evaluation suggests that aggregating judgments across multiple models can improve robustness on subjective tasks and reduce dependence on a single judge

[14,38]. This step is especially useful for ambiguous or politically sensitive cases, since disagreement between models can signal that the content should not be treated as a straightforward automated decision. The council result, together with the candidate rationales, can therefore provide a more robust basis for downstream review while preserving traceability of disagreement. In some implementations, models may also contribute unequally to the final aggregation, with greater influence assigned to those that show stronger empirical performance or closer policy alignment. This stage can also be analysed through agreement rate, escalation frequency, and score consistency across candidate models.

4.2 Experimental Analysis

To validate the proposed approach, a test set of 150 examples was considered and evaluated with four candidate models, llama3.2:1b, gemma3:1b-it-q4_K_M, atel3134/gpt2:1.5b, and deepseek-r1:1.5b, under a pointwise council configuration with three judges, score normalisation enabled, a tie margin of 0.10, and a minimum of one valid judge per candidate.

Table 2. Candidate level moderation and council selection results on 150 examples.

Metric	llama3.2	deepseek_r1	gemma3	gpt2	Council
Accuracy	0.6267	0.6133	0.4733	0.4533	0.5733
Correct/Total	94/150	92/150	71/150	68/150	86/150
Council wins	67	15	49	19	–
Avg. raw score	4.8480	2.9110	3.8764	3.2749	–

Table 2 presents the results obtained for the different models. At the individual level, llama3.2 achieved the highest accuracy, with 0.6267 (94/150), followed by deepseek_r1 with 0.6133 (92/150), while gemma3 and gpt2 reached 0.4733 (71/150) and 0.4533 (68/150), respectively. The candidate pool nevertheless shows strong potential, since the oracle accuracy reaches 0.9467 (142/150), indicating that correct answers are already present for most examples and that the main remaining challenge lies in the selection and aggregation stage rather than in the absence of viable candidate outputs.

At the council stage, the aggregated decision selected llama3.2 in 67 cases, gemma3 in 49, gpt2 in 19, and deepseek_r1 in 15, with no ties under the current configuration. The resulting council accuracy was 0.5733 (86/150), which does not yet surpass the best individual model. In the present implementation, the council acts as an exploratory aggregation layer based on pointwise judging, score normalisation, prior based adjustment, and fallback rules, rather than as a trained selector. Consequently, the current result is more informative as evidence of where the bottleneck lies, rather than as a final estimate of the council's value based moderation. In particular, the large gap between council's and oracle's accuracy suggests that the candidate pool is already sufficiently strong and that further gains are more likely to come from improving the consolidation rule, judge calibration, and escalation strategy. The final consolidated decision is then forwarded to a human moderator, preserving institutional oversight while keeping the workflow auditable, comparable, and suitable for iterative refinement.

5 Open Challenges and Research Directions

Despite advances in Transformer-based models and LLMs, moderating harmful content on e-participation platforms remains an open and evolving problem, particularly regarding the subjectivity and deliberative complexity of moderation itself [33]. The conducted review identifies several interrelated challenges shaping ongoing research, including the need to move beyond toxicity-only views of moderation towards broader support for deliberative quality [19].

Bias and fairness are primary concerns. Language models can reproduce or amplify demographic, cultural, or ideological biases from training data, potentially silencing specific groups or distorting deliberation. Methods to detect, measure, and mitigate these biases remain a key research focus [9,20]. Explainability and accountability are also critical. LLM-generated rationales may not reflect internal reasoning and can vary across similar cases. Ensuring moderation outcomes are interpretable, contestable, and institutionally accountable is essential in civic contexts [25].

Robustness and reliability pose further challenges. Prompt sensitivity, adversarial manipulation, and contextual ambiguity can produce inconsistent outcomes, undermining both technical performance and perceptions of fairness. Research must better characterise failure modes and develop safeguards to complement LLM reasoning [15]. Resource limitations constrain scalability, as LLM-based systems require substantial computation, large datasets, and specialised expertise. Future work should explore efficient, locally deployable solutions that maintain transparency and institutional independence [36].

Evaluation and validation remain complex. Harm is context-dependent and socially constructed, limiting the usefulness of conventional metrics and single majority-vote labels [9]. Research should develop methodologies incorporating deliberative quality, inclusiveness, and institutional trust alongside accuracy [6]. More empirical work is also needed in civic or realistically simulated participatory settings, since current evidence remains much stronger for general social-media moderation than for e-participation platforms specifically. Addressing these challenges requires interdisciplinary collaboration across AI, social science, HCI, and governance.

6 Conclusion

The moderation of harmful content in e-participation platforms should not be treated merely as a conventional text classification problem, but rather as a socio-technical governance challenge shaped by the need to balance user safety with the protection of legitimate democratic expression, procedural fairness, and deliberative quality. The literature review highlights that the evolution from rule-based methods to deep learning, Transformer-based architectures, and large language models has significantly improved the ability of automated systems to capture contextual meaning, implicit intent, and pragmatic nuance. However, these advances do not eliminate the core challenges of civic moderation, since issues such as bias, limited explainability, prompt sensitivity, adversarial manipulation, and misalignment with institutional norms continue to constrain the reliable deployment of such models in high-stakes participatory settings.

In this context, LLM-based moderation appears most valuable when embedded within structured and policy-aware workflows that combine automated analysis with model plurality, traceable reasoning, and human oversight. The proposed council-based approach reinforces this perspective by framing moderation as a supervised and accountable decision-support process rather than as a fully autonomous mechanism, thereby better reflecting the interpretive and contested nature of harmful content in democratic environments. Overall, effective moderation in e-participation platforms such as CoParticipation requires hybrid systems that integrate contextual language understanding with transparency, accountability, and institutional control, while future research should continue to develop evaluation methods and governance frameworks that are better aligned with inclusiveness, civic trust, and deliberative legitimacy.

Acknowledgements. This work was supported by national funds through the COMPETE 2030 Programme, co-financed by the European Union through the European Regional Development Fund (FEDER), under the CoParticipation project (COMPETE2030-FEDER-02208000). The views expressed in this work are those of the authors and do not necessarily reflect those of the funding bodies or the European Union.

References

1. Gemma. https://deepmind.google/models/gemma/. Accessed 20 Apr 2026
2. Llama. https://www.llama.com/. Accessed 18 Feb 2026
3. Openai. https://openai.com/. Accessed 18 Feb 2026
4. Arana-Catania, M., et al.: Citizen participation and machine learning for a better democracy. Digit. Gov. Res. Pract. **2**(3), 1–22 (2021)
5. Badjatiya, P., Gupta, S., Gupta, M., Varma, V.: Deep learning for hate speech detection in tweets. In: Proceedings of the 26th International Conference on World Wide Web Companion, pp. 759–760 (2017)
6. Banko, M., MacKeen, B., Ray, L.: A unified taxonomy of harmful content. In: Proceedings of the Fourth Workshop on Online Abuse and Harms, pp. 125–137 (2020)
7. Barandiaran, X.E., Calleja-López, A., Monterde, A.: Decidim: political and technopolitical networks for participatory democracy. White Paper (2019)
8. CoParticipation: Coparticipation: Enabling inclusive, smart, and secure participation. Project website. https://coparticipation.onesource.pt/. Accessed 20 Apr 2026
9. Davani, A.M., Atari, M., Kennedy, B., Dehghani, M.: Hate speech classifiers learn normative social stereotypes. Trans. Assoc. Comput. Linguist. **11**, 300–319 (2023)

10. Devlin, J., Chang, M.W., Lee, K., Toutanova, K.: Bert: pre-training of deep bidirectional transformers for language understanding. In: Proceedings of the 2019 Conference of the North American chapter of the Association for Computational Linguistics: Human Language Technologies, Volume 1 (Long and Short Papers), pp. 4171–4186 (2019)
11. DeYoung, J., et al.: Eraser: a benchmark to evaluate rationalized NLP models. In: Proceedings of the 58th Annual Meeting of the Association for Computational Linguistics, pp. 4443–4458 (2020)
12. Fortuna, P., Nunes, S.: A survey on automatic detection of hate speech in text. ACM Comput. Surv. (CSUR) **51**(4), 1–30 (2018)
13. Franco, M., Gaggi, O., Palazzi, C.E.: Integrating content moderation systems with large language models. ACM Trans. Web **37**(4), 1–21 (2024). https://doi.org/10.1145/3676508. https://dl.acm.org/doi/10.1145/3676508
14. Guo, Q., et al.: League of LLMs: a benchmark-free paradigm for mutual evaluation of large language models. arXiv preprint arXiv:2507.22359 (2025)
15. Hagendorff, T.: Deception abilities emerged in large language models. Proc. Natl. Acad. Sci. **121**(24), e2317967121 (2024). https://doi.org/10.1073/pnas.2317967121
16. Hsiao, Y.T., Lin, S.Y., Tang, A., Narayanan, D., Sarahe, C.: vtaiwan: an empirical study of open consultation process in taiwan. SocArXiv **4** (2018)
17. Inan, H., et al.: Llama guard: LLM-based input-output safeguard for human-AI conversations. arXiv preprint arXiv:2312.06674 (2023)
18. Jhaver, S., Birman, I., Gilbert, E., Bruckman, A.: Human-machine collaboration for content regulation: the case of reddit automoderator. ACM Trans. Comput.-Hum. Interact. (TOCHI) **26**(5), 1–35 (2019)
19. Jundi, I., Vecchi, E.M., Quensel, C., Falk, N., Lapesa, G.: It is not only the negative that deserves attention! understanding, generation & evaluation of (positive) moderation. In: Proceedings of the 2025 Conference of the Nations of the Americas Chapter of the Association for Computational Linguistics: Human Language Technologies (Volume 1: Long Papers), pp. 11360–11395 (2025)
20. Kiritchenko, S., Nejadgholi, I., Fraser, K.C.: Confronting abusive language online: a survey from the ethical and human rights perspective. J. Artif. Intell. Res. **71**, 431–478 (2021). https://doi.org/10.1613/jair.1.12590
21. Kolla, M., Salunkhe, S., Chandrasekharan, E., Saha, K.: LLM-mod: can large language models assist content moderation? In: Extended Abstracts of the CHI Conference on Human Factors in Computing Systems, pp. 1–8 (2024)
22. Liu, P., Yuan, W., Fu, J., Jiang, Z., Hayashi, H., Neubig, G.: Pre-train, prompt, and predict: a systematic survey of prompting methods in natural language processing. ACM Comput. Surv. **55**(9), 1–35 (2023)
23. Mathew, B., Saha, P., Yimam, S.M., Biemann, C., Goyal, P., Mukherjee, A.: Hatexplain: a benchmark dataset for explainable hate speech detection. In: Proceedings of the AAAI Conference on Artificial Intelligence, vol. 35, pp. 14867–14875 (2021)
24. Minaee, S., et al.: Large language models: a survey. arXiv preprint arXiv:2402.06196 (2024)
25. Mitchell, M., et al.: Model cards for model reporting. In: Proceedings of the Conference on Fairness, Accountability, and Transparency, pp. 220–229 (2019)
26. Palla, K., et al.: Policy-as-prompt: rethinking content moderation in the age of large language models. In: Proceedings of the 2025 ACM Conference on Fairness, Accountability, and Transparency, pp. 840–854 (2025)
27. Park, C.Y., et al.: Detecting community sensitive norm violations in online conversations. In: Findings of the Association for Computational Linguistics: EMNLP 2021, pp. 3386–3397 (2021)

28. Pavlopoulos, J., Sorensen, J., Dixon, L., Thain, N., Androutsopoulos, I.: Toxicity detection: does context really matter? In: Proceedings of the 58th Annual Meeting of the Association for Computational Linguistics, pp. 4296–4305 (2020)
29. Schmidt, A., Wiegand, M.: A survey on hate speech detection using natural language processing. In: Proceedings of the Fifth International Workshop on Natural Language Processing for Social Media, pp. 1–10 (2017)
30. Subramanian, M., Sathiskumar, V.E., Deepalakshmi, G., Cho, J., Manikandan, G.: A survey on hate speech detection and sentiment analysis using machine learning and deep learning models. Alex. Eng. J. **80**, 110–121 (2023)
31. Van't Riet, J., Van Stekelenburg, A.: The effects of political incivility on political trust and political participation: a meta-analysis of experimental research. Hum. Commun. Res. **48**(2), 203–229 (2022)
32. Vaswani, A., et al.: Attention is all you need. In: Advances in Neural Information Processing Systems, vol. 30, pp. 5998–6008 (2017). https://papers.neurips.cc/paper/7181-attention-is-all-you-need
33. Vecchi, E.M., Falk, N., Quensel, C., Jundi, I., Lapesa, G.: Perspectivemod: a perspectivist resource for deliberative moderation. In: Proceedings of the 2025 Conference on Empirical Methods in Natural Language Processing, pp. 34163–34186 (2025)
34. Wang, K., Lu, D., Han, C., Long, S., Poon, J.: Detect all abuse! Toward universal abusive language detection models. In: Scott, D., Bel, N., Zong, C. (eds.) Proceedings of the 28th International Conference on Computational Linguistics, pp. 6366–6376. International Committee on Computational Linguistics, Barcelona, Spain (Online) (2020). https://aclanthology.org/2020.coling-main.560/
35. Zangl, M., et al.: A multidisciplinary analysis of transparent ai-driven toxicity detection tools for civic engagement platforms. AI Soc. **41**(1), 527–544 (2026)
36. Zhan, X., Goyal, A., Chen, Y., Chandrasekharan, E., Saha, K.: SLM-Mod: small language models surpass LLMs at content moderation. In: Proceedings of the 2025 Conference of the NAACL-HLT, pp. 8774–8790 (2025)
37. Zhao, H., et al.: Explainability for large language models: a survey. ACM Trans. Intell. Syst. Technol. **15**(2), 1–38 (2024)
38. Zhao, J., Plaza-del Arco, F.M., Curry, A.C.: Language model council: democratically benchmarking foundation models on highly subjective tasks. In: Proceedings of the 2025 Conference of the Nations of the Americas Chapter of the Association for Computational Linguistics: Human Language Technologies (Volume 1: Long Papers), pp. 12395–12450 (2025)

Healthcare 5.0 and Challenges for 6G Mobile Technology

Lechosław Tomaszewski[1](✉) and Agnieszka Tomaszewska[2]

[1] Orange Polska S.A., Al. Jerozolimskie 160, 02-326 Warszawa, Poland
lechoslaw.tomaszewski@orange.com

[2] University Clinical Hospital No. 1, Medical University of Silesia in Katowice, 3 Maja 13-15, 41-800 Zabrze, Poland

Abstract. Healthcare (HC) 5.0 conditions and use cases create demands addressed to information and communication technologies, particularly mobile networks. This paper confronts HC 5.0 service requirements with the current state-of-the-art 5G System (5GS) and future 6G System (6GS) whose standardisation has only just begun. There are technological barriers to implementing extremely-high-data-rate and very-low-jitter HC services in 5GS, but more importantly, legal barriers for mobile operators ("Network neutrality") and common market strategy (focus on mass consumers and delayed deployment of network slicing support causing disappointment to industrial customers). 6GS has the technological potential to support HC 5.0 depending on the mutual synchronisation of 6GS and HC 5.0 development roadmaps. Examples of ETHER, 6G-PATH and ELIXIRION projects show how research initiatives contribute to the creation of specific 6GS enablers for HC 5.0 support.

Keywords: 5G · 6G · IMT-2020 · IMT-2030 · IoMT · healthcare 5.0 · eHealth · telemedicine · standardisation · use cases · services · mobile · requirements · ITU-R · 3GPP

1 Introduction

The 5th industrial revolution assumes a major paradigm shift. While the 4th revolution focused on the full digitisation and automation of online processes, Industry 5.0 introduces a new dimension – the humanisation of processes. As far as Industry 4.0 concentrated on the efficiency of processes designed as mass and standardised ones, thus eliminating individualisation, in Industry 5.0 the role of humans collaborating with artificial intelligence (AI), machine learning (ML) – for decision-making processes optimisation – and cobots – collaborative

ELIXIRION project has received funding from the European Union's Horizon Europe Marie Skłodowska-Curie Actions (MSCA) programme under Grant Agreement No. 101120135. Views and opinions expressed are, however, those of the author(s) only and do not necessarily reflect those of the European Union. Neither the European Union nor the granting authority can be held responsible for them.

Published by Springer Nature Switzerland AG 2027
A. Papaleonidas et al. (Eds.): AIAI 2026 Workshops, IFIP AICT 796, pp. 207–221, 2027.
https://doi.org/10.1007/978-3-032-30507-7_13

robots for safe human-machine interaction – becomes crucial, while processes evolve towards ones to be personalised (human-centric), resilient, and focused on sustainability [1]. The healthcare (HC) sector is a particular target of this vision – as it is extremely connected to humans both as whose who act there and whose are direct recipients of the actions associated with so fundamental values as life and health. Therefore, a fundamental question arises: "Does the evolution of information and communication technologies (ICT) industry (and especially mobile networks) provide readiness to implement the HC 5.0 vision?"

The paper is organised as it follows: the trends and drivers of HC 5.0, its vision and use cases (UCs) are presented in Sect. 2. The ICT enablers and service requirements of HC 5.0 are discussed in Sect. 3. Section 4 analyses present (5G) and foreseen (6G) support for HC 5.0 as well as selected research projects associated with HC demands. Section 5 summarises the paper.

2 HC 5.0 and its Demands

2.1 Trends and Drivers

The HC system is subject to multidimensional pressure – progress in medicine escalates the demand for increasingly expensive and more effective medical services. This is compounded by social changes on a global scale – growth of global population (1.60 bln in 1900, 5.33 bln in 1990, 8.09 bln in 2023, forecasted 8.88 bln in 2035, and 9.85 bln in 2055 [2]) demographic structure changes (ageing of societies represented by gradual transformation of the demographic pyramid into the shape of a biconvex lens [2]) and the extension of life expectancy (32 years in 1900, 64 in 1990, 73.2 in 2023 [3], while the forecast for the 2030s is 75, and for 2050s is 77–78 [4]). At the same time, an increasing spread of chronic and lifestyle diseases and the globalisation of epidemic risks due to the unprecedented mobility of people and goods ("global village") can be observed.

Changes in the HC system are described in subsequent phases, sometimes mapped to the sequence of industrial revolutions. Undoubtedly, the foundation of this process was the electronicisation and digitisation of both medical equipment and records – first, the local electronic medical records (EMRs) containing a patient's medical data from one facility, and then electronic health records (EHRs) designed to collect and share holistic information about a patient's health. Miniaturisation of equipment, advances in HC computerisation, and development of widely available mobile communication services have enabled the first remote health monitoring services implementation based on wearable devices. However, isolated digital islands did not constitute telemedicine. Only comprehensive digitalisation creates an integrated distributed on-line system of HC 4.0, including patients' with wearables, based on modern means of wired and wireless communication. This system started evolving towards "smart" due to the implementation of Big Data analytics and introduction of AI. In parallel, the therapeutic (*i.e.*, reactive care) approach has undergone a transition from doctor's individual experience- and judgment-based treatment to generic, population-derived treatment standards – resource-intensive, however.

At the political level, the United Nations have defined the sustainable development goals (SDGs) [5], among which SDG3 is "Ensure healthy lives and promote well-being for all at all ages", and SDG12 "Ensure sustainable consumption and production patterns" concerns HC in the context of how societies produce and consume goods and services. Within the area of "Public Health", the European Union (EU) is implementing, *i.a.*, the digitalisation program "eHealth" [6], that aims at enhancing HC efficiency and quality of care, empowering citizens to take a proactive role in managing their health, and supporting HC professionals. The program also covers the issue of common EU Health Data Space and EHRs.

The aforementioned factors and the vision of Industry 5.0 create the foundations for HC 5.0 – a new model that is intended to implement P4 Medicine (personalised, preventive, participatory, and predictive) in a smart, human-centric, and data-driven HC sustainable ecosystem providing individualised, holistic, precision, adaptive, proactive, and preventive care with patient empowerment.

2.2 Vision of HC 5.0

The HC 5.0 ecosystem is designed as a highly geographically dispersed, decentralised, distributed, and mobile multi-level ICT system covering the hardware layer (sensing/monitoring, imaging, analytics, treatment), individual actors (patients, medical doctors and surgeons, dentists, psychiatrists, nurses, paramedics, caregivers, pharmacists, physiotherapists, diagnostic and therapeutic technicians, electromedical technicians) and institutional actors (hospitals, clinics, sanatoriums, pharmacies, laboratories, medical factories), transport services (ground or air ambulances, delivery drones). However, the true heart of this system is the data layer encompassing the processes of multi-modal collection, processing, analysis, inference, aggregation, ML of AI algorithms, and multimedia presentation. The real-time (RT) integration of all layers is intended to implement a framework based on the closed-loop "sense-transmit-reason-act" model [7]. Another approach to exploiting AI in critical care is the "learn-predict-monitor-detect-correct" loop [8].

A system defined in this way will have several dimensions of operation:

Personalised and patient-oriented HC – customised approach that spans the patient's lifetime to continuously monitor health and provide holistic personalised guidance associated with lifestyle, prevention/prediction/early detection of health issues, and medical or pharmacological interventions based on individual medical history and genetic profile; in particular, in the case of co-occurring diseases, ensuring an optimal therapeutic approach that mutually takes into account the treatment processes of particular diseases. This approach can be supported with remote digital care (based on wearables) and telemedicine. Such a model can involve patient's context (*e.g.*, cultural, religious, or social background, personal values and goals) and includes patient's active participation and shared decision-making in the HC process.

Public health management – aggregation of individual data to the population level in order to track disease trends, detect health patterns and their correlation with socioeconomic patterns, predict and prevent epidemics as well as monitor and combat them, and create health policies.

HC system efficiency management – complex analytics aimed at optimisation of HC system resources allocation, multidimensional assessment of effectiveness of medical intervention types, avoidance of unnecessary/wasteful medical procedures (*e.g.*, redundant or resulting from a lack of coordination when treating simultaneously different co-existing diseases), and HC sustainability (both environmental and economic due to, *e.g.*, optimisation of HC costs, limiting in-person visits by telemedicine practices, *etc.*).

HC unit performance management – growth of clinical workflow efficiency, increased satisfaction of clinical staff (due to increase of treatment effectiveness and decrease of mortality rate, offloading of routine tasks, reduction of administrative burden by automation of monitoring and documentation, ability to focus on patient care itself) and lower burnout risk, optimisation of operational efficiency (earlier diagnosis and intervention, optimal treatment selection, better resources availability and utilisation).

2.3 UCs of HC 5.0

The above HC 5.0 ecosystem will be built around the following UCs:

Remote Monitoring. RT data acquisition from wearable medical devices – audio, video, motion, electrocardiography (ECG), electroencephalography (EEG), electromyography (EMG), cardiotocography (CTG), body temperature, blood glucose/pressure/oxygen saturation, heart/respiratory rate, *etc.* – will feed the patient's EHR for fitness-tracking, disease early detection or in-therapy health analytics systems to be further used by HC professionals supported by AI; the latter can provide personalised preventive HC to patients based on their long-term trends analysis, prediction of potential health risks, and delivering actionable notifications (pre-emptive alerts or advices).

Telemedicine. Remote consultations enabling medical advice and treatment without in-person visits; rehabilitation activities (kinesiotherapy) can be carried out in a similar way – exercises under remote supervision and instruction of a physiotherapist. With the additional use of immersive holographic projections, the diagnostic accuracy of teleconsultations and remote training of HC professionals can be much higher.

AI-Supported Behavioural Analytics. Based on remote monitoring of vocal features, gait/movement and posture parameters, tremor, bradykinesia, facial expression, eye movements, *etc.* optionally supported with vital parameters readouts, early detection of certain diseases (*e.g.*, respiratory, Parkinson's, depression [9], stroke) and musculoskeletal disorders can be provided, as well as support of biomechanical functional assessment of the musculoskeletal system or teleconsultations/telerehabilitations.

Remote Robotic Surgery. The use of remotely controlled surgical robots to bridge the geographic gap between the location of a patient requiring immediate or highly specialised surgery procedures and the location of the surgeon. For this purpose, it is necessary not only to remotely control the robot within appropriate delay regimes, but also to provide the operator with haptic feedback.

RT Medical Imaging. This area covers not only the transmission of images constituting a huge volume of data related to computed tomography (CT), magnetic resonance imaging (MRI), positron emission tomography (PET), ultrasonography (USG), optical coherence tomography (OCT), otolaryngological examinations, and diagnostic pathology (including ultra-high-resolution endoscopy based on OCT or near-infrared fluorescence) for on-line consultations or intra-operative pathological analysis. With remote robotic control of microscope or robotic-assisted USG, the consulting expert can adjust the magnification or manipulate the robotic arm at the patient end [10].

Intelligent/Smart Hospital. A complete and comprehensive ecosystem (exploiting the above UCs) based on connected sensors tracking patients, staff, assets (equipment), and hospital internal environment. The RT data flow feeds AI-powered automation platforms to improve therapeutic procedures and optimise management of hospital resources. In particular, this may involve predictive hospital resource orchestration and supply chain management to avoid bottlenecks and shortages, intelligent equipment maintenance for failure prevention/early warning, or automated infection/contamination control.

Connected Ambulance. As a remote and highly mobile part of smart hospital, apart from emergency medicine treatment on the go, it can perform remote triage (patient admission and initial diagnostics) – with on-board remote monitoring, telemedicine (including one or more on-board cameras), and means of remote imaging – for identification and preparation of appropriate hospital treatment path in advance before the patient is brought to the hospital admission room.

Patient Digital Twin. A virtual, dynamic model of a biological process, organ, part, or entire body of a specific patient, created using medical records, genetic profile, environmental data, and current sensory information. This allows for life-course and diseases prognosis with early detection of the latter ones, surgical procedures planning and simulation with assessment of complications risk, and RT testing of the effectiveness of pharmacological therapies.

Autonomous Mobile Service Robots. A wide class of autonomous devices designed to handle patient transport, surveillance and monitoring, material handling and logistics, telepresence for infectious disease control as well as cobots for patient monitoring and care (including living assistance and rehabilitation), for HC staff safety and assistance (support in patient-related activities to reduce the physical strain and injury risk), or for enhanced precision of therapeutical tasks to reduce complication rates.

3 HC 5.0 ICT Enablers and Service Requirements

3.1 ICT Enablers of HC 5.0

The HC 5.0 ecosystem is a complex ICT environment requiring key enablers:

AI and ML. AI supports HC professionals in analysing massive data sets, recognising disease patterns, predicting disease/biological processes progression, and making faster and more accurate diagnostic and therapeutic decisions. The main areas of AI application in medicine include imaging diagnostics, personalised clinical decision support, genetic data analysis, and HC management (automation and optimisation of processes in HC facilities).

Explainable AI (XAI). Classic AI algorithms act as opaque "black box"; the HC context imposes an exceptional dimension of transparency, justifiability, and interpretability of the results of AI used in clinical decision-making for facilitating clinicians' trust, safe human–AI cooperation, regulatory oversight, and error analysis. The emerging XAI research domain addresses this critical requirement.

Federated learning (FL). Training AI models centrally on large-scale, heterogeneous datasets often faces limitations not due to computing resources but lawful data privacy protection, especially in the case of HC. FL provides distributed collaborative training of shared model. The effectiveness of this approach is close to the central one; the key issues are communication within the cluster (high bandwidth for continuous model updating), heterogeneity of local data sets (their size and quality), and security ("model poisoning" attacks).

Edge Computing. The highly distributed and data-intensive HC 5.0 requires fast data processing infrastructure as close to the source as possible, supporting diverse service function chains (SFCs) and high mobility of Internet of medical things (IoMT) sources. Edge computing allows also for other enablers listed here, *e.g.*, augmented reality (AR), virtual reality (VR), semantic communication.

VR and AR. The expanding use of these technologies is associated with AI-supported consultations, examinations, diagnostics, surgical planning, therapy, rehabilitation, and medical training.

Tactile Internet. RT tactile sensations and physical impressions to provide remote "touch" – sensing the texture, resistance, and temperature of objects is crucial for remote robotic examination or surgery ("feeling" tissues) and medical training (learning manual skills with haptic feedback).

IoMT. A realm of mainly mobile, always connected medical devices/sensors, applications, and RT ICT systems that collect, process, and analyse patient health data, feeding the intelligence of HC 5.0.

Ubiquitous Connectivity. Ubiquity of network access everywhere is crucial to ensuring the continuous presence of patient's wearables in the HC 5.0 ecosystem.

Quantum Computing. Some optimisation/simulation problems or ML in computational medicine are intractable with conventional computers, due to exponential complexity growth with input dimensions. Solving them in reasonable time (timescale suitable for HC, very short for emergency cases) can be addressed with quantum computing, an emerging technology that proved its superiority by solving these classes of problems hundreds of millions of times faster.

Wireless Body Area Network (WBAN). Low-power wireless access and data exchange technology for both wearable and implantable IoMT objects.

Semantic Communication. A shift in the communication paradigm from the precise transmission of raw source data to the transmission of contextually relevant information. This may involve extracting key features of the source information (*e.g.*, a postural model of the remote patient) or adapting the information acquisition and transmission strategy to ensure it is most valuable to the recipient as well as energy- and network-efficient.

Blockchain. In HC, it ensures confidentiality, integrity (non-repudiation and non-tamperability), and security in data transmission and storage; it enables authorised access to decentralised EHRs, drug supply chain tracking (combating drug counterfeiting), and health insurance claims automation.

3.2 Requirements of HC 5.0 for ICT Services

The communication services' requirements for HC 5.0 are characterised by great diversity due to the richness of UCs and underlying technological enablers used, as described in Sects. 2.3 and 3.1, respectively. An additional difficulty is the fact that the literature presents a wide range of quality of service (QoS) parameters' values, which is related to the results of experiments under specific conditions imposed by the available technologies and equipment. Moreover, continuous technological progress systematically raises the crossbar of requirements.

Services for HC 5.0 can be classified as follows: **(A)** Conversational voice and video – typical interpersonal communication used, *e.g.*, for teleconsultations; **(B)** Non-RT data exchange – transmission of large volumes of data, *e.g.*, medical imaging, AI models, patients' EHRs; **(C)** IoMT exchange – transmission of data from wearables (vital signs) and other mobile medical equipment (*e.g.*, infusion pumps); **(D)** Cyber-physical systems – multi-sensory and control exchange for remote surgery and examination; **(E)** Autonomous mobile service robots – transmission for logistics or assistance robots in simultaneous localisation and mapping mode; **(F)** Remote and AI-assisted point-of-care imaging – bedside and on-board of connected ambulance imaging with remote consultation; **(G)** Immersion – VR/AR in HC procedures or trainings, and holographic communication in HC. Table 1 provides maximum QoS targets for these classes.

The gathered requirements' criticality is related to neurophysiological considerations or technological limitations. For telesurgery and similar applications, latency and jitter limitations directly impact the surgeon's performance, which increases the likelihood of errors, requires adaptation efforts and actions, *e.g.*, "move-and-wait" approach; hence, the procedure is prolonged and the risk to the patient increases. The criticality of jitter in holographic technology is related to the ability to render 3D images without distortion. Additionally, the latency

Table 1. List of QoS targets for HC 5.0 ICT services

Service class	Latency	Reliability	Data rate	Jitter
A_1 (audio, lossy compression, XU)	≤ 150 ms	$< 99.9\%$	≤ 128 kbps	< 30 ms
A_2 (audio, lossy compression, AN)	150–300 ms	99–99.9%	≤ 128 kbps	< 30 ms
A_3 (video, Full HD, 60 fps, lossy compression, XU)	< 150 ms	$\geq 99.5\%$	< 10 Mbps	< 30 ms
A_4 (video, Full HD, 60 fps, lossy compression, AN)	150–300 ms	98–99.5%	< 10 Mbps	< 30 ms
B (generic)	—	$\geq 99\%$	> 1 Gbps	—
C_1 (heart/respiration rate, blood pressure/oxygen, temperature, RT)	< 250 ms	$\geq 99\%$	< 10 kbps	< 20 ms
C_2 (ECG/EEG, RT)	< 250 ms	$\geq 99\%$	< 100 kbps	< 20 ms
C_3 (EMG, RT)	< 250 ms	$\geq 99.9\%$	1–2 Mbps	< 20 ms
D_1 (audio – communication with local team, compression) $\flat$	< 100 ms	$\geq 99.9\%$	≤ 200 kbps	< 30 ms
D_2 (video, 4K UHD, 60 fps, 3D camera, lossy compression) $\flat$	< 50 ms $\natural$ < 100 ms $\sharp$	$\geq 99.9\%$	< 1 Gbps	< 2 ms
D_3 (haptic control and feedback – force/vibration) $\flat$	< 50 ms $\natural$ < 100 ms $\sharp$	$\geq 99.99\%$	≤ 500 kbps	< 2 ms
E (simultaneous localisation and mapping)	≤ 20 ms	$\geq 99\%$	> 0.3 Gbps	≤ 1–2 ms
F_1 (connected ambulance)	≤ 10 ms	$\geq 99.999\%$	0.5–1 Gbps	≤ 2 ms
F_2 (point-of-care imaging, AI)	≤ 50 ms	$\geq 99.99\%$	≥ 1 Gbps	≤ 5 ms
G_1 (VR, surgical training, 60 fps)	≤ 20 ms	$\geq 99.999\%$	< 5 Gbps	≤ 2 ms
G_2 (AR, surgical navigation, 60 fps)	≤ 5 ms	$\geq 99.999\%$	< 5 Gbps	≤ 2 ms
G_3 (holography, 60–90 fps)	< 1 ms	$\geq 99.999\%$	< 10 Tbps	< 0.1 ms

Degradation: AN – noticeable but acceptable; XU – unnoticeable (excellent QoS)
$\flat$ – video stream must be synchronised with audio and haptic control within a range of $\pm$ 50 ms to avoid sensory conflict that cannot be ignored by the brain
$\natural$ – no delay perceived, automatic subconscious compensation [10]
$\sharp$ – awareness of "difference", automatic deliberate compensation [10]

and jitter values consider the total, end-to-end (E2E) limitations, *e.g.*, "glass-to-glass" for video – the entire SFC processing with image capturing, compression, transmission, decompression, AI-supported enrichment, and reproduction.

4 Support for HC 5.0 by Mobile Network Technology

4.1 3GPP 5G System (5GS) – The State of the Art and Reality Check

5GS or IMT-2020 according to ITU-R, *i.e.*, International Mobile Telecommunications for 2020s, is in its phase of maturity. Its standardisation by 3GPP, in fact, the only validated by ITU-R, spanned the 3GPP releases since the 15th (started in March 2016) until the currently on-going 20th (considered to be the final one for evolution of 5G/5G-Advanced, and to be finished in June 2027).

5GS has been defined as in-software solution, based on virtualisation technology and evolving towards cloud-native. It implements the paradigm of network access and service (application) layers separation; both are built on the Internet Protocol (IP). The 3GPP 5GS architecture [11] enables and provides the specification of 3rd-party systems integration, implementing applications, with the control mechanisms of the mobile network. While ITU-R has from the beginning assumed differentiation of usage scenarios characterised by different QoS parameters – Enhanced Mobile Broadband (eMBB), Massive Machine Type Communications (mMTC), Ultra-Reliable Low-Latency Communication (URLLC) – and implementation of this differentiation via the network slice (NS) mechanism, to date 3GPP has already defined a total of 7 different NS types, enabling deeper distinctions. The 5GS architecture implements a QoS management framework. Additionally, 3GPP supports Industry 4.0 and factory automation industrial applications through mechanisms of private networks (both separate implementation based on the local spectrum license or virtually separated from the resources of a public network), 5GS as a bridge for local area network (LAN) and IEEE Time-Sensitive Networking (TSN), and enhanced support of deterministic applications (beyond IEEE TSN). 3GPP 5GS was not originally designed to provide inherent seamless non-terrestrial access (specifically satellite one) and to natively include edge computing. The gradual integration of both, as external ones to the fundamental architecture, was added during the 5GS evolution.

Unlike in areas such as automotive or unmanned aviation, 3GPP has not created a consolidated vision of HC service requirements in a single document, but these requirements are dispersed (*cf.* [12] and its auxiliary-subordinate documents). Basic 5GS key performance indicator (KPI) targets are presented in Table 2 below; their confrontation with the service requirements collected in Table 1 leads to the conclusion that meeting the requirements of classes B, D_2, E, F, G in 5GS is unrealistic due to the required data rate, which should be stable and continuous. In class B, for the stationary systems integration, the service can be implemented in fixed networks. Maximum jitter tolerable by holographic communication (G_3) can never be achieved in 5GS. It should be mentioned that in some of these scenarios, the uplink traffic will dominate, while the typical downlink:uplink ratios in 5G networks vary from 7:3 to 4:1, correspondingly worsening the achieved data rate.

While for functional and performance reasons it seems possible for 5GS to support the remaining HC 5.0 service classes, there exist other key barriers. Implementation of the NS mechanism requires deployment of 5GS in the standalone (SA) variant. And although currently 24% (95 of 392) of 5GS operators worldwide have already implemented SA [13], only 2.8% of 5G traffic in Europe is handled in 5GS SA, compared to 32% in North America and 80% in China [14], which means that the availability of the NS mechanism in Europe is limited to small coverage islands. Moreover, there is still an unresolved conflict in Europe between the idea of NS and the EU directive on net neutrality, which prohibits privileging any traffic at the expense of QoS of public access to the Internet [15]. Implementing a private 5GS SA with its own spectrum license as a smart hospital campus network would be a form of workaround; however, it should be remembered that the idea of HC 5.0 essentially means geographic ubiquity.

Table 2. Comparison of selected IMT-2020 (5G) and IMT-2030 (6G) KPI targets [16].

Network performance requirement	5G KPI	6G KPI
Peak data rate per device	20 Gbps	50/100/200 Gbps ♭
User-experienced data rate	100 Mbps	300/500 Mbps ♭
Area traffic capacity	10 Mbps/m^2	30/50 Mbps/m^2 ♭
Connection density	10^6 dev./km^2	10^6–10^8 dev./km^2 ♮
Mobility support	500 km/h	500–1000 km/s ♭
Latency (over the air interface, user data)	1 ms	0.1–1 ms ♮
Jitter (over the air interface, user data)	1 ms ♯	1 μs ♯
Reliability	99.999%	99.999%–99.99999% ♮
Positioning accuracy	metre-level ♯	1–10 cm ♮

♭ – example values for research, by ITU-R ♮ – target range for research, by ITU-R
♯ – not defined by ITU-R – practical achievement (5G) or common expectation (6G)

4.2 3GPP 6G System (6GS) – The Future to Come

Publications about 6GS began to appear from the beginning of 2018, *i.e.*, more than a year before the commercial launch of 5GS in its first version. Several years of discussion and research on visions, ideas, and enablers are now being capitalised in the already ongoing standardisation process. The foundations for this process were defined by the ITU-R [16] in the document on framework and overall objectives of the future development of IMT for 2030s. Following that, the works on detailed minimum requirements related to technical performance for IMT-2030 radio interfaces have recently been concluded, consented, and sent to approval and publication (expected in December 2026). It is already known that 6GS will not be just 5GS with lifted KPI targets. Indeed, specific KPIs are expected to improve by 1, 2, or 3 orders of magnitude (*cf.* Table 2), the three existing usage scenarios (eMBB, mMTC and URLLC) are to be extended and accordingly renamed to "Immersive Communication", "Massive Communication" and "Hyper Reliable and Low-Latency Communication", respectively. ITU-R addresses the latter scenario to industrial environment communication for time-synchronised operations, including emergency services and telemedicine. However, new scenarios emerge: "Ubiquitous Connectivity" for currently uncovered or scarcely covered areas, "Artificial Intelligence and Communication" for, *e.g.*, digital twins or autonomous collaboration between devices for medical assistance, and "Integrated Sensing and Communication" for, *e.g.*, activity detection and movement tracking: people posture/gesture recognition or fall detection.

In the context of HC 5.0, ITU-R acknowledges such key trends as: ubiquitous connectivity, intelligence, and computing – immersive multimedia and multi-sensory interactions – integration of sensing and communication – digital twin and virtual world. Finally: the trend of digital-health and well-being, which benefits from all the aforementioned ones. Hence, IMT-2030 (6GS) is envisioned to be a versatile and ubiquitous platform of integrated communication, computing, intelligence, and sensing capable to support the HC 5.0 ecosystem entirely.

ETSI runs two industry specification groups (ISGs) dedicated to monitoring and also impacting the international standardisation in the fields of integrated sensing and communication (ISAC) and THz technologies considered as enablers for 6GS. Both of them have published their reports on UCs, which include those associated with HC. The ISAC ISG reports UCs on human motion recognition, RT monitoring of health hazard and disaster risk, emergency search and rescue, outdoor HC sensing and monitoring, remotely controlled robots for senior citizen monitoring and care, safe & economic transport with drones (including medical supply delivery), emergency vehicle route planning, and several UCs on robots in logistics [17]. Particularly, these UCs support contactless patient monitoring (fall detection, heart/breath rate monitoring), ambient assisted living (behavioural anomalies with privacy protection), precise positioning in hospitals. The THz ISG proposes UCs on remote surgery, cooperative mobile robots, hazardous material work (use of THz waves both for spectroscopy and remote control), interactive immersive and mission-critical extended reality [18].

3GPP has already initiated their works on 6GS – probably the only world-wide one to be validated as IMT-2030-compliant. The general roadmap assumes the study phase within the on-going Release 20, and the first normative phase within the Release 21 (in 2026–2028, detailed timeline to be decided in June 2026), which will allow for the 3GPP vision to be validated within the ITU-R time window. The unprecedented event is the recent delivery (March 2026) of a study on 6G UCs and their service requirements; the 595 pages-long document describes around 210 UCs (!) [19], demonstrating the importance the industry places this time on the adoption of 6GS. These are probably "lessons learnt" of the world-wide 5GS implementation; the common mobile operators' strategy of mass-consumer-oriented deployment (non-SA, NS-less, only eMBB, *i.e.*, boosted LTE) froze the implementation of advanced UCs and brought disappointment to industrial customers. Work has already been initiated on a normative document for the 6GS service requirements (6G equivalent of [12]), on studies on architecture, application enablement, management and orchestration, aspects of media, charging, and radio access. These documents are at a very early stage. In the case of architecture, the key issues include: AI for 6GS and *vice versa*, ISAC, 6G computing support, and support of non-terrestrial network (NTN) – clearly, 3GPP emphasises 6GS as a ubiquitous, natively integrated communication-computing-sensing-AI platform in line with the ITU-R vision [16].

The 3GPP vision on 6G UCs and their service requirements [19] distinguishes between different classes of UCs (sorted by number of UCs): AI (61), system and operational aspects including backward compatibility (51), specific UCs on industry and verticals (30), ISAC (25), ubiquitous connectivity (20), immersive communication (18), other UCs (5), and massive (machine) communication (2).

While many UCs generically support the needs of HC 5.0 and its enablers described respectively in Sects. 2.3 and 3.1, 31 of them (15%) explicitly address the context of HC, medicine, assisted living, and related, namely **system and operational aspects** (1): disaster risk-based network resilience; **AI** (15): personalised AI for health monitoring, home robots, exposing achievable QoS to aid computational resource selection, smart housekeeping, child health management assistant, network-assisted video-based AI inference task offloading for mobile embodied AI, smart home user-centric AI service, smart HC, energy efficiency for AI service, AI for disability support, AI agent management, proactive AI agent for personal safety, feasible intent achievement for AI agents, enhancement of AI-driven location services, AI agent-assisted rescue in the water park; **ISAC** (4): multi-sensor fusion-based sensing for drones takeoff and landing, safe and economic drone transport, network-assisted smart transportation, gesture recognition in industrial environments; **ubiquitous connectivity** (3): ubiquitous and resilient network, service continuity for wearable mobile devices, global mobile video; **immersive communication** (4): immersive gaming, holographic telepresence in HC, mixed reality gaming, smart life for aging population with immersive RT communication; **massive communication** (1): wide-area coverage; **specific UCs on industry and verticals** (3): RT digital twins, service robots in smart community, medical applications in 6G.

The 6GS specification by 3GPP is therefore in its early stages, and it appears that 3GPP is aware of the individual building blocks necessary for HC 5.0 creation. However, for the latter to be successful, it will be necessary for 3GPP to build its comprehensive and consolidated vision of the HC sector's needs. Prioritising UCs on the roadmap for future 3GPP releases will be crucial. Spot-deploying fragments of HC 5.0 using generic services instead of a systematic approach will probably dilute the vision and bring disappointment. Therefore, it seems necessary to establish cross-industry cooperation and representation of the HC industry at 3GPP, as well as political and regulatory support.

4.3 HC 5.0 Enablers for 6GS – Selected Research Projects

The recently concluded **ETHER** project [20] was dedicated to the integration of NTN with the ground mobile network. It demonstrated 3 UCs: (1) horizontal handovers for delay-tolerant mMTC applications (sparse low-orbit satellite constellations – store & forward mechanism and semantic analytics), (2) direct handheld device access and vertical handovers, and (3) air-space safety-critical operations using vertical handover and multi-link features as well as edge applications migration to follow aircraft users. Results of each of these UCs are relevant to the HC context in the aspect of ubiquitous connectivity support, respectively: non-RT remote health monitoring, continuous connectivity for HC based on handovers from terrestrial access to satellite one and back, and support of safety-critical high-mobility communication in HC (*e.g.*, connected ground or air ambulance).

The **6G-PATH** project [21] demonstrates, *i.a.*, the HC 5.0-related UCs: "3D hydrogel patches" and "Elderly care". The former UC provides the remote hospital care at home for patients with chronic wounds. It supports wounds detection and segmentation, their 3D scanning for documentation and visualisation, interfacing of 3D bioprinter for hydrogel patches application – to be used by a visiting nurse with on-line connectivity to hospital systems. The latter UC implements a teleconsultation platform and provides AI-supported remote elderly care and rehabilitation, vital signs monitoring, fall detection, automatic diagnostics, threat assessment and immediate intervention, contributing this way to the improvement of security and quality of life for the elderly.

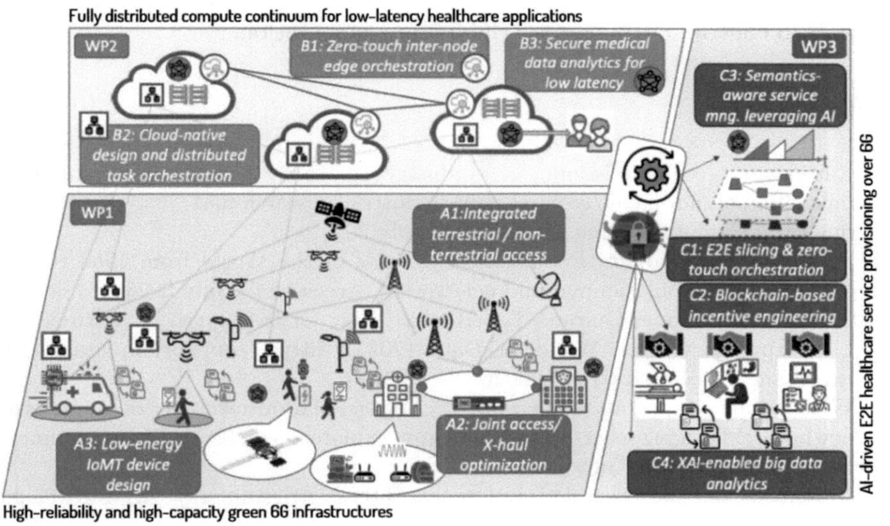

Fig. 1. Conceptual architecture of the ELIXIRION system.

The motto of the doctoral project **ELIXIRION** [22] is "realising HC 4.0 exploiting the 6G network evolution". The ELIXIRION system (*cf.* Fig. 1) integrates high-reliability and high-capacity green 6G infrastructures, fully distributed compute continuum for low-latency HC applications, and AI-driven E2E HC service provisioning over 6G. 10 doctoral candidates do research on specific enablers to support zero-touch and AI-optimised orchestration, ubiquitous connectivity, energy efficiency on both device and network sides, secure and XAI-enabled analytics, semantics-aware service QoS, and blockchain. The results of individual research will compose the HC support-oriented ICT platform to integrate communication, computation, and AI components of the IMT-2030 system envisioned by ITU-R.

5 Summary

This paper presents the HC 5.0 conditions, demands, and service requirements towards the ICT systems. These requirements were confronted with the current state-of-the-art 5GS and future 6GS whose standardisation process has only just begun. In the case of 5GS, there are technological barriers to implementing extremely-high data rate and very-low jitter HC services. However, the key factors are primarily regulatory barriers for mobile operators and their market strategies, which inhibit the NS mechanism necessary to enable the delivery of tailored services for HC with guaranteed QoS. 6GS has the technological potential to support HC 5.0, but the materialisation of this potential will depend on the proper recognition of the entire HC 5.0 ecosystem by the telecommunications industry and the mutual synchronisation of development roadmaps on both sides. The research activities presented on the examples of ETHER, 6G-PATH and ELIXIRION projects are perfectly suited to the creation of specific enablers for 6GS to contribute to support HC 5.0 implementation.

References

1. European Commission: Industry 5.0. https://research-and-innovation.ec.europa.eu/research-area/industrial-research-and-innovation/industry-50_en. Accessed 03 July 2026
2. PopulationPyramid.net: Population Pyramids of the World from 1950 to 2100. https://www.populationpyramid.net/world/. Accessed 03 July 2026
3. Dattani, S., Rodés-Guirao, L., Ritchie, H., Ortiz-Ospina, E., Roser, M.: Life expectancy. Our World in Data (2023). https://ourworldindata.org/life-expectancy. Accessed 03 July 2026
4. WHO: Life expectancy at birth. https://platform.who.int/data/maternal-newborn-child-adolescent-ageing/indicator-explorer-new/MCA/life-expectancy-at-birth. Accessed 03 July 2026
5. United Nations: Sustainable Development. https://sdgs.un.org/. Accessed 03 July 2026
6. European Commission: eHealth: Digital health and care. https://health.ec.europa.eu/ehealth-digital-health-and-care_en. Accessed 03 July 2026
7. Younesi, A., Oustad, E., Ansari, M., Fahringer, T., Buyya, R.: HealthCare 5.0: an industry 5.0 perspective for next-generation medical systems with synergistic integration of IoT, AI, and 6G. Internet of Things **35**, 101815 (2026). https://doi.org/10.1016/j.iot.2025.101815
8. Boussi Rahmouni, H., et al.: Healthcare 5.0-driven clinical intelligence: the learn-predict-monitor-detect-correct framework for systematic artificial intelligence integration in critical care. Healthcare **13**(20) (2025). https://doi.org/10.3390/healthcare13202553
9. Yuxuan, Z., et al.: Mobile systems for healthcare 5.0: applications, challenges and opportunities. High-Confid. Comput. 100392 (2026). https://doi.org/10.1016/j.hcc.2026.100392
10. Georgiou, K.E., Georgiou, E., Satava, R.M.: 5G use in healthcare: the future is present. J. Soc. Laparoendosc. Surg. **25**, e2021.00064 (2021). https://doi.org/10.4293/JSLS.2021.00064

11. 3GPP: System architecture for the 5G System (5GS). Technical Standard TS 23.501, ver. 20.1.0, 3rd Generation Partnership Project (2026)
12. 3GPP: Service requirements for the 5G system. Technical Standard TS 22.261, ver. 20.6.0, 3rd Generation Partnership Project (2026)
13. GSA: State of the Market April 2026. https://gsacom.com/paper/state-of-the-market-april-2026/. Accessed 03 July 2026
14. Cenerva: 5G News Round-Up for the Week to 12 April 2026. https://cenerva.com/articles/5g-news-round-up-for-the-week-to-12-april-2026/. Accessed 03 July 2026
15. Tomaszewski, L., Kołakowski, R.: Network slicing vs. network neutrality – is consent possible? In: Maglogiannis, I., Iliadis, L., Papaleonidas, A., Chochliouros, I. (eds.) Artificial Intelligence Applications and Innovations. AIAI 2023 IFIP WG 12.5 International Workshops, pp. 77–90. Springer, Cham (2023). https://doi.org/10.1007/978-3-031-34171-7_6
16. ITU-R: Framework and overall objectives of the future development of IMT for 2030 and beyond. Recommendation M.2160, International Telecommunication Union – Radiocommunication Sector (2021)
17. ETSI: Integrated Sensing And Communications (ISAC); Use Cases and Deployment Scenarios. Group Report ETSI GR ISC 001 V1.1.1, European Telecommunications Standards Institute (2025)
18. ETSI: TeraHertz modeling (THz); Identification of use cases for THz communication systems. Group Report ETSI GR THz 001 V1.1.1, European Telecommunications Standards Institute (2024)
19. 3GPP: Study on 6G Use Cases and Service Requirements. Technical Report TR 22.870, ver. 20.0.0, 3rd Generation Partnership Project (2026)
20. ETHER. https://ether-project.eu/. Accessed 03 July 2026
21. 6G-PATH. https://6gpath.eu/. Accessed 03 July 2026
22. ELIXIRION. https://elixirion-mc.eu/. Accessed 03 July 2026

Key Value Indicators in 6G for Societal Evaluation

Alexandros Kostopoulos[1](✉), Ioannis P. Chochliouros[1], Anastasia S. Spiliopoulou[1], Aitor Alcázar-Fernández[2], Kostas Ramantas[3], and Christos Verikoukis[4]

[1] Hellenic Telecommunications Organization S.A. (OTE), 99 Kifissias Avenue, 15124 Maroussi, Athens, Greece
alexkosto@oteresearch.gr
[2] Telefónica Innovación Digital SL, Madrid, Spain
[3] Iquadrat Informatica SL, Barcelona, Spain
[4] Industrial Systems Institute (ISI)/Athenà Research Center, Athens, Greece

Abstract. The FLECON-6G [1] project aims to develop an innovative blueprint for 6G architecture, characterised by its distributed, modular, open and collaborative frameworks. This architecture is built upon trustworthy principles and incorporates multi-layer Network Digital Twins (NDTs) which integrate seamlessly across various domains – from resource management to control and management planes, extending all the way to the business layer. FLECON-6G envisions an "Intelligent 6G Network of Networks" that seamlessly integrates Native and Trustworthy AI. This vision empowers the automated and scalable orchestration of services and capabilities across diverse networks, subsystems and technological domains, fostering collaboration among multiple stakeholders. In this paper, we consider a set of the Key Value Indicators (KVIs) for evaluating the societal aspects of the FLECON-6G use cases.

Keywords: 6G · Key Value Indicators (KVIs) · Societal Evaluation · Artificial Intelligence · Native AI · Network of Networks (NoN) · Network Digital Twins (NDTs) · Trustworthiness · Generalisability

1 Introduction

A plethora of technological innovations transformed the wireless communication landscape over the past decade. Technological advances under the 5G standard facilitated the introduction of extremely "data-hungry" enhanced mobile broadband (eMBB) services, as well as novel massive machine-type communication (mMTC) and ultra-reliable and low latency communication (uRLLC) services [11, 12]. 6G research is now underway to shape the new generation of Smart Networks and Services, aiming to further advance the state-of-the-art (SotA) with breakthrough technologies and new use-cases with extreme requirements. Most importantly, 6G is changing the way that future networks will be

Published by Springer Nature Switzerland AG 2027
A. Papaleonidas et al. (Eds.): AIAI 2026 Workshops, IFIP AICT 796, pp. 222–234, 2027.
https://doi.org/10.1007/978-3-032-30507-7_14

architected [13, 14]; the concept of an intelligent and fully adaptive "network of networks" [15] in 6G infrastructures, allows to aggregate multiple resources and subsystems, including not only communication technologies, but also computational resources and AI (Artificial Intelligence) models. This approach is the "foundation" for a digital ecosystem that becomes more and more complex, heterogeneous and intelligent, putting AI / ML (Machine Learning) [16] and Native AI-driven automation [17] at the forefront, while facilitating new business models for operators (e.g., Network Infrastructure as-a-service (NIaaS) [18]).

In line with EU's policies, FLECON-6G [1] will design, develop and validate – through relevant proofs of concept (PoCs) – several secure, trustworthy, resilient and reliable solutions across several and heterogeneous verticals, covering highly immersive and digital twinning applications that require 6G performance capabilities. PoCs deployment and validation will exploit, re-use and extend, where relevant, testbed infrastructures from current SNS projects [19]. FLECON-6G gathers key participants from Phase-1 and Phase-2 SNS JU projects, aiming to make the "Intelligent 6G Network of Networks" vision a reality, with Trustworthiness and Generalisability of Native AI and Network Digital Twins (NDTs) assisted approaches [20]. It aims to deliver key technological assets in the form of collaborative and distributed frameworks offering scalability and support for multi-domain, multi-stakeholder infrastructures, jointly with network infrastructure programmability that supports the offloading of network application logic.

FLECON-6G provides groundbreaking research to "drive" the next phase of 6G Native AI research, addressing Trustworthiness and Generalisability via novel intent-driven frameworks and robust Foundation Models, that not only deliver zero-touch orchestration [21] but also performance guarantees and robustness in multi-stakeholder infrastructures. A multilayer, multi-vendor NDT framework [22] will also assist online decisions and resolve conflicts among multiple closed control loops operating in reactive, proactive or predictive mode for zero-touch self-optimisation.

At the business layer, a Smart Marketplace will facilitate the creation of a wide, sustainable ecosystem of highly diversified stakeholders, through which, Mobile Network Operators (MNOs), digital service providers, verticals and software developers of AI or Digital Twins (DT) software applications will jointly collaborate to build more integrated and intent-driven service offers, composing a plethora of modular assets for their effective monetisation.

In this paper, we briefly present the main use cases (UCs) considered by FLECON-6G (Sect. 2), and we investigate a set of KVIs for societal evaluation (Sect. 3).

2 Use Cases

This section discusses the fundamental UCs being deployed in the framework of FLECON-6G ecosystem. These are described in the following subsections.

2.1 Seamless Immersive Reality (SIR)

The objective of this scenario is to test and validate the performance of the Smart Marketplace and Accelerated Programmable Edge Computing (APEC) technological components of FLECON-6G to support future seamless immersive reality application services [23].

The SIR experience proposed for FLECON-6G will leverage stereoscopic capture techniques to properly represent multiple human figures, in a real-time metaverse application for virtual presence meetings [24]. Metaverse attendees will be represented by their 3D silhouettes, captured in real-time via synchronised streams up to 16k at 100 frames per second. This will help support fully immersive teleconferencing experiences for all participants, creating the illusion of "presence" in a shared meeting room. In addition, this PoC will leverage the rendering capabilities of the future Virtual Reality (VR) headset capabilities. Spatial computing based on see-through methodologies [25], first implemented in VR headsets, allow to project augmented reality elements on the real surrounding environment or inside the virtual scene. The capability to create an unprecedented immersive experience projecting the connected and stereoscopically captured meet participants will be explored in this PoC. For each immersive conference participant two modules will be deployed and connected through different mobile connections. The rendering module (headset) will receive lightly compressed (on the edge with low latency and high ratio codecs, like High Efficiency Video Coding (HEVC) or JPEG-XS [26] to reduce the load on the final device) synchronised 16k video streams for every participant visualised. To support the stringent latency requirements, the SIR application will be disaggregated in the form of cloud-native functions supporting stereoscopic capture, transcoding, fusion and synchronisation functions that can be deployed at a multi-stakehoder continuum of resources. Thus, less latency sensitive functions can be deployed at edge sites coming from multiple stakeholders with different price points. The FLECON-6G Smart Marketplace and Accelerated Programmable Edge Computing technological components will be validated to: (a) *automatically negotiate edge resources that will host SIR services* and; (b) *dynamically interconnect them via the APEC data pane.* More specifically, during PoC execution:

- The **Smart Marketplace** component will be validated, exposing networking and computational resources from multiple Network Operators; these are emulated within a testbed environment via appropriate segmentation of resources in multiple resource pools. The Smart Marketplace allows the Metaverse vertical owner to propose the price they want/can pay for Connectivity and Computational capacity via intent Application Programming Interfaces (APIs). Brokers are involved in the negotiating process, offering the same service at the best price, where the best offer/price relation between Network Operator's offerings is selected automatically, via intent-driven consensus convergence mechanisms. The SIR application cloud-native functions are automatically deployed at Edge and Deep Edge nodes selected from the automated resource selection process.
- The **APEC component** will be validated by decomposing the SIR application into its different logical blocks and by offloading its network critical performance components down to the APEC acceleration stack. Here, the objective is to support high data rate traffic processing while not compromising with latency and jitter on the single

node. Whenever possible, the computation will be pushed down to the APEC hardware level, otherwise fall back in the software layer will be adopted. As for performance assessment, different scenarios, ranging from loaded (high network congestion) and unloaded (low network congestion) will be explored.

2.2 Machine Inspection Using Autonomous Robots and VR

The objective of this PoC is to showcase the usage of RAN (Radio Access Network) Network Digital Twin within a Zero touch network and Service Management (ZSM) [27] closed-control loop to guarantee constant quality for the video streams collected from the robots that do machine inspections [28]. In this PoC, we will demonstrate FLECON-6G's approach to resolve conflicts in a Native AI-driven closed loop ZSM system to guarantee that robots' video stream is not degraded, even in bad conditions (channel degradation or competition with other flows), by adapting the radio resources allocated to the robots' video stream in real-time.

We will use two robots, which is a robotics development kit designed specifically for advanced robotics applications, supporting a wide range of sensors commonly used in robotics, including cameras, LiDAR, radar and inertial measurement units (IMUs). These sensors can be interfaced with the platform to provide input for navigation, object recognition and environment perception. In this PoC, we will use cameras to capture video simulating a machine inspection. The captured video stream will be streamed through the DT to a human wearing a VR headset. The person should be able to see both streams in real-time and in excellent quality without degradation.

To represent the ZSM approach, we will develop a AI/ML-based Decision Engines (DEs) that collect Key Performance Indicators (KPIs) from the RAN and combine it with video quality statistics obtained from the client (buffer fullness, video freezing, etc.) to decide about the RAN resources (number of physical Resource Blocks (pRBs)) to be allocated to the User Equipment (UE), which are connected to the robots. The AI/ML model will correlate between the application level KPI (obtained from the video client) and the RAN KPI (channel statistics, PDCP (Packet Data Convergence Protocol) throughput, etc.) to detect degradation of the video streams; in that case, a decision is triggered to the RAN to update the dedicated pRB to the UE connected to the robot.

The closed control loop (achieving ZSM) is enforced as a rApp and deployed on top of a Non-RT RAN Intelligent Controller (RIC). The rApp runs the AI/ML application and collects RAN KPI via a xApp[1] [29] deployed on top of FlexRIC (Near-Real Time RIC) [30], which uses the KPM (Key Performance Metrics) service model[2] to collect RAN KPI and the RC (Remote Control) service model[3] to enforce the decisions of the rApp (RB allocation) on the RAN. From the video client (Oculus), the rApp collects

[1] Operating as specialist tools for the purposes of enhancing network automation and intelligence, xApps and rApps sit on a RAN Intelligent Controller (RIC). They are created by developers, to maximise the operational efficiency of the RAN – providing key management features and functionality.

[2] The Key Performance Metric is the O-RAN service model for monitoring.

[3] The RAN Control is the O-RAN service model to control the RAN. For further information also see: https://bubbleran.com/docs/devops-guide/flexric/developers-guide/xapp/xapp-programming/O-RAN-Standarized-SMs/

service-level KPI describing the quality of the video as perceived by the user. The closed control loop and NDT-assisted conflict resolution will be tested and validated through different scenarios possible with the RAN DT, such as UE (i.e., robots) mobility, channel conditions and models, as well as parallel traffic by increasing the number of simulated UEs that generate UDP (User Datagram Protocol) traffic.

2.3 Network Digital Twin with NTN

In this PoC, we intend to validate that a NDT for mobile communication adds benefit to a process digital twin "not only network planning and provisioning" (e.g., real-time optimisation based on process information). Moreover, we investigate the benefits of clustering DTs in categories, as well as the potential of an integrated NDT, computing digital twin, process digital twin. Last but not least, we intend to realise a mobile network infrastructure which is transparent to the application no matter which transport network technology is used, based on the example of combining terrestrial mobile communication and Non Terrestrial Network (NTN).

An industrial process emulator is leveraged which intricately models the complexities of an industrial system, using real operational data of a production system. This industrial process spans multiple network segments, incorporating equipment via a fixed network, a non-public mobile network and NTN. Each facet of the process, including the network, is meticulously emulated by the respective FLECON-6G Network Digital Twin, ensuring a comprehensive virtual representation. Industrial processes are engineered to be robust and maintain functionality, even amidst disruptions. They achieve this by establishing their own private communication and computing infrastructure, especially in isolated environments like the high seas or deserts. The system architecture is a fusion of computing and communication, designed to be hybrid in nature. It is adept at managing the mobility of resources and simultaneously offers a reliable platform that supports both edge and cloud computing capabilities. A pivotal component of this system is the FLECON-6G Network Digital Twin framework, which plays a crucial role in validating the configurations and operational scenarios of the end-to-end (E2E) industrial process. It achieves this by creating a seamless link between the process's digital twin and the NDT itself. The E2E NDT framework, is set to be showcased across industrial scenarios that exemplify mobile automation, device management, and alarm systems. In a significant collaboration, a NTN testbed will augment the use case with NTN functionalities, simulating global scenarios that feature mobile infrastructure and application nodes. This integration results in a dynamic connected computing system, where Cyber-Physical System (CPS) components and their digital twins are evaluated holistically.

The variety of technologies within the testbed environment provides an excellent environment to showcase the capability of the FLECON-6G NoN Collaborative Framework alongside NDTaaS (Network Digital Twin as-a-Service) [31] and AIaaS (Artificial Intelligence as-a-Service) [32] Marketplace components to dynamically compose and federate 6G networks of networks (NoN) in a recursive manner [33]. The PoC will show how resources and subsystems from multiple technological (edge, mobile networks, NTN) and administrative domains (Non-Public Network (NPN) administrator, MNO, satellite operator, edge computing provider) can be efficiently chained in end-to-end services and network topologies. The composition and network automation logic will be supported through the FLECON-6G Cognitive Closed Loops Coordination Framework, with the assistance of E2E NDTs dynamically provisioned through the FLECON-6G Service and Network DTaaS Orchestration Framework. At least 3 closed loops will be provisioned, operating at the resource, network and service level respectively, for automated re-allocation of edge components, self-recovery of E2E network connectivity and self-optimisation of service components distribution. Their coordination will be handled with the assistance of the (N)DTs to guarantee the consistency of the overall decisions and avoid the risk of enforcing conflicting actions in different layers or domains. Specialised (N)DTs will be instantiated and configured on-demand, enabling the creation of an end-to-end multi-layer and multi-domain digital twin covering 4 technological domains (industrial network domain, edge computing domain, 6G access/core network domain, satellite network domain as backhaul) and 3 layers (physical infrastructure, E2E network slice including edge computing resources, industrial application service). The NDTs' models will be parameterised according to performed parameter studies, so that different scenarios can be tested and evaluated. The PoC will also show how the interactions among different (N)DTs will allow to elaborate a consistent and fully synchronised representation of the end-to-end system. As part of the NDTs chain, the NDT of the NTN to be developed in the project will be specifically validated, exploiting the NTN-Testbed capabilities. The NTN testbed can emulate the orbital behaviour of NTN satellite constellations and configurable link characteristics for inter-satellite and satellite-to-earth links. The validation will use statistical analysis of both setups, including a comparison. More specifically, the following scenarios will be showcased:

- Validate representative industrial scenarios and configurations from the area of mobile automation, device management, and alarming of the industrial E2E process by interconnecting the process digital twin with the NDT framework.
- An NTN testbed will be used to add NTN capabilities to the use case and emulate global scenarios with mobile infrastructure and application nodes, which form together a highly dynamic connected computing system. CPS components and capabilities and its DT will be considered end-to-end.
- Demonstrate joint orchestration alongside AIaaS and NDTaaS jointly leveraged in the automation of system operation (simulation of process, updates, and commissioning/decommissioning of devices/services). Enable a co-design, operation, and maintenance of industrial applications and corresponding 6G systems based on a communication and computing pool across heterogeneous entities and its Digital Twins.

The outcomes of the FLECON-6G initiative will undergo rigorous validation to assess operational reliability, resilience, and efficiency, ensuring that the system meets the highest standards of industrial performance.

2.4 Public Safety Services

The primary objective of the Public Safety Services Proof of Concept (PoC) within the FLECON-6G project is to demonstrate the feasibility and efficacy of leveraging the novel FLECON-6G connectivity platform in addressing the critical communication needs of public safety end-users. Specifically, the PoC aims to validate the adaptability and robustness of the FLECON-6G architecture in supporting mission-critical communication services for public safety agencies [34, 35]. Through this PoC, we seek to assess the platform's ability to meet the stringent requirements of public safety applications, including uRLLC, seamless mobility and secure data transmission. Additionally, the PoC aims to showcase the potential of advanced AI-driven capabilities integrated into the platform to enhance situational awareness, response coordination, and decision-making in emergency scenarios. Overall, the objectives of the Public Safety Services PoC are centered around validating the FLECON-6G platform's suitability for supporting mission-critical communication requirements and enhancing the operational effectiveness of public safety agencies in emergency situations.

The corresponding PoC encompasses a comprehensive demonstration of the platform's capabilities in addressing the unique communication requirements of public safety agencies. The PoC scenario involves simulated emergency situations, such as natural disasters or large-scale incidents, where timely and reliable communication is paramount for effective response and coordination. In this PoC, the FLECON-6G platform will be deployed in a controlled testbed environment, mimicking real-world public safety operations. Various elements of the platform, including its open and flexible architecture, Native and Trustworthy AI technologies, privacy and security mechanisms, will be "put" to the test to evaluate their performance under different scenarios and stress conditions. During experiment execution, First Responders are connected to the network via Amarisoft gNBs, and roaming with their UEs. Network and infrastructure Faults and workload variations are created to test the system's reliability and adaptability to disaster scenarios. The platform will also demonstrate its ability to support seamless mobility, ensuring continuous connectivity to the Command & Control centre for personnel operating in dynamic environments. More specifically, during the PoC execution:

- The FLECON-6G Trustworthy AI mechanisms will be validated, in terms of ensuring the stringent Service Level Agreements (SLAs) required by the system offering guarantees via predictive service migrations, reconfigurations and handovers, while quantifying the various system uncertainties and monitoring model drift.
- The PoC will showcase Native AI integration into the platform, such as AI-driven planning, predictive modeling, decision support and infrastructure auto-configuration. This is achieved via the integration of the Cognitive Intent Management Function within all technological domains (Operation Support Systems (OSS) / Business Support Systems (BSS), Computational Infrastructure, Amarisoft gNBs).
- The security and privacy mechanisms will be validated by introducing simulated denial-of-service (distributed and single-source) attacks, network intrusion and resource exhaustion to evaluate the impact of the FLECON-6G's mechanisms on availability and disaster resilience. This will be achieved through the real-time deployment, configuration, and tuning of the Trustworthiness Evaluation Framework and the AI-driven security and privacy components that can understand sophisticated attacks and deploy appropriate contingencies.

Throughout this PoC, emphasis will be placed on evaluating the platform's performance in meeting the stringent requirements of public safety applications, including reliability, latency, security and coverage. Technical challenges, such as network congestion, interoperability issues, and resource optimisation, will be identified and addressed to ensure the platform's suitability for mission-critical communication tasks.

3 Key Value Indicators for Societal Evaluation

Several research efforts deal with the concept of Key Values (KV) and Key Value Indicators (KVIs) to address social challenges in technology design and development phases and to identify and estimate value outcomes from technology use [2–5]. These aspects aim to measure all this impact created not only in terms of performance, but also in terms of overall "societal/human" value, addressing issues such as democracy (fairness, digital inclusion), responsibility and energy efficiency.

According to [3], a list of KVs could include the following: *environmental sustainability, societal sustainability, economical sustainability and innovation, democracy, cultural connection, knowledge, privacy and confidentiality, simplified life, digital inclusion, personal freedom, personal health and protection from harm, trust.*

Similarly, HEXA-X II [6] addresses sustainability by comprehensively considering **environmental**, **social**, and **economic** factors. These factors extend beyond mere energy efficiency, which is crucial given the anticipated widespread adoption of the 6G ecosystem. The sustainability analysis qualitatively "outlines" the KVs and potential impacts for each use case. These impacts are categorised into *benefits* (sustainability handprints), and *costs* (sustainability footprints).

FIDAL's proposal for a High-Level Framework for KVs and example indicators are presented in [7]. FIDAL aims to adopt a standardized methodology to identify the parameters that maximise the impact of 5G evolution services on the community. KVIs [36] complement Key Performance Indicators (KPIs) [37, 38] to balance business and social performance metrics. The main KV clusters identified are: *democracy* (trustworthy, inclusiveness/equal opportunity, fairness, personal freedom, transparency, privacy); *economic* (sustainability, business value, tackling economic inequality); *innovation* (responsibility, open collaboration, flexibility); *environmental* (sustainability, waste management, mitigation strategies, compliance quality standards); *safety and security* (safety, security, data protection), and; *societal* (sustainability, healthier community, cultural connection, knowledge, quality of living / wellbeing).

CENTRIC's vision [8] has a strong emphasis on developing technological enablers that contribute to the goal of a sustainable 6G network. Such sustainability can be understood from, mainly, three dimensions: *environmental sustainability* (energy efficiency improvements, material efficiency improvements), *economic sustainability* (CAPEX reductions, OPEX reductions), and *societal sustainability* (electromagnetic fields- (EMF-) aware networks, user data protection and privacy).

SAFE-6G [9], ensuring the effective measurement and assessment of trust, security, privacy, resilience and reliability in future 6G networks, identifies the following aspects for KVI analysis: *trust, security, privacy and confidentiality, sustainable resource utilization, simplified life, digital inclusion, societal sustainability.*

FLECON-6G's KVIs are designed to evaluate the societal impact of 6G technologies, focusing on three major driving forces as follows (cf. Figure 1). These forces are related to the EU Sustainable Development Goals (SDGs) [39].

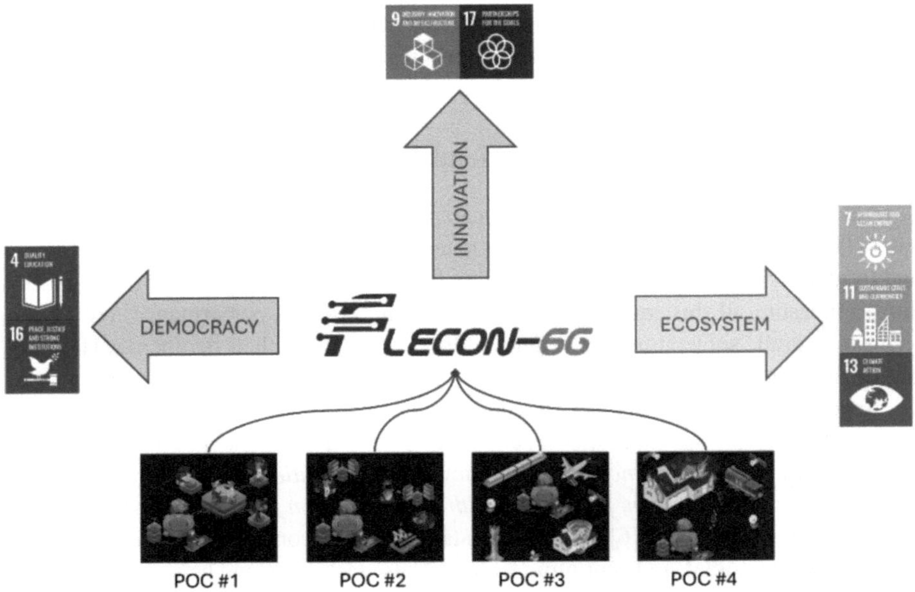

Fig. 1. Correlation between the three major driving forces of FLECON-6G KVIs and SDGs

The KVIs, mentioned in the SNS R&I Work Programme 2023–2024 [40], have been defined in the following Table, also by including an explanation on their relevance, aim and measurement method and quantitative evaluation metrics. These KVIs will show how FLECON-6G will provide societal impact to 6G vertical sector applications and to European industrial competitiveness.

The KVIs will be validated in the PoCs as well as externally through focused group surveys, workshops, webinars, interviews with relevant stakeholders, etc., as they relate to important human and societal key value areas (Table 1).

Table 1. Overview of the KVIs to be validated and their measurement method.

KV	KVI	Description
Innovation	*Safety*	Evaluates that unavailability or degradation of communication service does not negatively impact humans or the environment. Measures how 6G architectures improve confidence in technology acceleration regarding safety of people and processes
Innovation	*Security*	Protection of 6G networks and data against cybersecurity threats, ensuring robust design against attacks
Innovation	*Regulation*	Compliance with legal and policy frameworks, promoting network neutrality and adoption of 6G
Innovation	*Responsibility*	Ensures accountability and control in 6G networks through responsible innovation

(*continued*)

Table 1. *(continued)*

KV	KVI	Description
Innovation	*Energy Efficiency*	Reduces energy consumption at all architectural levels in 6G networks
Democracy	*Privacy*	Ensures appropriate use of end-user data, aligning with GDPR (General Data protection Regulation) and enhancing confidence in data protection
Democracy	*Fairness*	AI/ML algorithms perform decisions free from discrimination and bias, ensuring social justice and high-quality techniques
Democracy	*Digital Inclusion*	Deployment of technologies serving historically under-served populations; reducing digital divide
Democracy	*Trustworthiness*	6G networks support trust and distributed learning, ensuring end-to-end confidence in AI decisions
Ecosystem	*Sustainability*	Minimises resource consumption considering environmental, economic, and societal impacts
Ecosystem	*Business Value*	Demonstrates benefits of 6G networks to MNOs; supports value creation and Return of investment (ROI)
Ecosystem	*Economic Growth*	Supports competitive and resilient economy via next-gen 6G services, skills, and digital transformation
Ecosystem	*Open Collaboration*	Promotes knowledge sharing and collaborative methods across projects and stakeholders
Innovation	*New Value Chain*	Engages new stakeholders to enhance and expand existing 5G value chains

4 Discussion

In this paper, we considered a set of the KVIs for evaluating the societal aspects of the FLECON-6G use cases. A new paradigm shift is required for technology design and evaluation focusing not only on network related parameters and market opportunities, but equally important by addressing the Sustainable Development Goals. Hence, apart from the technical challenges, it is important to highlight the societal insights emerging from the 6G ecosystem.

The proposed KVIs will be validated in the corresponding PoCs as well as externally through focused group surveys, workshops, webinars, interviews with relevant stakeholders, etc., as they relate to important human and societal key value areas. The relevant external 6G stakeholders (e.g., MNOs, Mobile Virtual Network Operators (MVNOs), vendors, vertical applications providers, end-users, etc.) will be recruited through wide dissemination and communication means (e.g., from webinars, workshops, public events, joint events at 6G-IA and at SNS JU level) and incentivised to participate in surveys and/or in focused groups.

Our future work also includes our alignment with the TMV KVIs and 6G-IA SNVC (Societal Needs and Value Creation) Working Groups [41], by "matching" the considered KVIs to the corresponding KVs classification proposed in [10]. The identified categories of KVs are the following: environmental sustainability, societal sustainability, economic sustainability & innovation, democracy, cultural connection, knowledge, privacy & confidentiality, simplified life, digital inclusion, personal freedom, personal health & protection from harm, and trust. This categorisation utilised within [10] does not represent or stand for a final proposal of classification of the Key Values, rather, it is utilised as a "point of reference" for many of the research projects that participated in the questionnaires.

Acknowledgments. The paper has been based on the context of the SNS-JU "FLECON-6G" ("Flexible Open Architecture and AI-driven Enabling Technologies for a Novel 6G Connectivity Platform") Project (GA No.101192462), funded by the European Commission.

References

1. FLECON-6G (Flexible Open Architecture and AI-driven Enabling Technologies for a Novel 6G Connectivity Platform) Horizon SNS-JU Project, Grant Agreement No.101192462. https://flecon6g.eu/
2. Kostopoulos, A., Chochliouros, I.P., Verikoukis, C.: A business analysis framework for 6G Architectures. In: Proceedings of the 2024 IEEE 29th International Workshop on Computer Aided Modeling and Design of Communication Links and Networks (CAMAD), Athens, Greece, pp.1–6 (2024). https://doi.org/10.1109/CAMAD62243.2024.10942810
3. 6G Infrastructure Association (6G-IA): What societal values will 6G address? Societal Key Values and Key Value Indicators analysed through 6G use cases. Vision and Societal Challenges Working Group, Societal Needs and Value Creation Sub-Group (2022). https://doi.org/10.5281/zenodo.6557534
4. 6G Smart Networks and Services Industry Association (6G-IA): 6G-IA Emerging 5G and beyond ecosystem business models. White paper (2025). https://doi.org/10.5281/zenodo.14756404
5. Wikstrom, G., et al.: Key value indicators: a framework for values-driven next-generation ICT solutions. Telecommun. Policy **48**(6), 102778 (2024). https://doi.org/10.1016/j.telpol.2024.102778
6. HEXA-X II Project: Deliverable 1.3 "Environmental and social view on 6G". https://hexa-x-ii.eu/wp-content/uploads/2024/03/Hexa-X-II_D1.3_v1.00_GA_approved.pdf
7. FIDAL Project: Deliverable 2.1: "Requirements, Architecture And Methodologies (Initial Version)". https://fidal-he.eu/public-deliverables/d-21-fidal-requirements-architecture-and-methodologies-initial-version
8. CENTRIC Project: Deliverable 5.1: "Early results on KPIs/KVIs, testing methodologies and benchmarking". https://zenodo.org/records/10473249
9. SAFE-6G Project: Deliverable 2.4: "6G Trustworthiness KPI & KVI definition and validation methodology". https://zenodo.org/records/14943206
10. Smart Networks and Services Joint Undertaking (SNS JU): 6G KVIs – SNS Projects Initial Survey (Results 2025). Test Measurements and Validation Working Group (2025). https://doi.org/10.5281/zenodo.15220945

11. Tummala, M., Bekal, P., Kumar, P., Purid, S., Rawat, S., Kumari, A.: A systematic review on current and future prospects of 5G communications. Cogent Eng. **12**(1), 2547635 (2025). https://doi.org/10.1080/23311916.2025.2547635
12. Morgado, A., Huq, K.M.S., Mumtaz, S., Rodriguez, J.: A survey of 5G technologies: regulatory, standardization and industrial perspectives. Digit. Commun. Netw. **4**(2), 87–97 (2018). https://doi.org/10.1016/j.dcan.2017.09.010
13. Chowdhury, M.Z., Shahjalal, M., Ahmed, S., Jang, Y.M.: 6G wireless communication systems: applications, requirements, technologies, challenges, and research directions. IEEE Open J. Commun. Soc. **1**, 957–975 (2020). https://doi.org/10.1109/OJCOMS.2020.3010270
14. Bertin, E., Crespi, N., and Magedanz, T.: Shaping Future 6G Networks: Needs, Impacts, and Technologies. John Wiley & Sons Ltd. (2022)
15. Karimi, F., Green, D., Matous, P., Varvarigos, M., Khalilpour, K.R.: A Network of networks: a bibliometric analysis. Physica D **421**, 132889 (2021). https://doi.org/10.1016/j.physd.2021.132889
16. Smart Networks and Services Joint undertaking (6G SNS): AI/ML as a key Enabler of 6G Networks (White Paper) (2025). https://doi.org/10.5281/zenodo.14623106
17. Jiun, W., Wang, N., Zhang, L., Tian, X., Shi, B., Zhao, B.: A review of AI-driven automation technologies: latest taxonomies, existing challenges, and future prospects. Comput., Mater. Continua **84**(3), 3961–4018 (2025). https://doi.org/10.32604/cmc.2025.067857
18. Moussaoui, M., Bertin, E., Crespi, N.: Telecom business models for beyond 5G and 6G networks: towards disaggregation? In: Proceedings of the 2022 1st International Conference on 6G Networking (6GNet), 06–08 July 2022, Paris, France, pp.1–8 (2022). https://doi.org/10.1109/6GNet54646.2022.9830514
19. Smart Networks and Services Joint Undertaking (SNS JU). https://smart-networks.europa.eu/project-portfolio/#sns-ju-call-1-2022
20. Nguyen, H.X., Trestian, R., To, D., Tatipamula, M.: Digital Twin for 5G and beyond. IEEE Commun. Mag. **59**(2), 10–15 (2021). https://doi.org/10.1109/MCOM.001.2000343
21. Bello, R.C., Scivoletto, G., Landi, G., Mihai, R., et al.: Zero-touch cross-domain orchestration in the 6G compute continuum: a framework evaluation in real-life scenarios. IEEE Open J. Commun. Soc. **7**, 1376–1395 (2026). https://doi.org/10.1109/OJCOMS.2026.3662044
22. Raza, S.M., Minerva, R., Crespi, N., Alvi, M., Herath, M., Dutta, H.: A comprehensive survey of network digital twin architecture, capabilities, challenges, and requirements for edge-cloud continuum. Comput. Commun. **236**, 108144 (2025). https://doi.org/10.1016/j.comcom.2025.108144
23. Liao, S., Chaudhri, S., Karwa, M.K., Popescu, V.: SeamlessVR: bridging the immersive to non-immersive visualization divide. IEEE Trans. Visual Comput. Graphics **31**(5), 2806–2816 (2025). https://doi.org/10.1109/TVCG.2025.3549564
24. Hatami, M., Qu, Q., Chen, Y., Kholidy, H., Blasch, E., Ardiles-Cruz, E.: A survey of the real-time metaverse: challenges and opportunities. Future Internet **16**(10), 379 (2024). https://doi.org/10.3390/fi16100379
25. Xu. J., Papangelis, K., Tigwell, G.W., Lalone, N., et al.: Spatial computing: defining the vision for the future. In: Proceedings of the CHI EA '24: Extended Abstracts of the CHI Conference on Human Factors in Computing Systems, May 11–16 2024, Honolulu, HI, USA, pp.1–4 (2024). https://doi.org/10.1145/3613905.3643978
26. https://jpeg.org/jpegxs/documentation.html
27. Liyanage, M., et al.: A survey on zero touch network and service management (ZSM) for 5G and beyond networks. J. Netw. Comput. Appl. **203**, 103362 (2022). https://doi.org/10.1016/j.jnca.2022.103362
28. Patrashko, D.Y., Gurau, V.: Machine learning-powered vision for robotic inspection in manufacturing: a review. Sensors **26**(3), 788 (2026). https://doi.org/10.3390/s26030788

29. Acceleran Academy: An xApp and an rApp - What's the difference and what do they mean for RAN Automation? (2026). https://accelleran.com/xapp-rapp-2/
30. https://openairinterface.org/flexric-tutorial-xapp-development/
31. Talasila, P., Gomes, C., Mikkelsen, P.H., Arboleda, S.G., Kamburjan, E., Larsen, P.G.: Digital twin as a service (DTaaS): a platform for digital twin developers and users. Cornell University (2023). https://arxiv.org/abs/2305.07244
32. Lins, S., Pandl, K.D., Teigeler, H., et al.: Artificial intelligence as a service. Bus. Inf. Syst. Eng. **63**, 441–456 (2021). https://doi.org/10.1007/s12599-021-00708-w
33. SUNRISE-6G (SUstainable federatioN of Research Infrastructures for Scaling-up Experimentation in 6G) Horizon SNS-JU Project, Grant Agreement No.101139257. https://sunrise6g.eu/
34. Yu, W., Xu, H., Nguyen, J., Blasch, E., Hematian, A., Gao, W.: Survey of public safety communications: User-side and network-side solutions and future directions. IEEE Access **6**, 70397–70425 (2018). https://doi.org/10.1109/ACCESS.2018.2879760
35. Saafi, S., Hosek, J., Kolackova, A.: Enabling next-generation public safety operations with mission-critical networks and wearable applications. Sensors **21**(17), 5790 (2021). https://doi.org/10.3390/s21175790
36. Osman, H., Bradford, J., Mitchell, S., Chiavarino, C.: An approach for key value indicator evaluation: enabling consistent assessment of societal impacts. In: Proceedings of the 2025 Joint European Conference on Networks and Communications & 6G Summit (EuCNC/6G Summit), 03–06 June 2025, Poznan, Poland, pp.411–415 (2025). https://doi.org/10.1109/EuCNC/6GSummit63408.2025.11037055
37. 5G Infrastructure Public Private Partnership (5G PPP): White Paper - Beyond 5G/6G KPI Measurement (2023). https://5g-ppp.eu/wp-content/uploads/2023/06/white_paper_b5g-6g_kpi_measurement_FINAL.pdf
38. 5G Infrastructure Public Private Partnership (5G PPP): KPIs Measurement Tools. From KPI definition to KPI validation enablement (White Paper) (2023). https://5g-ppp.eu/wp-content/uploads/2023/05/TMV-KPI-Measurement-Tools_1.0-published.pdf
39. European Commission: Sustainable Development Goals https://commission.europa.eu/strategy-and-policy/sustainable-development-goals_en
40. Horizon Europe: SNS JU Phase (2023) call for proposals & related R&I Work Programme 2023–2024. https://horizoneurope.ie/sns-ju-2023/sns-ju-phase-2023-call-for-proposals
41. SNS JU Working Groups. https://smart-networks.europa.eu/sns-ju-working-groups/

Network Slicing-Enabled Architecture for Autonomous Inventory Verification in Smart Warehouses

Christina C. Lessi[1](✉), Gregory Mygdakos[2], Makis Stamatelatos[3], and Ioannis P. Chochliouros[1]

[1] Hellenic Telecommunications Organization (OTE) S.A, Athens, Greece
clessi@oteresearch.gr

[2] bSpoke Solutions, Thermi, Greece

[3] Diakinisis Logistics Services, Athens, Greece

Abstract. The transformation of warehouse operations through automation introduces new requirements for communication networks, particularly in terms of latency, reliability and scalability. Autonomous robotic systems performing real-time tasks, such as inventory verification, depend on continuous and efficient data exchange with centralized platforms. Beyond 5G (B5G) networks provide the necessary technological framework to support such applications, enabling flexible and service-oriented architectures. Among their key features, network slicing allows the deployment of multiple logical networks over a shared infrastructure, each tailored to specific service requirements. This paper presents a B5G-enabled architecture designed for autonomous inventory verification in warehouse environments, with a primary focus on network slicing. A detailed use case is introduced, where mobile robots perform real-time validation of load positions by interacting with Warehouse Management Systems (WMS). The proposed slicing framework ensures service differentiation, efficient resource utilization and high system reliability.

Keywords: B5G · Network Slicing · Automated Logistics · Smart Warehouses

1 Introduction

The increasing demand for efficiency and accuracy in logistics operations has driven the adoption of automation technologies within warehouse environments. Autonomous mobile robots are now widely used to perform tasks such as transportation, inspection and inventory management, significantly reducing human workload and operational errors.

A critical challenge in such environments is maintaining consistency between the physical placement of goods and the digital records stored in Warehouse Management Systems (WMS). Misplaced items or incorrect inventory data can lead to inefficiencies, delays and increased operational costs.

Published by Springer Nature Switzerland AG 2027
A. Papaleonidas et al. (Eds.): AIAI 2026 Workshops, IFIP AICT 796, pp. 235–241, 2027.
https://doi.org/10.1007/978-3-032-30507-7_15

To address these challenges, real-time monitoring and verification mechanisms are required. However, such mechanisms impose strict requirements on the underlying communication infrastructure, including low latency, high reliability and the ability to support multiple concurrent devices.

Beyond 5G (B5G) networks introduce advanced capabilities, such as virtualization and service-based architectures, that enable the support of these demanding applications. Network slicing allows the creation of isolated, service-specific logical networks over a shared physical infrastructure [1, 2].

In this context, 5G Standalone (SA) architectures follow a service-based design that enables flexible and modular deployment of network functions [3]. Network slicing has been widely recognized as a key mechanism for supporting heterogeneous services with strict QoS requirements [4]. Furthermore, edge computing paradigms improve latency performance by relocating computational resources closer to data sources [5].

This paper investigates the role of network slicing in supporting autonomous inventory verification systems and proposes a B5G-based architecture tailored to the requirements of smart warehouse environments (Fig. 1).

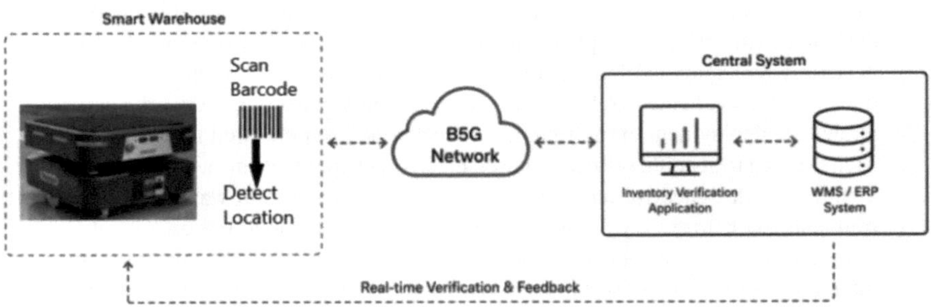

Fig. 1. Smart Warehouse Concept.

2 Autonomous Inventory Verification

2.1 Scenario Description

The examined use case focuses on the deployment of an autonomous robotic system within a modern warehouse environment, aiming to support and enhance inventory verification processes. The robotic platform operates without human intervention, navigating safely and efficiently through warehouse aisles while coexisting with human workers and other automated systems. Its operation is designed to be flexible, allowing both periodic inspections based on predefined schedules and on-demand missions triggered by warehouse management events or operator requests. This dual-mode functionality ensures continuous visibility of inventory status without disrupting normal warehouse workflows or affecting operational productivity [6].

The robot is equipped with advanced navigation and perception capabilities, including simultaneous localization and mapping (SLAM), obstacle detection and avoidance and high-precision indoor positioning. These features enable it to traverse complex warehouse layouts, dynamically adapt to environmental changes and maintain accurate positioning even in densely populated storage areas. During each inspection cycle, the robot systematically scans storage aisles and rack locations using integrated sensors such as cameras and barcode/QR code readers. By capturing both load identifiers (e.g., pallet IDs, product codes) and location identifiers (e.g., rack labels, bin positions), the system establishes a direct association between each inventory item and its physical placement.

The collected data are transmitted in near real time to a central application platform, typically deployed at the network edge or in a cloud infrastructure. This platform is responsible for data aggregation, processing and integration with backend enterprise systems. It interfaces with the WMS, which maintains the digital record of inventory, including the expected storage location, product classification and handling constraints for each load [7]. Data transmission is achieved through reliable wireless communication technologies, ensuring low latency and high availability for time-sensitive operations.

The primary objective of the system is to continuously verify whether each load is stored in its correctly designated location. This is accomplished through the correlation of three key data sources: (i) the identification data extracted from the load itself, (ii) the actual physical position derived from location-specific markers and the robot's positioning system and (iii) the expected storage information retrieved from the WMS. By comparing these datasets, the system can accurately determine discrepancies such as misplaced items, missing inventory, or incorrect slotting.

Furthermore, the system supports near real-time anomaly detection and reporting. When inconsistencies are identified, alerts are generated and forwarded to warehouse operators or management systems, enabling prompt corrective actions. The robot can also be configured to prioritize specific zones or high-value goods, thereby optimizing inspection efficiency based on operational priorities.

By performing multiple inspection rounds throughout the day, the robotic system enables continuous validation of inventory accuracy, significantly reducing the need for manual stock checks and periodic audits. This leads to improved operational efficiency, reduced human error and enhanced supply chain visibility. Ultimately, the integration of autonomous robotics with intelligent data processing contributes to the realization of smart warehouse environments, aligned with the principles of Industry 4.0 and beyond.

2.2 System Integration

The proposed solution relies on the seamless integration between the autonomous robotic system and existing warehouse information systems. It is assumed that each load entering the warehouse is assigned a specific storage position, which is recorded and maintained within the WMS or the underlying Enterprise Resource Planning (ERP) system [7]. This information constitutes the reference dataset against which real-time observations are validated.

To enable continuous and near real-time verification, the robotic platform is interfaced with the WMS through an application programming interface (API) or an equivalent data exchange mechanism. Through this integration, the system is able to retrieve up-to-date information regarding the expected storage location of each load, ensuring that the verification process is aligned with the latest operational state of the warehouse.

The data collected during the inspection process, including load identifiers and detected storage locations, are transmitted to a central application platform where they are processed and correlated with the corresponding WMS records. This platform is responsible for performing the consistency checks and identifying potential mismatches between observed and expected positions. In case of discrepancies, appropriate alerts or notifications are generated, enabling timely corrective actions and improving overall inventory accuracy.

2.3 Communication Requirements

The described use case generates heterogeneous communication demands, as it involves the continuous exchange of different types of data between the autonomous robots, the central application platform and the backend warehouse systems. These data flows include control-related information, identification data derived from barcode or QR code scanning, as well as, optionally, image or video streams used for supervision purposes.

From a networking perspective, the inventory verification process requires low end-to-end latency in order to support near real-time validation and timely system response. At the same time, high reliability and service availability are essential, as communication disruptions may lead to incomplete inspections or inconsistencies in the verification process. In addition, the transmission of scanning data and potential image streams introduces moderate to high throughput requirements, particularly in scenarios where multiple robots operate concurrently within the same environment.

Furthermore, the system must be able to scale efficiently with the number of deployed devices, as warehouse operations may involve a large fleet of robots and interconnected sensors. This results in varying traffic patterns and dynamic resource demands over time.

The coexistence of these diverse and, in some cases, conflicting requirements renders traditional one-size-fits-all network configurations inefficient. Instead, a more flexible and service-aware approach is required, capable of differentiating between traffic types and allocating resources accordingly. In this context, network slicing emerges as a key enabler, allowing the deployment of logically isolated network instances tailored to the specific performance requirements of each service category [4, 8].

3 Network Architecture

3.1 Network Components

The proposed system is based on a 5G Standalone (SA) architecture aligned with Release 16 specifications and extended towards Beyond 5G (B5G) capabilities, with the objective of supporting the stringent requirements of autonomous logistics applications. In this context, particular emphasis is placed on ensuring high service quality and reliability, which are critical for the uninterrupted operation of inventory verification processes [9]. To address these requirements, the architecture incorporates a network slicing framework, enabling the efficient support of heterogeneous services and preventing performance degradation under dynamic workload conditions.

The overall infrastructure consists of the Radio Access Network (RAN), the 5G Core (5GC), a cloud-based service platform and a slicing management framework. The

RAN leverages New Radio (NR) technology to provide high data rates and low latency, while advanced features such as beamforming and massive MIMO enhance coverage and capacity within the warehouse environment. The 5G Core is implemented following a cloud-native, service-based architecture, where network functions are deployed as containerized entities. This design enables flexible deployment strategies and supports the separation of control and user plane functions, facilitating edge computing capabilities and optimized data routing (Fig. 2).

The cloud infrastructure hosts the application layer, including the central platform responsible for inventory verification and enables the execution of latency-sensitive functions closer to the network edge. This distributed deployment contributes to reduced end-to-end latency and improved responsiveness of the system.

A key component of the architecture is the slicing management framework, which includes the Slice Manager and the Orchestrator. The Slice Manager is responsible for the lifecycle management of network slices, supporting operations such as slice creation, modification and termination, as well as maintaining information regarding available slices and their configuration parameters. This information is exposed to the Orchestrator, which is responsible for decision-making regarding slice selection and resource allocation.

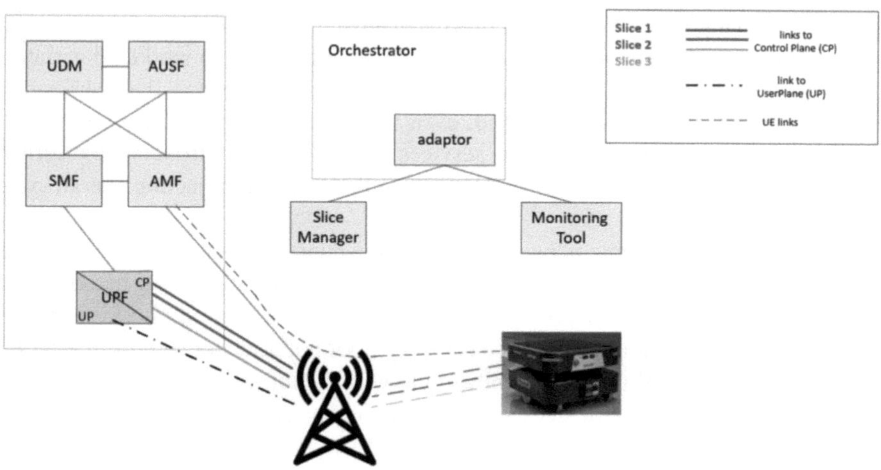

Fig. 2. Network Architecture

The Orchestrator maintains a global view of the network state and applies predefined criteria to determine when slice adaptation is required. Based on service requirements and network conditions, it can trigger slice reconfiguration actions through the Slice Manager, enabling dynamic adjustment of resource allocation. This interaction ensures that the communication needs of the autonomous logistics application are continuously met, even under varying traffic conditions and operational demands.

Overall, the proposed architecture enables end-to-end connectivity between robotic systems, control platforms and backend applications, while providing the flexibility and scalability required to support heterogeneous services through network slicing.

3.2 Dynamic Slice Adaptation

Given the dynamic nature of warehouse operations, static slice configurations are not sufficient to guarantee consistent service performance. The number of active robots, the generated traffic load and the priority of ongoing tasks may vary significantly over time, leading to fluctuations in network resource demands. To address these challenges, an automated slice adaptation mechanism is incorporated into the proposed architecture [10, 11].

The adaptation process is driven by the Orchestrator, which continuously evaluates the system state based on a set of predefined policies and service requirements. These policies capture key operational conditions, such as variations in the number of active robots, increased data transmission demands due to concurrent inspection processes and priority shifts in critical operations, for example when real-time control traffic must be prioritized over non-critical data flows. By maintaining a global view of network conditions and service requirements, the Orchestrator can determine whether slice reconfiguration is necessary.

When such conditions are met, the Orchestrator triggers appropriate adaptation actions through the Slice Manager. These actions include the dynamic reallocation of network resources across slices, the adjustment of Quality of Service (QoS) parameters and the reassignment of devices to different slices depending on their current service requirements. This closed-loop interaction between monitoring of system conditions and slice reconfiguration enables the network to respond effectively to workload variations.

Through this adaptive slicing mechanism, the system ensures that performance requirements are continuously satisfied, even under highly dynamic operational conditions. In particular, latency-sensitive services such as robot control can be prioritized when needed, while less critical traffic can be handled without impacting overall system performance.

The adoption of dynamic network slicing in the context of automated logistics provides several key benefits. It enables service differentiation by supporting heterogeneous applications with distinct performance requirements, while ensuring performance isolation so that congestion in one service category does not affect others. Furthermore, it enhances system flexibility and scalability, allowing the infrastructure to accommodate variations in the number of devices and workload intensity. Finally, it improves overall resource utilization by allocating network resources in a demand-driven manner.

4 Conclusion

This paper has presented a B5G-enabled network architecture for autonomous inventory verification in smart warehouse environments, with a particular focus on the role of network slicing as a core enabler for service differentiation and resource isolation. The proposed system supports real-time verification of load positions through the tight integration of autonomous robotic platforms with WMS, enabling continuous alignment between physical and digital inventory states.

By leveraging a slicing-based communication framework, the architecture is able to accommodate the heterogeneous and time-varying requirements of warehouse operations, including latency-sensitive traffic control, data-intensive scanning processes and scalable multi-device connectivity. The introduction of dynamic slice adaptation further enhances system robustness by allowing the network to respond to variations in workload, operational priorities and device density in a controlled and automated manner.

Overall, the proposed approach demonstrates how B5G network capabilities can be effectively exploited to support complex industrial automation scenarios, ensuring high levels of performance, reliability and operational flexibility.

Future research directions will investigate the integration of intelligent and predictive orchestration mechanisms, potentially leveraging machine learning techniques to anticipate network demand and proactively optimize slice allocation and resource utilization in highly dynamic environments.

Acknowledgments. This work has been performed in the scope of the 6G-PATH European research project and has been supported by the Smart Networks and Services Joint Undertaking (SNS-JU) by receiving funding form the European Union's Horizon Europe (HORIZON) Research and Innovation Programme under Grant Agreement No. 101139172.

References

1. Foukas, X., Elmokashfi, A., Patounas, G., Marina, M.K.: Network slicing in 5G: survey and challenges. IEEE Commun. Mag. **55**(5), 94–100 (2017). https://doi.org/10.1109/MCOM.2017.1600951
2. Chochliouros, I.P., et al.: Automated logistics in the B5G/6G era. In: AIAI 2025 IFIP WG 12.5 International Workshops: B5G-PINE 2025, Limassol, Cyprus, 26–29 June 2025, Proceedings, Part I. IFIP Advances in Information and Communication Technology, vol. 753, pp. 73–90. Springer, Cham (2025). https://doi.org/10.1007/978-3-031-97317-8_6
3. 3GPP. System architecture for the 5G system (5GS). 3GPP TS 23.501, Release 16. 3rd Generation Partnership Project, Sophia Antipolis (2020)
4. Popovski, P., Trillingsgaard, K.F., Simeone, O., Durisi, G.: 5G wireless network slicing for eMBB, URLLC and mMTC. IEEE Commun. Mag. **56**(7), 72–79 (2018). https://doi.org/10.1109/MCOM.2018.1701000
5. Abbas, N., Zhang, Y., Taherkordi, A., Skeie, T.: Mobile edge computing: a survey. IEEE Internet Things J. **5**(1), 450–465 (2018). https://doi.org/10.1109/JIOT.2017.2750180
6. Bonetto, M., et al.: Autonomous mobile robots in logistics and warehousing. IEEE Robot. Autom. Mag. **27**(3), 82–92 (2020). https://doi.org/10.1109/MRA.2020.2982111
7. Elsherif, E., et al.: Edge computing and industrial IoT for smart manufacturing. IEEE Access **7**, 168140–168152 (2019). https://doi.org/10.1109/ACCESS.2019.2954596
8. 3GPP. Policy and charging control architecture (QoS and traffic types). 3GPP TS 23.203, Release 16. 3rd Generation Partnership Project (2020)
9. ETSI. Network functions virtualisation (NFV): Architectural framework. ETSI GS NFV 002 V1.1.1. European Telecommunications Standards Institute, Sophia Antipolis (2013)
10. Afolabi, M., Taleb, T., Samdanis, K., Ksentini, A., Flinck, H.: Network slicing and softwarization: a survey on principles, enabling technologies and solutions. IEEE Commun. Surv. Tutor. **20**(3), 2429–2453 (2018). https://doi.org/10.1109/COMST.2018.2815638
11. Letaief, K.B., Chen, W., Shi, Y., Zhang, J., Zhang, Y.-J.A.: The roadmap to 6G: AI empowered wireless networks. IEEE Commun. Mag. **57**(8), 84–90 (2019). https://doi.org/10.1109/MCOM.2019.1900271

Optimizing Digital Resources Usage in Large Industries: a Telecommunications Use Case

Achilleas Marinakis[1(✉)], Christos A. Gizelis[1], Maria Panagiotidou[1], Eleanna Papakonstantinou[1], Konstantinos Nestorakis[1], Gary Joel Pereira[1], Vrettos Moulos[2], Vasileios Siopidis[3], Nikolaos Tepelidis[3], Charalampos Tsakiridis[3], Konstantinos Votis[3], and Dimitrios Tzovaras[3]

[1] OTE Group of Companies, Athens, Greece
{amarinaki,cgkizelis,mpanagiot,epapakonsta,knestorak,gpereira}@ote.gr
[2] AiNTIGONE, Athens, Greece
vrettos@aintigone.gr
[3] CERTH, Center for Research and Technology Hellas, Thessaloniki, Greece
{vasisiop,ntepe,chtsakiridis,kvotis,dimitrios.tzovaras}@iti.gr

Abstract. This paper describes the results of an innovative solution that aims to optimize the use of digital resources within a large industry in the telecommunications domain. It attempts to address the challenge of managing large amounts of data by a group of companies, which consists of many subsidiaries that collect, process, and store their own data across heterogeneous systems. The solution is part of an open-source modular framework, the main goal of which is to assist European companies in preparing their data for trading, exchange, and potential monetization. The proposed architecture is based on distributed data management for big data analytics, follows the data product paradigm, and has been validated against real-world business case scenarios. The findings presented in the article show how enterprises can benefit from cutting-edge technology and data-driven insights to achieve both economic growth and cost effectiveness, while respecting the principles of the digital circular economy. In this way, companies make a significant step towards achieving their sustainability and environmental goals, by reducing digital waste and making more efficient usage of their existing data and infrastructure resources.

Keywords: Data management · Digital resources optimization · Digital circular economy · Telecommunications · 3D-CIRCULAR EU project

1 Introduction

The digital transformation of large-scale industries has led to heavy utilization of integrated computational, storage, and network resources. This fact is even more

Supported by 3D-CIRCULAR EU Project – 101226256.

Published by Springer Nature Switzerland AG 2027
A. Papaleonidas et al. (Eds.): AIAI 2026 Workshops, IFIP AICT 796, pp. 242–254, 2027.
https://doi.org/10.1007/978-3-032-30507-7_16

challenging within the telecommunications sector, where almost all services and operations rely on digital infrastructure, and consequently the management of these resources has recently become a strategic priority. Besides the usual goals of cost reduction and performance improvement, special emphasis has been put on resources usage which should align with sustainability goals and the principles of the Circular Economy (CE), such as minimizing waste, conserving resources, and reducing environmental impacts [17].

However, CE principles cannot be implemented without the support of digital technologies [5]. To this end, Digital Circular Economy (DCE) is an emerging notion that expands the traditional CE concepts into the domain of digital systems. According to that notion, digital resources are no longer considered as infinitely renewable commodities, but as assets that have an environmental and economic cost during production, operation, and disposal. For telco providers, this notion introduces new opportunities and risks in minimizing resource over-provisioning, extending infrastructure utilization, and reducing energy consumption across complex, distributed environments [18].

Current telecommunication infrastructures work across heterogeneous systems that may include cloud platforms, virtual network functions, edge computing nodes, and legacy systems, while needing to support data-intensive and latency-sensitive applications, such as 5G/6G services, Internet of Things (IoT) deployments, and real-time media streaming. However, the unpredictable and dynamic nature of those workloads frequently results in resourcing patterns that are far from being optimal, like storage redundancy, and data duplication.

On one hand, cloud-native technologies and orchestration frameworks have led to smoother transformations and flexibility, but on the other hand they have ignored requirements related to sustainable and circular resource management. Their approaches mostly deal with elasticity and performance without considering efficiency, recapture, or environmental impact on a long term basis. As a result, operational optimization and sustainability-driven resource management gradually go in different directions. The paper attempts to fill this gap by delving into how digital deep tech driven circular economy [1] can be nested into deployment strategies in large-scale industrial settings, as exemplified by the telecommunications sector.

The rest of the document is structured as follows. Section 2 summarizes the related literature, while Sect. 3 briefly describes the conceptual architecture of the proposed solution, along with the datasets involved in the conducted research. Next, in Sect. 4 are analyzed the validation use cases and in Sect. 5 are presented the results that highlight the soundness of the solution. Finally, Sect. 6 concludes the paper.

2 Related Work

In recent years, much research effort has been spent to explore how swiftly evolving digital technologies can accelerate the transition of companies towards CE. More specifically, studies have proven that via the utilization of innovative and digital technologies, the circularity gap can be bridged in the short and medium term [8]. In addition, Khan et al. [10] have concluded in their survey that technological innovation is positively associated with CE practices, and that it leads to economic and environmental performance. Furthermore, according to Mamudu et al. [11], the integration of digital transformation technologies with CE principles presents a viable and promising path toward sustainable manufacturing. However, many researchers have identified that there exist diverse barriers to incorporate digital technologies for a CE, ranging from knowledge management and financial issues to challenges related to process management & governance or policies & regulations [20]. In addition, unclear benefits and lack of awareness have been also recognized as severe impediments against the adoption of digital technologies in a functional circular economy network [9]. Nevertheless, unlike theoretical studies, this paper tries to overcome those barriers by presenting an end-to-end applied methodology that highlights environmental, financial, and procedural benefits of digital deep tech driven circular economy, in a highly demanding industrial landscape.

3 Methodology

OTE Group [16] (hereafter OTE) handles a huge amount of data, as the largest technology company in Greece, offering a wide variety of digital services that extend far beyond telecommunications. Despite its ambitious trajectory, the rapid growth of OTE's services portfolio has been accompanied by certain challenges. In fact, many of the newly introduced services were deployed without extensive testing or the establishment of well-structured data models. This paper builds on our previous work [14], in which the aforementioned challenges have been analyzed, and in addition, an innovative solution that deals with them has been introduced. That solution is based on an open-source modular data management framework [7], which was developed in the context of DATAMITE EU project [6]. Unlike the previous paper [14] which focused mainly on analyzing the framework's architecture [2] tailored to OTE's internal systems as well as defining the validation scenarios, the current study presents the actual results when executing those scenarios, also emphasizing on how these results contribute to OTE's overall DCE strategy.

One of the main goals of the DATAMITE framework is to provide tools to improve data quality management [13] and to comply with the Findability, Accessibility, Interoperability and Reusability (FAIR) principles.

By adopting that framework, large organizations -such as OTE- can move towards a more agile, scalable, and policy-driven data ecosystem, where data is not only a passive asset but also an actively governed, continuously evolving resource. This concept shift fosters efficient data democratization, improves cross-functional collaboration, and ensures that AI-driven applications can be deployed quickly and effectively [14].

Towards that direction, Fig. 1 depicts the conceptual architecture of the proposed solution that aims to transform existing data management models into systems that follow the data product paradigm [4], thus boosting the adaptation to the rapidly changing Artificial Intelligence (AI) era.

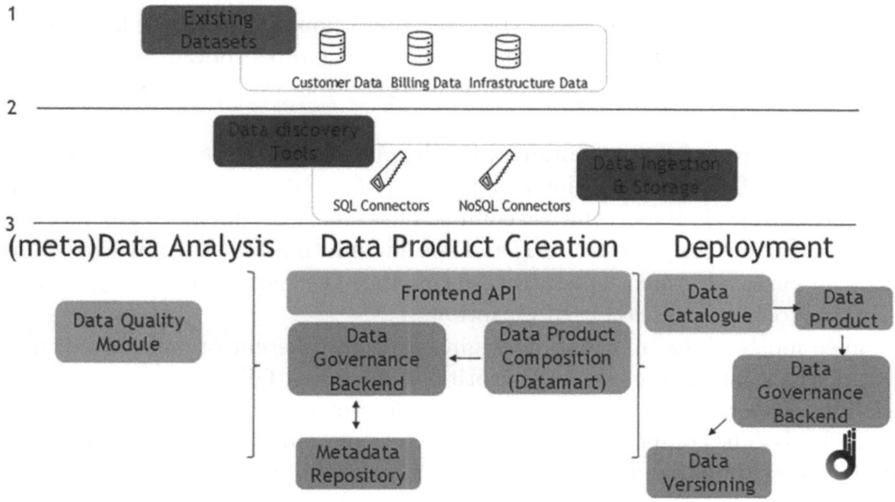

Fig. 1. Solution conceptual architecture

In the validation scenarios examined in this paper, the goal is to identify inconsistencies across three distinct and heterogeneous data repositories within OTE's environment, via the creation and analysis of complex data products, as illustrated in Fig. 1. This process leverages data discovery tools and ingestion pipelines to unify data from Structured Query Language (SQL) and NoSQL sources into a governed data product layer. Moreover, the depicted architecture incorporates data quality checks, metadata management, and versioning mechanisms to ensure consistency, traceability, and reliable deployment of the resulting data products.

Those repositories correspond to different operational units, each one managing critical aspects of the organization's infrastructure and services. The first repository, managed by the *Registry Unit* and implemented with MariaDB v12.1 relational database [12], contains the organization's customer data. This repository includes personal identification details of customers, their loyalty status, and information related to their relationship with the organization. Specifically, it tracks the number of services utilized by the customer, the duration of the relationship, and the total expenditure incurred by the customer on OTE services.

The second repository, overseen by the *Infrastructure Unit* and implemented with MongoDB v8.0 document database [15], facilitates the management of the organization's hardware and physical infrastructure essential for service delivery to end users. This repository maintains detailed information on the physical and operational aspects of the network, such as Fiber-to-the-Home (FTTH) cabinets, copper cables, Digital Subscriber Line Access Multiplexer (DSLAMs), and network operation centers. It encompasses data on the customer's router, including the model and firmware version, as well as the physical communication medium (e.g., fiber, copper, satellite) and its connection path to the network center. Additionally, it records physical constraints and operational analytics of the network lines, such as maximum bandwidth capacity, error rates, power supply limitations, and the presence or absence of Uninterruptible Power Supplies (UPS) at endpoints or intermediate nodes.

The third repository, maintained by the *Accounting Unit* and implemented with PostgreSQL v18.1 relational database [19], contains billing and financial information related to customer accounts. This repository includes details about invoicing, total sales per customer, and specific information that must be shared with the customer, such as contract terms and the Service Level Agreements (SLAs) associated with their subscription.

Since much of the information originates from different organizational units with distinct business goals and priorities, numerous failures arise due to the lack of interoperability in such a dynamic environment, where changes occur on a weekly basis. The competitive nature of the telecommunications market demands rapid processes and transformations, which inevitably lead to inconsistencies in data entry and discrepancies between various data stores. Unlike data entry errors, inconsistencies between repositories are often caused by logical errors that are much more challenging to detect and resolve.

4 Validation Case Studies

A comprehensive series of tests have been carried out to validate the solution in a reliable manner. The benchmarking datasets that were used in this assessment have been explicitly designed according to the particular characteristics of the solution's design. A synthetic AI script has been developed specifically for this purpose, taking into account various factors and cases that data analysts may face while querying the data. The importance of using benchmark datasets and synthetic tools in evaluating frameworks such as DATAMITE cannot be underestimated. In fact, they serve as critical references that facilitate the evaluation of performance and functionality across different systems, especially in Online Analytical Processing (OLAP) and Online Transaction Processing (OLTP) environments. Furthermore, synthetic tools can simulate diverse data scenarios, enabling a more robust analysis of how platforms respond to varying workloads and queries.

4.1 OLAP Scenario

The primary goal of this evaluation scenario is to analyze the telecom infrastructure and identify key insights regarding network providers, missing data issues, and location-specific deployment trends. More specifically, it aims to determine the number of network infrastructure components deployed by each one provider, detect instances where critical billing and order information is missing, and analyze devices deployed in specific regions. By executing such kind of queries, OTE can detect data inconsistencies, optimize network operations, and improve service provisioning.

Going a step further the analysis, by leveraging DATAMITE framework OTE can extract much more fruitful results. So instead of return only counts, the company can also determine a flow that produces multi-dimensional findings. These can be -provider wise- infrastructure concentration, anomaly rates per region, ratio of technically deployed versus commercially validated services, customer/service records with incomplete monetization paths, recurring combinations of missing attributes, hotspot detection for problematic cabinets, providers, or product types. All those are few indicative examples that can be developed using the add-on functionalities that are offered by DATAMITE. In that way, the developers could exploit the output of the result to leverage extra evaluations of the responses.

By identifying missing data in billing and order records, OTE can reduce errors that could lead to revenue losses. In addition, strengthening data governance and compliance ensures that network deployment records remain complete and auditable. Improved collaboration between network providers and internal teams allows for more efficient issue resolution. Furthermore, preventing delays in customer service and network provisioning enhances overall operational efficiency. This approach ensures that OTE operates with a data-driven strategy, reducing risk, increasing efficiency, and maintaining compliance with regulatory frameworks.

Fig. 2. Data product extra evaluation features

As depicted in Fig. 2, the results of the data products can be further evaluated using the modules that are provided by DATAMITE framework. Thus, data anonymization (to the output) or quality checks can be extracted as metadata, giving to the analyst the opportunity not only to export the results in a secure manner, but also to provide extra metadata to the end user. Consequently, rather than simply counting records, the evaluation results can generate a ranked cross-system anomaly profile that combines provider, location, service type, and data completeness indicators. This extra step allows OTE to distinguish between isolated missing values and structurally recurring issues that affect specific regions, providers, or deployment categories, which is one of the headaches that the business department faces during the year.

4.2 Visual and Strategic Scenario

This evaluation test shifts the focus towards metadata exploration and visualization. The queries described in the previous subsection have already established patterns in missing billing and order data across different network providers, highlighting inconsistencies in infrastructure records. In the context of the current scenario, the emphasis is put on leveraging metadata to provide data analysts with actionable insights by structuring the extracted information into a new data product.

The effectiveness of network management depends not only on raw query results but also on the ability to interpret and contextualize this data within an analytical framework. By developing a metadata-driven data product, analysts can benefit from a structured, abstracted view of data quality issues, thus enabling them to detect systemic trends, root causes of inconsistencies, and the overall impact on operations. The main advantage of this concept lies in the ability of Trino [21] module to export query results in a standardized format that is highly suitable for visualization and integration with external analytical tools (like those that OTE already uses in the everyday analysis). In more detail, Trino operates as a backend query layer capable of exporting structured results that can be consumed through Application Programming Interfaces (APIs) and reused across different analytical environments and products that OTE has acquired. This shift allows the results of the queries to be delivered in formats that internal teams can directly use, extend, or integrate depending on the needs of each service or analytical scenario. Given the high variability of telecom operational data and the diversity of analytical requirements across departments, a single generic visualization system cannot easily accommodate all use cases. Therefore, the system has been designed towards a more flexible backend architecture where the exported APIs and data structures allow teams to develop visualization interfaces that best fit their operational workflows.

Another important advantage of this approach is that the visualization layer can now integrate additional systems and services that are not strictly part of the original data product environment. This fact enables teams to combine operational, commercial, and analytical information in a single interface when needed. At the same time, these interfaces can be exposed through common and user-friendly environments tailored to specific teams, such as analysts, engineers, or operational managers.

4.3 OLTP Scenario

Customer retention is a critical factor for OTE to maintain profit stability and clients satisfaction. Customers who pay high monthly bills and subscribe to multiple services provided by OTE, such as fixed & mobile telephony, subscription TV, electronic payment, and insurance services, among others, represent a significant portion of the company's revenue. A common challenge arises when these high-value customers approach the end of their contracts, without making renewal attempts in a proactive way. If these people feel that the company neglected them, they may opt to switch to a competitor, which would lead to a crucial revenue loss.

Consequently, OTE must identify customers at risk of leaving, particularly those whose contracts will expire in less than 15 days. Additionally, tracking multi-service clients ensures that people who have invested more money in OTE's ecosystem receive personalized retention strategies. A metadata-driven approach is necessary not only to analyze customer contract statuses, and spending behavior, but also subscription engagement. In that way, proactive outreach is enabled before customer dissatisfaction increases a lot. By embedding this metadata analysis into the framework, analysts have a real-time view of at-risk customers and can take immediate action to maintain customer loyalty. A new data product can be created to identify those customers, enabling to download a targeted list that can be then forwarded to a dedicated retention team or an external contractor, who will implement risk mitigation strategies.

To this end, this evaluation scenario focuses on identifying high-paying customers at risk of contract termination and flagging them for engagement. By leveraging metadata exploration and automated categorization, DATAMITE framework allows analysts to detect which customers require immediate attention and prioritize outreach accordingly. This analysis is conducted through a recurring OLTP query.

A significant aspect and requirement of this scenario is the ability to monitor and evaluate the operational and financial impact of such kind of data products through the monitoring interfaces provided by the backend infrastructure and the Trino query engine. Through these interfaces, both the framework performance and the financial implications of executing a specific query can be analyzed in detail. More specifically, the system allows the FinOps [3] team of OTE as well as the analysts/operators to understand the computational cost associated with the execution of the queries that support a data product, leveraging the analytics of the backend like those that are depicted in Fig. 3.

Since the retention analysis may involve recurring queries and cross-system data federation, it is important to track how frequently the query is executed, the amount of resources consumed, and the corresponding cost implications. In fact, the framework provides the capability to directly access the Trino monitoring component, so that each query execution can be evaluated in terms of

Fig. 3. Backend performance indicator and analysis

performance metrics, resource utilization, and associated infrastructure costs. In particular, that feature enables the FinOps team to assess the financial footprint of the data product and determine whether the analytical value produced justifies the operational cost of continuously scanning the relevant datasets. Management teams and decision-makers can therefore gain a clearer understanding of the trade-offs between analytical insights and infrastructure consumption. In practice, this means that the execution frequency, recursion depth, or other query attributes can be adjusted according to both operational needs and cost-efficiency considerations. Furthermore, the monitoring framework enables the comparison between the computational cost of executing the query in cloud environments and the equivalent cost of running the same analytical workload on-premises infrastructure. This comparative analysis supports better infrastructure planning and helps determine the most efficient deployment strategy for each one data product.

By analyzing the cost and performance of each analytical step, the company can optimize query execution strategies, improve resource allocation, and ensure that the data product operates efficiently while delivering meaningful insights to the business.

5 Results

When validating DATAMITE against the scenarios analyzed in the previous section, the results demonstrate a big step forward concerning data governance, usability, and workflow management (Fig. 4). Particularly, the framework enables large industries to address bureaucratic inefficiencies with which they constantly struggle. Indeed, traditional data management models often introduce delays, redundant approvals, and compliance bottlenecks, making it difficult for businesses to efficiently utilize their data and infrastructure resources.

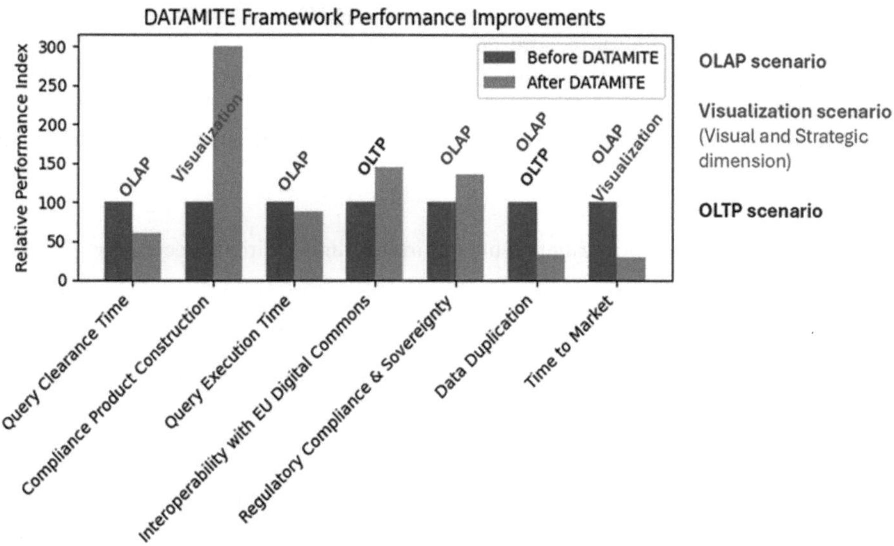

Fig. 4. Solution performance results

In detail, one of the most important improvements is in query clearance time, which has been reduced by 40%, due to faster query approval via governance automation, compared to manual multi-level approvals that cause long delays. Furthermore, a critical improvement is the 200% acceleration in the construction of compliance-ready products, due to automated regulatory tagging, metadata standardization, and interoperability validation. With legacy systems, manual efforts were needed to align with EU regulations. Moreover, it is worth noting the 12% reduction in query execution time across multiple databases. That reduction further enhances data accessibility and operational speed. Interoperability with EU Digital Commons has also improved by 45%, ensuring that datasets are easily integrated, shared, and monetized across European digital infrastructures. In addition, regulatory compliance and sovereignty have been significantly strengthened, with a 35% increase. In contrast with older systems that relied on manual data access reviews, DATAMITE framework offers continuous monitoring and policy enforcement, thus reducing the risk of data breaches and compliance violations.

Another key enhancement is the reduction of data duplication from three instances per data source to a maximum of one per data repository. In data models that are currently in use, many copies of the same data are often kept on different platforms, which makes storage costs go up and data becomes inconsistent.

DATAMITE makes sure that all metadata is managed in one place also enforcing deduplication mechanisms. In that way, the framework keeps each dataset in one authoritative source, improves data integrity, and cuts down on infrastructure costs. Finally, the time it takes to bring new data products to market has decreased from three to four weeks, to only one. On the opposite, before launching new services or insights, traditional systems often need long manual processes to prepare, validate, and combine data.

While Fig. 4 presents the quantitative Key Performance Indicators (KPIs) defined for the proposed solution, Table 1 explains how -by achieving those KPIs- companies can further enhance their adherence to digital circular economy principles.

Table 1. Key performance indicators for digital circular economy

KPI	Contribution to DCE	DCE effect
Query Clearance Time Reduction	Faster query clearance reduces idle data and processing waste, ensuring that data is used efficiently rather than remaining locked in approval or validation cycles	Improved use of existing digital assets with reduced operational overhead
Compliance-Ready Product Construction	Supports long-term reuse of data products across various use cases	Reduced digital waste and increased lifecycle value of data products
Query Execution Time Improvement	Efficient query execution lowers computing and energy consumption, thus reducing the environmental footprint of digital operations	More value extracted per unit of energy and infrastructure
Interoperability with EU Digital Commons	Interoperability enables cross-platform reuse of data, services, and digital assets	Data and services circulate freely across ecosystems rather than being used in silos
Regulatory Compliance and Sovereignty	Supports local value creation, while also enabling cross-border digital circulation under clear rules	Sustainable and trusted circulation of data within and across regions
Data Duplication Reduction	Minimizes redundant storage, processing, and maintenance	Reduced energy consumption and infrastructure costs
Reduction of Time to Market for New Data Products	Allows rapid reuse of existing data assets to create new value	Accelerated value creation from existing digital resources

6 Conclusion

The paper analyzes how large-scaled telecommunications companies may achieve efficiency through the best use of digital resources, leveraging the outcomes of

EU initiatives [1,6]. The proposed system combines resource-aware optimization methodologies, and advances in data management techniques, also considering the principles of the digital circular economy. As shown in the study, telecommunications infrastructures can avoid redundancy, extensive energy consumption, and high operational costs, while maintaining a high level of service, as validated in real-world case studies from which the presented findings are derived. The importance of adaptability in resource management and continuous monitoring is highlighted, so that enterprises accomplish sustainable digital transformation activities. Overall, the article proposes a coherent methodology to align the optimization of digital resource utilization with economic and environmental objectives. Furthermore, it provides a reproducible cross-sector architecture that can be exploited from other large industries, which seek to improve operational performance and sustainability in increasingly data-driven environments.

Acknowledgment. 3D-CIRCULAR project has received funding from the European Health and Digital Executive Agency under the Grant Agreement No 101226256. The contents of this publication are the sole responsibility of the authors and do not necessarily reflect the opinion of the European Union.

References

1. 3D-CIRCULAR EU project. https://3d-circular.eu/. Accessed 31 Mar 2026
2. Aroca, J.A., et al.: Boosting data monetisation with datamite. In: IFIP International Conference on Artificial Intelligence Applications and Innovations, pp. 33–46. Springer, Cham (2024)
3. Bhardwaj, P.: The role of finops in large-scale cloud cost optimization. Int. J. Sci. Res. Eng. Manag **9**(01), 1–5 (2025)
4. Blohm, I., Wortmann, F., Legner, C., Köbler, F.: Data products, data mesh, and data fabric: I. blohm et al. Bus. Inf. Syst. Eng. **66**(5), 643–652 (2024)
5. Chi, Z., Liu, Z., Wang, F., Osmani, M.: Driving circular economy through digital technologies: current research status and future directions. Sustainability **15**(24), 16608 (2023)
6. DATAMITE EU project. https://datamite-horizon.eu/. Accessed 31 Mar 2026
7. DATAMITE GitLab repository. https://gitlab.eclipse.org/eclipse-research-labs/datamite-project. Accessed 31 Mar 2026
8. De Felice, F., Petrillo, A.: Green transition: the frontier of the digicircular economy evidenced from a systematic literature review. Sustainability **13**(19), 11068 (2021)
9. Kandasamy, J., Venkat, V., Mani, R.S., et al.: Barriers to the adoption of digital technologies in a functional circular economy network. Oper. Manag. Res. **16**(3), 1541–1561 (2023)
10. Khan, S.A.R., Piprani, A.Z., Yu, Z.: Digital technology and circular economy practices: future of supply chains. Oper. Manag. Res. **15**(3), 676–688 (2022)
11. Mamudu, U.U., Obasi, C.D., Awuye, S.K., Danso, H., Ayodele, P., Akinyemi, P.: Circular economy in the manufacturing sector: digital transformation and sustainable practices. Int. J. Sci. Res. Arch. **12**(2), 129–141 (2024)
12. MariaDB. https://mariadb.org/. Accessed 31 Mar 2026

13. Marinakis, A., et al.: Ensuring data quality across heterogeneous systems: a large-scale telecommunication industry case study. In: Ventura, S., Luna, J.M., Martín-Castaño, A.R.M. (eds.) Data Quality Matters - Best Practices for Integrity and Assurance, chap. 14. IntechOpen, London (2026). https://doi.org/10.5772/intechopen.1013585
14. Marinakis, A., et al.: Transforming data management in telecommunications: the case study of OTE group's integration with datamite project. In: IFIP International Conference on Artificial Intelligence Applications and Innovations, pp. 287–300. Springer, Cham (2025)
15. MongoDB. https://www.mongodb.com/. Accessed 31 Mar 2026
16. OTE Group. https://www.cosmote.gr/static/otegroup/en/page/omilos_ote. Accessed 31 Mar 2026
17. Oyejobi, D., Firoozi, A., Fernández, D.B., Avudaiappan, S.: Integrating circular economy principles into concrete technology: enhancing sustainability through industrial waste utilization. Results Eng. **24**, 102846 (2024)
18. Piscicelli, L.: The sustainability impact of a digital circular economy. Curr. Opin. Environ. Sustain. **61**, 101251 (2023)
19. PostgreSQL. https://www.postgresql.org/. Accessed 31 Mar 2026
20. Trevisan, A.H., Lobo, A., Guzzo, D., de Vasconcelos Gomes, L.A., Mascarenhas, J.: Barriers to employing digital technologies for a circular economy: a multi-level perspective. J. Environ. Manage. **332**, 117437 (2023)
21. Trino query engine. https://trino.io/. Accessed 31 Mar 2026

ReUse-Telco: Turning Regulatory Compliance into Data Value

Christos A. Gizelis(✉), Nikolaos Tiniakos, Stavrina Sabati, Mihalis Kefalogiannis, Efstathia Deligeorgi, and Achilleas Marinakis

OTE Group of Companies, Athens, Greece
{cgkizelis,ttiniakos,ssabati,mkefalogiannis,edeligeorgi,amarinaki}@ote.gr

Abstract. Telecom operators process petabytes of distributed data daily, yet much of this potential remains buried under regulatory uncertainty and internal silos. Traditionally, the evolving European landscape, defined by General Data Protection Regulation (GDPR), the Data Act, and the AI Act, has been viewed solely as a compliance hurdle. This paper argues the opposite: these regulations are actually the blueprint for a new era of sovereign and trusted data exchange. We introduce ReUse-Telco, a pragmatic framework designed to shift the industry from a "one-off" data usage mindset toward a sustainable Circular Data Economy. The framework is built on three integrated pillars: privacy-preserving monetization, regulation-by-design, and data circularity. Instead of treating information as a disposable byproduct of network operations, we propose the creation of "Data Products", managed, reusable assets that carry their own Data Service Level Objectives (SLOs), semantic definitions, and embedded compliance metadata. Drawing from the operational objectives of EU-funded initiatives like DATAMITE and the workforce-reskilling focus of 3D-CIRCULAR, this research provides a comprehensive technical and governance roadmap. We detail actionable architecture patterns, including secure enclaves and Privacy-Enhancing Technologies (PETs), alongside a measurable KPI model for value capture and reuse readiness. By treating data as a circular resource that evolves through multiple lifecycles, operators can finally bridge the gap between strict legal compliance and sustainable commercial innovation.

Keywords: Data reusability · Sovereign data monetization · GDPR · EU Data Act · EU AI Act · Interoperable Europe Act · Circular economy · Data products · Data spaces · Privacy-Enhancing Technologies · Federated analytics · Workforce reskilling

1 Introduction: Breaking the Data Paradox

Data reusability is the ability to utilize the same digital asset multiple times across different contexts without losing its original meaning, legality, or the

Supported by 3D-CIRCULAR EU Project – 101226256.

Published by Springer Nature Switzerland AG 2027
A. Papaleonidas et al. (Eds.): AIAI 2026 Workshops, IFIP AICT 796, pp. 255–265, 2027.
https://doi.org/10.1007/978-3-032-30507-7_17

trust of the stakeholders involved. This capability is rapidly becoming the core of Europe's ambition for a competitive and sovereign data economy. Operators manage massive volumes of network telemetry and IoT events, but the granularity that makes this data valuable also transforms it into a compliance liability under GDPR and the EU AI Act.

For an organization like OTE Group managing complex connectivity layers across diverse geographical landscapes, the challenge is to move away from the traditional model of data silos. Historically, data was collected for a single purpose, such as billing or network maintenance, and then essentially frozen to avoid any regulatory friction or security risks. However, this one-off usage model is no longer sustainable. The European policy shift, led by the EU Data Act [6], now mandates fair access and interoperability, effectively forcing a transition from simply protecting data to enabling its trusted reuse.

This paper introduces ReUse-Telco, a framework designed to bridge the gap between strict compliance and commercial innovation. We propose that regulatory requirements should be treated as primary design constraints rather than external blockers. By adopting a circular economy lens, we suggest that data should be viewed as a reusable resource that can be recycled across multiple internal and external value chains. This approach ensures that information remains useful long after its primary purpose has been served.

Our framework is grounded in the operational objectives of the DATAMITE project [3] and the human-centric innovation focus of 3D-CIRCULAR [1]. We provide a roadmap that balances technical excellence with the commercial and regulatory realities of the modern telecom sector. Through the adoption of Data-as-a-Product strategies and Privacy-Enhancing Technologies, we demonstrate how operators can finally move from maintaining infrastructure to generating systemic value for the entire digital ecosystem.

2 Regulatory and Policy Context: Compliance as a Catalyst for Innovation

The modern European data landscape is defined by a shift from simple protection to the active promotion of data sharing. ReUse-Telco treats these regulations as a robust set of architectural requirements that, when integrated early in the design phase, can actually accelerate innovation by reducing legal friction.

GDPR remains the foundational pillar, emphasizing that any data reuse must respect the principles of purpose limitation and data minimization. For operators like the OTE Group, this means that the transition from personal data to reusable assets requires sophisticated strategies for anonymization and pseudonymization. By embedding these controls directly into the data pipelines, compliance becomes an automated feature rather than a manual audit task.

The EU Data Act introduces a new dimension [6] by establishing rights for fair access to data generated by connected products and services. It explicitly moves the industry toward interoperability, requiring that data holders provide machine-readable formats and standardized interfaces. This aligns with the Interoperable Europe Act [7,8], which encourages the creation of reusable building blocks for digital public services. For a Telco, this is an opportunity to standardize how information is shared with smart city ecosystems or emergency response units, ensuring that connectivity data can flow securely across different administrative borders.

Furthermore, the EU AI Act brings a risk-based approach to data governance. It demands that high-risk AI systems be trained on datasets that are transparent, documented, and free from bias. By treating data as a circular asset under the Ecodesign for Sustainable Products Regulation (ESPR) logic [4], information is continuously refined, remaining high-quality and audit-ready throughout its lifecycle.

3 ReUse-Telco: A Telecom Data Reusability Framework

To move beyond the constraints of traditional data management, we propose ReUse-Telco, a framework that operationalizes reusability through a structured, architectural approach. This framework is designed to transform the operator's internal infrastructure into a dynamic engine for value creation, shifting the focus from simply storing data to actively managing it as a reusable resource. ReUse-Telco is built upon four mutually reinforcing pillars (see Fig. 1).

Pillar A—Engineering Data-as-a-Product

The transition from treating data as a static asset to managing it as a dynamic product is the cornerstone of the ReUse-Telco framework. In traditional telecommunications environments, data sharing is often an ad-hoc process, characterized by manual extracts and inconsistent formats. By adopting a Data-as-a-Product mindset [18], we shift the responsibility of data quality to the source. A telecom data product is not merely a dataset; it is a self-describing, governed, and secure entity that includes the underlying data, its associated metadata, and the necessary access interfaces [12].

To ensure high reusability, these products must adhere to strict internal standards, often codified through Data Contracts. These contracts serve as a formal agreement between data producers and consumers, defining schemas, strict Data SLOs, and allocating Error Budgets. For an operator, this means that a mobility pattern feed or a network performance stream is treated with the same operational rigor as a customer-facing service. Consumers bypass weeks of data validation by simply subscribing to a trusted product, drastically reducing time-to-value.

Pillar B—Regulation-by-Design and Automated Policy Enforcement

Modern European regulations like GDPR and the AI Act are frequently viewed as obstacles to data agility. ReUse-Telco reframes these requirements as architectural constraints that must be integrated into the engineering lifecycle. We move away from manual legal audits toward a model of Regulation-by-Design, where compliance logic is embedded directly into the data pipelines.

This pillar utilizes automated policy enforcement gates to ensure that data reusability does not lead to privacy leaks. By implementing automated PII (Personally Identifiable Information) detection and anonymization scripts at the point of ingestion, we guarantee that any reusable data product is compliant by default. For high-risk AI workloads, the framework maintains an immutable ledger of data provenance and processing history, fulfilling the transparency requirements of the EU AI Act [5]. This systemic approach allows the operator to scale its data operations globally, knowing that the "legal guardrails" are enforced by code rather than manual oversight.

Pillar C—Building Interoperability Bridges

Reusability across different industries requires more than just technical connectivity; it demands a shared understanding of information. Our framework emphasizes both syntactic and semantic interoperability to ensure that telecom data can flow seamlessly into external ecosystems like Smart Cities or Energy Grids. Syntactic interoperability is achieved using standardized, machine-readable formats and stable, versioned Application Programming Interfaces (APIs) that follow European standards.

By aligning telecom data models with common European vocabularies and sector-specific ontologies, we ensure that a "location coordinate" or a "congestion indicator" has the same meaning for a network engineer as it does for an urban planner. This alignment reduces the "integration tax" that often kills cross-industry projects. It allows the operator to act as a central node in the EU data economy, providing interoperable building blocks that can be easily combined with third-party datasets to generate new, complex insights.

Pillar D—The Circular Data Lifecycle

The final pillar of ReUse-Telco introduces the concept of Data Circularity, mirroring the principles of a circular economy. In a traditional linear model, data is captured, used for a specific purpose (such as billing), and then archived or deleted, becoming "digital waste". Our framework promotes a lifecycle where data is treated as a renewable resource that gains value through successive reuse cycles.

This circularity begins with internal network optimization and extends to external monetization through data spaces. Crucially, the framework establishes a feedback loop where insights generated during the reuse phase, such as refined mobility models or identified data quality issues, are fed back into the primary collection systems. This creates a virtuous cycle of continuous quality improvement. By aligning with the Ecodesign for Sustainable Products Regulation (ESPR) logic [4], we ensure that the operator's data assets are not only reused but are also "designed for durability" and relevance, maximizing the return on every byte processed by the network infrastructure.

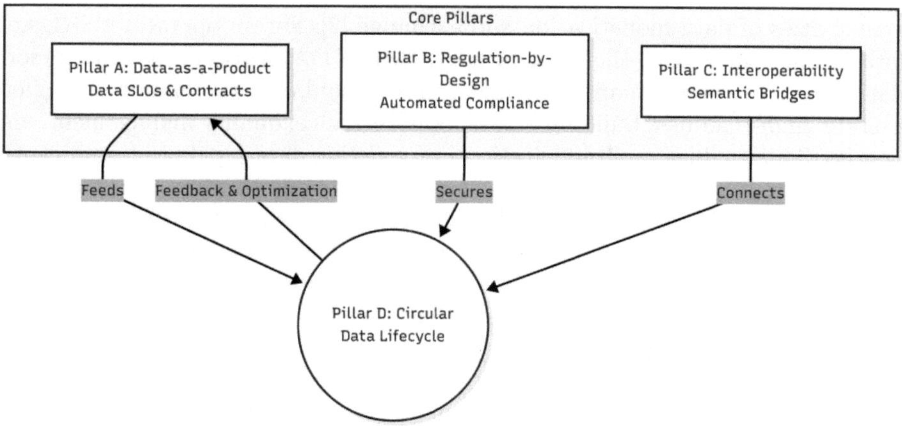

Fig. 1. The ReUse-Telco framework: Core enabling pillars driving the Circular Data Lifecycle.

4 Value Creation Models: From Selling Data to Orchestrating Insights

The strategic value of the ReUse-Telco framework is realized through its ability to enable sovereign value creation. Traditionally, telecommunications operators have struggled to maximize the operational and commercial utility of their data infrastructure, often hindered by the friction between commercial growth and privacy compliance. We propose a fundamental shift in mindset: moving away from the high-risk practice of exchanging raw datasets toward a model centered on orchestrating verified outcomes. This approach ensures that a leading operator, such as the OTE Group, retains total control over its assets while fueling the wider European data economy.

Monetization within our framework exists on a spectrum defined by trust and transparency. While some aggregated indicators can be shared for the public good, high-value commercial models rely on disclosure-minimal architectures. By utilizing a Data-as-a-Product strategy, we allow partners to query specific insights via policy-enforced APIs without ever interacting with the underlying sensitive records. The commercialization layer is built upon federated data marketplaces [13], targeting three primary growth areas: mobility analytics for smart cities, edge-based IoT services, and sustainability intelligence. This orchestration role allows the operator to move up the value chain, ensuring that data-driven insights are reliable, compliant, and actionable.

5 Strategic Benefits of the DATAMITE Framework

The DATAMITE project serves as the foundational toolkit for operationalizing the ReUse-Telco framework. As an EU-funded Horizon Europe initiative, it delivers a modular, open-source infrastructure specifically designed to navigate the complexities of data monetization and exchange [2]. For an operator's SRE and data engineering teams, the primary advantage of DATAMITE lies in this modularity. Rather than demanding a high-risk overhaul of legacy systems, it offers discrete, high-readiness building blocks for governance, quality management, and security. This enables rapid integration into existing data pipelines, significantly reducing the time-to-market for externally consumable services [11]. Crucially, it natively embeds "Sovereignty by Design" into the architectural fabric; by providing robust tools for consistent metadata management and automated lineage capture, it guarantees that every data asset remains transparent and fully under the operator's control, strictly fulfilling the accountability requirements of the GDPR and the EU Data Act.

Beyond technical governance, a significant hurdle in data reusability is determining the fair economic value of information. DATAMITE actively addresses this through structured KPI catalogues and valuation strategies that standardize how data products are priced and packaged. This capability simplifies the complex process of automated contracting, drastically reducing negotiation friction with external partners. Furthermore, the framework's plugin-based architecture supports seamless publication to multiple European destinations, enabling robust cross-sector interoperability. This is particularly vital for telecom use cases that intersect with smart energy grids or circular manufacturing ecosystems, ultimately allowing the operator to act as a central, highly trusted node within the multi-sector digital economy.

6 Governance for Trustworthy Reuse: Quality, Provenance, and Accountability

The commercial viability of telecom data reusability is inseparable from the governance structures that ensure its integrity. We move beyond simple legal compliance toward a model of "Trustworthy Reuse". This approach recognizes that the risks associated with data reuse are not only legal but also epistemic [17]; data may be available, yet it might not be of sufficient quality for a specific business decision. Therefore, governance must address both the provenance of the data and its ongoing methodological quality.

The first layer is a cross-functional Data Reuse Board, involving legal, security, and AI ethics experts, to oversee high-impact use cases and ensure strategic alignment. Supporting this board are the Data Product Owners, who are directly accountable for the lifecycle, metadata accuracy, and Data SLOs of individual data products.

The operational layer enforces governance through Policy-as-Code, natively integrated into CI/CD pipelines via GitOps practices. This layer continuously monitors data provenance and quality metrics, ensuring that every reusable asset remains compliant. By leveraging the KPI catalogues developed within the DATAMITE project [10], we measure both "Reuse Readiness" (metadata completeness) and "Value Impact" (revenue generation, internal cost avoidance). This integrated approach ensures that data reuse is methodologically robust and commercially scalable.

7 Architecture Blueprint: From Network Data to Reusable Assets

To operationalize the ReUse-Telco framework, we propose a reference architecture that treats the data journey as a continuous value chain. This blueprint ensures that the strategic goals of monetization and the strict rules of governance are embedded directly into the operator's technical infrastructure.

The End-to-End Data Value Chain

The process begins with an automated Ingestion and Classification Layer that collects raw logs from OSS/BSS systems and IoT gateways, immediately categorizing them by sensitivity. This is followed by a Minimization and Curation stage, where Privacy-Enhancing Technologies (PETs) are applied at the earliest possible point. By utilizing techniques such as k-anonymity and pseudonymization, we remove personal identifiers before the data reaches analytical environments. By embedding semantic metadata and capturing full data lineage at this stage, we transform raw network noise into high-quality, discoverable Data-as-a-Product offerings. Crucially, this stage requires robust, end-to-end observability (metrics, distributed tracing) to detect pipeline bottlenecks in real-time and prevent SLO violations (as illustrated in Fig. 2).

Secure Consumption and Trusted Execution

The consumption of these assets is managed through a multi-tier Access Layer designed to prevent data leakage. For standard operational needs, the framework provides versioned, stable APIs. For high-value AI and machine learning workloads, we implement the Compute-to-Data paradigm using Secure Enclaves (Trusted Execution Environments). In this model, the operator provides hardware-protected "clean rooms" where third-party algorithms are executed directly on the data. The access is strictly ephemeral; the external algorithm generates a result and is wiped from the system, ensuring raw information never leaves the infrastructure. Furthermore, to enable collaborative AI across sectors, we integrate Federated Learning (FL) and secure multiparty computation [14–16]. This "Privacy-by-Math" approach allows partners to train models locally and share only cryptographic updates, guaranteeing absolute confidentiality.

Interoperability-by-Construction and Automated Contracting

Through Interoperability-by-Construction, our data products are natively compatible with European Data Spaces. By enforcing canonical schemas and shared vocabularies during the design phase, the OTE Group can reduce the technical debt and integration overhead typically associated with cross-sector data exchange. This technical foundation is completed by an Automated Contracting and Enforcement layer, which translates legal licenses into machine-readable policies. Using usage metering and real-time policy enforcement, the architecture automates the billing and transaction processes, ensuring that all data reuse remains within permitted purposes and pre-defined privacy thresholds. This systemic approach turns the operator into a central, interoperable hub of the sovereign digital economy.

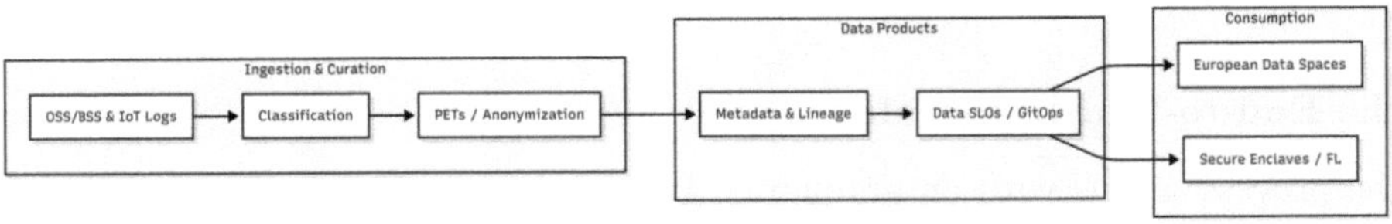

Fig. 2. The End-to-End Data Value Chain: From raw network telemetry to trusted execution and European Data Spaces.

8 Enabling Sustainability Through Data Circularity

The implementation of the ReUse-Telco framework is fundamentally aligned with the principles of the circular economy, where information is treated as a renewable resource rather than a disposable byproduct. This concept of Data Circularity directly addresses the environmental footprint of digital operations, a priority highlighted by the European Green Deal and the Ecodesign for Sustainable Products Regulation (ESPR) [4]. Internally, the OTE Group (Cosmote) leverages its vast network telemetry to optimize infrastructure capacity and automate predictive maintenance, anchoring our operations in the practice of Digital Sobriety [9]. By reusing high-quality, governed data products across multiple lifecycles, the engineering teams systematically eliminate the need for redundant, bespoke data pipelines. This architectural consolidation drastically reduces duplicated storage requirements and energy-intensive compute cycles, embedding FinOps principles directly into the organization's carbon reduction strategy and proving that lean infrastructure is inherently sustainable.

Externally, these optimized and interoperable telecom data products act as foundational catalysts for ecosystem-wide green transitions. When a telecom operator shifts from data hoarding to secure data publishing, the environmental Return on Investment (ROI) extends far beyond its own data centers. By exposing high-resolution, privacy-preserved mobility and IoT analytics to external partners via European Data Spaces, urban planners and public administrations are empowered to design highly resource-efficient routes and implement smart grid optimizations. This external circularity ensures that the computational effort and energy spent once by the operator fuels sustainable innovations across multiple sectors, effectively reducing society's overall energy consumption through data-driven transparency and shared systemic intelligence.

9 Implementation Roadmap and Operational Challenges

The implementation roadmap spans three evolutionary phases to balance rapid technical deployment with organizational readiness. The initial foundation (0–6 months) focuses on establishing a comprehensive data catalog and deploying baseline policy enforcement, ensuring new data products are "born" with correct governance markers. The growth phase (6–18 months) introduces Privacy-Enhancing Technologies, such as Federated Learning, allowing the operator to refine its Data SLOs via an internal data marketplace. Finally, reaching maturity (18–30 months) marks the transition to external sovereign monetization; the OTE Group integrates its infrastructure with European Data Spaces using secure enclaves and automated machine-readable contracting, fully aligning with the Data Act's requirements for interoperable access.

Despite this structured approach, achieving full data circularity presents complex operational hurdles. A primary concern is the robustness of anonymization under composition; as data products combine in open marketplaces, privacy engineering teams must guarantee mathematical privacy without destroying AI training utility. Furthermore, cross-sector semantic interoperability requires evolving canonical models to bridge disparate industrial domains. Finally, while the DATAMITE project provides initial KPI catalogues, accurately modeling the long-term ROI of data circularity and actively managing dataset bias remain critical frontiers. Addressing these challenges is a continuous process of technical innovation, essential for a responsible, sovereign EU data economy.

10 Conclusion: Toward a Sovereign and Sustainable Data Future

The ReUse-Telco framework marks a strategic turning point for the OTE Group, transforming data from a dormant byproduct into a high-value, sovereign asset. By integrating the modular tools of the DATAMITE project [3] with advanced Privacy-Enhancing Technologies, we have demonstrated that large-scale data monetization is entirely compatible with absolute subscriber privacy. This "Privacy-by-Math" approach allows the operator to move beyond traditional connectivity, establishing itself as a central intelligence hub within the European data economy.

Furthermore, by embedding the principles of Digital Sobriety and data circularity into our technical architecture, we ensure that digital growth directly supports the environmental goals of the European Green Deal. This "Twin Transition" reduces infrastructure waste while maximizing the social and economic utility of our network assets. Ultimately, the success of this framework relies on the continuous reskilling of our workforce through initiatives like 3D-CIRCULAR [1]. By combining robust governance with specialized expertise, the OTE Group is positioned to lead a more efficient, secure, and sustainable digital future for the telecommunications industry.

Acknowledgment. 3D-CIRCULAR project has received funding from the European Health and Digital Executive Agency under the Grant Agreement No 101226256. The contents of this publication are the sole responsibility of the authors and do not necessarily reflect the opinion of the European Union.

References

1. 3D-CIRCULAR EU project. https://3d-circular.eu/. Accessed 31 Mar 2026
2. Aroca, J.A., et al.: Boosting data monetisation with datamite. In: Maglogiannis, I., Iliadis, L., Karydis, I., Papaleonidas, A., Chochliouros, I. (eds.) AIAI 2024. IFIP Advances in Information and Communication Technology, vol. 715, pp. 33–46. Springer, Cham (2024). https://doi.org/10.1007/978-3-031-63227-3_3
3. DATAMITE EU project. https://datamite-horizon.eu/. Accessed 31 Mar 2026
4. Ecodesign for Sustainable Products Regulation. https://environment.ec.europa.eu/strategy/circular-economy/ecodesign-sustainable-products-regulation_en. Accessed 31 Mar 2026
5. EU Regulation - AI Act. https://eur-lex.europa.eu/eli/reg/2024/1689/oj/eng. Accessed 31 Mar 2026
6. EU Regulation - Data Act. https://eur-lex.europa.eu/eli/reg/2023/2854/oj/eng. Accessed 31 Mar 2026
7. Interoperable Act. https://commission.europa.eu/publications/interoperable-europe-act_en. Accessed 31 Mar 2026
8. Interoperable Europe Policy. https://interoperable-europe.ec.europa.eu/interoperable-europe/interoperable-europe-act. Accessed 31 Mar 2026
9. Lean ICT: Towards digital sobriety. The Shift Project Report. https://theshiftproject.org/en/publications/lean-ict/. Accessed 31 Mar 2026
10. Marinakis, A., et al.: Ensuring data quality across heterogeneous systems: a large-scale telecommunication industry case study. In: Ventura, S., Luna, J.M., Martín-Castaño, A.R.M. (eds.) Data Quality Matters - Best Practices for Integrity and Assurance, chap. 14. IntechOpen, London (2026). https://doi.org/10.5772/intechopen.1013585
11. Marinakis, A., et al.: Transforming data management in telecommunications: the case study of OTE group's integration with DATAMITE project. In: Papaleonidas, A., Pimenidis, E., Papadopoulos, H., Chochliouros, I. (eds.) AIAI 2025. IFIP Advances in Information and Communication Technology, vol. 753, pp. 287–300. Springer, Cham (2025). https://doi.org/10.1007/978-3-031-97317-8_21
12. Murphy, N.R., Beyer, B., Jones, C., Petoff, J.: Site reliability engineering: how google runs production systems. https://www.oreilly.com/library/view/site-reliability-engineering/9781491929117/. Accessed 31 Mar 2026
13. Manjula, N.J.: Federated data marketplaces: Enabling secure AI/ML workloads in a multicloud world. https://pubsonline.informs.org/do/10.1287/LYTX.2025.02.05/full/. Accessed 31 Mar 2026
14. Rahman, R.: Federated learning: a survey on privacy-preserving collaborative intelligence. arXiv preprint arXiv:2504.17703 (2025)
15. Shalabi, E., Khedr, W., Rushdy, E., Salah, A.: A comparative study of privacy-preserving techniques in federated learning: a performance and security analysis. Information **16**(3), 244 (2025)

16. Shenoy, D., Bhat, R., Krishna Prakasha, K.: Exploring privacy mechanisms and metrics in federated learning. Artif. Intell. Rev. **58**(8), 223 (2025)
17. Weissgerber, T.L., et al.: Understanding the provenance and quality of methods is essential for responsible reuse of fair data. Nat. Med. **30**(5), 1220–1221 (2024)
18. Dehghani, Z.: Data mesh: delivering data-driven value at scale. https://www.oreilly.com/library/view/data-mesh/9781492092384/. Accessed 31 Mar 2026

Smart Cities Evolutionary Progress in the B5G/6G Era: The 6G-PATH European Paradigm

Ioannis P. Chochliouros[1(✉)], Anastasia S. Spiliopoulou[1], Christina C. Lessi[1], Luís Cordeiro[2], Marilena Paraskeva[3], Jing Li[4], Imesha Wedikkara Gedara[4], Uthayasankar Sivarajah[5], and Vishanth Weerakkody[4]

[1] Hellenic Telecommunications Organization (OTE) S.A., 99 Kifissias Avenue, 15124 Maroussi-Athens, Greece
ichochliouros@oteresearch.gr

[2] OneSource Consultoria Informática Lda, Aveiro, Portugal

[3] eBOS Technologies Limited, Nicosia, Cyprus

[4] University of Bradford, Bradford, UK

[5] Kingston University, Kingston upon Thames, UK

Abstract. Technological solutions play a vital role in addressing urban challenges and transforming the city environment into a resilient, efficient and sustainable setup. The deployment of fifth-generation (5G) wireless networks has already laid the ground-work for futuristic smart cities but along with this, it has also triggered the rapid growth of a wide range of applications. However, continuous demands for higher throughput, lower latency and more energy efficiency have set the path towards B5G/6G, especially in the corresponding smart cities' vertical sector. Smart cities represent one of the most dynamic and strategically prioritised verticals for 6G adoption in Europe and their further evolutionary progress can be affected by a variety of factors ranging from technology and infrastructure readiness to specific regulatory and policy enablers. Our work focuses upon the specific ecosystem created by the innovative 6G-PATH EU-funded research framework, via assessing three selected use cases relevant to: (i) connected and sensing city; (ii) automated logistics, and; (iii) security coordination. For these, we provide a closer look at sector-specific market dynamics by highlighting concrete demand drivers, strategic challenges and adoption barriers. Then we identify potential pathways for businesses by assessing strategic visions and value propositions, market commercialisation channels and related key challenges for growth. The successful transition of the 6G-PATH project's innovations in the smart cities' vertical, from research excellence to real market deployment, requires a comprehensive understanding of market dynamics, business opportunities and strategic commercialisation approaches within the rapidly evolving 6G telecommunications landscape.

Keywords: 5G · B5G · 6G · Artificial Intelligence (AI) · automated logistics · connectivity · digital services · Internet of Things (IoT) · market verticals · security coordination · sensing · smart cities

Published by Springer Nature Switzerland AG 2027
A. Papaleonidas et al. (Eds.): AIAI 2026 Workshops, IFIP AICT 796, pp. 266–285, 2027.
https://doi.org/10.1007/978-3-032-30507-7_18

1 Introduction

The 5G network is supported by technological advances that transform the core of mobile communication networks. 5G enables a wide range of application scenarios by introducing a completely new network architecture [1]. 5G systems have widely entered the stage of commercial deployment, providing users with new services, improved user experiences as well as a host of novel opportunities to various industries. In this scope, to make immersive solutions possible and ubiquitous, new technologies such as Artificial Intelligence (AI) [2–4] and Multi-access Edge Computing (MEC) [5, 6] as well as the concept of network slicing [7, 8] and softwarisation technologies such as Software-Defined Networking (SDN) and Network Function Virtualization (NFV) [9], play critical roles.

However, while the rollout of 5G is still underway, the researchers across the world have started working to bring a new generation of wireless networks. The vision of 5G technologies is extended for the 6G networks by speculating the visionary technologies for next-generation wireless systems [10].

The sixth-generation (6G) wireless communication will be the successor of fifth-generation (5G) communication [11, 12]. From a technological point of view, it will make use of higher frequency radio bands and will provide a higher capacity combined with lower latency, enabling the integration into a single network with increased throughput and reliability. These characteristics make 6G networks ideal for the large-scale adoption of the Internet of Things (IoT) paradigm [13], especially considering that, in a short time, the devices connected to the IoT infrastructure are expected to reach billions of devices [14].

The 6G technology market represents the next evolutionary leap in wireless communications driven by transformative applications across diverse sectors, including *inter-alia* healthcare, education, agriculture, transportation, entertainment and smart cities. 6G is expected to deliver capabilities far beyond the limits of current 5G infrastructure which include ultra-low latency, massive machine-type communication, integrated sensing and AI-native networking which are essential for enabling the next generation of digital services and socio-economic transformation [15].

Digital technologies have the transformative power to deliver progressive, sustainable and positive impacts on urban life [16]. The present work examines some among the "key" industry sectors of 6G-PATH project's [17] by emphasising upon smart cities via demonstrating the highest adoption potential for 6G technologies, analysing their specific requirements for ultra-low latency, massive connectivity, and AI-native network functionalities; simultaneously, it assesses the market demand for the corresponding 6G-PATH project innovations through both quantitative market projections and qualitative demand drivers that "position" the project's technological contributions within the broader competitive landscape of next-generation wireless communication system. In particular, we focus upon the potential use of AI in the corresponding use cases (UCs) that will enable 6G networks to become more agile, intelligent, flexible, and resilient in solving network challenges [18]. AI can be used to analyse, manage and optimise resources and to efficiently support 6G networks.

The paper is structured around several separate sections: Sect. 1 introduces the current global framework where 5G systems have been widely deployed worldwide and became exploitable; however, as more requests appear by the markets, especially from the vertical sector, the transition towards a more enhanced framework beyond 5G, becomes a necessity. Section 2 "delineates" smart cities in the European B5G/6G ecosystem, as they represent one of the most dynamic and strategically prioritised verticals for 6G adoption in Europe; our work assesses both technology and infrastructure readiness as well as corresponding regulatory and policy enablers that can all influence the related scenery. Section 3 is dedicated to the detailed description of the 6G-PATH within the smart cities' vertical via three use cases being relevant to connected and sensing city, automated logistics and security coordination. Section 4 goes some steps further by providing a closer look at sector-specific market dynamics and by highlighting concrete demand drivers, strategic challenges and adoption barriers. Section 5 refers to potential pathways for making business by articulating the strategic vision and value propositions of the corresponding 6G-PATH UCs, by assessing market commercialisation channels as well as by examining "key challenges" and critical considerations. Here some strategic recommendations are also proposed, aimed at maximising adoption potential and long-term commercial success. Finally, Sect. 6 provides an overview of the entire work.

2 Smart Cities in the European 6G Ecosystem

A "smart" city is a municipality where communication networks and traditional services are made more efficient through the use of digital and real-time solutions, with various technical, economic and social benefits to residents and businesses. A smart city utilizes Information and Communication Technologies (ICT) to enhance the quality and performance of urban services, reduce costs and resource consumption and improve the interaction between citizens and the local government [19]. Smart cities employ digital technologies for better use of resources by ensuring, *among others*, smarter urban transportation networks, better monitoring and water supply facilities, optimised waste disposal and more efficient ways of lighting and heating buildings [20]. In addition, the respective city government becomes more interactive and responsive, being able to offer benefits such as ensuring safer public spaces and meeting the needs of an aging population.

The initiation of modern technologies such as the Internet of Things (IoT), Artificial Intelligence (AI), blockchain and 5G, has critically modified the scenery for smart cities. In particular, 5G technologies play very important roles in several aspects, including basic internet, broadband technology, video streaming, high-speed internet, connection to the world and vertical industries [21, 22].

Smart cities represent one of the most dynamic and strategically prioritised verticals for 6G adoption in Europe [23]. 6G-enabled technologies in the smart city can promote the inclusivity of citizens and elevate their quality of life by ensuring easy access to a great variety of services and/or applications. Current adoption readiness reveals both promising foundations and critical gaps that must be "addressed" for successful 6G deployment. This readiness is shaped by several factors as analysed below.

2.1 Technology and Infrastructure Readiness

The sixth-generation (6G) wireless communication will be the successor of 5G. From a technological point of view, it will make use of higher frequency radio bands and will provide a higher capacity combined with lower latency, enabling the integration into a single network with increased throughput and reliability. These characteristics make 6G networks ideal for the large-scale adoption of the IoT paradigm, especially considering that, in a short time, the devices connected to the IoT infrastructure are expected to reach billions of devices [14].

The ever-increasing computing power, together with the affirmation of 5G and the development of 6G, are "key ingredients" for the innovation of smart cities, designed around people and sustainability [24]. Blockchain, quantum computing, extended reality, and digital twins represent a non-exhaustive list of players that can also inspire for better cities. The key factors of smart cities "trace" several closely interrelated areas such as:

- *Artificial Intelligence (AI):* AI has the potential to play a major role in the development of smart cities by improving efficiency, sustainability, and the quality of life for citizens. The use of AI will enable 6G networks to become more agile, intelligent, flexible, and resilient in solving network challenges [18]. AI-powered solutions can help to reduce energy consumption, optimize traffic flow, and improve public safety.
- *Data:* Data analytics, data management, data storage, and data infrastructure are all critical components for development [25]. With the rise of the IoT and the increasing use of technology in cities, the amount of data generated is massive and is growing every day. These data sets can provide valuable insights into the functioning of a city (e.g., including traffic flow, energy consumption, and public safety). Data analytics allow cities to make sense of these data and make data-driven decisions to improve the efficiency and sustainability of the city.
- *Connectivity:* 5G, B5G, 6G, latency, Wi-Fi and IoT play a crucial role in the development of smart cities providing the foundation for a smarter and more connected future [26]. The roll-out of 5G and the upcoming B5G/6G networks will provide faster and more reliable connectivity [13], allowing for the efficient transmission of large amounts of data generated by IoT devices. Low latency is also important, as it enables real-time decision-making and responsive actions.
- *Digital services:* Simulated environments, digital twins, metaverse, virtual reality, robotics, and blockchain are all technologies that have the potential to revolutionise further development [27].
- *Cloud platforms:* City platforms, cloud computing, cloud storage, edge computing, hybrid data storage, IaaS (infrastructure as a service), and PaaS (Platform as a service) play critical roles in the development of smart cities [28].
- *Internet of Things:* IoT, machine-to-machine (M2M) communication, networked devices and sensing are among the critical actors for development [11, 13].

The smart cities sector presents a complex landscape of infrastructure readiness for 6G adoption [24], marked by significant variations across urban environments and technological domains. In general, European smart city infrastructure exhibits moderate readiness for 6G deployment, characterised by fragmented maturity and uneven development [29]. The global smart cities market demonstrated exceptional growth potential, with market size projected to grow from $767.75 billion in 2024 to $4,647.63 billion by 2032, representing a robust CAGR (Compound Annual Growth Rate) of 15.6% during the forecast period [30]. Nevertheless, the European smart cities market is also experiencing robust growth, projected to expand at a CAGR of 22.7% from 2024–2030 [31]. By that year, Europe is expected to account for over 70% of global smart city spending, alongside the U.S. and China [31]. These projections "reflect" substantial ongoing infrastructure investments and modernisation efforts across European municipalities.

European cities have already established comprehensive digital infrastructure ecosystems that provide a strong foundation for future 6G deployment. These ecosystems include extensive fiber optic networks, distributed edge computing nodes and integrated IoT sensor networks across domains such as transportation, energy, water management and public safety. Leading cities like Barcelona, Amsterdam, Copenhagen and Vienna have implemented sophisticated smart city platforms that manage thousands of connected devices and process vast amounts of real-time data. Such systems demonstrate both the technical capacity and operational maturity required for successful 6G integration [32]. Despite this progress, several infrastructure gaps must also be addressed. While many developed urban areas possess robust fiber-optic backbones and 4G/5G infrastructure that can serve as steppingstones to 6G, the ultra-dense network demands of 6G, especially for high-distribution video services as outlined in the 6G-PATH project [17], necessitate considerable upgrades. To enable seamless connectivity for mobile users consuming high-quality video content, network density must far exceed the current 5G capabilities. Moreover, the operational demands of smart city applications such as automated logistics and traffic avoidance systems highlight the critical importance of edge computing infrastructure. Although some cities have begun edge deployments, many still depend heavily on centralised cloud systems. The transition to a cloud-edge-IoT continuum is essential for enabling real-time, intelligent applications in 6G smart cities, such as Automated Guided Vehicles (AGVs) [33] and advanced traffic management [34]. This "shift" requires significant investment in distributed computing capabilities, robust orchestration, and new security models to meet the demands of low latency, scalability and reliability [35].

Additionally, while IoT sensor deployment has made notable progress, the sensing and communication demands of 6G applications are far more sophisticated. Mission-critical applications in smart cities [36, 37], such as real-time situational awareness, security coordination and dynamic resource tracking, will depend on ultra-low-latency integrated sensor networks, which many cities currently lack. Furthermore, the energy demands of 6G networks, particularly those associated with dense small-cell deployments in urban environments, present another critical infrastructure challenge [38]. Many cities' existing electrical grids are not optimised for the distributed power requirements of 6G, necessitating substantial upgrades to enable sustainable deployment.

2.2 Regulatory and Policy Enablers

The regulatory landscape for 6G adoption in smart cities presents both opportunities and significant challenges that will critically influence deployment timelines and implementation strategies. The European regulatory environment offers a favourable framework for 6G adoption in smart cities [39], underpinned by coordinated policy development and strategic technology leadership initiatives. The European Commission has laid out comprehensive 6G preparation strategies, positioning Europe as a global leader in next-generation telecommunications infrastructure through its Digital Strategy framework.

Regulatory bodies across EU member states have adopted harmonised spectrum allocation policies and standardised technical requirements, which support seamless 6G deployment across national boundaries. For example, the Radio Spectrum Policy Group (RSPG) [40] has reserved the 100–330 GHz bands for 6G trials, aligning with the International Telecommunication Union's (ITU) 2028 standardisation timeline [41]. However, international spectrum harmonisation remains a complex issue which could significantly affect deployment schedules.

The European General Data Protection Regulation - GDPR [42] ensures robust privacy protections that enhances public trust in smart city technologies, however it also introduces regulatory challenges. Although GDPR compliance is essential, it complicates data sharing practices such as federated learning within smart cities [43]. This requires advanced, dynamic data anonymisation protocols to manage cross-border data flows while preserving data sovereignty [44]. Although the regulatory clarity around privacy and data security helps to "address" public concerns related to data collection and processing in connected urban environments, it also introduces constraints that could slow the pace of innovation. Similarly, while the EU's Digital Single Market strategy aims to eliminate internal regulatory barriers, enabling interoperability and efficient cross-border deployment, current frameworks still create obstacles for cross-border data sharing and system integration, potentially limiting the effectiveness of 6G-enabled smart city services [45].

Regulatory support for 6G adoption is further "reflected" in targeted funding mechanisms and strategic policy initiatives. The European Investment Bank has introduced specific financing instruments for digital infrastructure projects, while various national governments have implemented tax incentives and procurement preferences for advanced telecommunications technologies [46]. These measures are designed to reduce implementation barriers and accelerate adoption timelines for municipal authorities exploring 6G deployment.

3 6G-PATH as B5G/6G Enabler for Smart Cities

The EU-funded 6G-PATH project [17] aims to foster the development of advanced technologies to support deployment towards B5G/6G, via an advanced infrastructure to be available and extended throughout the project duration for broader experimentation purposes. This takes place both in close collaboration with other 6G-IA projects [47] and through the process of Open Calls to engage European companies developing innovations for B5G and 6G systems, as well as bringing new UCs [48] and pilot sites to the corresponding ecosystem [49, 50]. Such technologies and pilots are combined in relevant testbeds used in UCs corresponding to the four verticals where 6G-PATH is actually present, that is: Farming, Education, Health and Smart Cities [51]. Such UCs and their corresponding applications will create demanding requirements from the trials, thus requiring a proper validation through dedicated KPIs [52, 53] and KVIs [54, 55].

The project also proposes an architectural scheme and a platform aiming at providing a unified interaction point for all UCs partners.

Overall, 6G-PATH builds an extensive B5G/6G infrastructure where a set of core architectures and domain-specific capabilities are brought together and made available for integration of applications and UCs of relevance, within the four addressed verticals, to "conduct" large-scale pilots and trials. The results of these pilots and trials are collected and analysed in detail, to generate appropriate lessons and requirements for future 6G communications, as well as to identify, characterise and refine leading-edge business models towards the commercialisation and exploitation of 6G UCs and technologies.

The Smart Cities vertical is composed of three UCs (i.e.: Connected and Sensing City (UC-CITIES-1); Automated Logistics (UC-CITIES-2) and; Security Coordination (UC-CITIES-3)) and focuses on exploring and testing the integration of large-scale extreme IoT-Edge-Cloud scenarios [35, 56]. This includes differentiated QoS support (e.g., massive machine-Type Communications (mMTC)) applied to MCX (Mission Critical) communications and extreme high-throughput video/data streaming. This vertical also serves for evaluating the emerging deterministic, reliable and high-resolution services and the resilience, safety and security of the next-generation networks, a key aspect for PPDR (Public Protection and Disaster Relief) and emergency-related applications.

UC-CITIES-1, relies upon a smart city platform, consisting of different types of vehicles [57] (some of them being autonomous), people and sensors around the city [58], such as environmental and mobility sensors (e.g., video cameras, radars, lidars), all being connected and sending real-time information [59]. This platform serves as "base" to the subset of scenarios that are further detailed next. Three separate scenarios are considered:

In a UC of *high-distribution video on the move,* we consider the scenario where people are travelling around while watching high-quality video [60]. The video coding and video distribution services are proactively orchestrated in the new points of access of the people before they arrive, so no video disruption is foreseen. The data of the vehicles, people, of the mobility and network will give information on the prediction of both mobility and network quality, providing an estimate of the needs of the services, in terms of quality and location, to travel with their users.

In a UC of *traffic avoidance,* we consider the scenario with autonomous vehicles and people, bicycles and motorcycles on the roads [61]. Vehicles, communicating with other vehicles and with the edge, "sense" their environment; the edge, through their sensors, also senses the environment. This data aggregation and processing can be performed in the cloud-edge-IoT continuum [35], integrating AI-network and edge processing, providing latency-critical services, advanced resource allocation, (re-)distribution of edge computing resources, and federated learning and computing in a continuum environment. The information of the environment will be made available to all the citizens and automations, allowing for the appropriate choice of paths to flow through areas with improved traffic performance.

In a UC of *enhanced city services,* AI is used to provide better services to citizens [27], such as detecting stolen cars, badly parked vehicles, cars parked in the carriageway and control of shared areas, to improve the quality of life in the urban spaces. This UC aims further developing various scenarios across the Smart Cities vertical, improving media content distribution, providing an increased awareness of traffic and mobility, as well as, increasing the overall performance of the network, while acting as a driver for new and increased 6G requirements [62].

In short, UC-CITIES-1 aims to realise: (i) enhanced safety in the roads; (ii) better decision-making, as AI detection and data fusion can provide the means to improve any decision systems; (iii) increased efficiency and effectiveness of the deployed services, and; (iv) better resource management, as the AI network slice-based resource management will improve the management of network and computing resources.

UC-CITIES-2 is relevant to the use of Industry 5.0 in smart cities [63, 64] that can bring significant benefits by enabling more efficient and sustainable production of goods and services and to better manage resources and infrastructure [65]. By integrating Industry 5.0's principles into their manufacturing processes, companies can reduce waste, lower energy consumption and improve overall productivity [66]. This UC explores automated logistics processes focused on the use of Automated Guided Vehicles (AGVs) [67] and essentially aims to improve both the production process and employee safety. By designing an automated sorting process, the time required to organise the produced goods/items during the last stage of the production process and before they are distributed is reduced. At the same time, the employees are disengaged from this process, avoiding the risk of injury during the transport of the produced items, especially if the products have a large volume and weight [68]. In this context, beyond 5G and 6G networks play an important role, improving UC's performance. In addition, network performance is expected to be advanced, offering low latency ($<5\%$), and high availability (99.999%).

UC-CITIES-3 deals with a traditional emergency response situation, where communication between public safety end-users can be slow and unreliable, potentially leading to delays and/or dangerous situations [69]. To "address" this problem, smart cities are leveraging advanced communication technologies – like 5G and B5G/6G – to create more secure, efficient and effective communication platforms for public safety end-users [70, 71]. The latter have access to a secure, mission-critical communication platform that leverages B5G/6G technologies to ensure fast and reliable communication [72], even in high-stress situations, while the advanced security features ensure that sensitive information remains private. This platform shall provide real-time communication, situational awareness and collaboration tools to help first responders on their day-to-day operations, quickly respond to emergencies, coordinate their efforts, and ensure public safety [36]. In addition, the platform is designed to integrate with other public safety agencies and systems, allowing for seamless communication and collaboration across multiple agencies and jurisdictions. Overall, the proposed platform has the potential to offer: (i) Enhanced Public Safety; (ii) improved response times via the inclusion of 5G/6G; (iii) better decision-making; (iv) increased efficiency, and; (v) better resource management.

4 Market Demand for 6G Innovation in 6G-PATH Smart Cities' Vertical

This section outlines the evolving market demand for innovations emerging from the 6G-PATH project in the smart cities' vertical. In particular, we provide a closer look at sector-specific market dynamics by highlighting concrete demand drivers, strategic challenges and adoption barriers. Together, these insights do form the foundation for aligning 6G-path technological developments with real-world market needs and policy frameworks.

4.1 Key Demand Drivers

There are several "key demand drivers" that affect the entire playground and these are identified as follows:

Digital Infrastructure Transformation: Cities are experiencing unprecedented demand for high-capacity, low-latency networks that can support massive IoT deployments and real-time data processing [11, 13, 14]. The proliferation of connected devices in urban environments requires network architectures that can handle diverse traffic patterns while maintaining consistent performance across different geographical areas and user mobility scenarios [23].

Exploding Data and Connectivity Needs: The rapid increase in mobile data traffic and the proliferation of connected devices are creating unprecedented demand for robust, high-speed networks [13, 26]. By 2028, global mobile data traffic is expected to increase underscoring the need for advanced infrastructure like 6G to support high-volume, real-time applications.

Public Safety and Mission-Critical Services: There is surging demand for secure, ultra-reliable communications for emergency response, real-time situational awareness and inter-agency collaboration [36, 70, 71]. 6G's ultra-low latency and enhanced security features directly address these requirements, as highlighted by the 6G-PATH security coordination use case.

Mobility and Logistics Automation: The need for advanced traffic management, autonomous vehicles, and automated logistics is accelerating. 6G's capacity for high-speed, distributed video processing and real-time data sharing is essential for connected and sensing city scenarios, as well as for Industry 5.0-driven logistics automation [63–65].

4.2 Use Case Specific Demand Analysis

In the scope of a UC specific demand analysis, we distinguish the following:

Connected and Sensing City (UC-CITIES-1): The demand for high-distribution video services and traffic optimisation represents a significant market opportunity. Urban populations increasingly expect seamless multimedia experiences while mobile, creating requirements for predictive content distribution and network quality management. The traffic avoidance use case demonstrates substantial economic potential, as improved traffic flow can reduce congestion costs, lower emissions and enhance productivity. Market demand is driven by the need for vehicle-to-everything (V2X) communication capabilities [73] that can process environmental data in real-time and provide city-wide traffic optimisation through cloud-edge-IoT continuum architectures.

Automated Logistics (UC-CITIES-2): The automated logistics market segment [74] shows strong growth potential, particularly in last-mile delivery and urban warehouse operations. Cities face increasing pressure to optimise goods movement while reducing environmental impact and improving worker safety. The demand for AGV-supported logistics systems [67] that can operate safely in mixed human-machine environments requires advanced 5G and 6G network features including ultra-reliable low-latency communication (URLLC), precise positioning services and distributed intelligence capabilities. This market segment is driven by e-commerce growth, labour shortage concerns and sustainability mandates.

Security Coordination (UC-CITIES-3): The market for mission-critical, real-time communication platforms is expanding rapidly [75], with cities seeking to enhance public safety, resource tracking and emergency response. Emergency services require communication platforms that can operate reliably during disasters, enable real-time resource tracking and support automated response coordination. The market demand is reinforced by regulatory requirements for improved emergency response capabilities and growing concerns about urban security threats. This segment values network resilience, security features, and interoperability across different agencies and technologies. 6G's ultra-reliable, low-latency connectivity is essential for these high-stakes applications.

The following summary table "maps" the key drivers of market demand to the relevant 6G-PATH Use Cases (Table 1).

4.3 Challenges and Considerations

Taking into account the existing 6G-PATH ecosystem for the smart cities' vertical, we can identify the following challenges:

Technical Implementation Barriers: Deploying 6G-PATH innovations in smart cities faces significant technical challenges including network infrastructure integration, spectrum management and ensuring consistent performance across diverse urban environments. Upgrading legacy systems and ensuring interoperability across diverse urban platforms remain significant challenges.

Social Acceptance and Privacy Concerns: Public acceptance of pervasive sensing and connectivity technologies remains a challenge. As cities become more connected, robust cybersecurity and privacy frameworks are critical to maintaining public trust and operational resilience. However, citizens' concerns about privacy, data security and potential surveillance implications can impact market adoption rates and require transparent governance frameworks.

Regulatory and Standards Alignment: The evolving regulatory landscape for 6G technologies, combined with varying municipal requirements and international standards, creates uncertainty for market development. Ensuring compliance with data privacy regulations, spectrum allocation policies and interoperability standards across different urban contexts requires careful coordination.

Economic and Investment Barriers: The high capital investment required for comprehensive smart city deployments creates market adoption barriers. Cities must balance

Table 1. Market Demand Mapping Table – 6G-PATH Smart City Sector Use Cases

Key Market Demand Driver	Relevant 6G-PATH Use Case(s)	Mapping Summary
Digital Infrastructure Transformation	UC-CITIES-1 & UC-CITIES-2	Supports massive IoT and edge-cloud integration for real-time city monitoring, traffic coordination and smart logistics infrastructure
Exploding Data and Connectivity Needs	UC-CITIES-1	6G's high-capacity bandwidth enables real-time HD video streaming, predictive content delivery and uninterrupted connectivity for mobile urban users
Public Safety & Mission-Critical Services	UC-CITIES-3	Provides ultra-reliable, secure communication during emergencies with agency-wide interoperability, real-time situational tracking and coordinated response
Mobility & Logistics Automation	UC-CITIES-1 & UC-CITIES-2	Enables V2X communications and AGV coordination for intelligent transport systems and last-mile delivery optimisation. Supports urban mobility transformation
Sustainability and Emissions Reduction	UC-CITIES-1 & UC-CITIES-2	Traffic and logistics optimisation reduce emissions and congestion. Real-time data enables energy-efficient urban flows
Security & Emergency Preparedness Regulations	UC-CITIES-3	Complies with urban safety mandates by enabling fail-safe communication and dynamic emergency resource allocation via 6G's ultra-reliable network features

the costs of advanced network infrastructure against limited municipal budgets and competing priorities. The business case for 6G-PATH innovations must demonstrate a clear return on investment and long-term sustainability.

In conclusion, there is robust and accelerating market demand for 6G-PATH innovations in the smart cities sector. The convergence of exploding data needs, IoT proliferation, public safety imperatives, and logistics automation is driving cities to invest in next generation 6G infrastructure and services. With strong policy support, substantial investment, and a rapidly maturing ecosystem, 6G is set to become a foundational enabler of future urban life in Europe and globally.

5 Pathways for Business Strategy in 6G-PATH

As B5G/6G technologies begin to take shape, a robust and forward-looking business strategy is essential to ensure that innovations developed within the 6G-PATH project can transition effectively from research to real-world application. This section "outlines" the key commercialisation pathways for the project, focusing on how the smart cities' vertical of the 6G-PATH project can translate technological advances into scalable, market-ready solutions.

The section begins by articulating the strategic vision and value propositions of the corresponding 6G-PATH UCs, defining the unique market benefits it offers through next-generation connectivity, intelligence and sustainability, *among others*. It then presents an overview and rationale for the main commercialisation pathways identified for the smart cities' sector, aligning these with current market practices, industry demand and evolving customer expectations. Further, it examines "key challenges" and critical considerations, including regulatory barriers, go-to-market timing, competitive dynamics and partner ecosystem development. Based on this analysis, the section concludes with a set of strategic recommendations tailored to the sector, aimed at maximising adoption potential and long-term commercial success.

This preliminary business planning analysis is based primarily on secondary data from recent market research, industry trend reports, and strategic publications, accompanied by the expert insights of the 6G-PATH consortium members. It provides an early-stage framework for commercialisation that will be refined in next version of the report due at the end of the project. It will incorporate primary data gathered through stakeholder interviews, pilot testing and market validation activities to deliver a more detailed and actionable commercialisation strategy.

5.1 Strategic Vision and Value Proposition

This section briefly discusses strategic vision and value proposition for each one among the three4 defined uses cases in the smart cities' vertical.

UC-CITIES-1 – Connected and Sensing City: This UC aims to build an intelligent urban ecosystem that seamlessly integrates mobility, media and infrastructure, enhancing both the citizen experience and operational efficiency of city services. Its specific value lies in the ability to deliver high-distribution, uninterrupted video streaming for commuters by leveraging predictive analytics and proactive network orchestration, ensuring a smooth media experience, even on the move. Simultaneously, the system enhances traffic management by fusing real-time data and applying AI-driven resource allocation and federated learning across cloud, edge and IoT layers. This allows both citizens and automated systems to make informed routing decisions, reducing congestion, optimising mobility and enabling smarter use of urban resources. In this context, 6G facilitates the value proposition by providing ultra-reliable, low-latency connectivity and intelligent network orchestration, enabling seamless media streaming and real-time, AI-driven traffic management across a highly integrated urban ecosystem.

UC-CITIES-2 – Automated Logistics: This UC envisions the realisation of Industry 5.0 principles in urban logistics by integrating automation, sustainability and connectivity. Its core value proposition lies in automating goods handling using AGVs, significantly enhancing operational efficiency while reducing human error and workplace accidents. These AGVs, coupled with advanced B5G/6G connectivity, support seamless integration of sensors and enable real-time remote control and route optimisation. This fosters more agile, data-driven logistics operations, capable of responding to the dynamic needs of smart cities, particularly in areas like last-mile delivery and municipal goods distribution. In this scope, 6G facilitates the value proposition by enabling ultra-reliable, real-time communication and precise coordination of AGVs through seamless sensor integration and low-latency connectivity, driving smarter, safer and more adaptive urban logistics operations.

UC-CITIES-3 – Security Coordination: With a strategic vision to elevate the capabilities of emergency services, this UC focuses upon providing ultra-reliable and low-latency B5G/6G communication infrastructure to support mission-critical operations. The value proposition practically centres on enhancing situational awareness through real-time data sharing and robust inter-agency collaboration tools. Moreover, this UC leverages advanced technologies to enable automated task assignment, resource tracking and dynamic information flows, ensuring timely and efficient crisis response. By integrating intelligent coordination and communication tools, emergency services can significantly improve their responsiveness, accuracy and overall effectiveness in various urban safety scenarios. 6G facilitates the value proposition by delivering ultra-reliable, low-latency connectivity that enables real-time data sharing, seamless inter-agency coordination, and intelligent automation, thereby significantly improving the speed, precision and effectiveness of emergency response operations.

5.2 Commercialisation Channels

This section discusses potential commercialisation channels for the 6G-PATH UCs in the smart cities' vertical, by performing both an overview and rational as follows:

Platform as a Service (PaaS): The PaaS model [76] offers a flexible, cloud-based approach for deploying smart city solutions by enabling municipalities and private enterprises to access cutting-edge tools such as mobility analytics, AI and automation without the need for heavy upfront investment. This subscription-based model supports the dynamic needs of smart cities by offering scalable solutions that can evolve with technological advancements and policy shifts. For example, UC-CITIES-1 can offer a PaaS for predictive mobility analytics and video orchestration; UC-CITIES-2 can deliver a logistics automation platform for managing fleets of AGVs; and UC-CITIES-3 can provide a real-time security coordination platform tailored for emergency response teams. These platforms can be continuously updated and integrated with third-party services, fostering adaptability and innovation in urban service delivery.

Direct Sales and Licensing: Direct sales and technology licensing offer commercialisation pathways that ensure control, customisation and revenue generation from smart city technologies. This approach is ideal for well-resourced city authorities and service providers seeking robust, tailored solutions. For instance, the predictive mobility algorithms developed under UC-CITIES-1 can be licensed to public transport agencies to enhance traffic flow and commuter services. Under UC-CITIES-2, direct sales of AGV fleet management systems to logistics providers enable efficient urban freight solutions. Similarly, UC-CITIES-3 can commercialise secure communication and coordination platforms through licensing to public safety agencies, ensuring mission-critical reliability and compliance with data governance regulations.

Public-Private Partnerships (PPPs): PPPs serve as a strategic commercialisation mechanism that aligns with public sector goals and unlocks investment for scaling complex smart city infrastructure. These partnerships combine governmental oversight with private innovation and efficiency, making them well-suited to EU policy priorities around sustainability, digital transformation and resilience. In UC-CITIES-1, PPPs can support joint investments in AI-powered urban mobility platforms. For UC-CITIES-2, city governments and private logistics firms can co-develop sustainable logistics hubs to reduce emissions and congestion. UC-CITIES-3 can benefit from PPPs focused on the co-development of secure, interoperable emergency response networks that integrate real-time data, sensor inputs and command coordination, improving urban safety outcomes.

5.3 Key Challenges, Critical Considerations and Strategic Recommendations

In this section we first assess three essential challenges that can affect deployment, including: (i) regulatory and data governance; (ii) market adoption, and; (iii) technical complexity. For each one we distinguish the following:

Regulatory and Data Governance – Both of these can be relevant to: (i) Privacy and Security, implicating for properly handling sensitive mobility, logistics and security of data, all conformant to GDPR and cybersecurity standards, and; (ii) Interoperability, implicating about ensuring compatibility with legacy systems and third-party tools to realize seamless integration and user satisfaction.

Market Adoption – This is related to: (i) High Upfront Costs, as the deployment of 6G infrastructure and advanced automation solutions may require significant investment, thus necessitating innovative funding models (e.g., PPPs, subsidies), and; (ii) Digital Divide which implicates about ensuring equitable access to smart city benefits across diverse urban and suburban populations.

Technical Complexity – This is mainly relevant to: (i) Integration Challenges that are relevant to the harmonization of AI, IoT, and edge computing across heterogeneous urban environments, and; (ii) Scalability, that is about effectively managing the growing demand for bandwidth and low-latency services as smart city applications proliferate.

Then we conclude with some strategic recommendations listed as follows:

- *Development of modular and scalable platforms*: To act in this way it should be necessary to prioritise platform-based delivery (PaaS) to support rapid deployment, integration, and continuous innovation.
- *Strengthening of Public-Private collaboration:* This implicates for leveraging PPPs and EU funding mechanisms (e.g., Horizon Europe, Digital Decade 2030) to co-invest in smart city infrastructure and pilot projects.
- *Investing in interoperability and standards:* This implicates for alignment with 3GPP and ITU standards to ensure compatibility and future-proof solutions.
- *Addressing data privacy and security:* This implicates for implementing robust data governance frameworks, including encryption, anonymisation and compliance with GDPR.
- Promoting inclusive growth: This implicates for design solutions "bridging" the digital divide and ensuring all citizens benefits from smart city advancements.
- *Monitoring and adaptation*: This implicates for establish feedback loops and KPI/KVI dashboards to "track" performance, stakeholder satisfaction, and societal impact.

6 Overview and Concluding Remarks

In the scope of the fast worldwide deployment of 5G, more challenges are now appearing, due to numerous innovative use cases originating from diverse vertical sectors of a fully converged market. In particular, 5G acts as the communication network to support the IoT infrastructure required by various smart city vertical industries and, consequently, will represent a "key turning point" in the evolution of smart cities as it enables high-speed connectivity, low latency, longer battery life and the ability to handle a massive number of connections, among others. Thus, 5G and smart city are at the forefront of a new wave of generational transformation driven by multiple factors, including technology and infrastructure readiness, regulatory and policy issues but also societal changes and economic challenges. However, the fast progress in a multiplicity of sectors together with the inclusion of modern innovative technologies like AI, sets new requirements for more enhanced and more efficient infrastructure in a path beyond 5G or towards 6G.

Smart cities and B5G/6G are technological areas that have the potential to transform the way we live and work in the years to come. The integration of advanced 6G communication technologies into smart city applications promises to usher in a new era of connectivity, efficiency and innovation. Smart cities leverage advanced technologies to enhance the quality of life for residents, optimise resource utilisation and improve overall urban governance, especially when correlated to AI inclusion into the corresponding services offered. The benefits of 6G technology with smart city systems are making city ecosystems sustainable, efficient, and responsive in terms of connectivity, data speed, and reduced latency, thus smart cities are among the most promising verticals to demonstrate 5BG/6G inclusion and readiness.

The ongoing EU-funded 6G-PATH project proposes a fully innovative framework for evaluating an effective and reliable transition towards B5G/6G via dedicated trials/tests in large scale pilots for the evaluation of selected use cases that cover four essential market verticals, among which is also the one referred to smart cities. In particular, 6G-PATH identifies three fundamental UCs related to: (i) connected and sensing city;

(ii) automated logistics, and; (iii) security coordination and focuses upon exploring and testing the integration of large-scale extreme IoT-Edge-Cloud scenarios.

The next part of our work was about examining the evolving market demand for potential innovations emerging from the above UCs. To this aim, a detailed look at sector-specific market dynamics has been provided by highlighting concrete demand drivers, strategic challenges and adoption barriers. Our approach has identified the existence of strong and increasing market demand for 6G-PATH innovations in the smart cities sector. A variety of factors is driving cities to invest in next generation 6G infrastructure and services.

In the rapid evolutionary framework of a fully converged landscape where B5G/6G technologies are gradually become real, a robust business strategy is critical to guarantee efficiency and beneficial inclusion of the 6G-PATH smart cities UCs into real world scenarios. Our work proposes potential pathways for business exploitation by assessing the strategic vision and the value propositions of the corresponding 6G-PATH UCs, by assessing market commercialisation channels and by examining "key challenges" and critical considerations.

The smart cities sector in the 6G-PATH project faces complex regulatory, technical and business challenges, but also offers transformative opportunities through advanced connectivity, AI-driven analytics and automation. The integration of 6G technologies into urban environments such as real-time video distribution, automated logistics and mission-critical security coordination implicates for suitable business models and appropriate commercialisation strategies, per case, being able to address both market needs and stakeholder concerns.

Acknowledgements. This work has been performed in the scope of the 6G-PATH European research project and has been supported by the Smart Networks and Services Joint Undertaking (SNS-JU) by receiving funding form the European Union's Horizon Europe (HORIZON) Research and Innovation Programme under Grant Agreement No. 101139172.

References

1. Ghosh, A., Maeder, A., Baker, M., Chandramouli, D.: 5G evolution: a view on 5G cellular technology beyond 3GPP release 15. IEEE Access **7**, 127639–127651 (2019). https://doi.org/10.1109/ACCESS.2019.2939938
2. 5G Public Private Partnership (5G PPP): AI and ML – Enablers for Beyond 5G Networks, version 1.0 (2021). https://zenodo.org/records/4299895
3. Wang, C.-X., Renzo, M.D., Stanczak, S., Wang, S., Larsson, E.G.: Artificial intelligence enabled wireless networking for 5G and beyond: recent advances and future challenges. IEEE Wirel. Commun. **27**(1), 16–23 (2020). https://doi.org/10.1109/MWC.001.1900292
4. Hossain, A.R., Liu, W., et al.: AI-native for 6G core network configuration. IEEE Networking Letters **5**(4), 255–259 (2023). https://doi.org/10.1109/LNET.2023.3302833
5. European Telecommunications Standards Institute (ETSI): Multi-access Edge Computing (MEC). https://www.etsi.org/technologies/multi-access-edge-computing
6. Li, M.: Application scenarios and deployment schemes of 5G multi-access edge computing. In: Proceedings of the 2023 3rd Asia Conference on Information Engineering (ACIE), 05–07 January 2023, Chongqing, China, pp. 54–58 (2023). https://doi.org/10.1109/ACIE58528.2023.00017

7. Chochliouros, I.P., Spiliopoulou, A.S., et al.: Dynamic network slicing: challenges and opportunities. In: Maglogiannis, I., Iliadis, L., Pimenidis, E. (eds.) AIAI-2020. AICT, vol. 585, pp. 47–60. Springer, Cham (2020). https://doi.org/10.1007/978-3-030-49190-1_5
8. Afolabi, I., Taleb, T., Samdanis, K., Ksentini, A., Flinck, H.: Network slicing and softwarization: a survey on principles, enabling technologies, and solutions. IEEE Commun. Surv. Tutor. **20**(3), 2429–2453 (2018). https://doi.org/10.1109/COMST.2018.2815638
9. Bouras, C., Killia, A., Papazois, A.: SDN & NFV in 5G: advancements and challenges. In: Proceedings of the 2017 20th Conference on Innovations in Clouds, Internet and Networks (ICIN), 07–09 March 2017, Paris, France, pp. 107–111 (2017). https://doi.org/10.1109/ICIN.2017.7899398
10. Viswanathan, H., Mogensen, P.E.: Communications in the 6G era. IEEE Access **8**, 57063–57074 (2020). https://doi.org/10.1109/ACCESS.2020.2981745
11. Kamruzzaman, M.M.: Key technologies, applications and trends of internet of things for energy-efficient 6G wireless communication in smart cities. Energies **15**(15), 5608 (2022). https://doi.org/10.3390/en15155608
12. Zhao, Y., et al.: A comprehensive survey of 6G wireless communications (2021). https://arxiv.org/abs/2101.03889
13. Qadir, Z., Le, K.N., Saeed, N., Munawar, H.S.: Towards 6G internet of things: recent advances, use cases, and open challenges. ICT Express **9**(3), 296–312 (2023). https://doi.org/10.1016/j.icte.2022.06.006
14. Akhtar, M.W., Hassan, S.A., Ghaffar, R., Jung, H., Garg, S., Hossain, M.S.: The shift to 6G communications: vision and requirements. Hum.-Cent. Comput. Inf. Sci. **10**, 53 (2020). https://doi.org/10.1186/s13673-020-00258-2
15. David, L.K., Wang, J., Brooks, W., Angel, V.: Digital transformation and socio-economic development in emerging economies: a multinational analysis. Technol. Soc. **81**, 102834 (2025). https://doi.org/10.1016/j.techsoc.2025.102834
16. Blasi, S., Ganzaroli, A., De Noni, I.: Smartening sustainable development in cities: strengthening the theoretical linkage between smart cities and SDGs. Sustain. Cities Soc. **80**, 103793 (2022). https://doi.org/10.1016/j.scs.2022.103793
17. Smart Networks and Services – Joint Undertaking (SNS-JU): 6G-PATH ("6G Pilots and TriAls THrough Europe") Project, Grant Agreement No.101139172. https://6gpath.eu
18. Du, J., Jiang, C., Wang, J., Ren, Y., Debbah, M.: Machine learning for 6G wireless networks: carrying forward enhanced bandwidth, massive access, and ultrareliable/low-latency service. IEEE Veh. Technol. Mag. **15**(4), 122–134 (2020). https://doi.org/10.1109/MVT.2020.3019650
19. Bibri, S.E., Krogstie, J.: Smart sustainable cities of the future: an extensive interdisciplinary literature review. Sustain. Cities Soc. **31**, 183–212 (2017). https://doi.org/10.1016/j.scs.2017.02.016
20. Silva, B.N., Khan, M., Han, K.: Towards sustainable smart cities: a review of trends, architectures, components, and open challenges in smart cities. Sustain. Cities Soc. **38**, 697–713 (2018). https://doi.org/10.1016/j.scs.2018.01.053
21. Gohar, A., Nencioni, G.: The role of 5G technologies in a smart city: the case for intelligent transportation system. Sustainability **13**(9), 5188 (2021). https://doi.org/10.3390/su13095188
22. Han, H., Zhao, J., Zhai, W., Xiong, Z., Lu, W. Smart city enabled by 5G/6G networks: an intelligent hybrid random access scheme (2021). https://arxiv.org/pdf/2101.06421
23. Sharma, S., et al.: The role of 6G technologies in advancing smart city applications: opportunities and challenges. Sustainability **16**(16), 7039 (2024). https://doi.org/10.3390/su16167039
24. Shafi, M., Jha, R.K., Jain, S.: 6G: technology evolution in future wireless networks. IEEE Access **12**, 57548–57573 (2024). https://doi.org/10.1109/ACCESS.2024.3385230

25. Ma, M., Preum, S.M., Ahmed, M.Y., Tärneberg, W., Hendawi, A., Stankovic, J.A.: Data sets, modeling, and decision making in smart cities: a survey. ACM Trans. Cyber-Phys. Syst. **4**(2), 1–28 (2019). https://doi.org/10.1145/3355283
26. Yang, C., et al.: Using 5G in smart cities: a systematic mapping study. Intell. Syst. Appl. **14**, 200065 (2022). https://doi.org/10.1016/j.iswa.2022.200065
27. Dahmane, W.M., Ouchani, S., Bouarfa, H.: Smart cities services and solutions: a systematic review. Data Inf. Manage. **9**(2), 100087 (2024). https://doi.org/10.1016/j.dim.2024.100087
28. Trigka, M., Dritsas, E.: Edge and cloud computing in smart cities. Future Internet **17**(3), 118 (2025). https://doi.org/10.3390/fi17030118
29. Correia, D., Marques, J.L., Teixeira, L.: The state-of-the-art of smart cities in the European union. Smart Cities **5**(4), 1776–1810 (2022). https://doi.org/10.3390/smartcities5040089
30. Fortune Business Insights: Smart Cities Market Size, Share - Global Growth Report. Fortunebusinessinsights.com (2024). https://www.fortunebusinessinsights.com/industry-reports/smart-cities-market-100610
31. Frost & Sullivan: Smart Cities to Create Business Opportunities Worth $2.46 Trillion by 2025, says Frost & Sullivan. Frost & Sullivan (2020). https://www.frost.com/news/press-releases/mobility-press-releases/smart-cities-to-create-business-opportunities-worth-2-46-trillion-by-2025-says-frost-sullivan/
32. Angelidou, M., Politis, C., Panori, A., Bakratsa, T., Fellnhofer, K.: Emerging smart city, transport and energy trends in urban settings: results of a pan-European foresight exercise with 120 experts. Technol. Forecast. Soc. Chang. **183**, 121915 (2022). https://doi.org/10.1016/j.techfore.2022.121915
33. Ullrich, G., and Albrecht, T.: History of automated guided vehicle systems. In: Automated Guided Vehicle Systems. Wiesbaden, Germany: Springer Vieweg (2023), https://doi.org/10.1007/978-3-658-35387-2_1
34. Nijim, M., Kanumuri, V., Alaqqad, W., Albataineh, H.: Advanced traffic management system for smart cities. In: Daimi, K., Al Sadoon, A. (eds.) Proceedings of the 2023 International Conference on Advances in Computing Research (ACR 2023). ACR 2023. LNNS, vol. 700. Springer, Cham (2022). https://doi.org/10.1007/978-3-031-33743-7_19
35. Gkonis, P., Giannopoulos, A., Trakadas, P., Masip-Bruin, X., Andria, F.D.: A survey on IoT-edge-cloud continuum systems: status, challenges, use cases, and open issues. Future Internet **15**(12), 383 (2023). https://doi.org/10.20944/preprints202311.0532.v1
36. Konstantopoulou, E., Sklavos, N., Ognjanovic, I.: Securing public safety mission-critical 5G communications of smart cities. In: Gupta, N., Mishra, S. (eds.) Internet of Everything for Smart City and Smart Healthcare Applications. Signals and Communication Technology. Springer, Cham (2024). https://doi.org/10.1007/978-3-031-34601-9_4
37. Freire, D.V.C.: Mission-critical communications from LMR to 5G: a technology assessment approach for smart city scenarios. Ph.D. thesis. NOVA University Lisbon, Portugal (2023). https://doi.org/10.13140/RG.2.2.35913.56167
38. Chochliouros, I.P., et al.: Energy efficiency concerns and trends in future 5g network infrastructures. Energies (MDPI) **14**(17), 5932 (2021). https://doi.org/10.3390/en14175392
39. European Commission: 6G networks in Europe. https://digital-strategy.ec.europa.eu/en/policies/6g
40. Radio Spectrum Policy Group (RSPG). https://radio-spectrum-policy-group.ec.europa.eu/index_en
41. International Telecommunication Union (ITU): IMT towards 2030 and beyond (IMT-2030) (2026). https://www.itu.int/en/ITU-R/study-groups/rsg5/rwp5d/imt-2030/Pages/default.aspx
42. European Parliament and European Council: Regulation (EU) 2016/679 of the European Parliament and of the Council of 27 April 2016 on the protection of natural persons with regard to the processing of personal data and on the free movement of such da-ta, and repealing

Directive 95/46/EC (General Data Protection Regulation). Official Journal (OJ) L 119 of 04 May 2016, pp. 1–88 (2016). https://eur-lex.europa.eu/eli/reg/2016/679/oj

43. Pandya, S., Srivastava, G., Jhaveri, R., Babu, M.R., et al.: Federated learning for smart cities: a comprehensive survey. Sustain.Energy Technol. Assess. **55**, 102987 (2023). https://doi.org/10.1016/j.seta.2022.102987
44. Murroni, M., et al.: 6G - enabling the new smart city: a survey. Sensors **23**(17), 7528 (2023). https://doi.org/10.3390/s23177528
45. Dąbrowski, L.D., Suska, M.: The European Union Digital Single Market: Europe's Digital Transformation. Routledge, London (2022). https://doi.org/10.4324/9781003262534
46. Fratto, C., Gatti, M., Kivernyk, A., Sinnott, E., van der Wielen, W.: The scale-up gap financial market constraints holding back innovative firms in the European Union. European Investment Bank (2024). https://www.eib.org/files/publications/20240130_the_scale_up_gap_en.pdf
47. The 6G Smart Networks and Services Industry Association (6G-IA). https://6g-ia.eu/
48. Next Generation Mobile Networks (NGMN) Alliance: Use Cases and Analysis v1.0 (2022). https://www.ngmn.org/wp-content/uploads/NGMN-6G-Use-Cases-and-Analysis.pdf
49. 6G-PATH SNS-JU Project: Deliverable 5.1: "Cascade Funding and training to third parties – Initial" (2025). https://6gpath.eu/wp-content/uploads/2025/09/6G-PATH-D5.1-August-2025-Final-EC-Version.pdf
50. 6G-PATH SNS-JU Project: Open Call 2 Winners (2025). https://6gpath.eu/open-call-2-winners/
51. Chochliouros, I.P., Cordeiro, L., Fernandes, J., Díaz Zayas, A., et al.: Promoting deployment of innovative use cases in market verticals for the support of 6G evolution: the 6G-PATH context. In: Maglogiannis, I., Iliadis, L., Karydis, I., Papaleonidas, A., Chochliouros, I. (eds.) AIAI-2024. AICT, vol. 715, pp. 154–176. Springer, Cham (2024). https://doi.org/10.1007/978-3-031-63227-3_11
52. 5G Infrastructure Public Private Partnership (5G PPP): KPIs Measurement Tools. From KPI definition to KPI validation enablement (White Paper) (2023). https://5g-ppp.eu/wp-content/uploads/2023/05/TMV-KPI-Measurement-Tools_1.0-published.pdf
53. 5G Infrastructure Public Private Partnership (5G PPP): White Paper - Beyond 5G/6G KPI Measurement (2023). https://5g-ppp.eu/wp-content/uploads/2023/06/white_paper_b5g-6g_kpi_measurement_FINAL.pdf
54. Fernandes, J., Rosa, L., Chochliouros, I., Cordeiro, L., Díaz Zayas, A., et al.: Paving the path to 6G: The 6G-PATH project's vision for advanced telecommunications' infrastructure and use cases. In: Proceedings of the 2024 IEEE Future Networks World Forum (FNWF), 15–17 October 2024, Dubai, United Arab Emirates, pp.1–6 (2024)
55. Wikström, G., et al.: Key Value indicators: a framework for values-driven next-generation ICT solutions. Telecommun. Policy **48**(6) (2024). https://doi.org/10.1016/j.telpol.2024.102778
56. Ray, P.P., Kumar, N.: SDN/NFV architectures for edge-cloud oriented IoT: a systematic review. Comput. Commun. **169**, 129–153 (2021). https://doi.org/10.1016/j.comcom.2021.01.018
57. Roger, S., Botella-Mascarell, C., Martín-Sacristán, D., García-Roger, D., Monserrat, J.F., Svensson, T.: Sustainable mobility in B5G/6G: V2X technology trends and use cases. IEEE Open J. Veh. Technol. **5**, 459–472 (2024). https://doi.org/10.1109/OJVT.2024.3375451
58. Arshi, O., Mondal, S.: Advancements in sensors and actuators technologies for smart cities: a comprehensive review. Smart Construct. Sustain. Cities **1**, 18 (2023). https://doi.org/10.1007/s44268-023-00022-2
59. Rafique, W., Rani Barai, J., Fapojuwo, A.O., Krishnamurthy, D.: A survey on beyond 5G network slicing for smart cities applications. IEEE Commun. Surv.Tutor. **27**(1), 595–628 (2025). https://doi.org/10.1109/COMST.2024.3410295
60. Khan, I., Tran, T.X., Hiltunen, M., Karagioules, T., Koutsonikolas, D.: An experimental study of low-latency video streaming over 5G (2024). https://arxiv.org/abs/2403.00752

61. Gherardini, L., Cabri, G.: The impact of autonomous vehicles on safety, economy, society, and environment. World Electr. Veh. J. **5**(12), 579 (2024). https://doi.org/10.3390/wevj15120579
62. Elassy, M., Al-Hattab, M., Takruri, M., Badawi, S.: Intelligent transportation systems for sustainable smart cities. Transp. Eng. **16**, 100252 (2024). https://doi.org/10.1016/j.treng.2024.100252
63. Sharma, I., Garg, I., Kiran, D.: Industry 5.0 and smart cities: a futuristic approach. Eur. J. Mol. Clin. Med. **7**(8), 2750–2756 (2020). https://web.archive.org/web/20210625184908/https://ejmcm.com/article_4786_fecb7ce33d6d11d7edb41c14e699c263.pdf
64. Kasinathan, P., Pugazhendhi, R., Elavarasan, R.M., et al.: Realization of sustainable development goals with disruptive technologies by integrating industry 5.0, society 5.0, smart cities and villages. Sustainability **14**(22), 15258 (2022). https://doi.org/10.3390/su142215258
65. Chochliouros, I.P., Spiliopoulou, A.S., Verrios, P., Doukoglou, T., Lessi, C., et al.: Automated logistics in the B5G/6G era. In: Papaleonidas, A., Pimenidis, E., Papadopoulos, H., and Chochliouros I.P. (eds.) AIAI-2025. AICT, vol. 753, pp. 73–90. Springer, Cham (2025). https://doi.org/10.1007/978-3-031-97317-8_6
66. Adel, A.: Unlocking the future: fostering human–machine collaboration and driving intelligent automation through industry 5.0 in smart cities. Smart Cities **6**(5), 2742–2782 (2023). https://doi.org/10.3390/smartcities6050124
67. Bhargava, A., Suhaib, M., Singholi, A.S.: A review of recent advances, techniques, and control algorithms for automated guided vehicle systems. Jo. Braz. Soc. Mech. Sci. Eng. **46**, 419 (2024). https://doi.org/10.1007/s40430-024-04896-w
68. Lessi, C., Chochliouros, I.P., Verrios, P.: B5G network implementation for automated logistics. In: Papaleonidas, A., Pimenidis, E., Papadopoulos, H., Chochliouros I.P. (eds.) AIAI-2025. AICT, vol. 753, pp. 91–100. Springer, Cham (2025). https://doi.org/10.1007/978-3-031-97317-8_7
69. Diaz Zayas, A., del Mar Moreno, M., Jimenez, J.A., Delmas, S: Demonstration of slicing for PPDR communications. In: Proceedings of the 2024 Joint European Conference on Networks and Communications & 6G Summit (EuCNC/6G Summit), 03–06 June 2024, Antwerp, Belgium, pp.1–2 (2024). https://fidal-he.eu/publications/general-papers/demonstration-slicing-ppdr-communications
70. Chochliouros, I.P., Spiliopoulou, A.S., Lazaridis, P.I., et al.: 5G for the support of public safety services. Wireless Pers. Commun. **120**, 2321–2348 (2021)
71. SNS Telecom & IT: The public safety LTE & 5G Market: 2020–2030 – Opportunities, challenges, strategies & forecasts. Research and Markets (2020). https://www.marketresearchreports.com/signals-and-systems-telecom/public-safety-lte-5g-market-2020-%E2%80%93-2030-%E2%80%93-opportunities-challenges
72. Borsatti, D., Grasselli, C., Controli, C., et al.: Mission critical communications support with 5G and network slicing. IEEE Trans. Netw. Serv. Manage. **20**(1), 595–607 (2023). https://doi.org/10.1109/TNSM.2022.3208657
73. Reports and Data: Automotive Vehicle-to-Everything (V2X) Market Summary (2025). https://www.reportsanddata.com/report-detail/automotive-vehicle-to-everything-v2x-mar ket
74. Grand View Research: Logistics Automation Market (2026–2033) (2026). https://www.grandviewresearch.com/industry-analysis/logistics-automation-market-report
75. The Business Research Company: Mission Critical Communication Market Report 2026 (2026). https://www.thebusinessresearchcompany.com/report/mission-critical-communication-global-market-report
76. Susnjara, S., Smalley, I.: What is platform as a service (PaaS)? IBM (2026). https://www.ibm.com/think/topics/paas

Together, these requirements define the operational constraints for AI-driven security systems and motivate the need for integrated, distributed security architectures in the Edge–Cloud continuum.

2.2 Design Dimensions

Based on these requirements, AI-driven security in the Edge–Cloud continuum can be characterised along key design dimensions that capture the trade-offs of distributed intelligent systems.

A first dimension is distributed intelligence, where decision-making is decentralised across edge and cloud nodes to enable scalability and localised threat detection [4]. Closely related is edge-centric inference and training, where AI models are deployed and updated near data sources, often through federated learning, improving privacy and reducing communication overhead [11]. Privacy preservation forms another critical dimension, supported by mechanisms such as federated learning and trusted execution environments, enabling secure data processing in distributed environments [2]. Low-latency operation is also essential, requiring efficient execution through hardware acceleration and in-kernel mechanisms such as eBPF to support real-time security enforcement [12]. In addition, resource awareness ensures that security functions are adapted to constrained edge devices through lightweight models and optimised deployment strategies [9]. Finally, high autonomy enables dynamic adaptation through advanced orchestration mechanisms, allowing security functions to scale and evolve with changing system conditions [13].

These dimensions define the design space and guide the development of integrated AI-driven security architectures for the Edge–Cloud continuum.

3 AI-Driven Security Mechanisms in the Edge–Cloud Continuum

Building upon the security requirements and design dimensions presented in Sect. 2, this section introduces the AI-driven security mechanisms that realise these principles in the Edge–Cloud continuum. These mechanisms constitute the core building blocks of the proposed framework, enabling distributed intelligence, privacy-preserving operation, low-latency enforcement, and autonomous security management.

3.1 Monitoring and Telemetry Collection

The foundational step in any AI-driven intrusion detection pipeline for cloud-native environments is the capture and injection of network data and derived metrics into downstream processing stages. Traffic traversing edge and cloud nodes must be intercepted and forwarded to the intrusion detection pipeline, making the choice of capture mechanism critical in terms of fidelity, latency, and scalability.

Smart Manufacturing Meets Data Spaces: A New Paradigm

Maria Belesioti(✉), Jason Diakoumakos, and Ioannis P. Chochliouros

Hellenic Telecommunications Organization (OTE) S.A., 99 Kifissias Avenue, 15124 Maroussi-Athens, Greece
mbelesioti@oteresearch.gr

Abstract. Data is a critical asset in today's world. As the global data environment is rapidly evolving with substantial proportion of internet data to be machine-generated, the extensive volumes of real-time industrial data have the potential to improve operational efficiency and to drive innovation enabling transformation in the manufacturing landscape. This paper examines the role of data as a "key driver" of economic growth within the European data economy, highlighting the strategic vision behind the European Strategy for Data. It explores the concept of data spaces as decentralized, trusted ecosystems that enable secure and sovereign data sharing across sectors. Additionally, it outlines "key initiatives" such as IDSA, DSSC and Gaia-X. Finally, it explores the SM4RTENANCE EU-funded project, which is designed to exploit cross-sector manufacturing assets to deploy a data space federation that will enhance collaboration within the industrial ecosystem strengthening data sovereignty.

Keywords: Data Spaces · IDSA · Data sovereignty · GAIA-X · Data sharing

1 Introduction

Data is the backbone of economic development, worldwide. It constitutes the basis for new products and services, thus fueling productivity across sectors. Moreover, the exponential growth of infrastructures and technologies [1] have led to the increase of diverse data sources, leading the data driven innovation in the European economy. This concept of data everywhere, resulted in the introduction of data space back in 2005 [2]. Following to this and considering the continuous European and global volatile landscape and the complexity of data produced, have led Europe to create a framework necessary to support the emerging data economy and to define a solid policy vision for data protection, exploitation and harmonization. Under this framework, the European strategy for data [3] has been created, aiming to "position" the EU as the leading player by enhancing data utilization among various stakeholders & sectors, creating ultimately a unique and single market for data that will strengthen Europe's global competitiveness while preserving its data sovereignty [4].

At its core, this strategy emphasizes in ensuring that data can move freely across borders and sectors within the EU, remaining accessible and usable for innovation

Published by Springer Nature Switzerland AG 2027
A. Papaleonidas et al. (Eds.): AIAI 2026 Workshops, IFIP AICT 796, pp. 286–300, 2027.
https://doi.org/10.1007/978-3-032-30507-7_19

while ensuring that European legislation and values – such as privacy, fairness, and transparency – are fully upheld. For realizing this, interdependent legal instruments as depicted in Fig. 1 are considered: (i) the Data Governance Act [5], for processes and structures creation used to facilitate voluntary data sharing provided by companies, individuals as well as the public sector; (ii) the Data Act [6], used for establishing rules and creating proper conditions for a fairer access to and reuse of data from industry, and; (iii) the latest European Commission's initiative on high-value datasets [7], complementing the Open Data Directive [8] with a list of technical requirements and datasets that public sector bodies are required to publish in machine-readable format, for free, and under open licenses.

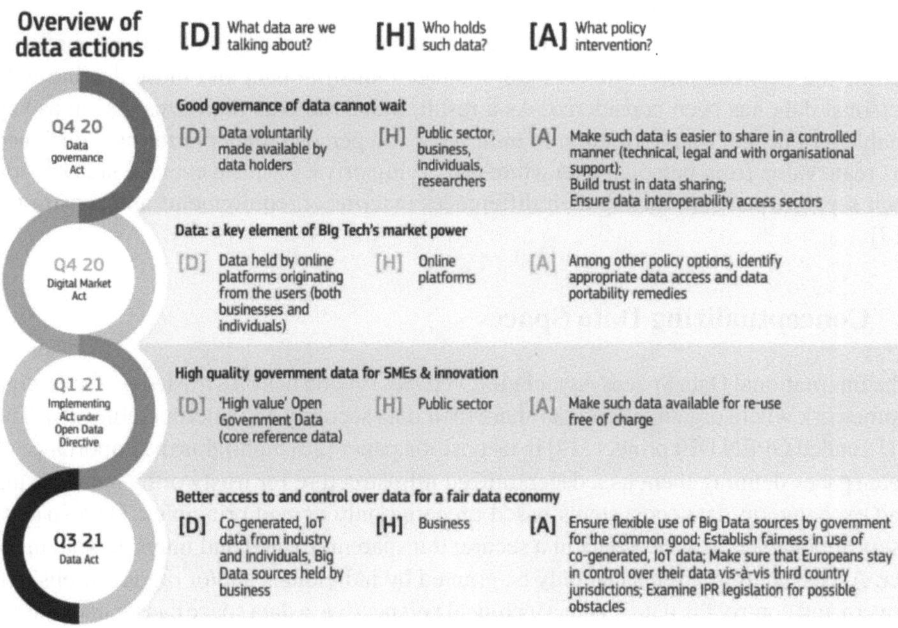

Fig. 1. Legislative initiatives defined within the context of the European strategy for data. (Source: European Commission, 2020 [9]).

A central pillar of this vision is the development of Data Spaces [10]. They facilitate access under clearly defined conditions, thereby shifting the paradigm from data ownership to data usage. This approach enables organizations to collaborate without relinquishing control, fostering new forms of value creation across sectors such as mobility, healthcare, and industry. In this sense, data spaces do not merely encourage cooperation; they actively reduce the structural and perceived risks that have historically hindered it [11].

Data spaces are a key concept of the European Strategy [12] and it is gaining increasing attention worldwide, both in industry and in academia. The term can be understood as an umbrella concept of a unified ecosystem of data elements that enable trusted data and knowledge sharing. This includes not only technical components –such as data models, datasets, ontologies, data-sharing agreements, and management services (for example, those provided by data centres, repositories, or data lakes) – but also the softer dimensions, such as governance frameworks, organizational processes, and stakeholder interactions [13]. On the other hand, the concept of data platforms [14] are typically understood from a more technical, software-oriented perspective referring to architectures and repositories of interoperable hardware and software components, following an approach that enables creation, transformation, evolution, curation, and exploitation of static and dynamic data [15, 16], providing the operational backbone that enables data spaces to function. The two concepts cooperate closely representing two complementary dimensions of the same data economy: data spaces define the ecosystem and governance framework, while data platforms provide the technological means to implement and operate it.

At the same time, due to the increasing attention to privacy and data protection a distinction between infrastructures that manage industrial data and those dealing with personal data has been considered. As a result, industrial data platforms – seen as key enablers of digital transformation in industry – and personal data platforms – designed to create value from personal data while preserving privacy – have evolved side by side their separate paths, reflecting their differences in terms of requirements and constraints [17].

2 Conceptualizing Data Spaces

The International Data Spaces Association's (IDSA) vision lies on a trusted and sovereign framework where organizations can share their data securely and interoperable [18]. The EU-funded OPEN DEI project [19] in its position paper [20] highlights the importance of data spaces defining them as a decentralized infrastructure for trustworthy data sharing and exchange in data ecosystems based on commonly agreed principles. Data spaces' users are enabled to access data in a secure, transparent, trusted and interoperable manner. Access & usage rights can only be granted by individuals and/or organizations that govern and control the data. From a technical perspective, a data space can be understood as a data integration concept that does not rely on shared database schemas or physical consolidation of data. Instead, it is based on distributed data sources, and on demand integration on a semantic level. Realizing interoperable data spaces is primarily a coordination challenge [21] that requires agreement on specific standards and design principles accepted by all participants. While interoperability can be demonstrated relatively easily in projects' demonstrators, proofs of concept and living labs, the main difficulty lies in its establishment as a default norm that enables large-scale adoption and scalability.

2.1 Data Space Design Principles

In sensitive sectors such as healthcare and finance, sharing data remains a challenge. These difficulties often stem from strict regulatory requirements, concerns regarding data ownership and control, and a lack of trust between data providers and data users. However, European data spaces are expected to introduce entirely new data-driven services, enhanced by increased transparency and stronger data sovereignty, aiming to establish a more level playing field for data sharing and exchange, thereby reducing the dominance of and dependency on large, quasi-monopolistic actors. Due to this, they are focused in fostering new user behavior as participants become more accustomed to exchanging and using data in an ethical and responsible manner [20].

Data space development requires the navigation through the stages of exploration, preparation and implementation according to the Data Space Development Processes [22] introduced by the Data Spaces Support Centre (DSSC). As multiple approaches could be considered in delivering data spaces, development processes can be applied in a modular manner, meaning that each data space may selectively adopt development processes or parts of them, based on their operational demands and requirements. Within these development processes, the components of a data space are designed and specified. In addition, thirteen design principles have been identified, covering seventeen building blocks distributed across six key pillars (i.e.: Business, Governance, Legal, Data Interoperability, Data Sovereignty and Trust, and Data Value Creation Enabler). These principles are categorized into two groups: (i) pillar-specific design principles and (ii) cross-pillar design principles, thus forming a structured foundation for the development and operation of data spaces [23].

Pillar-specific design principles are focused on guiding the implementation and functionality of building blocks within a specific pillar, ensuring that each domain is designed according to its requirements. On the other hand, cross-pillar design principles consider aspects of multiple pillars, promoting alignment across the overall data space architecture. Table 1 provides a comprehensive overview of these design principles along with their respective classification.

These principles are closely related to architecture requirements and standard building blocks steaming from a decentralized and trusted framework that enables secure data sharing. This framework outlines the key elements needed to build effective data-sharing ecosystems [24] promoting a more decentralized approach where different stakeholders can actively participate in decision-making through governance structures, data sovereignty, and federated systems. Moreover, it emphasizes on the importance of trust, ensuring that security, privacy, and compliance are built into systems from the very beginning rather than added later.

In addition, the framework supports making data easy accessible and useable, while encouraging sustainable data exchange through both financial and non-financial incentives. Last but not least, interoperability plays a central role by enabling different systems to exchange and understand data consistently.

At the same time, flexibility in system design allows developers to adapt and extend platforms to meet evolving needs. Finally, the framework highlights the value of open, reusable, and community-driven solutions to ensure long-term sustainability and wider adoption.

3 Current Challenges of Data Spaces

Data spaces can offer a trustworthy, decentralized, and interoperable data sharing platform and enable secure data exchange among organizations and systems [25]. They aim to establish trust through transparent rules, verifiable claims, and shared governance

Table 1. Data spaces design principles [23]

Category	Design Principles	Building Blocks
Pillar – specific	Reusability of Data	Data Value Creation Enablers Building Blocks
	Pursuit Quality by Design	
	Adaptable data space governance framework	Governance Building Blocks
	Establish a fit-for-purpose contractual framework	Legal Building Blocks
	Ensure Data Interoperability in data spaces	Data Interoperability Building Blocks
Cross-pillar	Incentives and Synergies Between Data Space Participants	Business and Data Value Creation Enablers Building Blocks
	Ensure Compliance with EU Legal Framework and Norms	Legal, Governance, and Data Sovereignty and Trust Building Blocks
	Discoverability, Availability, and Accessibility of Data	Business, Data Interoperability, Data Value Creation Enablers Building Blocks
	Transparency	Governance, Data Interoperability,Data Sovereignty and Trust, and Data Value Creation Enablers Building Blocks
	Establishing Trust and Security in Data spaces.	Legal and Data Sovereignty and Trust Building Blocks
	Ensure Participants Rights Through Data Sovereignty	Governance, Data Interoperability, andData Sovereignty and Trust Building Blocks
	Promote Participation Through Inclusivity	Governance and Data Value Creation Enablers Building Blocks
	Promote Environmental Sustainability	All building blocks

mechanisms. This understanding is consistent with ISO/IEC 20151's [26] definition of data spaces and in full alignment with IDSA's approach [27] to trusted data sharing and the terminology curated and harmonized by the DSSC [28]. Concerning European Data Spaces, the Big Data Value Association (BDVA) [29] has identified a number of challenges that should be considered in order for added value to be generated [13]. These challenges can be clustered into four distinct groups namely technical challenges, business and organizational challenges, legal compliance challenges, and last but not least, national and regional challenges.

The ambition to enable cross-border and cross-sector data spaces that will be able to support the processing of proprietary, personal and open data, has introduced new technical challenges while amplifying the already existing ones. The traditional four "Vs" of Big Data (volume, velocity, variety, veracity) [30] must be revisited in the light of data-sharing demands including besides raw data, metadata, models and algorithm as well. Since data lifecycle management is not yet designed with sharing in mind, data producers rarely anticipate reuse at the point of creation, limiting downstream interoperability and discoverability. Under this framework, related lifecycle models should evolve to better support data preparation, sharing, and reuse, while ensuring the availability of mature data services [13].

Data security and privacy are directly related to the concept of data sovereignty, ensuring that data is handled in a way that preserves its confidentiality, availability, and integrity [31]. In practice, this requires trusted mechanisms for data sharing [32] while ensuring that offering FAIR policies are followed [33], in conjunction with reliable ways to control how data is accessed and used within complicated data sharing spaces such as dataspaces. In addition, the decentralized architectures used, may ensure that data remains with its originator ensuring sovereignty but in this context, scalability and real-time data operations remain challenging with standardized data exchange protocols to be considered crucial.

In particular, data sovereignty is often understood as the control of data flows through national jurisdiction, but this interpretation is too narrow to capture its full scope. The concept can be extended further so as to include diverse contexts, such as governmental authority over stored data in domestic or overseas clouds [34] and indigenous data governance [35].

When it comes to trust and reliability in data spaces several challenges related to veracity, security, and privacy should be considered. Given their data sharing demands and distributed nature, robust mechanisms for data verification and provenance, are essential towards ensuring that data remains traceable and auditable throughout its life-cycle are of high importance. At the same time, secure data sharing should consider strong guarantees of confidentiality, access control, and digital rights management, challenging requirements in decentralized environments, where secure communication across nodes depends on interoperable protocols and trusted infrastructures. Moreover, privacy issues add an additional layer of complexity despite the fact that privacy-related technologies are well established. This is due to the fact that they cannot be fully integrated into the distributed and cross-functional environment of data spaces so they remain incomplete, requiring further development to ensure regulatory compliance without limiting innovation [36].

Beyond these aspects, additional challenges exist such as potential performance limitations due to the lack of centralized indexing & optimized data partitioning, and the need for advanced AI-based techniques to automate data integration tasks [37].

3.1 Data Spaces Initiatives

Data spaces were conceived as a response to the reluctance of organizations, providers and Industry 4.0 partners to share their data [38], despite acknowledging their value for fostering innovation and collaboration. This reluctance was – and still is – driven by several concerns related to loss of control, security and privacy risks, and legal issues. By "addressing" these obstacles, data spaces aim to create an environment in which data sharing becomes both feasible and attractive, and thus viable, especially in the current complex, multi-stakeholder ecosystem.

At their core, data spaces provide both the infrastructure and the governance framework that enables controlled and trustworthy environment for data exchange. As already mentioned, their main principle is data sovereignty meaning that organizations retain control over their data and determine the conditions under which it can be accessed and used. Standardization, interoperability in parallel with international regimes and practices [39] ensure that data exchange can be efficient while, at the same time, compliance with regulations is maintained.

Under this framework, The IDSA [27] has defined a data sharing framework that includes a reference architecture, open-source building blocks, and a certification process for the development and operation of Data Spaces. It aims to create a global standard for International Data Spaces (IDS) [40], as well as to foster technologies and business models that will drive the data economy of the future not only in Europe but also worldwide. Moreover, the association defines the technical and governance foundations that enable organizations to share data securely, in a self-determined manner, and being interoperable across industries and national borders.

The DSSC [28] is a "key implementation initiative" of the European Data Strategy delivered through the Digital Europe Program. One of the objectives of the DSSC is to accelerate the deployment, scaling and adoption of Data Spaces in Europe. In attaining that objective, the DSSC aims to fully respect European values, and supporting the European economy and society. The DSSC is fostering the development of Common European Data Spaces through exploring the needs of Data Space initiatives. Additionally, it defines common requirements and establishes best practices to accelerate the formation of sovereign Data Spaces. Herewith, the DSSC contributes to realizing the vision of a genuine European single market for data.

The Gaia-X European Association [41] unites a variety of organizations (such as large companies and SMEs, developers and users of technology, industrial players, and academic members) to achieve one common goal: to enhance the European data economy by enabling the creation of common Data Spaces, in full alignment with the EU's data strategy. Gaia-X is committed to the development of a common standard for a digital ecosystem that is open, transparent, and secure. This standard will serve as the foundation for a new data infrastructure that ensures the safe and trustworthy exchange of data. Gaia-X strives for innovation through digital sovereignty aiming to provide the European Single Market with unparalleled opportunities for innovative data-driven business models, thereby reducing the reliance on non-controllable technologies and reflecting Europe's need for data and cloud sovereignty.

Based on the principles of European data and cloud sovereignty, Gaia-X intends to build a federated open data infrastructure. Gaia-X seeks to create a digital governance system that can be implemented on any existing cloud or edge technology platform, thereby enabling data and service transparency, controllability, portability, and interoperability.

The Gaia-X vision [41, 42] is expressed through the creation of two ecosystems: data and infrastructure, which are interconnected by federations. The three conceptual pillars for the achievement of this vision are:

- Gaia-X Compliance: Decentralized services that foster objective and measurable trust.
- Data Spaces/Federations: Interoperable and portable cross-sector datasets and services.
- Data Exchange: Established contract rules for access and data usage, aiming to enable the portability, exchange, and sovereignty of services and data among providers, thereby opening the European Data Market to enhance competitiveness and ultimately foster growth and social equality.

This vision will only become a reality if all three pillars are fully realized.

4 SM4RTENANCE Overview

Europe hosts a highly competitive and comprehensive manufacturing ecosystem, forming the backbone of its economy by driving growth, exports, and employment. However, the sector is increasingly operating in a volatile, uncertain, complex, and ambiguous (VUCA) global environment, where challenges such as supply chain disruptions and geopolitical conflicts place growing pressure on industries. In this context, the effective use and exchange of industrial data emerges as a key asset. Data-driven approaches can contribute to intelligent decision-making enabling autonomous, self-optimizing systems, such as predictive maintenance enhancing resilience and efficiency across manufacturing processes.

4.1 The Vision

Looking ahead, Europe's manufacturing vision for 2030 [43] focuses on strengthening global competitiveness, productivity and technological leadership through deeper integration into interconnected value chains. This requires primarily collaboration among stakeholders across the entire lifecycle of manufacturing processes and increased integration of digital technologies. Central to this transformation is the concept of "data as a resource" [44] which underpins the development of industrial intelligence. To fully realize this potential, Europe must establish trustworthy and interoperable ecosystems based on common data spaces for manufacturing enabling seamless data sharing, supporting flexible data value chains and facilitating collaboration.

Recent European initiatives and platforms have already demonstrated the potential of digital manufacturing solutions to enhance automation, sustainability and operational excellence. The SM4RTENANCE EU funded project [45] aims to establish a neutral, cross-sector data space for the manufacturing industry, enabling multiple stakeholders – including service providers, manufacturers and OEM (Original Equipment Manufacturer) customers – to share and exchange data throughout the entire asset lifecycle in support of maintenance services. Its mission is to connect key ecosystems, standards, experimentation facilities and data space building blocks in order to foster scalable and sustainable data-sharing environments. By aligning with common European data space principles, technical infrastructures, shared vocabularies, data models and business agreements, SM4RTENANCE seeks to support the development of interoperable, multi-stakeholder predictive maintenance and supply chain data spaces.

4.2 The Objectives

The project's goal is to contribute in the building of a more connected, trustworthy, and value-driven data-sharing ecosystem in the field of European manufacturing. Within this context, SM4RTENANCE defines key objectives to support the development and operation of such ecosystems. More specifically, it aims to establish a coherent industrial and service framework for data space operations. This includes creating a legal entity to manage the data space, simplifying participation for users across multiple data spaces, and ensuring that stakeholders retain full sovereignty over their shared data. Additionally, it aims to support the expansion of data space services at a pan-European level while seeking to increase data sharing across manufacturing companies and service providers.

In addition, SM4RTENANCE promotes the harmonization of data space blueprints and the development of common guidelines to enable federation, trusted data flows, and interoperable services across sectors. This includes defining shared specifications, governance models, and compliance frameworks aligned with European standards. The project also focuses on improving the practical use of data spaces by making access to data, services and computing resources more transparent and easier to manage. This is to be realized by supporting increased data sharing from industry, enhancing the reuse of data products, and by encouraging the adoption of digital twins and Artificial Intelligence- (AI-) driven predictive maintenance solutions [46, 47]. Last but not least, it aims to operationalize these concepts by deploying a functioning data space federation [48]. This involves simplifying user access through mechanisms such as single sign-on, enabling on-demand data sharing under clear conditions, and continuously evaluating interoperability and system performance. Together, these actions aim to make data spaces more usable, efficient and impactful for industrial stakeholders.

4.3 Challenges Addressed

Digital manufacturing platforms are increasingly enabling data access and peer-to-peer exchange, fostering more collaborative industrial ecosystems. At the same time, advances in Internet of Things (IoT) ecosystems, the extended use of artificial intelligence, and the robotics are driving a shift from traditional automation toward more autonomous operations. Despite this progress, data remains largely isolated, and several key barriers continue to hinder effective data sharing. SM4RTENANCE seeks to bridge this gap between the potential of data-driven manufacturing and the current limitations, enabling scalable, secured collaborative data-sharing ecosystems.

As trust issues between companies persist, under the fear of misuse due to unauthorized redistribution or accidental exposure and due to the limited control mechanisms implying that once data is shared, organizations rely heavily on contracts, which cannot fully guarantee compliance trust cannot be established. In addition, low interoperability enhanced by the lack of common standards and scalable solutions restricts seamless data exchange across all sectors and ecosystems. Finally, as long as data protection mindsets prevail, since companies often treat data as a critical internal asset, with unclear valuation and high-perceived risks associated with sharing the promise of data-driven manufacturing adoption remains limited.

As a response to these challenges, SM4RTENANCE aims to provide practical guidance and operational frameworks for deploying industrial data spaces that support autonomous, collaborative maintenance and circular services. Beyond technical solutions, it addresses challenges at multiple levels: structural (ecosystem complexity and transition to Industry 4.0), organizational (collaboration and governance issues), and technical (data quality, lifecycle management, interoperability, security and trust).

Structural Challenges for Collaborative Digital Value Chains (DVC):
Considering the increasing complexity of modern manufacturing systems, driven by the transition toward smart, connected and collaborative industrial ecosystems, as well

as the demand for interoperable data-sharing infrastructures across sectors and value chains, the project proposes a unified operational blueprint for data space interoperability, enabling seamless data exchange and user mobility across heterogeneous industrial data ecosystems. This approach introduces modular and customizable "data rooms" built upon federated data infrastructures, supporting flexible governance, data sovereignty, and diverse revenue-sharing models. These data-sharing environments will facilitate the creation and exchange of standardized data products governed by machine-readable and legally enforceable contracts, ensuring trust, compliance and secure collaboration (Fig. 2).

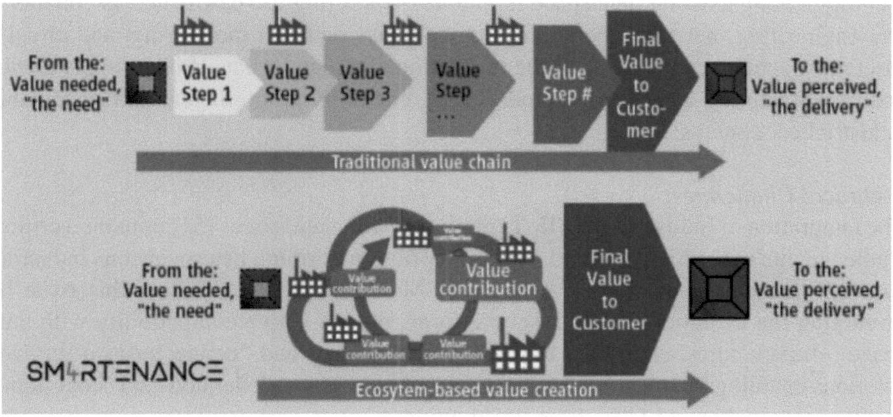

Fig. 2. Asset 4.0 Data Space Collaborative Digital Value Chains Structural Challenges [45]

More specifically, the project "targets" advanced asset management and predictive maintenance applications, leveraging shared data to enhance AI-driven analytics. By enabling multilateral data sharing, SM4RTENANCE improves the performance of predictive and prescriptive maintenance models, supporting the transition from reactive and condition-based maintenance toward autonomous, self-healing industrial systems. Furthermore, it aligns with Industry 5.0 principles [49] by integrating sustainability objectives, including energy efficiency, circularity, and lifecycle optimization through mechanisms such as digital product passports.

Organizational Challenges:
The implementation of data-driven maintenance and asset management across industries remains fragmented due to heterogeneous priorities and limited cross-sector interoperability. Current practices are largely dominated by preventive maintenance approaches, while the transition toward predictive and prescriptive maintenance is hindered by the lack of scalable, collaborative data-sharing mechanisms. Although initial efforts have enabled the creation of "data bridges" within isolated factory environments, the development of multilateral Data Value Chains (DVCs) across supply chains and sectors is still at an early stage.

SM4RTENANCE "addresses" these limitations by promoting interoperable and federated data space infrastructures that support standardized data products and collaborative service models. It emphasizes the evolution from bilateral and siloed data exchange toward multilateral data ecosystems, enabling advanced condition monitoring and autonomous maintenance capabilities. This transition requires enhanced federation services, interoperability mechanisms and scalable governance models that allow multiple data space operators to collaborate without monopolistic constraints. To validate this, the project implements cross-sector, pan-European pilot demonstrators across key industries, including automotive, aeronautics, electronics, and textile manufacturing. These pilots focus on enabling multilateral DVCs and testing interoperability among existing data space initiatives, supporting use cases such as collaborative engineering, net-zero operations, autonomous condition monitoring, and circular asset management contributing to the realization of dynamic, data-driven supply chains and Manufacturing-as-a-Service models [50], enabling more efficient and sustainable industrial ecosystems.

Technical Challenges:
The integration of Industrial IoT (IIoT) platforms with data spaces [51] remains a critical challenge due to the high cost and complexity of transforming heterogeneous industrial data into shareable, standardized formats. SM4RTENANCE addresses this issue by promoting the evolution of IoT asset platforms toward native compatibility with data space infrastructures, supported by certified connectors and "connector-as-a-service" solutions enabling seamless integration of data products into federated data ecosystems, facilitating scalable and SME-friendly adoption.

A key enabler of data spaces is the availability of high-quality, semantically interoperable data. Industrial environments generate large volumes of heterogeneous data, often affected by inconsistencies, human factors, and context-specific usage patterns. SM4RTENANCE aims το enable standardized data collection pipelines and cross-sector data sharing to ensure data quality, ecological validity, and robustness of AI-driven predictive maintenance models. To this end, it leverages a Smart Data Model (SDM) and an Information Management Framework (IMF), supporting metadata standardization, schema validation and the development of shared ontologies aligned with Industry 4.0 standards. Furthermore, it integrates digital twin technologies with data spaces, enabling collaborative training of AI/ML models and multi-stakeholder optimization of asset performance across the lifecycle. Finally, it enforces trust and compliance through certification and governance mechanisms aligned with Gaia-X and International Data Spaces Association frameworks, ensuring data integrity, sovereignty, and interoperability, thus providing a secure foundation for scalable and cross-sector industrial data ecosystems.

5 Conclusion

With a significant part of the industry adopting automation, the continued development of data-driven ecosystems will be critical for ensuring Europe's long-term competitiveness. The concept of "Data as a Resource" becomes crucial for Europe's vision for a sovereign data market enabled through Common European Data Spaces. This paper focuses on European initiatives like Gaia-X and IDSA, which aim to establish an ecosystem, where data is shared and made available in a trustworthy environment, enhancing digital sovereignty.

In this framework, SM4RTENANCE project deals with the growing need for trusted, interoperable, and scalable data spaces within Europe's manufacturing ecosystem. It promotes federated data-sharing infrastructures, sovereign, and interoperable data exchange across sectors and cross-sector collaboration by enabling structured, discoverable, and reusable data products. Overall, the paper highlights how data spaces can enable the transition toward a federated, trustworthy environment that will be beneficial for the European economy.

Acknowledgement. Part of this paper has been based on the context of the "SM4RTENANCE" ("European Deployment of Smart Manufacturing Asset 4.0 MultilateRal DaTa Sharing SpacEs for an AutoNomous Operation of CollAborative MainteNance and Circular SErvices") Project. This project is funded by the European Commission's Digital Europe Programme (DIGITAL) under Grant Agreement No. 101123490.

References

1. Välilä, T.: Infrastructure and growth: a survey of macro-econometric research. Struct. Changed Econ. Dyn. **53**, 39–49 (2020). https://doi.org/10.1016/j.strueco.2020.01.007
2. Franklin, M., Halevy, A., Maier, D.: From databases to dataspaces: a new abstraction for information management. SIGMOD Rec. **34**(4), 27–33 (2005). https://doi.org/10.1145/1107499.1107502
3. European Commission: Communication from the Commission to the European Parliament, the Council, the European Economic and Social Committee and the Committee of the Regions: A European Strategy for Data. COM(2020) 66 final (2020). https://eur-lex.europa.eu/legal-content/EN/TXT/?uri=celex:52020DC0066
4. Kalvet, T., Toots, M., Krimmer, B.: Contributing to a digital single market for Europe: barriers and drivers of an EU-wide once-only principle. In: Proceedings of the 19th Annual International Conference on Digital Government Research: Governance in the Data Age, Article No. 45, pp. 1–8 (2018). https://doi.org/10.1145/3209281.3209344
5. European Commission: Commission Staff Working Document Impact Assessment Report. Accompanying the document Proposal for a Regulation of the European Parliament and of the Council on European data governance (Data Governance Act) SWD(2020) 295 final (2020). https://eur-lex.europa.eu/legal-content/EN/TXT/PDF/?uri=CELEX:52020SC0295
6. European Commission. Proposal for a Regulation of the European Parliament and of the Council on harmonised rules on fair access to and use of data (Data Act) (Text with EEA relevance) 2022. SWD(2022) 34 Final. https://www.europarl.europa.eu/RegData/publications/trilogue/2022/0047/NEGO_CT(2022)0047(2023-03-28)_XL.pdf
7. European Commission: Commission Implementing Regulation (EU) …/... of 21.12.2022 laying down a list of specific high-value datasets and the arrangements for their publication and re-use. C(2022) 9562 final. https://eur-lex.europa.eu/legal-content/EN/TXT/?uri=PI_COM:C(2022)9562
8. European Parliament and Council of the European Union: Directive (EU) 2019/1024 of the European Parliament and of the Council of 20 June 2019 on open data and the re-use of public sector information (recast). Official Journal of the European Union L172, pp. 56–83 (2019). https://eur-lex.europa.eu/eli/dir/2019/1024/oj

9. Minghini, M., Kotsev, A., et al.: A European approach to the establishment of data spaces. Data **7**(8), 118 (2022). https://doi.org/10.3390/data7080118
10. Bacco, M., Kocian, A., Chessa, S., Crivello, A., Barsochhi, P.: What are data spaces? Systematic survey and future outlook. Data Brief **57**, 110969 (2024). https://doi.org/10.1016/j.dib.2024.110969
11. Otto, B., ten Hompel, M., Wrobel, S. (eds): Designing Data Spaces: The Ecosystem Approach to Competitive Advantage. Springer,Cham (2022). https://doi.org/10.1007/978-3-030-93975-5
12. European Commission: Data spaces are a key concept of the European Strategy. https://digital-strategy.ec.europa.eu/en/policies/strategy-data
13. Scerri, S., Tuikka, T., et al.: Common European Data spaces: challenges and opportunities. In: Curry, E., Scerri, S., Tuikka, T. (eds.) Data Spaces. Springer, Cham (2022). https://doi.org/10.1007/978-3-030-98636-0_16
14. Gieß, A., and Hutterer, A.: The Future of data management: a delimitation of data platforms, data spaces, data meshes, and data fabrics. Inf. Syst. e-Bus. Manage. **23**, 971–997 (2025). https://doi.org/10.1007/s10257-025-00707-4
15. Curry, E.: Real-Time Linked Dataspaces. Springer, Cham (2020). https://doi.org/10.1007/978-3-030-29665-0
16. Curry, E., Derguech, W., Hasan, S., et al.: A real-time linked dataspace for the internet of things. Futur. Gener. Comput. Syst. **90**, 405–422 (2019). https://doi.org/10.1016/j.future.2018.07.019
17. Zillner, S., Curry, E., Metzger, A., Auer, S., Seidl, R. (eds.): European Big Data Value Strategic Research & Innovation Agenda. Big Data Value Association (2017). http://www.edwardcurry.org/publications/BDVA_SRIA_v4_Ed1.1.pdf
18. International Data Spaces Association (IDSA). https://internationaldataspaces.org/
19. OPEN DEI. https://www.ehtel.eu/activities/eu-funded-projects/opendei.html
20. International Data Spaces Association (IDSA): Design Principles for Data Spaces (Position Paper, 2021). https://doi.org/10.5281/zenodo.5105744
21. European Union: Interoperability in data spaces: Building Europe's digital future. https://data.europa.eu/en/news-events/news/interoperability-data-spaces-building-europes-digital-future
22. Data Spaces Support Centre (DSSC): Data Space Development Processes (2024). https://dssc.eu/space/bv15e/766063009/Development+Processes
23. Data Spaces Support Centre (DSSC): Introduction to Data Space Design (2024). https://dssc.eu/space/DSDPV2/766181416/1.+Introduction
24. Kazantzsev, N., Islam, N., et al.: Data sharing for business model innovation in platform ecosystems: from private data to public good. Technol. Forecast. Soc. Chang. **192**, 122515 (2023). https://doi.org/10.1016/j.techfore.2023.122515
25. Curry, E., Scerri, S., Tuikka, T. (eds.): Data Spaces: Design, Deployment, and Future Directions. Springer, Cham (2022). https://doi.org/10.1007/978-3-030-98636-0
26. International Organization for Standardization (ISO)/International Electrotechnical Committee (IEC): ISO/IEC DIS 20151 – Dataspace concepts and characteristics, https://www.iso.org/obp/ui/en/#iso:std:iso-iec:20151:dis:ed-1:v1:en
27. International Data Spaces Association: International Data Spaces. https://internationaldataspaces.org/
28. Data Spaces Support Centre (DSSC). https://dssc.eu/
29. Big Data Value Association (BDVA). https://bdva.eu/
30. Abraham, G.: The 4Vs of big data (2025). https://www.georgescifo.com/2025/07/the-4-vs-of-big-data-understanding-the-core-characteristics-that-define-modern-data/
31. Gan, S.K., Wong, T.L., Goh, C.P., et al.: A review on the development of dataspace connectors using microservices for cross-company secured data exchange. In: Proceedings of the

International Conference on Digital Transformation and Applications (ICDXA 2021), 25–26 October 2021, Kuala Lumpur, Malaysia (2021). https://doi.org/10.56453/icdxa.2021.1010
32. Hernandez, J., McKenna, L., Brennan, R.: TIKD: a trusted integrated knowledge dataspace for sensitive healthcare data sharing. In: Proceedings of the 2021 IEEE 45th Annual Computers, Software, and Applications Conference (COMPSAC), 12–16 July 2021, Madrid, Spain, pp.1855–1860. IEEE (2021). https://doi.org/10.1109/COMPSAC51774.2021.00280
33. Martella, C., Longo, A., et al.: Dataspaces in urban digital twins: a case study in photovoltaics. In: Proceedings of the 31st Symposium on Advanced Database System (SEBD 2023), 02–05 July 2023, Galzignano Terme, Padua, Italy, pp.1–8 (2023). https://ceur-ws.org/Vol-3478/paper52.pdf
34. Irion, K.: Government cloud computing and national data sovereignty. Policy Internet **4**(3–4), 40–71 (2012). https://onlinelibrary.wiley.com/doi/10.1002/poi3.10
35. Kukutai, T.: Indigenous data sovereignty: toward an agenda (2016). https://www.researchgate.net/publication/310214035_Indigenous_Data_Sovereignty_Toward_an_Agenda
36. Dutkiewicz, L., et al.: Privacy-preserving techniques for trustworthy data sharing: Opportunities and challenges for future research. In: Curry, E., Scerri, S., Tuikka, T. (eds.) Data Spaces. Springer, Cham (2022). https://doi.org/10.1007/978-3-030-98636-0_15
37. Nargesian, F., Zhu, E., Miller, R.J., et al.: Data lake management: challenges and opportunities. Proc. VLDB Endow. **12**(12), 1986–1989 (2019). https://doi.org/10.14778/3352063.335211
38. Möller, F., Jussen, I., et al.: Industrial data ecosystems and data spaces. Electron. Mark. **34**, 41 (2024). https://doi.org/10.1007/s12525-024-00724-0
39. Krasner, S.D.: Sovereignty: an institutional perspective. Comp. Polit. Stud. **21**(1), 66–94 (1988). https://www.critical-juncture.net/uploads/2/1/9/9/21997192/krasner_soverignty.pdf
40. International Data Spaces Association: IDSA Rulebook – Introduction. https://docs.internationaldataspaces.org/ids-knowledgebase/idsa-rulebook/idsa-rulebook/1_introduction
41. Gaia-X European Association: About Gaia-X. https://gaia-x.eu/
42. Bundesministerium für Wirtschaft und Energie: Franco-German Position on GAIA-X (2020). https://www.bundeswirtschaftsministerium.de/Redaktion/DE/Downloads/F/franco-german-position-on-gaia-x.html
43. ManuFuture: ManuFuture Vision 2030. Competitive, Sustainable and Resilient European Manufacturing (2018). https://www.manufuture.org/wp-content/uploads/2022/04/Manufuture-Vision-2030_DIGITAL.pdf
44. Surblyte, G.: Data as a digital resource. SSRN Electron. J. **16–12**, 1–40 (2016). https://doi.org/10.2139/ssrn.2849303
45. SM4RTENANCE ("European Deployment of Smart Manufacturing Asset 4.0 MultilateRal DaTa Sharing SpacEs for an AutoNomous Operation of CollAborative MainteNance and Circular SErvices Digital Europe Programme") DIGITAL Program, Grant Agreement No.101123490. https://sm4rtenance.eu/
46. Chen, S., Bekar, E.T., Bokrantz, J., Skoogh, A.: AI-enhanced digital twins in maintenance: Systematic review, industrial challenges, and bridging research–practice gaps. J. Manuf. Syst. **82**, 678–699 (2025). https://doi.org/10.1016/j.jmsy.2025.07.006
47. Ismail, L., Abdelmoti, A., Basu, A., Berini, A.D.E., Naouss, M.: Systematic review of digital twin-driven predictive maintenance in industrial engineering: taxonomy, architectural elements, and future research directions (2025). https://arxiv.org/pdf/2509.24443
48. Hutterer, A., and Krumay, B.: The adoption of data spaces: drivers toward federated data sharing. In: Proceedings of the 57th Hawaii International Conference on System Sciences (HICSS-57), 03–06 January 2024, Honolulu, Hawaii, pp. 4506–4515 (2024). https://doi.org/10.24251/HICSS.2024.542
49. Ghobakhloo, M.,Iranmanesh M.,: Behind the definition of industry 5.0: a systematic review of technologies, principles, components, and values. J. Industr. Prod. Eng. **40**(6), 432–447 (2023). https://doi.org/10.1080/21681015.2023.2216701

50. Bulut, S., Wende, M., Wagner, C., Anderl, R.: Impact of manufacturing-as-a-service: business model adaption for enterprises. Procedia CIRP **104**, 1286–1291 (2021). https://doi.org/10.1016/j.procir.2021.11.216
51. Lam, A.N., Nguyen, P.H., Ma, X.: Context-driven edge-based data sharing for industrial IoT data spaces. In: Proceedings of the 40th ACM/SIGAPP Symposium on Applied Computing (SAC 2025), 31 March–04 April 2025, Catania, Italy, pp. 498–505. ACM (2025). https://doi.org/10.1145/3672608.3707988

Towards AI-Driven Security in the Edge—Cloud Continuum: A Unified Architectural Perspective

Pedro R. Tomas[1], João Fernandes[1(✉)], Davide Miola[2], Grigorios Chrysos[3], Rajat Kandoi[4], Amir Javadpour[5], Riccardo Sisto[2], Matthias Dippold[6], Despina Kopanaki[3], Sotiris Ioannidis[3], Sofia Maragkou[6], Luís Cordeiro[1], and Tarik Taleb[7]

[1] OneSource, Consultoria Informática, Lda., Coimbra, Portugal
{pedro.tomas,joao.fernandes,cordeiro}@onesource.pt
[2] Politecnico di Torino, Turin, Italy
{davide.miola,riccardo.sisto}@polito.it
[3] Technical University of Crete, Chania, Greece
{gxrysos,dkopanaki,sioannidis}@tuc.gr
[4] Ericsson Research, Helsinki, Finland
rajat.kandoi@ericsson.com
[5] MOSA!C Lab/ICTFICIAL Oy, Espoo, Finland
[6] TU Wien, Vienna, Austria
e1609401@studenttuwien.ac.at, sofia.maragkou@tuwien.ac.at
[7] Ruhr University Bochum, Bochum, Germany
tarik.taleb@rub.de

Abstract. The evolution towards Beyond 5G (B5G)/6G systems is accelerating the emergence of distributed Edge–Cloud environments, where computation and intelligence span heterogeneous and dynamic infrastructures. While this enables latency-sensitive and data-intensive services, it also expands the attack surface, rendering traditional perimeter-based security insufficient.

In this context, Artificial Intelligence (AI)-driven security is emerging as a key approach for enabling adaptive monitoring, intelligent threat detection, and automated response. This paper presents an integration-oriented perspective on AI-driven security in the Edge–Cloud continuum. It identifies the main security requirements and design dimensions, and analyses representative building blocks, including eBPF-based monitoring, hardware-accelerated intrusion detection, federated intelligence, and privacy-preserving mechanisms.

Based on these elements, the paper outlines a unified architectural framework that integrates telemetry collection, AI-driven detection, distributed learning, and trusted orchestration into an end-to-end security pipeline. The approach is further supported by insights from the ELASTIC and 6G-PATH projects, highlighting its applicability in realistic deployment scenarios. Finally, the paper discusses key challenges related to scalability, trust, and robustness in next-generation Edge–Cloud systems.

Published by Springer Nature Switzerland AG 2027
A. Papaleonidas et al. (Eds.): AIAI 2026 Workshops, IFIP AICT 796, pp. 301–315, 2027.
https://doi.org/10.1007/978-3-032-30507-7_20

Keywords: Edge–Cloud Continuum · AI-Driven Security · eBPF · AI-Based Intrusion Detection · Federated Learning · 6G

1 Introduction

The evolution towards 6G networks is driving the emergence of a highly distributed computing paradigm, where intelligence, storage, and processing capabilities are seamlessly deployed across the Edge–Cloud continuum. This transformation enables a wide range of latency-sensitive and data-intensive applications, but also significantly expands the attack surface, introducing new security challenges that cannot be addressed by traditional, perimeter-based approaches [17]. In such environments, security must be intrinsically embedded across all system layers, from resource-constrained edge devices to cloud-native infrastructures.

AI is increasingly recognised as a key enabler for addressing these challenges, providing advanced capabilities for anomaly detection, threat prediction, and automated response. However, the adoption of AI in security introduces a set of new complexities. Security mechanisms must operate under strict latency and resource constraints, ensure data privacy across distributed domains, and remain robust against adversarial manipulation [3]. At the same time, they must remain deployable, scalable, and trustworthy in operational Edge–Cloud environments.

1.1 Research Gap and Paper Scope

Although substantial progress has been made in areas such as telemetry collection, AI-based intrusion detection, federated intelligence, and privacy-preserving analytics, these directions are often studied in isolation. As a result, fewer works address how such mechanisms can be combined into coherent, end-to-end security pipelines for practical Edge–Cloud environments.

This paper addresses this gap by analysing and positioning a set of complementary AI-driven security mechanisms within the Edge–Cloud continuum. In particular, we consider kernel-level telemetry collection through AI- based monitoring, AI-based intrusion detection techniques, and distributed intelligence approaches based on federated learning and privacy-preserving mechanisms. These components are examined not as standalone solutions, but as building blocks of a broader security pipeline. Accordingly, the scope of this paper is not to provide an exhaustive survey of all security solutions for 6G systems, but rather to focus on a representative set of complementary mechanisms that support an integration-oriented architectural perspective.

1.2 Main Objective and Contributions

Building on this analysis, we outline a unified architectural perspective that organises these mechanisms into a layered framework, highlighting their interactions and identifying key challenges related to interoperability, scalability, and trust. While full integration remains an open issue, this work provides a structured foundation for understanding how such technologies can be combined in future systems. More specifically, the main objective of this paper is to clarify how monitoring, intelligent threat detection, distributed intelligence, and privacy-preserving security functions can be positioned and connected within a common Edge–Cloud security architecture.

The main contributions of this paper are as follows. First, we identify key requirements and design dimensions for AI-driven security in the Edge–Cloud continuum (Sect. 2). Second, we analyse a set of complementary building blocks, including eBPF-based monitoring, AI-driven intrusion detection, distributed intelligence via federated learning, and privacy-preserving mechanisms (Sect. 3). Third, we outline a unified architectural perspective integrating these elements into an end-to-end security pipeline (Sect. 4). Finally, we discuss deployment perspectives and open challenges based on insights from the ELASTIC and 6G-PATH projects (Sect. 5). Section 6 highlights open challenges and research directions, and Sect. 7 concludes the paper.

2 AI-Driven Security in the Edge–Cloud Continuum

Building on the challenges outlined in Sect. 1, this section outlines the key requirements and design dimensions that underpin AI-driven security in the Edge–Cloud continuum.

2.1 Security Requirements

The transition to AI-driven security in the Edge–Cloud continuum requires a fundamental shift from perimeter-based protection to distributed, trust-centric architectures. In such environments, security mechanisms must satisfy several key requirements.

First, security solutions must be trustworthy and robust against adversarial manipulation. As AI becomes both a defensive tool and a potential attack target, systems must ensure resilience against poisoning, evasion, and model manipulation attacks [10]. Second, scalability and decentralisation are essential. The massive scale and distribution of connected devices in 6G environments require security intelligence to be distributed across edge and cloud domains, avoiding central bottlenecks while preserving data locality [24]. Third, explainability and verifiability are critical for operational deployment. AI-driven decisions must be interpretable and auditable, particularly in mission-critical scenarios where opaque behaviour may lead to unreliable or unsafe outcomes [8]. Fourth, security mechanisms must be resource-aware and low-latency. Edge devices operate under strict computational and energy constraints, requiring lightweight models and efficient execution while maintaining real-time responsiveness [18]. Finally, end-to-end trust and identity management must be ensured across the entire service chain. This includes consistent policy enforcement, secure identity propagation, and integrity guarantees across heterogeneous domains [7].

Two principal strategies exist. Hardware-assisted traffic replication relies on specialised equipment such as managed switches or SmartNICs to mirror traffic without CPU overhead, but assumes the availability of compatible infrastructure. In contrast, software-based capture intercepts traffic directly on the host using mechanisms such as network taps and Berkeley Packet Filter (BPF), offering greater flexibility for heterogeneous Edge–Cloud environments.

However, network interface-level capture becomes ineffective in cloud-native infrastructures where (CNI) plugins or Service Mesh frameworks enforce pervasive encryption. In such settings, traffic is encrypted within the application namespace before reaching the host network interface, rendering it opaque to traditional capture mechanisms. A possible mitigation is the deployment of capture agents within each Pod to intercept traffic prior to encryption. However, this approach introduces operational complexity, potential interference with workloads, and scalability limitations in dynamic environments.

To address these limitations, we adopt an eBPF-based traffic capture mechanism that operates at Layer-4 within the host kernel, providing uniform visibility across all co-located workloads without per-Pod instrumentation. The key advantage of this approach lies in its position relative to the encryption boundary imposed by Service Mesh and CNI components (Fig. 1). For outbound traffic, interception occurs before encryption, while for inbound traffic it occurs after decryption, ensuring visibility of cleartext data in both directions.

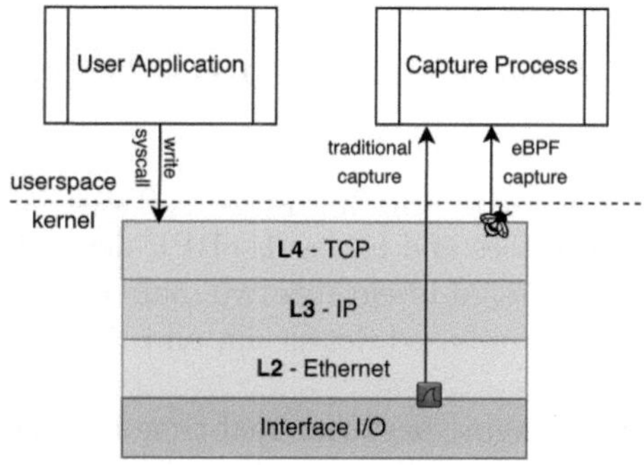

Fig. 1. Comparison of traditional traffic capture versus eBPF-based capture.

Furthermore, because eBPF programs execute within the shared host kernel rather than individual container namespaces, the system achieves comprehensive monitoring through a single, non-intrusive instrumentation point. This design is well suited to dynamic cloud-native environments, balancing deployment transparency, encryption-agnostic visibility, and scalability.

3.2 Hardware AI-Based Threat Detection Framework

AI driven intrusion detection enables the identification of both known and previously unseen attack patterns through data-driven analysis, complementing traditional rule-based approaches.

AI-IDS (Fig. 2) is a hardware-accelerated intrusion detection framework that combines (FPGA)- based processing with (ML)-driven analytics to address both known and emerging threats. The system integrates low-latency hardware monitoring with adaptive detection mechanisms, enabling real-time traffic analysis and high-precision intrusion detection.

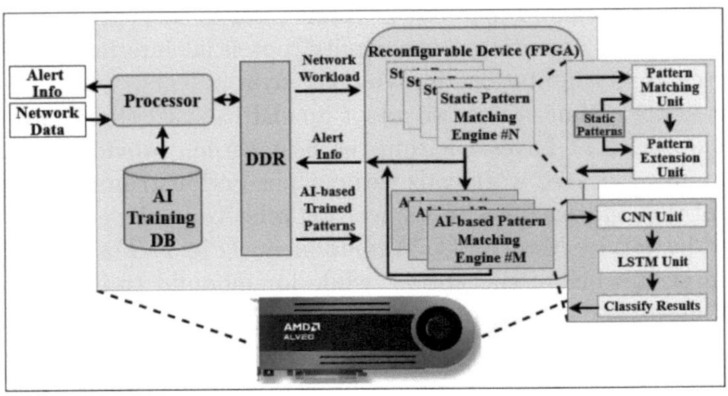

Fig. 2. Hardware-based AI-IDS architecture.

The framework adopts a hybrid hardware–software architecture, where a host-side interface preprocesses and forwards eBPF-derived traffic to the FPGA subsystem. The hardware design integrates two main components: (i) a pattern-matching engine for signature-based detection, and (ii) an AI-based module for adaptive pattern refinement.

The pattern-matching engine performs real-time inspection using predefined signatures, enabling deterministic, line-rate detection of known attacks with minimal latency [16].

The AI-driven module complements this capability through semi-supervised learning (e.g., (CNNs) and Long Short-Term Memory (LSTM)) to identify anomalous traffic patterns [5]. Suspicious instances are collected and used to periodically retrain the models, generating new signatures corresponding to previously unseen threats. These are translated into hardware-compatible representations and deployed to the FPGA, forming a closed-loop adaptation mechanism.

The FPGA-based implementation leverages parallel processing to enable high-throughput, low-latency inspection of multiple data streams, making it suitable for Edge–Cloud and (IoT) environments. Overall, this approach supports key design dimensions identified in Sect. 2.2, including low-latency operation, resource awareness, and adaptive intelligence.

3.3 Distributed and Federated Intelligence

The rapid growth of connected devices and distributed infrastructures has led to massive volumes of data that must be processed across the Edge–Cloud continuum [1]. Traditional centralised machine learning approaches, where data is aggregated and processed at a single location, are increasingly inadequate in such environments due to bandwidth constraints, latency requirements, and privacy concerns.

Federated Learning (FL) has emerged as a key paradigm to address these challenges by enabling collaborative model training across distributed nodes without requiring the exchange of raw data. Instead, each participant trains a local model and shares only model updates, which are aggregated to produce a global model. This approach reduces communication overhead while preserving data locality and privacy, making it particularly suitable for edge-native security applications. Different FL configurations can be adopted depending on the system architecture and data distribution, including hierarchical approaches that introduce intermediate aggregation layers at the edge to improve scalability and reduce latency.

DeepGuardian: A FL-Based Approach. DeepGuardian (DG) is a Network Intrusion Detection Prevention System (NIDPS) with a strong focus on data security and privacy. Relying on the core foundations of the Holistic Security and Privacy Framework (HSPF) [20], DG extends its core principles by combining FL, (CL), and unsupervised ML, with supervised ML to perform network traffic attacks classification, PETs to ensure data privacy and security, an intuitive dashboard and policy enforcement mechanisms, aiming to provide scalable, privacy-preserving, and (E2E) adaptive security for cloud-native environments.

Figure 3 presents the DG architecture, which is composed of the following key architecture components: (i) Aggregator, (ii) Agent, (iii) Collector, (iv) Policy Enforcer, (v) Dashboard. The Aggregator acts as the main framework unit, coordinating the Federated Training process and handling the management and distribution of the various ML models used for anomaly detection across federated agents. The Collector component gathers inbound and outbound network traffic traversing the primary network interface. This data is aggregated into flows and stored until classification occurs. Subsequently, the Agent, where the federated logic resides, is responsible for performing inference on the stored data and detecting potential malicious flows. Additionally, the Agent periodically executes federated training rounds to keep the ML model updated and effective in identifying anomalies within the continuously evolving network communication landscape. The Dashboard provides system observability over all the applications being protected, while also enabling the Human-in-the-loop functionality by allowing the human operator to override the AI's classification on a flow basis. Lastly, the Policy Enforcement [21] mechanism enables the enforcement of network traffic policies in cloud-native environments, supporting different policy enforcement mechanisms (i.e., OPA, Istio, Calico, Cilium, Kyverno).

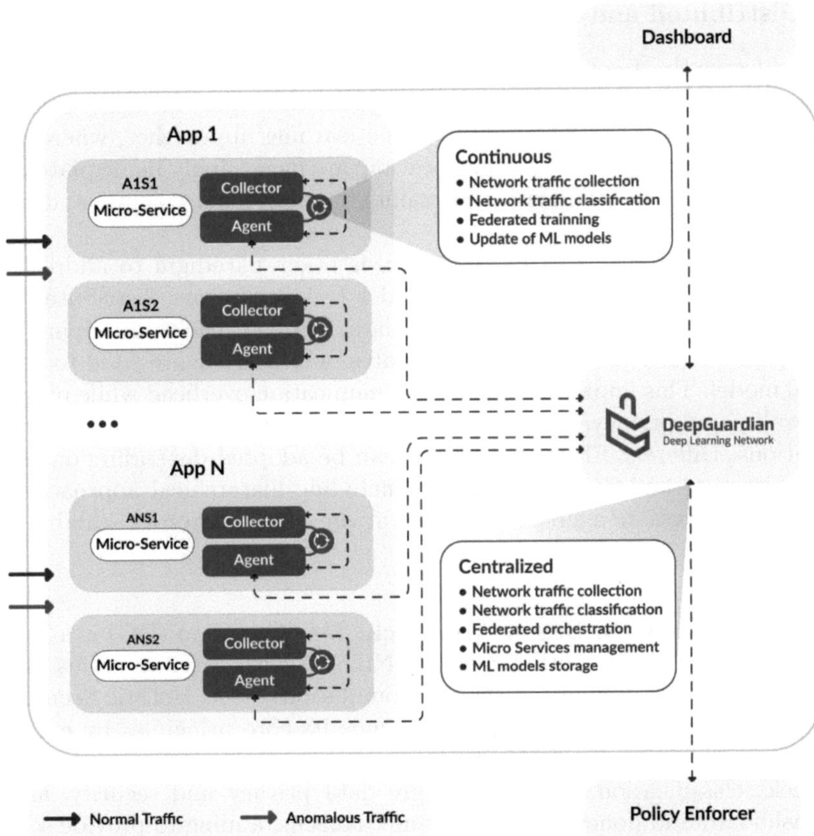

Fig. 3. DG Architecture

3.4 Privacy-Preserving Security Mechanisms

In distributed AI-driven security environments, sensitive data and model updates are exchanged across multiple domains, raising significant privacy and trust concerns. To address these challenges, a range of PETs can be integrated into the security pipeline.

Secure Multi-Party Computation (MPC) enables collaborative computation across multiple participants without exposing their private inputs, supporting secure aggregation and distributed analytics [25]. (DP) provides formal guarantees against information leakage by introducing controlled noise into model updates, making it particularly suitable for federated learning scenarios [15]. (HE) allows computations to be performed directly on encrypted data, ensuring confidentiality throughout the processing pipeline [6,14]. Zero-Knowledge Proof (ZKP) enable the verification of computations without revealing underlying data, facilitating trust across administrative domains [23]. Finally, Trusted Execution

Environments (TEEs) provide hardware-based isolation and attestation mechanisms to ensure the integrity and confidentiality of sensitive operations [19].

These mechanisms are complementary and can be combined to enforce privacy and trust at different stages of the AI-driven security pipeline. In particular, they play a critical role in enabling secure model training, aggregation, and deployment across distributed edge–cloud environments.

DG currently supports MPC, HE, ZKP and DP to ensure the data privacy and security of the data, especially of the model weights that are being shared through the network and that contain a bigger exposure to potential data breaches. Moreover, Tomas et al. [22] describe some preliminary work reporting on the impact of adding PETs to the DG foundations, the HSPF framework.

4 Towards a Unified Edge–Cloud Security Architecture

This section proposes a unified architecture that integrates the individual components from Sect. 3, including traffic capture, hardware-accelerated threat detection, distributed intelligence, and privacy-preserving mechanisms, into a cohesive Edge–Cloud security framework that relies on the key principles of continuous training, detection, and reaction. This architecture, Fig. 4, is organised into four functional domains: monitoring and telemetry collection via eBPF, AI-driven threat detection, distributed intelligence through federated learning and privacy-enhancing technologies, and system observability with policy enforcement. These components are connected through continuous data and control flows, enabling a closed-loop security pipeline across the Edge–Cloud continuum.

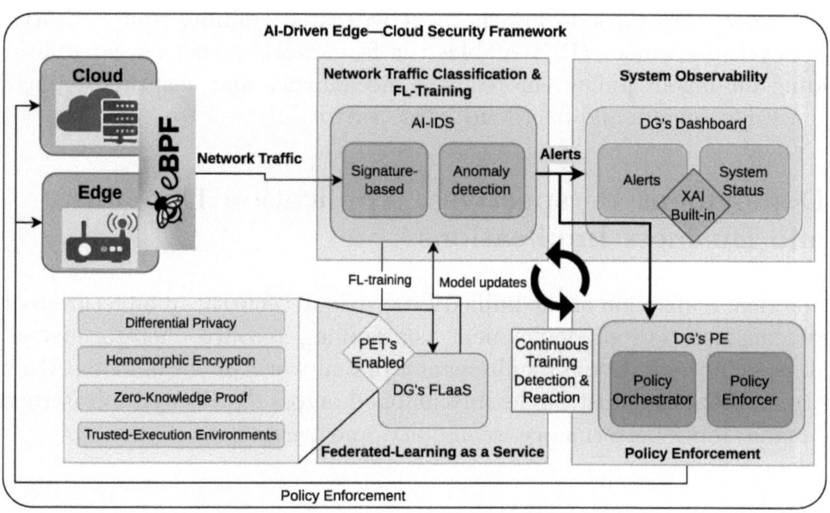

Fig. 4. Unified Edge AI-based security framework

At the data plane level, the system utilises an eBPF-based traffic capture mechanism (Sect. 3.1) to intercept traffic at the transport level directly within the operating system kernel. Captured traffic is then forwarded to the AI-IDS framework (Sect. 3.2), which is in charge of performing network traffic classification, via encrypted Kafka brokers supporting authentication and authorisation mechanisms. Leveraging its underlying FPGA support, the AI-IDS enables deterministic, line-rate inspection through hardware-accelerated signature matching while simultaneously incorporating adaptive machine learning models to detect both known and previously unseen threats.

To support large-scale and distributed deployments, the framework employs the DG FLaaS, an on-demand federated and distributed intelligence mechanism, which enables edge nodes to collaboratively train intrusion detection models while keeping raw data local. The FLaaS mechanism also supports hierarchical aggregation via intermediate edge aggregators, which improves scalability and reduces communication overhead.

Privacy and trust within the framework are reinforced by the integration of PETs, including DP, HE and ZKP, which protect sensitive data and model updates during both training and inference. Additionally, TEEs provide secure enclaves for critical operations such as secure aggregation and policy enforcement, utilising remote attestation to establish trust across the Edge-Cloud continuum.

The DG Dashboard provides system observability by presenting generated alerts complemented with known vulnerabilities linked to the source systems being protected. To ensure transparency, the Dashboard incorporates AIXAI by leveraging post-hoc methods to provide interpretability over the algorithms' decisions. The Dashboard also enables Human-in-the-Loop interaction within this architecture by enabling the operator to override the algorithm's decision, which is also considered during the next federated training round. Lastly, the DG Policy Enforcement (PE) enables the framework's reaction capabilities by providing intelligent policy enforcement mechanisms and ensuring deployment both on Edge devices and on Cloud infrastructures.

5 Deployment Perspectives, Application Domains, and Business Implications

The practical realisation of the unified Edge–Cloud security architecture requires careful consideration of deployment constraints, resource heterogeneity, and domain-specific operational requirements. In real-world environments, AI-driven security mechanisms must be flexibly mapped across distributed infrastructures while maintaining performance, scalability, and trust.

5.1 Deployment and Validation Scenarios

Edge–Cloud infrastructures are inherently heterogeneous, encompassing resource-constrained gateways, edge servers with hardware acceleration capabilities, and cloud platforms offering high computational capacity and confidential computing features. This diversity necessitates adaptive deployment strategies in which security functions are placed according to available resources and operational requirements.

In the considered framework, monitoring and low-latency threat detection are performed at the edge, where FPGA-based acceleration enables real-time processing of network traffic. More computationally intensive tasks, such as model aggregation and global training, are executed in cloud environments, which provide the required scalability and processing capabilities. Policy enforcement mechanisms are deployed at gateway nodes, enabling control over data flows at trust boundaries. Confidential computing technologies, such as TEEs, are selectively employed to protect sensitive operations depending on data confidentiality requirements and trust assumptions. These deployment principles have been validated in smart factory scenarios, including equipment health monitoring and cross-site energy optimisation. In such settings, sensor data is processed locally at edge nodes, while collaborative model training is performed across multiple sites without transferring raw data. This approach enables low-latency inference while preserving data privacy. Furthermore, the use of heterogeneous TEE technologies (e.g., AMD SEV-SNP and Intel TDX) demonstrates that trust can be established across administrative domains through remote attestation, even in environments with diverse hardware platforms.

5.2 Application Domains and Business Implications

The proposed architectural approach is applicable across multiple domains that share requirements for distributed processing, real-time decision-making, and privacy preservation. In industrial environments, such as smart manufacturing, the framework supports predictive maintenance and operational optimisation through distributed analytics. Similarly, telecommunications infrastructures, including 5G and 6G networks, can leverage the framework to support distributed, AI-driven security functions across operator domains. In this context, projects such as 6G-PATH provide testbed-driven environments for validating these capabilities in realistic conditions, enabling the experimentation of Edge–Cloud security mechanisms across multiple vertical use cases and deployment scenarios.

From a business perspective, this architecture enables new operational models for security deployment. Network operators and service providers can offer security-as-a-service solutions, where intrusion detection, model management, and policy enforcement are orchestrated across distributed infrastructures. By centralising intelligence while preserving data locality, the framework reduces operational complexity and enables scalable deployment of advanced security capabilities across diverse environments.

6 Open Challenges and Research Directions

The proposed framework highlights several open challenges that must be addressed to enable scalable and operational deployment in real-world Edge–Cloud environments.

At the monitoring layer, scalability remains a primary concern. The combination of eBPF-based telemetry, AI-driven detection, and federated learning generates large volumes of data and coordination overhead. This necessitates efficient mechanisms for filtering, feature extraction, and data reduction to prevent overwhelming downstream components. Additionally, tracing-based eBPF instrumentation introduces portability and maintainability challenges, as probes attached to internal kernel functions are sensitive to changes across kernel versions. Ensuring robustness therefore requires continuous adaptation to evolving system environments.

At the detection layer, hardware-accelerated AI-IDS solutions provide high performance but reduce flexibility in heterogeneous deployments, highlighting the need for adaptive hardware–software co-design. Similarly, federated learning introduces challenges in dynamic and adversarial environments, including robustness to poisoning attacks, handling non-IID data distributions, and ensuring reliable model convergence across distributed participants.

From a trust and privacy perspective, establishing secure collaboration across administrative domains remains a key challenge. Mechanisms such as TEEs and remote attestation are essential for ensuring integrity, but their integration into large-scale distributed systems introduces additional complexity. Furthermore, privacy-enhancing technologies (e.g., differential privacy, homomorphic encryption, and secure computation) introduce trade-offs between privacy, performance, and detection accuracy, requiring context-aware optimisation.

Finally, system-level orchestration of distributed security functions remains an open issue. Coordinating monitoring, detection, learning, and enforcement across heterogeneous environments demands advanced and adaptive orchestration strategies, potentially leveraging AI-driven control loops.

Addressing these challenges will be critical to enabling robust, scalable, and trustworthy AI-driven security architectures for future Edge–Cloud and B5G/6G systems, and represents a key direction for ongoing research and standardisation efforts.

7 Conclusion

This paper presented an integration-oriented perspective on AI-driven security in the Edge–Cloud continuum, addressing the increasing complexity and distributed nature of B5G/6G environments. Rather than treating monitoring, threat detection, distributed intelligence, and privacy-preserving mechanisms as isolated components, the paper positioned them as complementary elements of an end-to-end security pipeline.

Building on this view, we outlined a unified architectural framework that connects telemetry collection, AI-driven detection, federated intelligence, and trusted orchestration within a coherent Edge–Cloud security architecture. The relevance of this approach was further illustrated through deployment perspectives and validation insights, highlighting its applicability in realistic environments. At the same time, several challenges remain open, particularly in terms of scalability, adversarial robustness, explainability, privacy–utility trade-offs, and trust across heterogeneous infrastructures. Addressing these challenges is essential for moving from fragmented solutions towards fully integrated and operational AI-driven security systems.

Overall, this work provides a structured foundation for advancing AI-driven security in the Edge–Cloud continuum and supports future research towards scalable, trustworthy, and deployable security architectures for next-generation distributed systems.

Acknowledgments. This work was supported in part by: Smart Networks and Services Joint Undertaking (SNS JU) under the 6G-PATH (Grant No. 101139172) and ELASTIC (Grant No. 101139067) projects; the Horizon Europe Research and Innovation programme HORIZON-CL3-2022-CS-01-01 under the MIRANDA project (Grant No. 101168144); PNRR-NGEU, which has received funding from the MUR - DM 117/2023. The views expressed in this work are those of the authors and do not necessarily reflect the official position of the projects or the funding bodies.

Disclosure of Interests. The authors have no competing interests to declare that are relevant to the content of this article.

References

1. Al-Quraan, M., et al.: Edge-native intelligence for 6G communications driven by federated learning: a survey of trends and challenges. IEEE Trans. Emerg. Top. Comput. Intell. **7**(3), 957–979 (2023). https://doi.org/10.1109/TETCI.2023.3251404
2. Albshaier, L., Almarri, S., Albuali, A.: Federated learning for cloud and edge security: a systematic review of challenges and AI opportunities. Electronics **14**(5), 1019 (2025)
3. European Union Agency for Cybersecurity (ENISA): Artificial intelligence cybersecurity challenges. Technical report, ENISA (2020)
4. Feng, Y., Qi, Y., Li, H., Wang, X., Tian, J.: Leveraging federated learning and edge computing for recommendation systems within cloud computing networks. In: Third International Symposium on Computer Applications and Information Systems (ISCAIS 2024), vol. 13210, pp. 279–287. SPIE (2024)
5. Imani, F., Kargar, M., Assadzadeh, A., Bayani, A.: Integrating CNN-LSTM networks with statistical filtering techniques for intelligent IoT intrusion detection. In: 2024 8th International Conference on Smart Cities, Internet of Things and Applications (SCIoT), pp. 189–195. IEEE (2024)
6. Javadpour, A., et al.: Deploying testbed docker-based application for encryption as a service in kubernetes. In: 2024 International Conference on Software, Telecommunications and Computer Networks (SoftCOM), pp. 1–7. IEEE (2024)
7. John, W., Karapantelakis, A., Mouradian, C.: Supporting AI-driven mobile applications with a 6G AI compute continuum. Technical report, Ericsson Research (2026)
8. Kaur, N., Gupta, L.: Securing the 6G-IoT environment: a framework for enhancing transparency in artificial intelligence decision-making through explainable artificial intelligence. Sensors (Basel) **25**(3) (2025)

9. Kostopoulos, S., Papatsaroucha, D., Kefaloukos, I., Markakis, E.K.: eIDPS: a real-time eBPF-based and machine learning-powered network intrusion detection and prevention solution. In: 2025 6th International Conference in Electronic Engineering & Information Technology (EEITE), pp. 1–8. IEEE (2025)
10. Kumar, R., Dutta, J., Vamsi, N., Varri, U., Puthal, D.: Next-generation security in the 6G era: the role of ai in safeguarding future networks. IEEE Access 1 (2026). https://doi.org/10.1109/ACCESS.2025.3650208
11. Li, H., Ge, L., Tian, L.: Survey: federated learning data security and privacy-preserving in edge-internet of things. Artif. Intell. Rev. **57**(5), 130 (2024)
12. Lim, S.Y., Prasad, T., Han, X., Pasquier, T.: SafeBPF: hardware-assisted defense-in-depth for eBPF kernel extensions. In: Proceedings of the 2024 on Cloud Computing Security Workshop, pp. 80–94 (2024)
13. Liyanage, M., et al.: A survey on zero touch network and service management (ZSM) for 5G and beyond networks. J. Netw. Comput. Appl. **203**, 103362 (2022)
14. Marcolla, C., Sucasas, V., Manzano, M., Bassoli, R., Fitzek, F.H.P., Aaraj, N.: Survey on fully homomorphic encryption, theory, and applications. Proc. IEEE **110**(10), 1572–1609 (2022). https://doi.org/10.1109/JPROC.2022.3205665
15. Ouadrhiri, A.E., Abdelhadi, A.: Differential privacy for deep and federated learning: a survey. IEEE Access **10**, 22359–22380 (2022). https://doi.org/10.1109/ACCESS.2022.3151670
16. Papadogiannaki, E., Chrysos, G., Georgopoulos, K., Ioannidis, S.: A reconfigurable IDS framework for encrypted and non-encrypted network data in supply chains. In: 2023 International Conference on Engineering and Emerging Technologies (ICEET), pp. 1–6. IEEE (2023)
17. Pérez Palma, N., Skarmeta Gómez, A., Bisson, P.: Innovative approaches for 6G security: challenges, solutions, and impact (2025). https://doi.org/10.5281/zenodo.14619619
18. Rabbi Ahmed, K., et al.: AI-enhanced adaptive network security for 6G and edge computing. In: 2025 International Conference on Quantum Photonics, Artificial Intelligence, and Networking (QPAIN), pp. 1–6 (2025). https://doi.org/10.1109/QPAIN66474.2025.11172162
19. Tariq, A., et al.: Trustworthy federated learning: a comprehensive review, architecture, key challenges, and future research prospects. IEEE Open J. Commun. Soc. **5**, 4920–4998 (2024). https://doi.org/10.1109/OJCOMS.2024.3438264
20. Tomas, P.R., Felix, P., Rosa, L., Gomes, A.S., Cordeiro, L.: A novel approach for continual and federated network anomaly detection. In: Arai, K. (ed.) FTC 2024. LNNS, vol. 1157, pp. 212–225. Springer, Cham (2024). https://doi.org/10.1007/978-3-031-73128-0_14
21. Tomas, P.R., et al.: Network policy enforcement in cloud-native environments. In: Papaleonidas, A., Pimenidis, E., Papadopoulos, H., Chochliouros, I. (eds.) AIAI 2025. IFIP Advances in Information and Communication Technology, vol. 753, pp. 195–208. Springer, Cham (2025). https://doi.org/10.1007/978-3-031-97317-8_15
22. Tomás, P., et al.: Enhancing federated learning with homomorphic encryption and multi-party computation for improved privacy. In: 2024 IEEE Future Networks World Forum (FNWF), pp. 891–896 (2024). https://doi.org/10.1109/FNWF63303.2024.11028749
23. Xing, Z., et al.: Zero-knowledge proof-based verifiable decentralized machine learning in communication network: a comprehensive survey. IEEE Commun. Surv. Tutor. **28**, 985–1024 (2026). https://doi.org/10.1109/COMST.2025.3561657

24. Yalli, J., Hasan, M., Badawi, A.: Internet of things (IoT): origins, embedded technologies, smart applications and its growth in the last decade. IEEE Access **12**, 91357–91382 (2024). https://doi.org/10.1109/ACCESS.2024.3418995
25. Zhou, I., Tofigh, F., Piccardi, M., Abolhasan, M., Franklin, D., Lipman, J.: Secure multi-party computation for machine learning: a survey. IEEE Access **12**, 53881–53899 (2024). https://doi.org/10.1109/ACCESS.2024.3388992

Author Index

Published by Springer Nature Switzerland AG 2027
A. Papaleonidas et al. (Eds.): AIAI 2026 Workshops, IFIP AICT 796, pp. 317–318, 2027.
https://doi.org/10.1007/978-3-032-30507-7

MIX
Papier aus verantwortungsvollen Quellen
Paper from responsible sources
FSC® C105338

If you have any concerns about our products,
you can contact us on
ProductSafety@springernature.com

In case Publisher is established outside the EU,
the EU authorized representative is:
Springer Nature Customer Service Center GmbH
Europaplatz 3, 69115 Heidelberg, Germany

Printed by Libri Plureos GmbH
in Hamburg, Germany